SAN DIEGO SYMPHONY
from Overture to Encore

A Fairly Comprehensive History

SAN DIEGO SYMPHONY

from Overture to Encore

A Fairly Comprehensive History

Melvin G. Goldzband
Archivist
San Diego Symphony

San Diego Symphony from Overture to Encore
Copyright ©2007 by Melvin G. Goldzband
All rights reserved. First edition 2007

Publisher: San Diego Symphony Orchestra Association
Book and cover design: Armadillo Creative
Production Coordinator: Jennifer Redmond
Printed in the United States of America

San Diego Symphony
1245 Seventh Avenue
San Diego, CA 92101
(619) 235-0800
sandiegosymphony@sandiegosymphony.org
www.sandiegosymphony.com

09 08 07 06   5 4 3 2 1

Cataloging-in-Publication Data

Goldzband, Melvin G.
  San Diego Symphony: from overture to encore/ by Melvin G. Goldzband.-- 1st ed.
     p. cm.
Includes bibliographical references and index.
  ISBN-13:
  ISBN-10: 0-916251-79-9
  1. San Diego (Calif.)--History. Symphonic Music. I. Title.
  F869.S22E543 2005
  979.4'985--dc22
                          2006005473

Cover Photograph: San Diego Symphony, Jahja Ling Conducting by Ken Jacques. Courtesy San Diego Symphony. Cover Photograph (inset): "San Diego Philharmonic Orchestra at Spreckels Organ Pavilion, 1927" Courtesy San Diego Historical Society Photo Archives

Inside front cover photograph: San Diego Symphony by Ken Jacques. Courtesy San Diego Symphony. Inside back cover photograph: San Diego Symphony Summer Pops. Courtesy San Diego Symphony.

On Behalf of the Author, the Board of Directors,

the Musicians of the Orchestra, the Administrative Staff and

the Entire San Diego Symphony Family,

this True Labor of Love is Dedicated to

JOAN AND IRWIN JACOBS

Whose Incredible and Incomparable Generosity

Provides the Highest Degree of Support and Encouragement

to the Performance of Great Music in Our Community.

TABLE OF CONTENTS

PREFACE

First, the explanation. The subtitle was justly chosen. This is only a fairly comprehensive history because, in doing my research for it, I found that it is likely that many San Diegans still living, or their descendants, may have memorabilia or recollections that ought rightfully to find their places in here. As I went on my merry way collecting materials from the San Diego Historical Society, from newspaper archives in the San Diego Public Library, and at the News Library of the *San Diego Union-Tribune*, I would receive calls from people who had heard about my endeavors. They had stuff — plenty of stuff. Fortunately, many of them had the same stuff, so that the extra work of adding more new material was minimized, and the history was held to a fairly (that word again!) civilized length. But it is amazing how many people have memories in their attics. I am truly grateful to all of them.

Second, the disclaimer. Another subtitle could easily have been added. That would have made it, "A Fairly Comprehensive and Somewhat Personal History." Because I had been heavily involved with the goings on in San Diego Symphony Orchestra circles since 1962, with a few gaps, I had a great deal of personal knowledge about it. I also had a great many opinions about what went on, and, I admit, plenty of biases. On the other hand, all history is personal to a more or less great extent, even if it is about things that happened long before the writers' times. Certainly, everything must be taken these days with a heavier grain of salt than ever before, but I will continue to defend my own stances as given herein.

In the late 1990s, paradoxically at the end of what one San Diego music critic referred to as the "golden age" of the San Diego Symphony, the orchestra folded and went into bankruptcy. One day, the librarians of the orchestra, Nancy Fisch and her assistant, Pat Francis, came to check their bailiwick, the Florence and Fred Goss Memorial Music Library in Copley Symphony Hall. They found that during their absence, a huge pile of records, programs, other memorabilia and materials had simply been taken from the symphony offices upstairs and had been unceremoniously and very messily dumped onto the floor of the Copley Symphony Hall lobby. They were appropriately horrified, and, even more appropriately, they contacted Welton Jones, then Arts Section Editor of the Sunday *Union-Tribune*. His series of articles about the bankruptcy had been, in the most polite description, excoriating.

Welton had long been involved with the San Diego Historical Society. He knew the historical value of all that dumped material and arranged for it to be brought to the Society Archives in Balboa Park. Some time much later he called me. We had gone back a long way together. Jointly, we had even fought the good fight against what we believed would have been the disastrous results of a proposed Chapter 7 bankruptcy for the symphony. He told me about the material in the Historical Society, and he took blatant and deliberate advantage of my having been newly retired from a long practice of clinical psychiatry. He knew that I would have both the time and the interest to look into this material that had not been able to be sorted by the shorthanded Historical Society archival staff.

John Panter, then the Historical Society's Archivist, and his assistant, Dennis Sharp, were enormously helpful to me in my initially unlearned attempts to sort things out. After a time, during which my wife and I shuffled through an enormous number of clippings, programs, office records, minutes, and all sorts of other materials, things ran a bit more smoothly and a semblance of order was developed. Now, since the summer of 2006, it is all safely stored on the shelves of the Special Collections and University Archives Division of the Malcolm Love Library at San Diego State University.

But then, Welton did me further damage; he put a bug in my ear about preparing a history based upon those materials and all the other research findings so readily available in the sources I mentioned above. He had written some articles about varied bits of symphony history for the newspaper during his editorship, and he was very much aware of other sources that gave more information. But, as he said, there had never been a definitive, comprehensive history written about the San Diego orchestra, its triumphs and its incredible travails. Older, outdated master's theses had been prepared and were available at San Diego State or elsewhere, but even those were incomplete regarding many fascinating details about the orchestra and the city in which it tried to become a fixture.

I confess that as I perused the materials in the archives of the Historical Society, I became fascinated. I certainly recognized the sometimes severely limited aspects of the prior histories that had been put together. Besides, although I may not have been present at the creation, I was involved for a long enough time to have been a primary, participating combatant/advocate. That should count for plenty, as I rationalized it.

So I began, and as I went along the piles of sources and resources became higher and increasingly enthralling. My own love of history was my downfall here. Had I not been admitted to medical school in the years after World War II, I would probably have become a history teacher on some college campus. And now look — I'm a historian!

The real historians, though, were John and Dennis at the Historical Society, whose help verged on the enormous. I am terribly grateful to them for their patience and understanding. Welton, of course, pushed, as is his usual wont, but I was grateful for that, as well as for his touting one or another source.

So here it is, and what do we learn from it? The travails of the San Diego Symphony were brought on in great part by ignorance of the people, including myself, who were entrusted with its governance. The American Symphony Orchestra League might just as well have been whistling into the wind as far as our attention was being paid to its warnings and directions to symphony boards. Most of our managers were of little help in straightening us out. God bless the near-starving musicians who stuck with us, often while understandably hating us.

This history is not solely one of travail. There are plenty of good times described, and a lot of the music made was remarkable. Now, of course, our governance is far more sophisticated and dedicated. Our new conductor is wonderful. The orchestra is better than ever, and optimism reigns supreme. If this history teaches us anything, it is hoped that it will cause the people responsible for the orchestra not to make the mistakes that had been made before — sometimes over and over.

I worry, though, even with the current good times and an optimistic symphonic future. Regardless of the good governance of any American symphony orchestra, a major problem exists that may not be able to be fixed by even the best boards or executive directors.

Who is going to teach our children and grandchildren about music and the arts? Who is going to work hard to create discerning, critical audiences for symphonic music in future years? Will America continue to be dumbed down? That is a question well beyond the scope of this magnum opus, but I sure worry.

Meanwhile, I take leave here with overwhelming gratitude to my wife, Marilyn, the English teacher/editor who arm-wrestled with me, mostly satisfyingly, to cause me to try making sentences shorter than I have in this preface. God bless her. But the blessings in her direction must be accompanied by blessings for a few others as well, whose help and encouragement have been essential. E. B. "Ward" Gill, the Executive Director of the San Diego Symphony Orchestra Association, has been a constant source of encouragement and a force applied continually and constructively to get me to do this work. He recognizes the needs served by a history of such an organization, and he used a valued comparable history of his former bailiwick, the Minnesota Orchestra, as a stimulus here. He worked hard with the Symphony Association's executive committee and board to provide the funds needed to publish this work.

Others in the symphony administration also must be thanked for their encouragement and their work, most notably Eric Meyer, Vice President and Director of Development, and especially Jackie Anderson, Marketing Coordinator. She faithfully scanned the numerous historical pictures I had gleaned from many sources for this work — all despite the tremendously heavy pressures of busy seasons that needed her to do other work. I am tremendously grateful to her.

Finally, when the time eventually came to turn this mess into a formatted manuscript with photos, my good friend (who turned out to be an even better friend), Dr. Richard Rowen, applied his computer expertise to this job to great effect. I have no idea how I can possibly express my appreciation to him for that. It is wonderful to recognize how many people love the San Diego Symphony and recognize its importance and the necessity of preserving and learning from its history.

Melvin G. Goldzband, M. D.
San Diego, California
August 2006

CHAPTER 1

Beginnings and Quick Endings: Trial and Error

T he beginning of organized symphonic music making in San Diego centers around two hotels and a theatre. The Hotel del Coronado furnished the momentum for the organization of one of the early concert bands, and the U. S. Grant Hotel provided the venue for the first performances of the progenitor of the San Diego Symphony Orchestra. The Spreckels Theatre stimulated a vision of a hometown symphony orchestra playing there. But none of these contributed to the very earliest musical history of our city.

From the time of the Mission era, music played a significant role in the community life of the early settlement of San Diego. *The New Grove Encyclopedia of Music and Musicians (2001)* notes that an organ was played in the second mission established in San Diego in the late eighteenth century. The music of that instrument (more likely a primitive harmonium) was said to have attracted many of the indigenous peoples to the church and led to a number of conversions, as did the plain-chanting of the priests. The garrisons, Spanish, Mexican and American, all had bands of various sizes and instrumentations and, as reported in early histories, they often played for civic and social events aside from military purposes. Just as in nearly all communities throughout the world from time immemorial, the presence of some kind of music was important to the people living in pioneer San Diego. Certainly, the indigenous people displaced by the early San Diego colonists played their own kinds of music on their own instruments. Some of them can be seen in local museums.

In his 1953 article in the *San Diego Sound Post*, celebrating the fiftieth anniversary of the founding of San Diego's Local 325 of the American Federation of Musicians, Edward Ortiz, Jr., observed, "Bands have come and gone, but bandsmen remain and go on from one band to another." San Diego's first non-military band was organized in 1868 when clarinetist Matt Alderson hired his first cornet player off a side-wheeler steamship that had just sailed into the Bay! Alderson had arrived in San Diego somewhat before that, and had sent for his friend, "Doc" Martin, to join him here.

Winifred Davidson, author of *Where California Began*, contributed an article about old San Diego's first band in the *San Diego Union* of August 23, 1931, and described the Alderson-Martin reunion. Alderson had settled in San Diego, opened a bar and, "…had induced his friend Martin…to follow, and with his family, consisting of a wife and seven children, 'Doc' arrived on the Orizaba two weeks earlier than Alderson had anticipated. Off Ballast Point, when the old side-wheeler had boomed announcement of her approach, 'Doc' produced his cornet, saying, 'I don't know where the town of San Diego is, but if Matt Alderson is still in it, he'll know I'm on my way,' and began playing the difficult 'Shepherd's Quickstep.' Sure enough, Alderson, in his saloon in New Town, halted in the midst of pouring drinks and said, 'There's Doc!'"

Almost immediately, Alderson and Martin formed a band. A wonderful old daguerrotype showing the first seven members was reproduced for the Davidson *Union* article. The original members deserve mention here: W. B. Carlton, E-flat clarinet; Ed Eyry, tuba; Judge John Porter, baritone horn; (unknown first name) Thompson, violin; Billy McKeen, bass drum; as well as Alderson and Martin. Shortly afterwards Ed Gregg joined the band as drummer. As a youth he borrowed a snare drum and a bass drum, and, with his brother, according to Davidson, "started out one day drumming for dear life up and down New San Diego streets. About 40 boys joined in procession behind them; and they continued marching, stopping only to make collections for the band. 'Father' Horton gave them five dollars…" That makeshift (and profitable) parade was enough of a positive audition for Gregg who immediately joined the band.

The *San Diego Union* of October 22, 1869, provided a banner headline, "Our Distinguished Guests! A Great Day for San Diego!" A day-long and nighttime reception was given for the visiting Hon. William Seward and his party. Seward had been Secretary of State in Lincoln's and Andrew Johnson's cabinets. He was notably instrumental in the purchase of Alaska from Russia, a major reason for increased feelings of security among west coast residents. "The brass band of New Town enlivened the occasion with soft strains of charming music, which floated softly over the beautiful bay…" The band had also played earlier that day at the reception at the Gregg home, at Fifth and F Streets, where the visiting General William S. Rosecrans was also being honored.

Martin became increasingly influential in creating considerable music during San Diego's nineteenth century days. As a "professor" of music he taught music and dancing, according to a memoir written by his daughter, J. G. Martin, known affectionately to all as "Tude." She wrote that the band took part in every parade, including those for funerals, weddings and torchlight extravaganzas. When Matt Alderson was killed, the band played for that funeral, described by "Tude" as, "one of the biggest we ever had in this town."

Concerts by the New Town Band were beginning to be given for paid admission, and it was also hired for social events. In 1882 the City Guard Band

San Diego City Guard Band, 1885. *Photo courtesy San Diego Historical Society.*

was organized. The City Guard was a branch of the National Guard, a part of the Army Reserves, and the original members of the band had joined the Guard before requesting permission to form a band. Permission was granted by the National Guard, and a public subscription was raised to support the music. An 1885 photo shows the members in their snappy, military-style uniforms. One of the band members was Jack Dodge, whose memoir, *Jack Dodge: His Life and Times*, was dictated to William Holcomb and published by Sherman Danby Publications in Los Angeles, in 1937. Dodge was a very colorful character in San Diego through the years surrounding the turn of the century, and was very influential in developing musical and theatrical events.

Dodge arrived in San Diego in 1887 and immediately joined the band, now enlarged to thirty men, just in time to be a part of the trans-continental tour it was to take to many of the principal cities of the eastern United States as San Diego's first cultural ambassadors. They left San Diego in their private railroad car on September 1, 1887, and returned forty days later covered with glory. In his memoir Dodge described the gala welcomes received by the band wherever it played. He devoted considerable narrative to the band's great parade up Pennsylvania Avenue in Washington, D. C., where they were received by President Cleveland and members of Congress.

Part of the underwriting for that tour came from the then-new Hotel del Coronado to publicize its opening in 1887. How much the hotel actually benefited from the tour itself is unknown, but it and the city prospered. The band had been a great ambassador. The population of the city jumped five-fold by 1890. It had been demonstrated again that music indeed hath charms to move the not-so-savage citizens as well as the earlier music had moved the indigenous denizens. Soon after the turn of the twentieth century, the management of the Hotel del Coronado developed a novel idea to lure more visitors, the famous and eventually exceedingly popular Tent City. An article by Jerry Mulligan in the June, 1949, *Westways* Magazine called attention to the gaily-striped tents with their palm-leafed roofs that had stretched in the Tent City's heydays from the hotel's front porch down the Silver Strand for nearly a mile. The tents rented for twenty-seven dollars weekly, and more substantial cabins could also be had for forty dollars. Basic furnishings and maid service were provided along with a gasoline stove for cooking. A community sink was available in the midst of each block of tents.

A dance pavilion and a bandstand were located in the center of Tent City. Mulligan wrote of the "bandstand fashioned in the shape of a sphere." The Tent City Band played every night and on weekend afternoons, but not just for the renters of the tents and cabins. Citizens of San Diego flocked to hear the music.

Tent City Band, 1915. *Photo courtesy San Diego Historical Society.*

The *Coronado Journal* of June 4, 1959, in an article about the history of Tent City, noted that on Sunday afternoons, twelve thousand people came to listen. Mildred Lyman Tracy, in her San Diego State University thesis on the history of the San Diego Symphony Orchestra (1962) indicated that the emphasis in the band concerts was on classical or light classical music. Sousa marches were played as encores.

In brief, the concerts were a sensation. Because they were publicized across the country, the Tent City Band toured widely, increasing its fame — and the hotel's. The First World War led to decreasing interest in Tent City and its music, however, and the concerts gradually ceased. Some of the structures remained for a number of years — but not the bandstand. Everything was finally demolished by 1939. The Tent City Band, however, had provided a remarkable stimulus to the growth of professional music making in San Diego. Other bands were soon formed and they played frequently and busily around town.

Around the time of the Tent City Band's initial organization, a youth band and, subsequently, a youth orchestra were organized at Madame Tingley's famous Theosophical Institute on Point Loma. Katherine Tingley was born in 1841 in Massachusetts, but she left home in early adolescence in order to fulfill what she had felt to be her calling, that of a nurse for the wounded of both sides in the Civil War. She was said to have performed nobly on the battlefields with her charges. She became entranced with the philosophy known as Theosophy, then widely popular, as were a number of other neo-mystical ideologies. Theosophy encompassed spiritualism, reincarnation, and an attempt to recapture the mysterious lost knowledge of past ages. After having been married three times, she came to California and met General John Fremont to whom she described her vision of, "A white city on the banks of the Pacific." The General encouraged her, and Mrs. (known permanently thereafter as "Madame") Tingley located her spot on Point Loma. She was forty-five years old when she founded her Institute.

Mrs. A. J. Spalding, the very wealthy widow of the "Sporting Goods King," had also become interested in Theosophy and especially in Madame Tingley's work. She also moved to Point Loma, settling into facilities in the new Institute. Her financial contributions allowed the development of a number of buildings that eventually housed and trained hundreds of adherents over nearly half a century. The Institute also built the first open-air Greek theatre in the United States, still an eloquent representation of Madame Tingley's aspirations that always included uplift and enlightenment. In order to achieve those goals, she established (with the help of Mrs. Spalding and a number of other wealthy donors she had attracted) the Raja-Yoga College, in which classes were held in the Theosophical points of departure of many academic subjects.

Music education was important to Madame Tingley. At the time, there was little, if any musical education in America's public schools. The Raja-Yoga College taught younger children as well as college-aged young adults. Each student was required to learn to play at least one instrument and eventually had to join the band or orchestra. The ensembles Madame Tingley founded must have exemplified her goals and apparently allowed some to reach fruition. The orchestra gave some concerts during its short life, but how many, how often and under whom remain unknown. However, the photographs available of those groups certainly demonstrate their impressive appearances, especially the snow-white, flowing neo-Grecian gowns of the female players, with their floral head wreaths. The male members of the orchestra and band (the band was all male) wore high-collared military style uniforms.

The Theosophical Society purchased the old Fisher Opera House on Fifth Street in downtown San Diego. When it had opened in 1892, the Fisher Opera House was considered to be the most beautiful and best equipped theater on the Pacific Coast. Until the Spreckels Theater was built early in the next century, the Fisher was the city's largest. Madame Tingley was able to purchase it because Mr. Fisher had lost a great deal of money in unprofitable real estate investments and more in the panic of the later 1890s. She had the place refurbished and, characteristically, renamed it as the Isis Theatre. Ancient Greek and Egyptian deities were often referred to, even revered in Theosophical writings. Concerts were given at the Isis, as well as student recitals and lectures. Eventually, the theatre began to book traveling shows.

Theosophical Institute Orchestra, 1915. *Photo courtesy San Diego Historical Society.*

Jack Dodge had organized many theatrical and musical presentations in San Diego, at first using the old Horton Hall at Sixth Street and F. Only twenty-seven when he determined to become an impresario, he soon became quite successful. He became the manager of several of the newer theaters being built in town. Leach's Opera House had been opened on Broadway in 1887, the year of Dodge's arrival. Dodge successfully booked many traveling events into that house before he became manager of the Fisher Opera House. He continued in that capacity under the Theosophical Society's ownership. He and Madame Tingley formed a collabor-

Isis Theatre, 1900. *Photo courtesy San Diego Historical Society.*

ative partnership that allowed traveling shows and other features to be booked into the theater during the week, but Sundays were strictly reserved for performances and lectures by the Theosophical Society.

Madame Tingley died in 1920, but the Institute she founded remained an integral but decreasingly active or influential part of San Diego history until 1942. World War II brought the Federal Housing Administration into the picture. That agency took over many of the buildings that were no longer being used, and eventually the remaining structures became targets for curious sightseers. The Institute and the Raja-Yoga College were disbanded. The property now is used by the Point Loma Nazarene College, which purchased it from California Western University in the late 1970s.

Theaters began to sprout in San Diego during the decade of the 1890s. They all had orchestra pits and some had their own, permanent orchestras. Some of the pit orchestras neared concert size, especially those of the Empire and Grand Theaters. Those larger pit orchestras provided employment to many string players who, in turn, taught many youngsters who would eventually replace them. Wind and percussion instrument players from the Tent City and other bands had also taught eager San Diego youngsters. The turn of the century era of boys' bands, celebrated so brilliantly in Meredith Willson's *The Music Man*, found its niche in San Diego as well as in Iowa.

Edwin G. Mann, then secretary-treasurer of San Diego's Local 325, was interviewed in 1961 by Mildred Lyman Tracy for her SDSU thesis, a copy of which is available in that University's library. He recalled that sporadic concerts were given by the pit orchestra musicians, some of whom joined with other pit orchestras and musicians from the Tent City Band in order to create larger bodies of sound. In 1902, an orchestra of fifty-four members was conducted by R. F. Trognitz and was considered the first professional symphonic orchestra in San Diego's history, according to the *New Grove Encyclopedia of Music and Musicians*. Concerts such as those were sporadic, however. They were generated in great part by the needs of the musicians themselves to play symphonic music. Admission was charged and any profit after expenses was divided evenly among the orchestra members. In those days in San Diego, principal or first desk players were treated financially just like the rear stand musicians. The needs of the musicians to play good music eventually gave rise to the formation of the Musicians' Protective Association, the progenitor of the San Diego Local 325 of the American Federation of Musicians organized in 1903.

The organization of a musicians' union, as well as the 1912 opening of the Spreckels, then the largest and finest theater in San Diego (at the time, many said on the entire Pacific coast or even west of the Mississippi!), further stimulated the development of an orchestra that would give a regular series of concerts. Likewise, the opening of the U. S. Grant Hotel in downtown San Diego, allowed the planners of that orchestra to consider it a temporarily suitable venue for the group until the Spreckels became available.

An article in the *San Diego Union* of August 21, 1910, related that, "The noted German violinist ('the second Paganini'), Herr Richard Schliewen, who is to be the organizer and director of the projected symphony orchestra, has arrived from Berlin (Germany) here, and is especially encouraged in regard to the large amount of available material for the organization of a symphony orchestra." Schliewen was, indeed, reputedly an excellent violinist. He was brought to San Diego by the backers of the new orchestra not directly from Berlin but from Brenau College in Gainesville, Florida, where he held a faculty position. No information is currently available regarding how the backers had heard of him or had determined his availability for the San Diego post.

It should be noted that the president of the newly organized Symphony Society of San Diego was Mrs. Will Douglas. Mr. W. B. Gross was listed as vice-president, Mrs. Morton B. Fowler was secretary and her husband, Morton B. Fowler, was treasurer. These pioneers should be remembered.

The first concert by the orchestra of a couple of dozen players was given in the ballroom of the new U. S. Grant Hotel on December 6, 1910. The musicians called themselves the San Diego Symphony Orchestra. The music played during that initial concert included the Beethoven First Symphony and the "descriptive cantata," *Fair Ellen*, in which the orchestra was augmented by a chorus. The anonymous reviewer, in a brief column in the December 7, 1910, issue of the *San Diego Union*, noted the vitality demonstrated in the playing of the Beethoven. He or she felt that this trait attested to the thorough preparation of the orchestra. The composer of the "descriptive cantata" was not mentioned, nor was the name given of the specific participating choir.

In their next concert, on February 28, 1911, the orchestra played Mendelssohn's Wedding March from *A Midsummer Night's Dream* and his Overture, *Fingal's Cave*, as well as Schubert's "Unfinished" Symphony and several shorter works. The venue for that presentation was Madame Tingley's Isis Theater. That theatre was also the site of the next program, on May 5, 1911, when the concert opened with Massenet's *Phedre* Overture, a venturesome choice for a still under-sized group (forty-four members). A copy of the program for that concert was preserved at the San Diego Historical Society. Like all of the historic San Diego Symphony Orchestra material originally at the Historical Society, it was transferred in 2006 to the Special Collections and University Archives facility at the San Diego State University Library. All of the stored, preserved material there is available for public viewing and research.

The soloist at that second concert was Marshall Giselman, who played Liszt's thunderous *Hungarian Fantasia*. The orchestra played an Andante by Beethoven, as well as Mascagni's Intermezzo from *Cavalleria Rusticana*, a fairly contemporary piece in 1911. The concert concluded with Weber's *Invitation to the Dance*, a fantasy from Wagner's *Lohengrin,* and two Hungarian Dances by Brahms. By the time of its last concert for that initial season, back at the U.S. Grant Hotel, the orchestra seemingly had progressed enough to attempt Beethoven's Fifth Symphony. The *San Diego Union* of July 2, 1911, reported that the "hall was hardly large enough for the volume of the orchestra."

Schliewen remained with the orchestra through the following season that began in the fall of 1911. There were three concerts, all performed in the U. S. Grant Hotel. Dissension among a number of the players led to Schliewen's leaving after the third concert, in March, 1912, and another conductor was sought. Another violinist originally from Berlin, Lionel Gittelson, was hired and led the orchestra through its third season. Six concerts were given during that 1912-13 season with an orchestra enlarged to thirty-three members. A *San Diego Union*

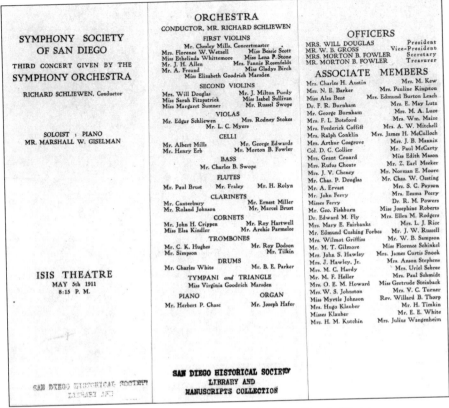

Symphony Society Program, 1912. *Photo courtesy San Diego Historical Society.*

article of September 18 1912, related that an Angelotti organ was acquired to provide, "added volume and color" to the orchestral fabric, although the personnel listing of the orchestra in the May 5, 1911, program lists Mr. Joseph Hafer as organist.

Eventually, stimulated by the popularity and successes of the first three seasons, a community organization was formed to back the orchestra and to try making it into a permanent asset for the city. The Spreckels Theater, just opened, provided a definite lure to the orchestra's backers who visualized their players performing in that acoustically and visually flattering venue. The members of that pioneering community group deserve to be remembered for their vision, foresight and energy. The president of what was re-named the San Diego Symphony Society was Mrs. M. B. Fowler, who had been secretary of the earlier Symphony Society of San Diego. Mr. Tyndall Gray became vice-president, Mrs. Rufus Choate was secretary and Mr. M. B. Fowler remained treasurer. Among the small board of directors was Mrs. H. B. Thearle, whose family's downtown music store was a San Diego fixture for many decades. Auxiliary members included such local eminences as Julius Wangenheim and Melville Klauber.

After incorporating the Symphony Society in 1912, the group contacted Buren Roscoe Schryock, conductor of the Riverside Symphony Orchestra that he had founded in 1908. Schryock was interviewed by the *San Diego Union's* James Frampton for a retrospective article published on September 10, 1960. In it, Schryock recalled that Tyndall Gray "...came to Riverside to see me and offered me a three-year contract to take over the orchestra. San Diego seemed to have a marvelous future. I accepted." Music was alive and well in town, and under Schryock's new, dynamic leadership it would, for a time, grow even healthier and stronger.

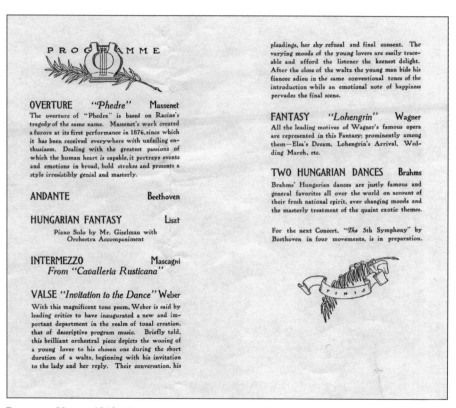

Program Notes, 1912. *Photo courtesy San Diego Historical Society.*

CHAPTER II

Temporary Permanence: The Schryock Regime

T he San Diego Symphony Orchestra's first permanent conductor (i.e., with a three-year contract) came to San Diego from Riverside where he appeared to have a successful career as the organizer and conductor of a symphony orchestra. In 1973, the year before his death at ninety-two, Schryock gave an extended interview to Elizabeth MacPhail. The interviewer, with ties to both the San Diego Historical Society and the California Room of the San Diego Public Library, left a highly-flavored memorandum of the dates and vital statistics regarding her subject as well as many of his recollections and opinions.

Born in 1881 on a farm near Sheldon, Iowa, the son of a Civil War veteran, Buren Schryock had little if any musical stimulation at home. However, when he was seven years old his family moved to Salem, Oregon, where he began piano and voice lessons. After graduating high school in Salem, he joined his older brother and sister in Battle Creek, Michigan, where he studied music at a local college. After his graduation there, he obtained a position as director of the Keene Musical Academy near Dallas, Texas. Two years later he left that post in order to attend the Landon Conservatory in Dallas. After his graduation from the Landon Conservatory, Schryock became the Musical Director and eventually Dean of Music at Union College, a Seventh Day Adventist School near Lincoln, Nebraska, where he conducted the student orchestra and choirs.

With wry humor, Schryock recalled to Ms. MacPhail his leaving that job. He had gone on a vacation to New York where he attended the opera for the first time. A music newspaper published in New York ran a small, probably patronizing article about this man from College View, Nebraska, attending the opera. When that news reached Nebraska, Schryock was fired because the Seventh Day Adventist administration opposed opera as sinful. The music Schryock conducted in his last Union College concert may provide a reasonable picture of his musical tastes and ambitions. With his student orchestra and choir, he conducted Beethoven overtures, Grieg's *Peer Gynt Suite* Number One, and Handel choruses. Schryock returned to Oregon to stay with his family but then decided to seek his future in southern California. He arrived in Riverside during the summer of 1908 and immediately began to organize a symphony orchestra that eventually grew to sixty-five musicians. By 1911, as he recalled, the orchestra had progressed to the status of inviting soloists at the level of Josef Hoffman and Arnold Krauss. In his last program as conductor in Riverside, he led his orchestra in excerpts from Wagner's *Tristan und Isolde*, as well as Tchaikovsky's "Pathetique" Symphony. Schryock maintained considerable pride in the group he founded there long after he left. In the retrospective memoir he sent to the Executive Committee of the San Diego Symphony Orchestra Association in 1952, he noted that when he left Riverside his first flutist left as well to become the first chair flutist of the Los Angeles Symphony Orchestra, the predecessor to the Los Angeles Philharmonic.

In the previously noted 1960 retrospective *San Diego Union* article by James Frampton, Schryock recalled that he had been contacted in Riverside by Tyndall Gray, a member of the newly formed San Diego Symphony Society. In the 1973 MacPhail interview he was more expansive, stating that D. C. Collier, the Director of the Panama-California Exposition that was to take place in San Diego in 1915-16, also came to Riverside to convince him to come to San Diego. Schryock noted that most of the advance activities promoting the Exposition began in 1913, and, according to Collier, the development of a symphony orchestra before the opening of the Exposition was an important goal. Schryock signed a three-year contract with the Symphony Society.

The 1915 Panama-California Exposition succeeded, just as had the tour of the City Guard Band three decades before, once again in putting San Diego firmly on the map. Dirk Sutro, in his book, *San Diego Architecture*, written in 2002 for the San Diego Chapter of the American Institute of Architects Guidebook Project, noted that San Diego had a population of 39,000 in 1909, when the initial ideas for a large exhibition began to crystallize. Sutro wrote, "…Chamber of Commerce President G. Aubrey Davidson proposed an international expo to celebrate the 1915 christening of the Panama Canal. When San Francisco announced its own expo, San Diego decided on a fair with a regional flavor. 'City Park,' the 1,400 acre, as yet mainly undeveloped parcel set aside as a parkland reserve by foresighted city fathers in 1868, was renamed 'Balboa Park' in 1910, in honor of the explorer who crossed Panama in 1513 and reached the Pacific Ocean." Schryock was a little off regarding the dates of the initial planning for the big fair, but he was certainly correct in pointing out Collier as the man particularly responsible for the formation of an orchestra that he felt strongly was to be a necessary part of the fair activities.

The Spreckels Theater, designed by Harrison Albright as the most modern theater in the west, with no obstructing columns to mar the viewing, and excellent acoustics, opened in 1912, prior to the California-Pacific Exposition. Its sadly faded glory can still be appreciated during its relatively infrequent shows, but when it was new it was a sensation. In the fantasies of the valiant members of the San Diego Symphony Society, it was to be the spectacular home of the new San Diego Symphony Orchestra in ever-increasing successful seasons. Only one concert was given there, however, during Schryock's first season, on May 22, 1913. Sadly, the orchestra was only rarely able to set foot on that theater's stage again because the Spreckels became a very busy "road house," featuring many traveling shows from Broadway and elsewhere, and also presenting many distinguished musical soloists in recital. It was seldom available for the fledgling San Diego orchestra, most often restricted to playing matinee concerts where it could in other venues. Evening performances would, of course, conflict with the musicians' regular jobs in hotels and dance palaces. The continuing dream of regularly scheduled concerts at the Spreckels, however, continued to provide an impetus to the new Symphony Society and stimulated it to function, often struggling, for eight years. One must never demean the power of dreams.

The first permanent conductor of the first orchestra officially called the San Diego Symphony (by virtue of the incorporation of the Symphony Society) was a real go-getter. His dreams at least matched those of the sponsoring organization if they did not actually exceed them in their spectacular vision. He brought his own extensive music library to San Diego, and he used most of it and more during his regime here. Throughout his time in San Diego, he was also able to bring in a number of "ringers," mainly from Los Angeles, to buttress the sound and performance level of the local orchestra. San Diego's Local 325, still young and generally ineffective, mounted only occasional weak protests, but to no avail. Schryock, himself, became a member of the Local right away.

Schryock's first program with the San Diego Symphony Orchestra, given in March, 1913, at the U.S. Grant Hotel ballroom, then only three years old, consisted of two movements from Mendelssohn's Italian Symphony, Tchaikovsky's *Andante Cantabile* for String Orchestra, Popper's *Hungarian Rhapsody*, and shorter pieces by Wagner and Thomas. The concert was successful, so he decided that the next concert should make a very big splash. It did.

In the longed-for Spreckels Theater, Schryock mounted what he called, somewhat grandiosely but hopefully, the First Annual San Diego May Music Festival. Cincinnati, an older and more wealthily establishmentarian city than 1913 San Diego, had a considerably deeper and more productive musical tradition based upon its large population of German immigrants. They had been mounting May Festivals there for a number of years by then in the enormous auditorium they had constructed for just such occasions. The Cincinnati May Music Festivals, given annually before several thousands in their Music Hall, were the largest and most successful orchestral/choral festivals yet to be given in the United States. To his enormous credit, Schryock believed that there was no reason why San Diego should not be able to duplicate that success.

With an orchestra of fifty-eight, the San Diego Choral Society and the Philomel Chorus (the chorus of the Normal School, eventually to become San Diego State University), a lengthy program was offered for the initial San Diego Annual May Music Festival, on May 22, 1913, featuring the Bruch G Minor Violin Concerto with Miss Nina Fletcher as violin soloist. There were also a number of vocal presentations. Many of those were of the "parlor song" genre, although the massed choruses (184 voices) joined the orchestra in the *Festmarsche* from Wagner's *Tannhauser*. The concert concluded with performances of Schryock's own *Adagio-Caprice* for Strings and the Overture to *Oberon* by Weber. In his 1952 memoir, Schryock recalled the concert as a "very great success."

One of Schryock's early programs ought to be specifically mentioned because of its novelty, although it must be recalled that program styles then differed considerably from those of our present day. The concerts of December 11 and 12, 1914, began with a performance of the Grand March from *Tannhauser*, played by sixteen pianists at eight keyboards. After the stage was cleared, the orchestra assembled and began its own program under Schryock's baton.

Internal dissension within the orchestra soon dampened some of the hopes held for it. According to Schryock's 1952 memoir, Chesley Mills, concertmaster since the earlier concerts under Schliewen and Gittelson, "…suddenly announced that he was to become conductor of a new orchestra of all union members. I had planned to use a gradual increase of union musicians, as our guarantee would permit. But I had walked the streets and had gotten a three-year guarantee for the San Diego Symphony Orchestra and knew that San Diego at that time could not support an all union scale for concerts and rehearsals…" In his memoir, Schryock commented that in those days most of the orchestras in America were cooperative, at least in their earliest days, and were only fitfully organized after considerable strife. He wrote about the New York Philharmonic, the Chicago Symphony and the Los Angeles Symphony, in which, ". . .all the members got for the full first season was a free dinner and a decision to go with it for the next year!"

Schryock reported, "I would have to give Chesley Mills a run for it. We strengthened the membership of the orchestra. We were now free to have all the rehearsals we needed, and came up with a better playing group than before. I rehearsed sections, selected new players and soon had a fine string section. I was now free to select the best of the local musicians. The union was not very strong at that time, and the best professional musicians were employed at night at the Hotel del Coronado and other spots. I had not been able to use these men at the night performance of the May Festival at the Spreckels. Chesley Mills started his orchestra, but after a short season it went *boom*, leaving quite a deficit….."

"Our orchestra was willing to give part and full rehearsals to satisfy me. The playing of the orchestra was precise and rich in tone. I had a number of violin teachers in the orchestra, and they backed me in my demand for more and more rehearsals..."

Sure enough, the next concert, on November 30, 1913, was given in the afternoon at the First Unitarian Church. The program consisted of the first movement from the Beethoven "Pastoral" Symphony, followed by two short numbers played by the cello soloist of the afternoon, Merrill Baldwin. The first half ended with the orchestra's playing Berlioz' *Dance of the Sylphs* from the *Damnation of Faust*. After the intermission, four local vocalists sang the Quartet from Verdi's *Rigoletto*. The soloists were Mrs. J. Perry Lewis, soprano; Mrs. L. L. Rowan, contralto; Mr. Harry Hammond, tenor; and Mr. Roy Dodson, baritone. The orchestra finished with Weber's Overture to *Der Freischuetz*. Other local vocal soloists appeared with the orchestra in the March 17, 1914 program, when they sang the Sextet from Donizetti's *Lucia di Lammermoor*. They were Mrs. F. Leavenworth, soprano; Mrs. C. N. Anderson, contralto; Mr. A. Besser, tenor; Mr. Glen Hall, tenor; Mr. Arthur Hughes, baritone; and Mr. K. S. Markham, bass. The Sextet was preceded by Brahms' D-Major Hungarian Dance and was followed by Sibelius' *Valse Triste*. After the intermission, pianist Wilhelm Kreuz played the Beethoven "Emperor" Concerto with the orchestra. The program ended with Schryock conducting his own *Adagio-Caprice* and, again, Weber's Overture to *Der Freischuetz*.

Amold Krauss, then-concertmaster of the Los Angeles Symphony, played the Beethoven Violin Concerto with the orchestra in a paired concert, December 11 and 12, 1914. The second of these was on a Saturday night, and represented one of the several exceptions to the standard of only matinee performances throughout Schryock's tenure. It was also exceptional in that this pair of concerts was played in the Spreckels Theater. The program also included the Beethoven Eighth Symphony, as well as the Berlioz *Dance of the Sylphs* (Schryock never minded programming frequent performances of pieces he especially enjoyed) and the Cherubini *Anakreon* Overture.

The rival orchestra, Chesley Mills' "San Diego Popular Symphony," gave its opening concert on November 25, 1914. Four more concerts were given during 1915, but, as Schryock joyfully noted, financial stresses led to its abandonment. Schryock was able to claim the services of several of Mills' musicians. Mills, himself, remained in San Diego and conducted the Juvenile Orchestra of the San Diego Conservatory, according to a January, 1917, article in the *San Diego Union*.

More May Festivals followed over the next several summers. The programs were increasingly lengthy and even adventuresome. The Beethoven Ninth

Spreckels Theatre, 1914. *Photo courtesy San Diego Historical Society.*

Symphony received its first San Diego performance during the 1915 Festival. It was, in fact, given in both the first and third concerts of the 1915 May Festival, initially at the U.S. Grant Hotel, and finally at the Spreckels Organ Pavilion in Balboa Park, completed in 1915 as a gift to the city by the Sugar King as his major contribution to the Panama-California Exposition. It became the favored site for subsequent May Festival performances and any performances associated with the Exposition.

Harrison Albright, the architect responsible for the Spreckels Theater, had been commissioned by Adolph Spreckels to build a suitable home for the world's largest outdoor organ that he was to donate to the city for the Exposition. The pavilion has 2,000 seats, and the center arch houses the console. The stage is vast and can easily hold large musical forces, which it does frequently to this day. It served as the home of concerts in subsequent years by the reorganized San Diego Symphony beginning a decade later and continuing through the 1930s. In his aforementioned book, Dirk Sutro describes the Organ Pavilion as, "…a fantasy flight back to ancient times…Rosettes, stars, satyr heads, floral sprays and musical motifs are among the decorative details." Although obviously not quite in the same style as Bertram Goodhue's grand Spanish colonial *palacios* lining the *Prado* in the park, it still looks terrific and goes well with them visually. Acoustically, it was less than adequate for orchestral music because there was no shell and little intrinsic structure in the pavilion to reflect sound out to the audiences. Twenty years later a newer site became far more favorable.

For Schryock's performances of the Beethoven Ninth Symphony in 1915, a children's chorus of a thousand voices was organized and it joined the so-called Festival Chorus of nearly five hundred voices and an orchestra augmented to eighty players. Schryock must have, indeed, been quite an organizer!

The performance of the Ninth Symphony during the 1915 Exposition was preceded by the playing and singing of Sir Arthur Sullivan's old chestnut, *The Lost Chord*! Today, this would appear to be a very strange juxtaposition, but, again, in the early years of the twentieth century things were often done like that. The Beethoven Ninth was repeated in the 1916 Festival as part of the California-Pacific Exposition, again at the Spreckels Organ Pavilion. That time it was preceded in concert by renditions by a male quartet of Van der Water's *Sunset* and by the male Orpheus Club's performance of Bullard's *Sword of Ferrara*.

Other, even more extravagant concerts were given in the Stadium in Balboa Park, presumably the antecedent to Balboa Stadium. Following is the program for one of the 1916 May Festival Stadium presentations as recalled by Schryock in his 1952 memorandum:

1. March into the Stadium by the San Diego County Children's Chorus of over five thousand trained singers, with their teachers, and headed by a large band.

2. Review of the large chorus before the grandstand by Mayor Edwin M. Capps, president of the May festival, as well as by numerous officers of the city and county school districts. The City Council was also present; they were Directors of the Festival.

3. The children march to their seats, except for those involved in contests.

4. Novelty events and prize singing by a number of county rather than city schools. The children from the Coronado schools formed a column a hundred and twenty feet long and fourteen feet wide, spelling the word, "Coronado."

5. The La Mesa children wore surplices and sang through trumpets. All of the schools competed in choral singing, each in distinctive costume.

6. Part two began with an address by the Mayor, who uncovered a bust of Shakespeare. The bust was then crowned with a laurel wreath by a teacher from the Lincoln School.

7. Massed singing by the "great chorus of over five thousand voices," including Handel's "See, the Conq'ring Hero Comes," from *Judas Maccabeus*, *The Bright Dove of Peace*, to music by Chopin, and the "Ode to Joy" from the Beethoven Ninth Symphony.

8. Three novelty athletic acts by the *Concordia Turnverein*, including the flower drill, the jumping jack dance, and buck-vaulting and pyramids.

9. Verdi's "Anvil Chorus" from *il Trovatore*, "Welcome, Sweet Springtime" to Rubenstein's *Melody in F*, and the Prayer and Finale from Wagner's Act I of *Lohengrin*, all sung and played by the massed chorus and the orchestra.

10. Introduction of Edward Hyatt, the State Superintendent of Public Instruction, who gave an address and also presented the prizes to the winning schools.

11. Solo by the winner of the boy soprano competition, singing through a megaphone to the audience and children's chorus.

12. Singing of the first and last stanzas of *America* (then the National Anthem) by the choruses and the audience.

Interior of Spreckels Theatre, 1914. *Photo courtesy San Diego Historical Society.*

Concerts were given throughout the year during Schryock's stay. Many of the standard orchestral repertoire pieces were featured as well as pieces that would be described today as salon music. He appeared to have a soft spot in his heart for the music of Wagner, and often played excerpts from that composer's music dramas. Chamber concerts were also given, played by orchestra members. Then, in 1917, came the First World War. At the age of thirty-seven, Schryock enlisted in the army and went overseas to France. Schryock's last concert before leaving for the army was given in February, 1917, at the San Diego Women's Clubhouse. The soloist was Helen Babson, who played the Mendelssohn Violin Concerto. The orchestra played the Overture to *Oberon* by Weber and the first movement of Mozart's "Jupiter" Symphony.

When he returned from military service, Schryock wasted no time in re-instituting a regular series of concerts. The orchestra had given no concerts during his absence. A number of the musicians had also been drafted. Most returned to continue playing in San Diego. The first concert of the truncated 1918-1919 season was given at the San Diego Women's Club House on Thursday night, March 6, 1919. The Mendelssohn Violin Concerto was played again, this time with Dorothy Fisher as soloist. A novelty was the unison playing of Schubert's *The Bee* by four of the orchestra's violinists. The concert concluded with Weber's Overture to *Euryanthe*.

Despite its struggling to succeed, the Symphony Society was unable to raise adequate funds during the hard times that followed the end of the war, and eventually Schryock was forced to disband the orchestra. The Symphony Society attempted to mount several concerts after that but was unable to hire the musicians who met Schryock's standards, so he never conducted them again. A couple of concerts were actually given under other conductors, but soon the Society folded, too. Schryock's own last concert with that orchestra under the auspices of the San Diego Symphony Society was given, appropriately at the Spreckels Theater, at noon on November 27, 1920.

The *San Diego Sun*, in its issue of November 26, 1920, provided consider-able publicity to that concert and to the orchestra itself. The unsigned newspaper article deserves some abridged mention here. Following a headline, "First Symphony Concert Tomorrow Noon at the Spreckels," the text began with, "The San Diego Symphony Orchestra, with a list of 53 members, all professionals and most of them soloists on their respective instruments, will open the symphony season tomorrow…The large picture of the orchestra, which is on display near Fifth and Broadway, gives the grouping of the musicians, and has aroused much interest, due to the fact that a large number of the men have been identified with the best symphony orchestras in this country.

"Among these are Clifford A. Webster, concertmaster, who studied under prominent violin masters in Philadelphia and was a member of Edwin Brill's Quartet, and the Schubert Symphony Orchestra, the Philadelphia Operatic Society, and other organizations. Joseph A. Vilim, violinist, graduated from the Prague Conservatory in 1882. While abroad he played under the great master, Tschaikowsky, then came to Chicago and was first violinist with the Thomas Orchestra for several seasons. James Seebold, solo flutist, was associated with the First Regiment Philadelphia Band, Thunder's Philadelphia Symphony Orchestra and Klinger's Concert Band, and for many

ORCHESTRA WILL PLAY

First Symphony Concert Tomorrow Noon at the Spreckels

"*Sun*" —— 11-26-20

The San Diego Symphony orchestra, with a list of 53 members, all professionals and most of them soloists on their respective instruments, will open the symphony season tomorrow noon at the Spreckels theater. The large picture of the orchestra, which is on display near Fifth and Broadway, gives the grouping of the musicians, and has aroused much interest, due to the fact that a large number of the men have been identified with the best symphony orchestras in this country.

Among these are Clifford A. Webster, concertmaster, who studied under prominent violin masters in Philadelphia and was a member of Edwin Brill's quartet, and the Schubert Symphony orchestra, the Philadelphia Operatic society and other organizations. Joseph A. Vilim, violinist, graduated from the Prague conservatory in 1882. While abroad he played under the great master Tschaikowsky, then came to Chicago and was first violinist with the Thomas orchestra for several seasons. James Seebold, solo flutist, was associated with the First Regiment Philadelphia band, Thunder's Philadelphia Symphony orchestra and Klinger's Concert band and for many years solo with Ohlmeyer's band at Tent City.

THE PERSONNEL

The complete personnel of the orchestra:

B. Roscoe Schryock, conductor.

First violins—Clifford A. Webster, concertmaster; Fred Olson, Joseph A. Valim, Lavina Lien, Harold Lindoft, Owen A. Bartlett, Charles Krieger and David Forrest.

Second violins — Lew Keyser, principal; Mrs. Franz Rath, Wm. J. Meader, Frederick W. Smith, W. A. Mark, Russo Rinaldo and W. A. Hutton.

Violas—August Wolf, principal; Emil C. Reinbold, Luella Fracker and Frank Cain.

Violoncellos—John Childs, principal; Jane S. Johnson, Pauline V. Holmes, Harold Hruska and Harvey Ball.

Basses — Earl Grainger, J. W. Armstrong, K. Markham, George Nagle and Ernest Camp.

Flutes — James Seebold and Franz Rath.

Oboes—A. A. Marsh and R. E. Trognitz.

English horn—R. E. Trognitz.

Clarinets—George T. McGuire, Robert R. Johnson and George Fish.

Bassoon—Roy Dodson.

Horns — Wendell Hoss, Frank Bollo, Fritz Erbe and C. B. Rodman.

Trumpets — F. A. Groves and Jules Jacques.

Trombones—Henry Simpson, F. Ruggieri and F. C. Kendall.

Tuba—Ernest Owen.

Tympani—E. P. James.

Percussion—R. E. Donaldson.

Harp—Marie Hughes Macquarrie.

Piano—Royal A. Brown.

The first chair men from the Los Angeles Symphony orchestra will play with the local professionals, Wendell Hoss, horn, and A. A. March, first oboe.

Barney & Barney, 208 Scripps Bldg. Insurance and Bonds.

1920 article from the *San Diego Sun*. *Photo courtesy San Diego Union-Tribune archives.*

years solo with Ohlmeyer's Band at Tent City..."

The article continued with a complete list of the personnel of the orchestra, and noted that "the first chair men from the Los Angeles Symphony Orchestra will play with the local professionals, Wendell Hoss, horn, and A. A. March, oboe." Surprisingly, no mention of the program was made in the article, otherwise so detailed regarding the musicians.

In his 1952 memorandum, Schryock recalled that he had to give the concert at noon because he could no longer employ musicians who needed their hotel and other work at night. The program was demanding and generous; the fifty-three member Symphony, all union members by then, ended its era with considerable glory. It began and ended with Wagner, the *Lohengrin* Prelude at first and the *Tannhauser* Overture at the end. Before the intermission, the Dvorak "New World" Symphony was played, and after the intermission the orchestra ren-

1920 San Diego Symphony Orchestra poster. *Photo courtesy Mildred Lyman Tracy Thesis.*

dered Debussy's *Prelude to the Afternoon of a Faun,* followed by more Wagner pieces. The novelty this time was the unison performance by the entire string section of Bach's *Air for the G String.*

Partially duplicating the list given in the *Sun* article, Schryock provided the names of many of his musicians in his own 1952 memoir. Notable among the partial list he could recollect of those who played in the final concert, R. E. Trognitz played the oboe. It may be recalled that Trognitz conducted the 1902 concert, considered to be the first symphonic concert given by the fledgling orchestra. Whereas Trognitz at least played in the orchestra after his conductorship, Schryock had no contact with any later developments that led to the re-formation of a new San Diego Symphony Orchestra under a different auspice. He certainly never conducted it. He remained in San Diego, however, as an active member of the musical community.

Very soon after disbanding the San Diego Symphony, Schryock took over the position of conductor of the San Diego Grand Opera Company. The company had been in existence, off and on, for a number of years under several different names, including the San Diego Civic Grand Opera Company. Schryock continued in that position until 1936, when the company disbanded in the midst of the depression. Until then it had been reasonably successful, producing annual seasons of operas from the standard repertoire in their original languages. Of note and seemingly characteristic of Schryock's attitude was that he took pains in the 1973 MacPhail interview to criticize the more recently founded San Diego Opera Company because, under Walter Herbert's direction, all of its performances were given in English translations.

Schryock expressed great pride in the quality of the productions given by his opera company. He was able to hire experienced performers — sometimes even stars — after they appeared on tour in San Francisco and Los Angeles. When the company gave *Rigoletto*, the title role was assumed by the world-famous baritone, Giuseppe de Luca. Schryock was proud, too, of the venues. Unlike most of the concerts he led with the Symphony, the operas were given in his beloved Spreckels Theater, as well as in the Russ Auditorium and in the Balboa Park Auditorium, which later became a fire casualty.

After 1936, Schryock taught voice and also turned to writing. He joined the Federal Writers' Project, a WPA subsidiary, and eventually completed several operas about ancient Rome, the Civil War, pioneer Iowa and Oregon, and the trek of Mongols across the Bering Straits into North America. There is no record of any of them having been performed. When the war came, he left San Diego to work in the Naval shipyard in Long Beach from which he retired in 1950. He returned to San Diego and remained a San Diegan until his death.

His last years appear now to have been somewhat lonely. He lived in a single room and was known to have taken the bus downtown every day in order to have his main meal at mid-day at a specific Chinese restaurant. He died at ninety-two on January 20, 1974. The obituary in the January 26 *San Diego Union* noted that he was survived by a brother, a nephew and three nieces, one of whom lived in Chula Vista. The impression is gained that he had been a widower for some time. In the list of musicians in the Riverside Orchestra that he included in his 1950s memorandum to the Executive Committee of the San Diego Symphony, a Mrs. B. Schryock was listed as a cellist. On another occasion, in Riverside in 1911, she was a piano soloist, playing the Grieg Concerto. Apparently there were no children.

Elizabeth MacPhail wrote in 1973, "He is convinced that nobody in San Diego has the slightest interest in his past endeavors in the music world in San Diego." Schryock's impression was probably quite true,

Buren Roscoe Schryock. *Photo courtesy San Diego Symphony.*

and he must have felt considerable, understandable bitterness. It is tragic that someone who expended such remarkable efforts to make symphonic music in San Diego should have been forgotten as he was. The orchestra he conducted provided an eight-year taste of the future. At times, he was able to fulfill his big ideas and impress the public with triumphs. At other times, at a minimum he kept his orchestra going — no insignificant feat. Buren Schryock deserves remembering on a strongly positive note. He made San Diegans appreciate the presence of a good concert orchestra.

D-2   **THE SAN DIEGO UNION**   Saturday, January 26, 1974

Buren Schryock Services Monday

Memorial services will be at 1 p.m. Monday in Berge-Roberts Mortuary for Buren Roscoe Schryock, 92, of 6599 Alvarado Road, former conductor of the San Diego Symphony Orchestra and founder of the San Diego Opera Co., which he headed from 1919 to 1932. He died Sunday in a hospital.

A native of O'Brien County, Iowa, Schryock moved with his family to Salem, Ore., and began studying piano and organ at the age of 8. He attended Battle Creek, Mich., College and later headed the music departments at Keene Academy at Keene, Tex., and Union College in Lincoln, Neb. He also was dean of music at Union College.

He moved to Riverside in 1908 and organized the Riverside Symphony Orchestra, which he conducted for five years. In 1913, he was named conductor of the San Diego Symphony Orchestra and of the San Diego Choral Society.

While head of the San Diego Opera Company, he presented performances of opera, mainly Italian, in the Spreckels Theater and Russ Auditorium. He wrote several operas about ancient Rome, the Civil War, pioneer Iowa and Oregon, and the trek of Mongols across

BUREN SCHRYOCK
... former conductor

the Bering Straights into Western America.

An Army veteran of World War I, Schryock was a member of Veterans of World War I, Barracks 240, and a member of Sons of Union Veterans of the Civil War. He was a former member of American Legion Post 6.

Survivors include a brother; a nephew, and three nieces, including Mrs. Elizabeth Hockin of Chula Vista.

Private inurnment will be in Greenwood Memorial Park.

Schryock obituary. *Photo courtesy San Diego Union-Tribune archives.*

CHAPTER III

Nino Marcelli, the Real Father of the San Diego Symphony

The financial stresses leading to Buren Schryock's 1920 departure from the podium prevented the Symphony Society from planning for any continuing seasons. The Society disbanded as well as the orchestra, and the city was left without any concert orchestra of its own for a number of years.

A truly remarkable man came to the rescue of the city's musical scene. Born in Rome in 1890, Giovanni Marcelli was an infant, the eleventh of twelve children, when his family emigrated to Santiago, Chile. Giovanni's name was changed to Juan in Spanish-speaking Chile but his family and friends always called him Nino. Eventually he used it as his official given name. His exceptional precocity in music was evident at an early age. When only ten years old, Nino followed his much older brother, Ulderico, into the National Conservatory in Santiago where he studied horn, as well as all aspects of music theory and harmony. At twenty Nino became a member of the faculty, teaching brass instruments and eventually *solfeggio* and theory. By 1913, he had developed so strongly that he conducted the Conservatory Orchestra in a concert series featuring all nine Beethoven symphonies!

Pietro Mascagni, the composer of *Cavalleria Rusticana*, visited Chile and was impressed enough by Marcelli to encourage him to come to Italy to study further and also to perform before more sophisticated audiences. Nino followed Mascagni's advice and enjoyed his patronage. He was able to support himself by playing cello with the orchestra of a traveling Italian opera troupe, eventually becoming its conductor. During the troupe's American tour, Marcelli left the company to make his mark in New York. He succeeded, conducting theater orchestras. He led the premiere and initial season of Sigmund Romberg's classic, *Maytime*, and also conducted the orchestra accompanying D. W. Griffith's *Birth of a Nation*.

Marcelli became Griffith's Musical Director, arranging scores for theatre orchestras to play in accompaniment to the grandiose silent film epics, and auditioning players for the theatre orchestras in America's principal cities. In Chicago, he was conducting the orchestra accompanying Griffith's *Intolerance* when he learned of the disastrous World War I Italian defeat by the Austrians

Nino Marcelli *Photo courtesy San Diego Symphony.*

and their subsequent retreat at Caporetto. The next day he led a group of his Italian musicians to the Italian Consulate in Chicago. They all offered to sail to Italy to join the Italian Army. The group's offer was refused, however, and they were all advised to continue working.

When America was brought into the war soon afterwards Marcelli became an American citizen. He enlisted as an infantryman in the AEF, joining the famous "Black Hawk" Division, the 344th Infantry, and was sent after training to France. Soon after he arrived in France with his unit, he entered a competition for an appointment as the Bandmaster of the Paris Band of the AEF. He won handily over thirty-five competitors. He was able to hand pick ninety-eight instrumentalists and fulfilled General Pershing's wish that the Americans should have a band that compared favorably with the world famous band of the French *Garde Republicaine*.

He continued composing when he could. Aside from several widely played marches, he also wrote *Ode to a Hero*, in honor of General Pershing, the commander of the AEF. Shortly before the Armistice, he was selected to conduct the Headquarters Band in Paris in a series of concerts before many dignitaries.

Upon his discharge, Nino went to the San Francisco home of his older brother, Ulderico, whose compositions were given repeated hearings in the Bay Area. Nino joined Alfred Hertz's San Francisco Symphony Orchestra as a cellist. The San Francisco fog, however, led to a chronic bronchial condition that caused Nino to think of moving to dryer, warmer southern California. San Diego beckoned when B. O. Lacey retired as Director of Music at San Diego High School, and a search was made for a successor. San Diego was blessed when Marcelli was chosen. In late 1920 he took the coastal steamer to his new city and began building what was to become one of the most exceptional, nationally recognized high school music departments in the country.

Although it may sound like the plot of a "feel good" Hollywood movie, it really is true that the San Diego Symphony Orchestra developed from an exceptional high school orchestra. It is also true that the development of the high school orchestra and its descendent San Diego Symphony Orchestra resulted from the exceptional efforts and charisma of Nino Marcelli.

When Marcelli came to San Diego High School from San Francisco in 1920, he found that a small group of students had formed an ensemble of twenty-two members. Three years later, he was able to take an enlarged group to Santa Ana where they received a warm critical notice in the *Pacific Coast Musician*. The notice referred to a "…revelation of what might be accomplished in our high schools under such efficient direction…" By dint of Marcelli's heroic efforts, the San Diego High School Orchestra grew to ninety players by 1926. Marcelli combed the school. He recruited any and all students who could or wanted to play any instrument, taught them to play better, pressured them to take private lessons outside of school, or persuaded them to start on a different instrument that was needed more by the orchestra. Often, he had to scrounge instruments from any source for his students to play. He was a tough taskmaster who demanded much from his players but also provided warmth and encouragement. The students responded.

Constance Herreshoff, music critic for the *San Diego Union* in later years, wrote an article for the January 6, 1952 paper, in which she quoted a former Marcelli student, Lois Wann, who had written to her. Ms. Wann had become a professional oboist, playing with a number of groups in the New York area, to which she had moved. In her article, Constance Herreshoff reported on how very grateful Ms. Wann had always been to Marcelli, but that recently the measure of her gratitude had jumped markedly. She played an oboe solo with the Pittsburgh Symphony Orchestra, in the Johann Strauss Overture to *Die Fledermaus*. The conductor, Fritz Reiner, stopped the orchestra and asked Lois how and where she had learned to play that passage and the oboe so well. She told Reiner (who rarely, if ever, had a kind word for his musicians until he reached the podium of the Chicago Symphony Orchestra — and even then, not too often!), "Nino Marcelli impressed this interpretation on me during a rehearsal of our San Diego High School Orchestra." The great Fritz Reiner becoming positively impressed is a meaningful criterion.

After a few years of Marcelli's hard work the San Diego High School Orchestra was good enough for the public to hear. Marcelli took his students to the Spreckels Theatre in December, 1925, and showed them off. The response was enthusiastic even among the musically sophisticated. The program was exceptional for any high school orchestra; it included Wagner's *Rienzi* Overture and his Prelude to Act Three of *Lohengrin*, as well as Tchaikovsky's *Nutcracker Suite* and *Marche Slave*! The next year the orchestra opened the high school's new Russ Auditorium, which became the city's major venue for concerts. Aside from the

San Diego High School, 1926. The new Russ Auditorium is the light-colored building. *Photo courtesy San Diego Historical Society.*

annual visits of the Los Angeles Philharmonic Orchestra, Marcelli's high school orchestra provided its own concerts there as well. There were even reviews. When Marcelli took them to Los Angeles for a concert, Bruno David Ussher of the *Los Angeles Times* expressed considerable amazement at the proficiency and seeming professionalism of the San Diego High School Orchestra. Later, when Ussher worked at music criticism for the *San Diego Evening Tribune*, he continued to praise Marcelli and his orchestra. Journals such as *Musical America* noted the development of the San Diego High School Orchestra and expressed praise for its prowess. One of Marcelli's successors as Director of Music in the San Diego Unified High School District, Kenneth Owens, paid tribute to him, saying, "Nino's school orchestra set the pattern for other schools."

In April, 1960, Marcelli responded to a letter from Joseph W. Landon, then-president of the California Music Educators' Association. Mr. Landon requested a brief outline of Marcelli's professional activities in music education, preparatory to a presentation to be made to Marcelli later that year in Monterey, California. In reply, Marcelli noted that demands for participation by the San Diego High School Orchestra became increasingly frequent. After 1922, the orchestra participated, "...numerous times at conventions for music teachers, high school principals, superintendents of schools, and many times at sectional, regional and state musical educators' conferences, and even at nationals. Some auditoriums remain in the 'visual memory,' such as the Hollywood High School Auditorium many years ago; the Redlands High School auditorium; Bridges Auditorium at Pomona College; the Biltmore Hotel Bowl during the 1940 National Conference..."

Marcelli became famous throughout southern California because of his work with his high school students, and also because of his composing, which he refused to neglect. The *San Diego Union* of March 28, 1924, provided an enthusiastic review by Daisy Kessler Biermann of a concert given at the Spreckels Theatre the evening before by the Los Angeles Philharmonic Orchestra, which had begun their annual series of performances in San Diego a few years before. This particular program was notable for Marcelli's conducting the orchestra in his own composition, the *Suite Araucana,* described as,

> "...a revelation of the genius of this young artist. The four movements of the suite may be considered to be the last word in modernist composition, the new mode in tone painting which seeks for vivid and realistic expression. Daring and original in orchestration, most novel in themes, and characteristic in creative construction, this composition is fascinating from varied angles. Realistic in the extreme, like the blustering winds over the high plateaus of the savage south American tribe which gave the piece its inspiration, with a pathetic crooning melody like the crooning squaw, the savagery of tom-toms and warring demons and men, the barbarous conflicts of the primitive jungles — these are the mingling elements in this stirring composition. And the modernist does stir unplumbed things in the inner consciousness that the metered and measured music of the older schools scarce flecks the surface. Whether you like it or not, there is that singular dynamic vitality that grips something elemental and basic beneath the appreciation of polished grace of musicianship..."

One must wonder what has happened to music criticism in the interim.

At any rate, the *Suite Araucana* figured on a number of programs conducted by Marcelli over the years, generally to enthusiastic response. As a guest conductor of the San Francisco Symphony Orchestra in 1925, he conducted the suite there, as well as with the Los Angeles Philharmonic Orchestra in the 1926-27 season. Marcelli also conducted it with the Los Angeles Philharmonic again, this time in a Hollywood Bowl concert in 1934. John Barbirolli also conducted the *Suite Araucana* with the Los Angeles Philharmonic when he was its guest conductor in the early '30s, and Leopold Stokowski conducted it in Philadelphia. It should be noted that the *Suite Araucana* had been premiered in 1924 by the New York Philharmonic. Willem van Hoogstraaten conducted.

Apparently, the *Suite Araucana* made the rounds of some of the top orchestras of the nation in the 1920s and 1930s, indicating that it was a piece of consider-

San Diego High School Orchestral Society, 1926. *Photo courtesy San Diego Historical Society.*

able substance and musical merit. How interesting it might be to hear it now, played by the San Diego Symphony Orchestra. The performance would certainly provide a fitting memorial to Marcelli.

The *San Diego Union* of February 28, 1926, printed a lengthy article praising Marcelli in glowing terms. The occasion was the forthcoming presentation of Rossini's *Stabat Mater* by the San Diego Oratorio Society, a group founded and trained intensively by Marcelli. No by-line was provided for the article, but the unknown writer extolled Marcelli's previous efforts with the Oratorio Society since he had organized it the prior year. They had already given Handel's *Messiah*, Humphrey Stewart's *The Hound of Heaven*, and, in concert form, Saint-Saens' *Samson et Dalila*. All had been enthusiastically and gratefully received. The article further praised Marcelli for bringing excellent vocal soloists for those performances, including the distinguished American baritone, Charles Marshall, as well as the then up-and-coming tenor, Richard Crooks.

The article continued:

> "What Marcelli has done here since 1921 is important musical history in this city. His high school orchestra concerts are events of real significance, and can be measured by the highest musical standards. He has instilled in the young musicians of the high school and the other schools of the city the ambition to achieve the best and highest in music. He has taken them when they are young and pliant, has indoctrinated them with high standards, and has made real musicians out of them. He is rightly proud of what they are doing, and he has the inspiring ability to get the very most of loyalty and enthusiasm into their work. When he is satisfied with the results he is getting, there

can be no question but that they are valuable, for there is no more strict or able judge of musicianship and interpretation than Marcelli in San Diego, or in this part of the country for that matter…"

By 1926 Marcelli began to be aware of the continuing needs of the orchestra's alumni to play. No other ensemble was available to them. The lack of a junior college in those days prevented the development of a post-high school graduate orchestra. Many musicians opted for a fifth high school year in order to play in the orchestra! Others, because of Marcelli's training and enthusiasm, chose to go to conservatories in order to become professional musicians. The solution, as Marcelli saw it, was to organize a permanent symphony orchestra for San Diego. He called it the San Diego Philharmonic Orchestra, but it is not to be confused with the much later group of the same name that tried establishing an ongoing series of winter seasons in the early 1950s.

Marcelli's San Diego Philharmonic's first concert, at the Spreckels Theatre in April, 1927, was financed by a local philanthropist, A. B. Bridges, who had married into the Timken family. The eighty-member orchestra was composed of many of the high school orchestra's graduates as well as the best of the city's professional musicians. The principal second violinist, however, had yet to graduate, but Joe Kirshbaum was extraordinarily talented, as befitted a member of one of the city's eminent musical dynasties. A mortician played first trombone, and a jazz drummer played the cymbals. An article written by Henry

ORCHESTRAL SOCIETY

UNDER the splendid leadership of Signor Nino Marcelli, composer and former director of some of the world's greatest symphony orchestras, The Orchestral Society, composed of students of the advanced and beginners' orchestras, has made its place in Hilltop activities as one of the most active, as well as one of the most talented organizations.

The orchestra, which is said to be one of the finest of its kind in the United States, has brought many honors to the San Diego High School by its superior performances, due to the untiring efforts and compelling personality of Mr. Marcelli, and to the diligent work of the sixty students who compose the advanced orchestra, and also the smaller group of beginning pupils.

By giving its aid to various dramatic performances, club activities, and assembly programs, the orchestra has rendered a great service to the school. Many of its members are regular entertainers at Camp Kearny, where they find a warm reception.

But the most important event of the season was the semi-annual and annual concert, given at the Spreckels Theatre on June 6. The difficult selections were perfected only after constant, persistent efforts on the part of the director and pupils.

San Diegans were justly proud of the achievement of the orchestra and of its distinguished director.

Beatrice Rogers
Helen Boyd
Geraldine Haddock
Norman McBride

Page one hundred sixty-two   *The Gray Castle*

Article from the 1926 San Diego High School Annual. *Photo courtesy Philip Klauber archives.*

Schwartz for the April, 1977 issue of *Applause Magazine*, formerly the publisher of program books for San Diego's cultural offerings, described the scene at the Spreckels. The theatre was filled. The audience included all the members of the San Diego Oratorio Society, organized and conducted for the previous several years by Marcelli. They had purchased a bloc of seats and sat together as a cheering section. KFSD had placed three microphones on the stage and, at 8:15 p.m., they went on the air from the theatre and broadcast the entire concert. How wonderful it would have been had they been able to have recorded it for posterity. As it is, we have no aural records of any of the Marcelli orchestras, but the recollections of the listeners are quite vividly enthusiastic.

As Schwartz remembered, "And on the night of April 11, 1927, his orchestra gave its best. Marcelli conducted with fire and enthusiasm. His players responded..." Marcelli's longstanding friendship with Dusolina Giannini led the distinguished dramatic soprano to donate her services. The orchestra accompanied her in arias from *la Forza del Destino* and *Cavalleria Rusticana*. She also sang three Neapolitan songs and then gave eight encores! The orchestra played Liadov's *The Enchanted Lake*, and Tchaikovsky's "Pathetique" Symphony, as well as his *Marche Slave*, which brought the concert to a rousing conclusion. *Time Magazine* reported that the audience cheered, and Marcelli had to quiet them — after taking several bows. Then, from the stage, he introduced Austin Adams of the soon-to-be-formed San Diego Symphony Association, who urged the audience to undertake a community commitment to a permanent orchestra with summer and winter seasons. According to Schwartz, the audience cheered some more.

Daisy Kessler Biermann, music critic for the *San Diego Union*, crossed Second Street to the old *Union* offices and typed her review, published the next morning. It began, "San Diego has her symphony orchestra. They played with hearts and souls as well as brains and fingers."

A series of summer concerts were given that year at the

FIRST SEASON
SUMMER CONCERTS
Philharmonic Orchestra
of SAN DIEGO

Maestro Nino Marcelli, Conducting

Organ Pavilion, Balboa Park
Sunday, July 10th, 1927, at 5 P. M.

OFFICERS *of* THE PHILHARMONIC ORCHESTRA
ED. H. CLAY, *President*   MADELINE B. CHILDS, *Secretary*
CLAUDE WOOLMAN, *Vice-President*   RONALD W. FAULKNER, *Treasurer*
E. P. JAMES, *Manager*

1927 Summer Concerts Program Cover.
Photo courtesy San Diego Historical Society.

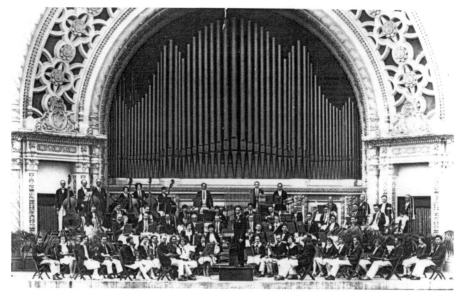

1927 San Diego Philharmonic Orchestra at Spreckels Organ Pavillion. *Photo courtesy San Diego Historical Society.*

Spreckels Organ Pavilion. The orchestra's programs were mainly what we would today call light classical in nature, very different from those with which Marcelli characteristically showed off the San Diego High School ensemble. He believed that the outdoor venue invited lighter fare, at least at first.

Nino Marcelli's dream of establishing a permanent professional symphony orchestra in his adopted city of San Diego seemed to approach reality. In the same year as the founding of the Philharmonic, Marcelli found personal as well as professional happiness. He married Adelaide Burns Vogel, a wealthy widow and a shrewd businesswoman in her own right. She proved to be the perfect helpmeet. Her social position enhanced his, and she organized much of Marcelli's professional life during the succeeding decade.

In 1928 a group of concerned San Diegans met to incorporate a new Civic Symphony Orchestra. A *San Diego Union* article of January 1, 1930, reflected on the origins and growth of Marcelli's orchestra. The writer was Wallace Moody, then the main arts columnist for the paper. He wrote:

> "While the success of the first venture [i. e., the first year of Marcelli's San Diego Philharmonic] was not as pronounced as it might have been, the germ of the idea had been implanted and it only required the right kind of encouragement to bring it above the ground. In the autumn of that year, 1927, Mrs. Mary Kimball Kutchin, in an inspired moment, conceived the idea

of putting the orchestra upon a permanent basis by arranging for one concert each week throughout the year on Sunday
afternoons, believing that adequate support would be forthcoming from public interest in the plan. It was obviously too
early to achieve such an ambitious program. Nevertheless, her
interest and enthusiasm in the matter was largely responsible
for crystallizing public attention and in serving as inspiration in
putting the orchestral forces upon a more solid foundation the
following year."

Moody continued, "Owing to Mrs. Kutchin's prolonged absence abroad
that winter, the late W. S. Dorland, who had become so intensely interested
in the project that he was willing to head it up, found himself faced with the
necessity of starting a movement for a new start early enough in the spring to
insure the summer season of park concerts. A survey of possible affiliations was
made and the work of reorganization was begun. Organization of the Orchestra
Association was at once effected..."

The Executive Committee were W. S. Dorland as president, with Havrah
Hubbard, Orville McPherson, Marnie Sullivan, Alice B. Stevenson and, repre-
senting the Musicians' Union, W. J. Meader and Dr. W. C. Newton. The new
society determined that the prior summer's backing and organization was,
according to its minutes, "conducted rather casually," and they determined that
a tighter organization was needed to establish a permanent orchestra. They
obtained the sponsorship of the San Diego Musicians' Protective Association and
named Marcelli conductor, "with such guest conductors as the board may see fit."
The Articles of Incorporation of the new, so-called Civic Symphony Orchestra
of San Diego were approved by the State on March 28, 1928.

Even though a change would eventually be made in the name of the group,
the charter from the state remained secure and permanent, and the current
San Diego Symphony Orchestra Association continues to function under that
charter's aegis. To many, March 28, 1928 is considered the birth date of the contemporary San Diego Symphony Orchestra. To others, 1910 is considered the
birth year of the orchestra because it was then that a group was first organized.
The backers of the 1928 date point to the fact that the orchestra of the 1910-
1920 years disbanded, as did the organization sponsoring it. They note that the
Marcelli orchestra was a totally new group with totally new backing. To some,
this minor dispute may appear to be a tempest in a teacup, although to historians
it might prove to be a situation to ponder.

The Civic Symphony Orchestra gave eight Sunday afternoon light classical concerts at the Organ pavilion during its first year. According to Moody's

San Diego Union article, the "most generous" financial guarantee given by the Musicians' Union was entirely fulfilled by the enthusiastic ticket sales. It was notable, however, according to Moody, that Miss Ellen Browning Scripps donated twelve hundred dollars to underwrite one of the concerts, and that San Diego's favorite musical resident (aside from Marcelli), the great contralto, Mme. Ernestine Schumann-Heink, donated her services as soloist for the final concert of that season. The first guest conductor came the next year, no less than Alfred Hertz, the famed Music Director of the San Francisco Symphony. He led a little more serious program, featuring Schubert's "Unfinished" Symphony.

"Noteworthy improvement in the playing of the orchestra" was commented upon by Moody in his 1930 article. "It may be said, in passing, that Nino Marcelli has had the cooperation of the Association's program committee in upholding the high standard of program material, keeping the concerts free of mediocrity while making them, at the same time, of wide appeal..." Moody noted the increased audience response in 1929 and pointed out that the final concert of that summer season was, "...in the nature of a tribute to Nino Marcelli. One of the largest audiences in the history of the association gathered at the Organ Pavilion to hear the orchestra alone, there being no feature on that day other than the orchestra itself...With another generous contribution by Miss Scripps the season closed with all financial obligations met and with the satisfaction of marked advance in artistic accomplishment on the part of the orchestra..."

Like its predecessor, the long-disbanded first San Diego Symphony Orchestra of twenty years before, the Civic Symphony Orchestra was a cooperative group for its first three years. The members were paid for their two-hour rehearsals but earned varied, usually small amounts of money from the concerts themselves. The proceeds from tickets, advertising and contributions were usually very sparse. The Musicians' Union insisted that the cooperative basis could no longer be tolerated and that contracts must be signed for a minimum wage scale. With that, the board voted to discontinue the concerts and it cancelled the 1930 season, giving the lie to Moody's premature, final sentences in his article, "With its second successful year now passed into history, the San Diego Civic Symphony orchestra may now be counted as one of our permanent cultural institutions. The committee intends to carry on."

As it always seems with orchestras, problems were difficult to overcome, but somehow these were handled. Great efforts were made by new officers of the board to find more money, more guarantors, more advertising and more subscriptions. The resulting 1930 Civic Orchestra season became the longest yet.

The Orchestra's programs had begun to be increasingly demanding as the summer seasons progressed. On his own, based upon the Orchestra's playing increasingly serious music, Marcelli determined that the ensemble should be known as the San Diego Symphony Orchestra instead of the Civic Orchestra. In 1931, he contacted Buren Schryock, the original San Diego Symphony's only permanent conductor during its short-lived, pre-1920 existence. Schryock, always a good promoter, had continued to live in San Diego, teaching music and various instruments, and also conducting choruses. He even formed San Diego's first opera company and presented several performances of standard repertory in the Savoy and Spreckels Theatres. There is no record of his attitude toward the new orchestra that he never conducted. Nonetheless, on April 11, 1931, he wrote to Nino Marcelli as follows: "Inasmuch as the San Diego Symphony Orchestra has not been active for several years, we find no objection to your organization assuming the name."

Marcelli thereafter called his orchestra the San Diego Symphony, and often the music writers in the media referred to it in the same way. The name change, however, became official only on March 30, 1937, when a group of concerned citizens reorganized the prior Civic Orchestra Board and incorporated the San Diego Symphony Orchestra Association. They continued the same organization, newly renamed, that remains the official backbone of today's San Diego Symphony. From that point to the present, our orchestra has been, officially and otherwise, the San Diego Symphony Orchestra.

A program of one of the 1931 concerts is available at the San Diego Historical Society. On August 11 of that year, Marcelli led the orchestra in the Beethoven *Egmont* Overture and a novelty, a *Concerto Gregoriano* for Organ and Orchestra, by a composer listed only as Yon. No first name was given in the program and there is no listing for him in *Grove*. After intermission, the orchestra gave its first ever performance of Rimsky-Korsakoff's suite, *Sheherazade*. To end the program, Elgar's *Pomp and Circumstance* March No. 1 was played, with Royal Brown at the organ.

The great depression came upon the orchestra and its community in the early 1930s. Money was tighter than ever. Audiences had increased needs for entertainment in those times of enormous job loss statistics. However, a nation, "Ill-housed and ill-fed," as described by FDR upon his assumption of the presidency early in 1933, had little spendable income. All the arts suffered. Not only the San Diego orchestra was put upon. In Philadelphia, the home of what was then called the world's greatest symphony orchestra, Leopold Stokowski had to cut the ranks of his sections and play a season and a half with a significantly reduced complement of musicians. He also took a significant cut in his own salary so that the salaries of those musicians he could keep would be augmented, at least a little. Other orchestras simply went under.

An orchestra such as the San Diego Civic Symphony did not even have the luxury of reducing its forces who were accustomed to splitting whatever was left in the pot after costs were taken out. Musical jobs were no longer available in the evenings at hotels, themselves victims of lower censuses and poor tourism. Would the musicians of the orchestra play for nothing?

At this point the first of the government programs began that would attempt to provide funds to employ unemployed musicians. The State Emergency Relief Administration (SERA) began to serve San Diego musicians on June 1, 1934. The musicians' project, sponsored by the City of San Diego, aimed to employ an average of fifty-one employees. A budget planned for the first six months was over seven thousand dollars. According to the extensive Master's Thesis written for a degree at the University of California, Davis, by Peter W. Mehren in 1972, that first allocation provided for a band. However, on October 12, SERA approved a sixty-three member orchestral project, also sponsored by the city. That was budgeted for more than twenty thousand dollars for the first six months.

In 1935, SERA was replaced by a newly organized federal program, the Works Progress Administration (WPA). The WPA was organized into several subsections for the arts, one of them being the Federal Music Project (FMP). It was the FMP that provided most of the employment for musicians throughout the country, adding to and augmenting severely cut or even absent salaries that may have been paid by the orchestras and bands in which they performed. The FMP also organized orchestras of its own, and so-called "WPA Symphonies" gave important series of concerts throughout the country.

The situation in San Diego was generally comparable. On November 18, 1935, the San Diego FMP registered more than 350 local musicians to play in a symphony orchestra, a fifty-eight member dance orchestra pool, an opera company, and a federal civic band. William Dean came to town to assume the administration of the local FMP. He was very sympathetic toward the new symphony orchestra formed by the FMP and encouraged it to give more concerts, while the band became restricted to one concert per week. The FMP orchestra was directed for the most part by Julius Leib.

The FMP orchestra did not replace the San Diego Symphony that, while struggling to just barely make it financially, continued playing its weekly programs under Marcelli's baton every summer through 1934, with its continued, constant personnel totaling eighty-two players. Russell Keeney remained the orchestra's concertmaster and Paul Henneberg, who served for many years as a bassist in the orchestra was another constant. Other factors fortunately intervened that allowed the San Diego Symphony to continue its progress.

The California-Pacific Exposition (or the California-Pacific International Exposition, as it was called in its second year, 1936) provided a needed shot in the arm to San Diego's still-struggling orchestra and to the depression-ridden city that was its home. World's Fairs were always hot items in those days before the development of rapid trans-world transportation and communication. The San Diego Exposition of 1935 was no exception, even though it was never officially a real "world's fair," never having been sanctioned by the international committee that oversees such issues and grants the titles. It was a great success nonetheless and provided an exceptional venue for San Diego's Orchestra and for Nino Marcelli, its conductor.

The ensemble's new (still unofficial) name, the San Diego Symphony Orchestra, was not the only change. Somehow in those difficult days, a little more community financial support was obtained. New musicians, especially section principals, were recruited from major orchestras across the country that did not play summer seasons. When the 1935 Exposition was planned, the Ford Motor Company contracted to sponsor the San Diego Symphony's summer concerts at the new Ford Bowl in Balboa Park, a much more acoustically favorable venue than the Organ Pavilion. With 4,000 seats, the bowl was designed by Vern Knudsen, an acoustical engineer and co-founder of the Acoustical Society of America. Ford provided the salaries for the musicians, conductor and soloists. The San Diego Symphony Orchestra — and it was referred to by that name over the air as well as in the program booklets — played nightly broadcast concerts for the first two weeks and for the last week of the Fair. The Los Angeles Philharmonic and the San Francisco, Portland and Seattle Symphonies played during the intervening weeks.

Ford Bowl, 1935. *Photo courtesy San Diego Historical Society.*

The Exposition was repeated in 1936, and the San Diego Symphony presented thirty-two concerts. These Exposition summers were the first real high times for the San Diego Symphony. Not only were the concerts given with guaranteed payment, the Columbia Broadcasting System again broadcast some of the concerts to a nationwide audience. The programs were no longer the "light classical" presentations characteristic of Marcelli's 1920s summer concerts. On July 12, 1936, the concert opened with Weber's Overture to *Der Freischuetz*, and continued with Schubert's "Unfinished" Symphony and Borodin's *Polovetzian Dances* from *Prince Igor*. The Pilgrim's Chorus from Wagner's *Tannhauser* was played after the intermission. That was succeeded by several shorter works, and the concert concluded with Tchaikovsky's *Marche Slav*.

The pattern of somewhat heavier works prior to intermission and some shorter but definitely not necessarily lighter works after intermission continued through that summer. The season finale, titled "Farewell Night," was on Sunday evening, August 9. Dvorak's *Carneval* Overture opened the program that continued with Siegfried's Funeral March from Wagner's *Gotterdammerung*, and the Prelude and *Liebestod* from Wagner's *Tristan und Isolde*. After the intermission, requests that had been mailed to the orchestra were played. These included more Wagner, with the *Ride of the Valkyries* from *Die Walkuere*, Liadov's *Enchanted Lake* and the *Valse Triste* by Sibelius. Special concerts abounded, such as "All-American Night," and "Jazz Night." Most of the soloists came from the ranks of the orchestra. Concertmaster Russell Keeney (who was local and who had been Marcelli's concertmaster at San Diego High School) played Mozart, and Enzo Pascarella, the assistant concertmaster, played Mendelssohn.

One of the CBS broadcast concerts, on Saturday evening, July 18, 1936, was notable for the inclusion of Marcelli's own *Ode to a Hero*. That piece ended the first half that began with Wagner's *Lohengrin* Prelude and the Franck Symphony in D Minor. After the intermission, the orchestra played some ballet music from Schubert's *Rosamunde*, the Liadov *Enchanted Lake* and Chabrier's *Espana* Rhapsody. Symphonies and concertos were featured as part of the first half of nearly every concert. The program of July 28 indicated that the performance that evening was the first in San Diego of Mendelssohn's Third, "Scotch" Symphony.

Fortunately, there were always good relations between Marcelli and Julius Leib, the conductor of the FMP orchestra. Leib "lent" Marcelli twenty-five musicians for the 1936 summer series. Those musicians rejoined the FMP orchestra after the summer season and the closure of the Fair, and they played in that orchestra's fall and winter season in the Savoy Theatre. The orchestras were simply not in mutual competition. The era of a group consisting mainly of San Diego High School alumni was over. Although many of the longstanding players were retained, including some who formed musical dynasties in San Diego such as

Savoy Theatre, 1914. *Photo courtesy San Diego Historical Society.*

the Kirschbaums and Leibs, the 1936 orchestra featured some players who later became stars in their own rights in a number of major American orchestras. Robert Hester eventually became principal oboist in several great orchestras, and Norman Herzberg served for many years as the principal bassoonist of the Los Angeles Philharmonic. John Barrows eventually became principal horn of several eastern orchestras including the New York Philharmonic, and percussionists Frederic Fennell and Royal A. Brown each developed further distinguished careers. Fennell became internationally famous as Director of the Eastman-Rochester Wind Ensemble and the Cleveland Symphonic Winds, and his recordings sold in the hundreds of thousands. Royal A. Brown developed into a distinguished writer on musical matters whose articles were published in numerous magazines and trade journals.

For the summer season of 1936, the San Diego Symphony musicians were paid a salary of $36.00 weekly — not bad for depression wages, albeit, of course, for only seven weeks. Nino Marcelli had developed an ensemble that captured the interest and enthusiasm of San Diego audiences during some of the worst times this nation ever suffered, and through the medium of radio he let it be heard throughout the nation.

Marcelli led the first concert of the newly-reorganized and officially-named San Diego Symphony Orchestra on July 13, 1937, before an audience of 4,000 in the Balboa Park Bowl. The program consisted of Dvorak's *Carneval* Overture, two pieces from Mendelssohn's *Midsummer Night's Dream*, the *Swedish Rhapsody* by Alfven, and, after the intermission, Tchaikovsky's Fifth Symphony. It was the first of twelve summer concerts. An all-Wagner concert was presented on July 20, 1937. The vocal soloists, both local singers, were Blythe Taylor Burns, soprano, and Clemence Gifford, Contralto. Another local singer, Marie Link Elmore, sang Puccini and Gounod arias during the July 30, 1937, concert. That night the orchestra played the Beethoven Seventh Symphony and concluded with Tchaikovsky's *Francesca da Rimini.*

The orchestra consisted of seventy-two musicians, paid in part by funds from the Federal Music Project. Again, a number of musicians had rotated through the FMP Orchestra, but in 1937 a pool of money had been granted to the San Diego Symphony to augment the income gained by the musicians from ticket sales.

Although loved by his audiences, revered by the city and adored by his musicians, the 1937 season was Marcelli's last as conductor of the San Diego Symphony. In sum and substance, Marcelli was trashed by the director for San Diego and Orange Counties of the Federal Music Project, Charles H. Marsh, who had replaced William Dean. Marsh had originally come to San Diego to work in the FMP as a choral director. Under pressure, Marcelli conducted Marsh's *Three Fairy Tales* during one of the 1937 concerts, much against his will because he felt it was inferior music. As would be expected, mutual resentment developed, a power struggle ensued and the person with the money won. The Association complied with Marsh's desires, and at the end of 1937 it was announced that the orchestra would play a winter season beginning in January, 1938, under the direction of Julius Leib.

In his memoir, J. M. Vogel, Marcelli's beloved stepson, relates that a very aggressive new board member, identified only as a general's wife, had determined on her own that in the tenth 1937 summer concert, in which the Tchaikovsky *1812 Overture* was to be played, a group of soldiers would march down the side aisles with lit smoke pots and would fire howitzers during the last part of the piece. These plans were made without Marcelli's knowledge. He did not learn about this until the intermission of that concert. Although he refused to continue, Marcelli was persuaded to finish the concert and the season. The aggressive board member did not interfere any more after that, but at the end of the season she worked with Marsh to remove the conductor.

The orchestra continued to play during the succeeding summer under Leib's guidance, and also under the batons of some extraordinary guest conductors. The Federal Music Project was a fine benefactor. In the 1938 summer season, Modest Altschuler guest conducted, as did, of all people, Arnold Schoenberg, the great musical revolutionary who had developed the twelve-tone system. In July of that year, Schoenberg conducted the orchestra in his own *Verklaerte Nacht* for string orchestra, as well his his orchestral transcriptions of the Bach "Saint

Anne" Prelude and Fugue, and the Brahms Piano Quintet. The reviews were little short of ecstatic. In the *San Diego Union* of July 27, F. M. headlined his review,
"Orchestral Heights Scaled by Schoenberg," and described the pieces performed
as "supermusic!" His and several other reviews emphasized the rapt attention
paid to the music by what was described as an enthused audience.

Just a few days later, Erich Wolfgang Korngold led the orchestra. He was
also a very eminent composer who was making a new, even more famous name
for himself as a movie composer. That year he won the Oscar® for his score
for Warner Brothers' *Robin Hood*, starring Errol Flynn and Olivia de Havilland.
The music for that film remains as famous today as it was when it was new,
and a number of contemporary recordings of it have been prepared. William
Grant Still, America's foremost African-American composer of the time, guest
conducted the season finale on August 9, featuring his own *Lenox Avenue*, which
included a large African-American choir as well as full orchestra.

Marcelli continued to live in San Diego after leaving the San Diego
Symphony. He continued conducting the San Diego High School Orchestra. He
also scored a great personal success when he conducted the premiere of his light
opera, *Carmelita*, at the Balboa Park Bowl in August, 1938. The performances
were sponsored by the San Diego PTA in recognition of Marcelli's services to
young musicians. Marcelli continued composing and published several new
works and a folio of band music. His 1917 *Ode to a Hero* was played in 1942 by
the Los Angeles Philharmonic. Constance Herreshoff, Music Critic for the *San
Diego Union*, wrote admiringly on December 27, 1942, about the Los Angeles
Philharmonic presenting that work in Los Angeles and Pasadena, as well as in San
Diego, all conducted by John Barbirolli, a longstanding Marcelli admirer.

Herreshoff also noted in that 1942 article that Marcelli was planning to
develop a training orchestra in San Diego and that rehearsals would be held
weekly at San Diego High School. No professional level orchestra had been playing in San Diego since 1940. Seventy local musicians signed up immediately after
Marcelli made his announcement, according to the article. Marcelli stated, "I am
organizing this orchestra in response to many requests from musicians who wish
to play symphonic music for their own pleasure. Concert giving is not our objective. The orchestra will be a sort of workshop for those who love to play." A year
into America's World War II efforts was not the best time to start an orchestra.
Too many players were drafted and shipped out, and the orchestra disbanded
after a short time.

A short-lived community symphony orchestra of volunteer players was
organized after World War II. Marcelli was asked to conduct what turned out to
be its only concert, given in Balboa Park Bowl (renamed by then from the former Ford Bowl) in the summer of 1947. More time was to pass before the San

Diego Symphony Orchestra was revived, but Marcelli was no longer involved in either its formation or its concerts.

Marcelli retired from the school system in 1948, the year of his wife's death. He guest-conducted several high school and collegiate orchestras in Oregon and Washington, and in 1949 he left for Chile where he stayed for a year. There he was the recipient of many honors and was recognized as a musical pioneer. In Santiago he was made an honorary faculty member of the *conservatorio* where he had been a student so many years before. Upon his return to San Diego in 1950 he guest-conducted the maintenance fund concert of the newly organized, short-lived San Diego Philharmonic Orchestra and was honored in the press as "San Diego's first musical citizen."

Although not unheralded in his lifetime, since his death in 1967 Nino Marcelli's memory has not been celebrated as it should be, even though he is definitely, legitimately considered the real "father" of the San Diego Symphony. The current, fine Orchestra is perhaps his most fitting memorial, but it is actually only one of a number of his remarkable legacies to have benefited San Diego. Single-handedly he created a musical climate that allowed the development of a very high order of home grown performance in this community. The community should remember him better. Statues have been raised to lesser contributors.

CHAPTER IV

Nicolai Sokoloff, the Federal Music Project — and Silence

J ulius Leib, later to be known with his son, Robert, as the Musical Directors of the San Diego Light Opera Company that eventually became Starlight Opera, led the San Diego Symphony Orchestra in a rather irregular concert series for a season following the departure of Nino Marcelli from the orchestra. Several other guest conductors, including Ferde Grofé, also served, but the planning and real artistic direction of the orchestra and the season remained haphazard until the arrival of Nicolai Sokoloff.

Born in Kiev in 1886, Sokoloff was brought to the United States as a young adolescent. He lived with his émigré family in Boston where he studied music. At Yale he studied the violin and continued his musical studies in Boston with the distinguished composer, Charles Martin Loeffler. He became a member of Karl Muck's Boston Symphony Orchestra and also began to conduct several community orchestras in New England. These ventures having proved successful, he went to England and the continent to conduct more professional groups. He returned to the United States with a growing reputation.

David Ewen, in his 1940 *Living Musicians*, related that in 1911 Sokoloff became the concertmaster of the Russian Symphony Orchestra in New York City. New York at the time had a number of independent symphonic groups, including the New York Philharmonic under Gustav Mahler and Josef Stransky, the New York Symphony under Leopold and Walter Damrosch, and the Russian Symphony (a cooperative organization) under a series of guest conductors, mainly from Russia. The Russian Symphony had organized after the opening of Carnegie Hall in 1893 when Tchaikovsky came to conduct the Philharmonic, creating a great sensation. The Russian orchestra hoped to capitalize on the ongoing Russian trend. Sokoloff conducted the Russian Symphony several times and attracted the attention of the San Francisco Symphony, which hired him to be its Music Director in 1916. He resigned soon afterwards, however, due to the American entry into World War I. He left for France to play for the troops, gaining increased popularity and fame. Upon returning to America he was extremely successful as a guest conductor in Cincinnati and was immediately engaged as Music Director of the new Cleveland Orchestra.

The famously waspish Nicolas Slonimsky, as editor of *Baker's Biographical Dictionary of Musicians (7th Edition)*, wrote about Sokoloff. "To the extent of his limited abilities, he discharged his duties [in Cleveland] until 1933." A glance at the record indicates that Slonimsky may have been unfair, as he was often wont to be. In his own book, for example, Ewen reported that Sokoloff did very well in Cleveland. He created an excellent orchestra that toured and garnered considerable praise from critics. Sokoloff also created enough commercial interest in town to build Severance Hall, still the Cleveland Orchestra's

Nicolai Sokoloff *Photo courtesy San Diego Symphony.*

home, and an endowment. An annual concert series by the orchestra in Carnegie Hall has continued uninterrupted to this date. With the Cleveland Orchestra, Sokoloff made a number of recordings for Columbia, including the first ever made of the uncut Rachmaninoff Second Symphony. Sokoloff was in frequent demand as a guest conductor during his tenure in Cleveland. He was quite successful leading a number of American, English and Russian orchestras.

In 1933 Sokoloff left Cleveland. The orchestra he had worked with there was in fine shape, even in the depression, and came under the strict discipline of Artur Rodzinski, the next music director. In a successful attempt to gain work for a number of unemployed New York musicians, Sokoloff organized an orchestra there that operated on a cooperative basis. This led to considerable publicity. Sokoloff came to the attention of the Works Projects Administration in Washington. He was called to that agency to help form the Federal Music Project (FMP), which he organized and instituted in 1935. The purpose of the FMP was to provide some work for the large number of unemployed musicians caught in the depression. Apparently the same administrative and financial acumen that had characterized Sokoloff in Cleveland and elsewhere was put to good use in Washington. Orchestras, bands, choral and operatic groups, as well as popular music and jazz groups were formed throughout the country. At its peak in 1936, the FMP employed more than fifteen thousand people in forty-two states and the District of Columbia. Sokoloff remained as director of the FMP until 1938.

In San Diego, the FMP provided considerable help to beleaguered musicians. In 1936 alone, according to the Mehren Master's Thesis referred to in the previous chapter, two hundred thousand dollars had been given as salaries to the musicians employed by the FMP. Even before the formation of the WPA and the FMP, SERA (the State Emergency Relief Administration) sent funds from Sacramento to set up musical groups, including a forty-piece orchestra that began giving weekly concerts at Broadway Pier and the auditorium of Roosevelt Junior High School. A large concert band was also created, and these and other groups toured neighborhood schools as well. Mehren's thesis quotes a November 22, 1936, *San Diego Union* article: "....Some of [the musicians] had finally despaired of ever again finding work in their profession and were toiling with picks and shovels to earn money for their families...Suicide among educated musicians, reduced to a state of hopelessness and too proud to accept charity, was all too frequent at the time the project was started. Now that is all changed..."

The FMP Symphony Orchestra in San Diego developed out of the SERA orchestra that had been organized in 1934. On November 18, 1935, Federal funds began to be available in San Diego, and all of the relief approaches were collected under the aegis of the FMP. The prior orchestra regrouped. Dr. Charles O. Breach was its conductor then, and because considerable rehearsal time was provided under the FMP guidelines, the performance level became quite high. Wallace Moody, the music writer for the *San Diego Union* reported on December 27, 1935, on one of the FMP orchestra's first programs: "The orchestra touched a degree of perfection equal to that of many prominent symphony organizations." A number of the musicians were members of the San Diego Symphony, but that orchestra was engaged in presenting concerts only during several months in the summer. Nino Marcelli, the Symphony's conductor, was busy with his high school duties during the times given over to the FMP orchestra. The degree of cooperation between the groups was remarkable.

Two concerts a month were planned for the FMP orchestra, all to be given in the Roosevelt Junior High School auditorium. Early in 1936, Dr. Breach resigned as conductor in order to "...devote his entire attention, instead of only a part of it, to the arranging bureau and the government music library here..." (*San Diego Union*, April 20, 1936). Julius Leib took his place and continued to direct the orchestra until it disbanded with the end of the FMP nationally in 1939. One particular aspect of the FMP was its promotion of new music by American composers. In southern California, William Grant Still, the famous African-American composer, was able to get repeated hearings of much of his music in Los Angeles and San Diego. Still had been the recipient of a Guggenheim Fellowship and had several of his works produced by the nation's premier orchestras, including the Philadelphia under Stokowski. In San Diego, Still came to conduct the FMP orchestra in his three-part suite, *Africa*, described by him as presenting, "…an American Negro's concept of the land of his ancestors based largely upon its folklore and influenced by his contact with American civilization…" (Wallace Moody, *San Diego Union*, May 1, 1938). The following year, Still returned to conduct the San Diego Symphony in his Second Symphony in its west coast premiere. According to Frances Imgrund, in the *San Diego Evening Tribune*, on August 2, 1939, the composer/conductor praised the orchestra for its ability to master the work in only two rehearsals.

Nicolai Sokoloff had become the Music Director of the Seattle Symphony orchestra in 1938, but that orchestra had no summer season. Therefore, Sokoloff was free to come to San Diego and indulge himself in the community with which he had fallen in love. He left the Seattle Symphony in 1940 and resided happily thereafter in La Jolla. But in early summer, 1939, the year after he had resigned as Director of the FMP (although he still maintained some ties to it), Sokoloff came to San Diego from Seattle to lead a conductors' seminar that attracted sixteen aspirants, including five San Diegans. The *San Diego Union* described the planned seminar on April 9, 1939, as "…free to members of any Federal Music Project and open to any musicians from any locale who qualify." It was during that period of the conductors' seminar that Sokoloff conducted the San Diego Symphony in conjunction with the FMP orchestra in five weeks of concerts in Ford Bowl. He had also conducted the Bonham Boys' Band and had embarked on a series of lectures as well, and social appearances that continued through the rest of his active life in this area. Both of his wives (he was widowed by his first wife in 1955) were very active socially and strong club members. They obviously helped him in his community endeavors.

The 1939 series of concerts was sponsored jointly by the San Diego Symphony Orchestra Association and the Federal Music Project. The FMP provided forty musicians and so did the San Diego Symphony. According to an article in the *San Diego Union* on June 8, 1939, only twenty five percent of the gate receipts would go to the FMP. The Symphony Association began a campaign to raise funds to supplement the gate receipts. George Scott headed that committee (*the San Diego Union*, June 10, 1939). The Association planned what the paper called an impressive list of artists to appear with the orchestra but, although ticket sales were reported as "normal," subscriptions and donations did not come up to expectations. However, Sokoloff proved very popular, and the *San Diego Union* reported on August 16 that he received an ovation following the final concert. He was said to have "…attained astonishing results!"

When the concert series ended in August, 1939, the San Diego FMP project started coming to a close as well. In September, 1939, musicians from Los

Angeles and San Diego combined to form a forty piece orchestra to accompany singers from several southern California FMP units in a light opera festival that never got off the ground. By the spring of 1940, most of the members of the orchestra had been dropped from the rolls. Under the heading, "Federal Music Project Cut," a *San Diego Union* article of January 26, 1940, described the end of the project and its programs. Money from Washington was being spent instead in extraordinary amounts on defense planning and the eventuality of getting into the war that was spreading havoc throughout Europe.

The new mood in the country was being shaped by the fact that jobs were beginning to be available again. Defense plants opened their gates and hired as many men (and — something new — women!) as they could find. Tremendous population migrations occurred from the rural south to the industrialized north, midwest and west coast. Amazingly, the new mood, coupled with a little bit of spendable income, allowed the San Diego Symphony Orchestra Association to sponsor its own series of summer concerts in 1941, again under the direction of Nicolai Sokoloff, who had become quite popular in San Diego and especially in La Jolla. George Scott's fund-raising committee did much better in 1941, and eight subscription and one special concert were planned and given.

Sokoloff's programs for the 1941 season are interesting and sometimes provocative. They bear repeating here.

July 18th, with John Powell, Piano
Massenet, *Phedre*, Overture
Powell, *Rapsodie Negra*
Moussorgsky, *The Fair at Sorochinsk*, Overture
Franck, Symphony in D Minor

July 25th, with Simmons & Scharl, Duo-Pianists
(postponed to August 3 due to fog)
Rossini, *la Gazza Ladra*, Overture
Henry Gilbert, Symphonic Prologue, *Riders to the Sea*
Jarnefeldt, *Berceuse* and *Praeludium*
Homer Simmons, *Partita Americana*
Rimsky-Korsakoff, *Capriccio Espagnole*

August 1st, Orchestral Program
Wagner, *Parsifal*, Prelude and Good FridaySpell
Traume
Die Goetterdammerung, Siegfried's Rhine Journey
Tchaikovsky, Symphony No. 5

August 5th, with Naoum Blinder, Violinist

Humperdinck, *Hansel & Gretel*, Overture

Debussy, Two *Noctournes*

Chausson, *Poeme*

Tchaikovsky, Violin Concerto

Delibes, Excerpts from *Coppelia*

August 8th, with Ruth Reynolds, Soprano

Grieg, *Peer Gynt* Suite No. 2

Arias

Sibelius, Symphony No. 2

August 12th, with Ramona Gerhard, Pianist

Wagner, *Die Meistersinger*, Overture

Smetana, *The Moldau*

Liszt, Piano Concerto No. 1

Debussy, Prelude to *The Afternoon of a Faun*

Ippolitov-Ivanov, *Caucasian Sketches*

Herbert, *American Fantasy*

August 15th, with Mona Paulee, Mezzo-Soprano

Goldmark, *In Springtime*, Overture

Handel, *Xerxes, Largo*

Strauss, Waltz, *Roses From the South*

Arias

Liszt, *Les Preludes*

August 19th, Orchestral Program

Tchaikovsky, *The Nutcracker*, Suite

Debussy, Two *Noctournes* (by request)

Mendelssohn, *A Midsummer Night's Dream, Noctourne & Scherzo*

Wagner, *Tannhauser*, Overture

Cadman, *Dark Dancers of the Mardi Gras*

August 22nd, Benefit Concert; Alec Templeton, Pianist

Thomas, *Mignon*, Overture

Smetana, *The Moldau*

Franck, *Symphonic Variations*

Liszt, *Hungarian Fantasia*

By the time of the last concert in that series, plans were being drawn up by the Navy for its own use of Balboa Park. The Naval Hospital, formerly occupying only a small portion of the great park, now was to spread out over the entire area. The psychiatric wards were to take up most of the room, making Balboa Park the world's largest outdoor mental hospital.

Pearl Harbor was bombed less than four months after the last 1941 concert, and no more concerts were to be given in Balboa Park during the war. Music, however, was plentiful. Small bands played in the park to entertain the many patients, but the bulk of the music played was martial or popular. Some of the musicians who had formerly been in the Symphony or in the FMP orchestra combined under Robert Leib's direction to form a swing band, and they played regularly in the park and in ballrooms throughout the town until they were drafted. The Ford Bowl, later to become the Balboa Park Bowl and the home of future symphony concerts and performances by Starlight, was appropriately dark. For anyone old enough to recall the famous radio commercial played so frequently during World War II, the San Diego Symphony Orchestra went to war just like Lucky Strike green. There was much more to do other than planning concert seasons.

That is, for most people but not for Nicolai Sokoloff. From his La Jolla home he planned and organized a new group, the Musical Arts Society. He successfully sought financing for summer seasons of music played by a virtuoso orchestra of about forty musicians, a number of whom would be imported from Los Angeles. In the first summer, 1941, only twelve were imports, but eventually the bulk of the players came down from the north. Sokoloff's contacts were many, partly based upon the good will he had generated as director of the Federal Music Project. Those contacts allowed him to contract some of America's biggest musical stars for his La Jolla concerts, at first given in the La Jolla High School Auditorium and subsequently, after Sokoloff's era, in the new Sherwood Hall of the Contemporary Arts Museum. In his first season, Josef Szigeti and William Kapell were soloists. The first winter season of concerts was given in 1958-59, consisting mainly of chamber music performances. The summer was reserved for the remarkable orchestra Sokoloff had assembled.

A heart attack felled Sokoloff in the summer of 1960. He returned to conduct in 1961, but it was apparent that his health was not what it had been. The strain of conducting an entire summer season was too much. Jan Popper succeeded him as conductor in 1962, and Milton Katims followed Popper in 1963. In 1965, Sokoloff succumbed to another heart attack, and the Musical Arts Society lost its strongest continuing force. Several summers of occasional concerts followed, but in 1969, the Board of Directors voted to give a scholarship to a deserving music student in lieu of presenting another season. Even after that, though, sporadic concerts were given in conjunction with the La Jolla Museum of Contemporary Art, functioning as Trustee for the inactive Musical Arts Society.

It is some kind of tribute to Nicolai Sokoloff that the music performances he had stimulated continued after his own life had ceased. Looking at his life and at the contributions he had made to the musical life of San Diego and, via the Federal Music Project, to the country as a whole, Nicolas Slonimsky's mean comments ought best to be forgotten. Sokoloff did well by all of us.

CHAPTER V

Back to Work Under Fabien Sevitzky

In great part, World War II, especially the War in the Pacific, was fought out of San Diego. The burgeoning Naval and Marine training and shipping-out facilities, combined with the enormous development of defense industry in the area, changed the pace of the city for all time. Its population increased by twenty five percent. Dynamism reared its head in the formerly small, sleepy city, but the energy was not directed toward the continuation and further development of a symphony orchestra.

The history of the San Diego Symphony indicated that summer seasons were the rule. Concerts were played only in Balboa Park Bowl. When the Naval Hospital commandeered the entire park as an adjunct facility, Balboa Bowl was off limits to San Diegans not in uniform. The end of the war against Japan in August, 1945, did not mean that the park was automatically again open to the public. It took a long time to slow down the pace of activity at what was then the world's largest military medical establishment. Until the patient population reduced itself considerably there could be no thought of eliminating the greater space needed by the facility referred to by many San Diegans as the "Pink Palace in the Park."

Nonetheless, San Diegans had become used to symphonic concerts in the park, and they missed them. A committee organized itself late in 1948 to determine if a summer series of concerts could be resumed the next year. Dr. G. Burch Mehlin, a local pediatrician and a dedicated music-lover, started the ball rolling. He was joined by a number of other San Diegans whose names are familiar to many contemporary concert goers because of their long service on the board of the San Diego Symphony Association. Many descendants of earlier board members continued the work of their parents. The Armours, Ledfords, Klaubers, Clarks, Fetters, Stewarts *et al* worked hard for many years, contributing considerable time, money and effort. Their post-war generation began their service with Dr. Mehlin.

One other name needs special mention. Florence Goss began her own service on the San Diego Symphony Association Board with Burch Mehlin, and she continued working hard for the Symphony into the 1970s. She probably served longer (and probably worked harder) than any other board member. The

San Diego Symphony Orchestra was her continuing pride and she focused her attention on it fully. Florence Goss was a lady of considerable and remarkable charm, However, she was not always easy to get along with, basically because of her tunnel vision about the Symphony and her very personal views about how it should be run. She organized a large group of San Diego women and kept them active as Symphony supporters for many years, at least nominally. The Rules and Regulations of the Women's Committee of the San Diego Symphony Orchestra Association outlined the purposes of the group in Article II.

> "The purposes of the Women's Committee are to plan and sponsor such fund-raising and other events as requested by the Board of Directors of the San Diego Symphony Orchestra Association and to work in close cooperation with said Association through its Board of Directors, its Executive Committee, and other committees and its officers in support of the objectives of the Association; and to create and extend interest in music in the community at large."

The Women's Committee attempted to fulfill its role mainly by planning social events to which the public was often invited but which in the main were attended by members of the Committee and their guests. The planning sessions for these events were also social events and reported upon as such in the newspapers, often with photos. A perusal of the events sponsored by the Women's Committee during the 1976-77 season provides a good overview of their activities. An opening night party was given at the beginning of the summer season, followed by an orchestra picnic. The "Sound-Off Luncheon" was held in early September to promote the sale of season tickets, and an "Overture Dinner" preceded the opening concert of the fall/winter concert season. Receptions were also held subsequently for donors who gave over five hundred dollars. Other luncheons and dinners were given throughout the season, as well as several post-concert receptions, held either in members' homes or, after 1965, in the Civic Theatre Grand Salon (now the Beverly Sills Salon). Special fund-raisers, e.g., the Viennese Ball and cookbook compilations and sales, were also significant.

The most important sponsorship provided by the Women's Committee was their partial underwriting of the children's and young people's concerts. Often, a Women's Committee subcommittee would contact a civic leader who could afford a good donation, and would credit him and his business with partial sponsorship if they were successful in getting him to donate a significant amount of money. Women's Committee members would also provide needed help in the Symphony Association office whenever there was a mailing. Envelopes would be stuffed, stamped and addressed by those members. Office staffs to do that kind of work were unheard of in San Diego through the 1950s and 1960s, into the early 1970s. Photos of those hard-working members of the Women's Committee often found their way into the society pages of the local papers. Although their names and pictures would be there, the accompanying articles always provided information about whatever symphony activity or event was being planned. The public relations aspect of the Women's Committee was all-important to the Association in those pre-marketing director days.

The Rules and Regulations specified that dues of $10.00 per year were to be paid by members. It must be recalled that the Women's Committee was formed early in the Sevitzky era when that amount seemed like a reasonable dues figure. However, the dues schedule was not changed during most of the long life of the Women's Committee, until the later 1970s. Regardless of the remarkable rise of expenses in the orchestra framework, with annual increases in the budget to amounts never dreamed of in 1949, the Women's Committee dues remained the same. Moreover, there was never any obligation for members to buy tickets to the concerts or to be active in any way other than to give their ten dollars! It is important to note that the present-day organization of women functioning as a volunteer auxiliary to the Symphony Association (the "Symphony Stars") is not the same organization. Each member of the present organization contributes a considerable amount of money, and they are all concert goers.

Through the 1950s, and even into the early 1960s, the few thousand dollars contributed by the Women's Committee were urgently important to the Association. After the Association budgets began to climb rapidly, however, the proportion of Symphony funds created by the Women's Committee lessened, although the Committee's activities continued after Florence Goss left the scene. In 1976, for example, the Women's Committee had 898 paid members, and the balance in their bank account was $8,048.18. The amounts raised by the different fund-raising activities, such as the Viennese Ball, varied according to how much external sponsorship contributions the Women's Committee could generate. It must be emphasized, however, that any and all funds or other contributions provided to the Association by the Women's Committee during the first twenty post-war seasons were extremely valuable to the fledgling organization. That provided considerable clout to the organizer of the Women's Committee, Florence Goss, who remained as its head into the early 1970s regardless of who might be the titular president.

By virtue of the muscle provided by her position as the continuing head of the Women's Committee, Mrs. Goss asserted herself into all planning conferences for the orchestra, including conductor selection, and even into program decisions. She had very strong feelings about nearly all aspects of the Symphony Association — and Symphony Orchestra — activities. Most of the time her wishes were granted, but often they resulted in some difficult issues with which the rest of the organization had to wrestle. One example was her staunch belief that the numerous generous federal grants offered in those days must be avoided at all costs, although the finances of the Symphony Association were always very fragile. Federal grants were considered a step toward socialism, a concept held by a number of influential board members, and characteristic of the more conservative bent of the city in those days. She also successfully fought against a program of providing some free tickets to community

Fabien Sevitsky *Photo courtesy San Diego Symphony.*

agencies as an attempt to promote greater community support and better public relations for the orchestra. She said, "Sevitzky told us that we should *never* give away seats! It reduces the worth of what we do." Sometimes, her wishes became demands to which the Association usually eventually acceded. She had the clout, at least in the early days.

Unfortunately, Mrs. Goss manifested considerable overt resentment against those women who formed the San Diego organization that sponsored the local performances of the Los Angeles Philharmonic Orchestra, especially after 1959, when the San Diego Symphony began to present winter concerts as well as the Balboa Bowl programs. She saw the Los Angeles supporters directly as saboteurs of the efforts of the San Diego Symphony Association, and bitter society battles raged for many years — actually until the Philharmonic finally ceased its annual San Diego seasons in the 1980s.

Many of the women belonging to the Los Angeles Philharmonic support organization were markedly antagonized by the hostile attitudes expressed by Florence Goss. Many chances were lost thereby to ease them into the San Diego Symphony fold of backers. As differentiated from most members of the San Diego Symphony Women's Committee, some might even have bought tickets for the local orchestra's concerts.

She was a tough lady who crossed many swords with many board members,

musicians, conductors and, certainly, with the Los Angeles Philharmonic backers. But she always felt that her wishes and goals were positive for the Symphony.
She became the walking embodiment of the San Diego Symphony Orchestra
Association in the minds of many observers, with results that were beneficial as
well as negative. Despite all of the difficulties emanating from some of her attitudes and approaches, no one could ever deny Florence Goss's energy and the
devotion with which she exercised it for the San Diego Symphony Association
and its Women's Committee.

By 1948, many of the musicians who had formerly played in the pre-war
San Diego orchestra had returned from their wartime service. Some had been
musicians in the armed services and were able to continue their practicing and
honing of their skills. A pool of musicians was present, but there was no available
local conductor. I have no idea if anyone even considered Marcelli, still reasonably well and living in town. Nicolai Sokoloff had alienated some of the members
of the Symphony Association board by forming the Musical Arts Society, a separate organization that gave concerts in La Jolla. He was also a favorite of many of
the La Jolla society women who were backers of the Los Angeles Philharmonic
appearances. Many of Sokoloff's musicians were imported from Los Angeles
for the Musical Arts Society programs. It was obvious that a conductor search
needed to be instituted for the local orchestra.

The choice fell on Fabien Sevitzky, the musical director of the Indianapolis
Symphony Orchestra. Since assuming that post in 1937, he had built that orchestra into a fine performing unit ranked among the best in the country. He was an
active and respected guest conductor, often seen on symphony podiums in New
York, Philadelphia and Chicago. RCA Victor selected his orchestra as one of
several with which they contracted for recordings in the later 1930s. RCA had
previously concentrated solely on the Boston Symphony under the direction of
Sevitzky's uncle, Serge Koussevitzky, as well as the then-new NBC Symphony
formed to play under Arturo Toscanini. The Philadelphia Orchestra, RCA's longest contractee, was waffling between two conductors. Eugene Ormandy had
been selected as Leopold Stokowski's replacement, but then Stokowski decided
to remain in Philadelphia at least part of the time. They each wanted to record,
and RCA wisely did not want to enter that arena.

RCA contracted with several fine groups, including the Cincinnati Symphony
under Eugene Goosens, the St. Louis Symphony under Vladimir Golschmann,
the San Francisco Symphony under Pierre Monteux, and Sevitzky's Indianapolis
Symphony. Frederick Stock's Chicago Symphony, having recorded through most
of the 1930s with Columbia, also joined RCA's roster at the end of that decade.
Sevitzky and his orchestra found themselves in excellent company. Sevitzky's
recordings were always praised, not only because they were well played but also

because he often chose neglected or new works to present on disc. For example, he and his orchestra made the first American recording of Tchaikovsky's First Symphony, as well as many other lesser-known Russian works. Gershwin, Gould and other American composers also were part of their recorded repertoire.

Sevitzky, whose real name was the same as his more famous uncle's, Koussevitzky, was born in Tver, Russia, in 1893. To his credit, he dropped the first syllable of his last name after his uncle became world-famous as a musician. Sevitzky rarely spoke about his relationship with his uncle, preferring to speak of his own career that he had made into a good one on his own. After studying with Siloti in St. Petersburg, he joined his uncle's Moscow orchestra where, like his distinguished relative, he played the string bass. He entered the Russian Army in 1916 and stayed in Russia through the revolution, escaping to the United States in 1923. He immediately joined Stokowski's Philadelphia Orchestra as a bassist. Always hoping to give up instrumental music for conducting, in 1925 he was able to organize the Philadelphia String Chamber Sinfonietta. His local successes there led him to guest conduct Russian operas for the Philadelphia Grand Opera Company. He also made two relatively successful European tours in the early 1930s as a guest conductor of some notable orchestras. From 1934 to 1936 he was active in his uncle's town, not with his uncle's orchestra but with the People's Symphony of Boston, a Federal Music Project-funded group.

The Indianapolis Symphony Orchestra had begun playing as a cooperative ensemble in 1930. Several conductors had presided over it until 1937, when Fabien Sevitzky was hired as its Musical Director. Because of his growing reputation, it was something of a coup for the reorganizing San Diego Symphony to be able to hire him. However, the Indianapolis Orchestra had no summer season. It played only a twenty to twenty-four-week winter season and then disbanded, only to come together again the next autumn. Most American orchestras lacked summer venues in those years, nor could they afford the year-around contracts that are increasingly common today. Sevitzky would make occasional summer guest appearances at Lewisohn Stadium in New York, at the Robin Hood Dell in Philadelphia, and at Ravinia or Grant Park in Chicago. Notably, he never appeared at Tanglewood, the summer bailiwick of his famous uncle and the Boston Symphony. Neither uncle nor nephew ever discussed that issue in public.

Sevitzky conducted his first season here in 1949, lured by the prospect of a steady, five-week period of employment in a delightful place that had fine weather and beautiful surroundings. Parenthetically, those same unique lures were the frequent bait held out to musicians by San Diego Symphony board members for many years. The idea of paying decent wages, however, was rarely, if ever considered. The orchestra and its conductors often had difficulties in attracting the best musicians because of the low pay schedules. Labor problems

would eventually result. The concept of long-term, adequately negotiated contracts did not become part of San Diego's hiring practices for several decades.
Sevitzky, however, had available to him a pool of local musicians who were not
used to being paid very well, and he was also able to attract others who badly
needed summer jobs. The 1949 season consisted of only five concerts at Balboa
Bowl, played by an orchestra that, for the most part, had either never played
together before or else had not played together for more than eight years. It was
composed of sixty-five musicians, some of whom became fixtures in the future
years of the developing orchestra.

A canny program-maker, Sevitzky attracted good audiences to the park
to hear his concerts. The season was deemed enough of a success to allow the
Symphony Association to promise a somewhat expanded season for the next
year, also under Sevitzky, who returned every summer through 1952. Sevitzky's
first programs for his introductory 1949 season demonstrate the wide range of
his interests and sympathies.

August 9th:
Glinka, Overture, *Ruslan and Ludmilla*
Rachmaninoff, Second Piano Concerto (Lyell Barbour, soloist)
Tchaikovsky, Fifth Symphony, two movements.
Sibelius, *Finlandia*
Strauss, J., Waltz, *Voices of Spring*
Deems Taylor, Suite, *Through the Looking Glass*
Bizet, Suites from *l'Arlesienne*

August 16th:
Berlioz, Overture, *Roman Carnival*
Beethoven Fifth Symphony, First Movement
Grieg, Suite from, *Sigurd Jorsalfar*
Bruch, First Violin Concerto (Jerome Kosin, concertmaster, soloist)
Lionel Barrymore, *Variations on a Wabash River Song*
Arcady Dubensky (Vernon Duke), *Steven Foster*
Brahms, Hungarian Dances

August 23rd:
Thomas, Overture, *Mignon*
Mendelssohn, "Italian" Symphony
Weinberger, *Schwanda, the Bagpipe Player*, Polka and Fugue
Strauss, J., *Emperor Waltz*
Delibes, Suite from *Coppelia*

Kreisler (orch. Sevitzky), *Praeludium and Allegro*
Opera Arias sung by Brian Sullivan

August 30th:
Wagner, Overture, *Rienzi*
Dvorak, "New World" Symphony, first movement
Smetana, *The Moldau*
Gershwin, Symphonic Picture, *Porgy and Bess*
Opera Arias sung by Marina Koshetz

September 8th:
Bach (orch. Sevitzky), "Giant" Fugue
Manuel Ponce, *Chapultapec* Suite
Tchaikovsky, First Piano Concerto (Holda Zepeda, soloist)
Tchaikovsky, Fourth Symphony

Obviously, Sevitzky was testing not only his musicians that first season, but the audience as well. "How much could they take?" he must have wondered, and found out that they could take more than symphony snippets. His later seasons presented generally more stable, classically oriented programs, but he always tried to incorporate some local and contemporary color. As an example, the program for August 1, 1950, was as follows.

Kabalevsky, Overture, *Colas Breugnon*
Brahms, First Symphony
Liszt, First Piano Concerto (Leonard Pennario, soloist)
Paul Creston, *Frontiers*
Berlioz, *The Damnation of Faust*, Three Orchestral Fragments

Creston, of course, was not only one of America's most significant composers but he also had the great advantage of living in the San Diego area.

Sevitzky's final season here was in the summer of 1952. He came to San Diego early and gave a press conference, reported by Constance Herreshoff for the *San Diego Union*, whose July 6, 1952 headline trumpeted, "Superb Program Slated by Symphony." Sevitzky was riding high early that summer. He had just signed a new, five-year contract with his Indianapolis Symphony, had just presented the first symphony orchestra concert series ever given on television, in Indianapolis with his orchestra, and was continuing to record for RCA. The *Union* reported that the San Diego Symphony's personnel for the coming 1952 season would show few changes from the fine roster of musicians Sevitzky had chosen over the previous couple of seasons. Constance Herreshoff praised the quality of the musicians, and on Sundays during the summer season, in her news-paper column she would usually profile several, and not only the principals.

Robert Gerle had been the concertmaster the previous year and continued in 1952. He would go on to a distinguished solo career, marked significantly by making the first recording of Samuel Barber's beautiful Violin Concerto. Aside from the concertmaster, twenty-one other violinists were in the orchestra, including some who were to serve there long and loyally over many subsequent years. Among those were Gail Glancy, Gerita Hanna, John Metzger, Al Pierno and, not only as a violinist but as a distinguished guest conductor, Dan Lewis. Edward Janowsky led the viola section in which Selma Kammerdiner began to play. The principal cellist was Fritz Bruch, formerly of the Cincinnati Symphony, and behind him sat Morris Kirshbaum (of the distinguished San Diego musical dynasty), Mary Louise Moore, Jean Moe, Gene Sacks and Victoria Bettencourt. Bernard Kestenbaum, Lloyd von Haden and Eugene Holloway (he doubled on tuba) became familiar figures as bassists. Fritz Baker began his long tenure as first flute, Carlos Mullenix and Floyd Grant were the oboists, Dan Magnusson was starting his own lengthy term as principal clarinet, and Lawrence Christianson played in the horn section. Arthur Avery was a trombonist then and for many years afterwards. Leo Hamilton, who had played in the Marcelli orchestras, was the tympanist, and among the percussionists was William Kraft, later to become tympanist for the Los Angeles Philharmonic as well as a distinguished composer.

Sevitzky, with more confidence in the orchestra and in the audience as well, programmed a fairly adventurous season. Constance Herreshoff, the *San Diego Union* critic, reviewed all of the concerts but provided little specific information about the playing other than in the most general terms. For example, in her review of the first concert of the 1952 season, she praised, "The finesse of the conductor." The programs are as follows:

July 22nd:
> Dvorak, *Carnaval* Overture
> Frances McCallin, Two Chorale Preludes
> Saint-Saens, Piano Concerto No. 4 (Grant Johannesen, Pianist)
> Tchaikovsky, Symphony No. 4
> (encore) Liadov, *The Musical Snuffbox*

July 29th:
> Beethoven, Overture, *Leonore,* No. 3
> Don Gillis, Symphony Number 5-1/2
> Gounod, *Faust,* Ballet Music
> Rachmaninoff, Piano Concerto No. 3 (William Kapell, Pianist)

August 5th:
   Bach (orch. Sevitzky), *Toccata and Fugue*
   Mendelssohn, Violin Concerto (Robert Gerle, Violinist)
   De Falla, *El Amor Brujo* (Nan Merriman, Mezzo-Soprano)
   Opera Arias by Nan Merriman
   Gershwin, *An American in Paris*

August 12th:
   Ravel, *Pavane for a Dead Princess*
   Brahms, Symphony No. 4
   Robert Russell Bennett, *Suite of Old American Dances*
   Arias and songs sung by Thomas L. Thomas, Baritone
   Ponchielli, *Dance of the Hours*, from *la Gioconda*
   (encore) Wagner, *Entrance of the Meistersingers*
   (Hereshoff noted in her review, "Praise for the free-spirited
       performances.")

August 19th:
   A Spanish Dance Program, featuring Antonio and Luisa Triana and
   their Troupe

August 26th:
   Rossini, Overture, *The Barber of Seville*
   Beethoven, Symphony No. 7
   Songs, opera arias and duets, sung by Vivian della Chiesa, Soprano, and
       Robert Hoffman, tenor
       Verdi (orch. Sevitzky), *Aida*, Suite
   John Alden Carpenter, *Song of Faith* (with un-named chorus)
   Wagner, Overture, *Tannhauser*
   (encore, sung by audience as well as chorus) *The Battle Hymn of the Republic*

When compared to his first season, it can be recognized that Sevitzky programmed in a more standard, symphonic manner in 1952. The 1952 novelties were not the excerpts or the "semi-classical," lighter fare he had used during his inaugural season here. Don Gillis, not only a composer but actually the producer of Toscanini's NBC Symphony concerts, wrote a fun work (but not an easy one to play) that was programmed by many orchestras throughout the country, including Toscanini's own. John Alden Carpenter and Robert Russell Bennett were longstanding, eminent American composers. I have no access to any information about Frances McCallin.

Sevitzky's personality, always acerbic but apparently growing increasingly so over the last couple of seasons here, made him no favorite of the musicians. The late Leo Hamilton, the Symphony's long-time tympanist, spoke with me about him, and noted that he was a very demanding conductor. Other conductors, he said, might be demanding, too, "But they would demand *with* the orchestra, *not against* them." Hamilton acknowledged that Sevitzky had brought in a number of good new players and that his programs were interesting. However, his relationship with the players and, as Hamilton intimated, with some Association Board members as well, deteriorated to such a point that in the middle of the 1952 season he was not offered a contract for the following year. That led to some considerable gossip and a minor scandal among the music-loving populace of San Diego, and a large crowd gathered at Balboa Bowl for his last concert to show their support. Constance Herreshoff reported in her review of his final 1952 concert that Sevitzky gave a curtain speech following the encore, saying, "This is not goodbye. I know I will be back. Remember MacArthur!"

Unlike MacArthur, Sevitzky did not return. Moreover, three years later he left Indianapolis, even though his contract with that orchestra had two more years to run. The trade papers reported then that he had been dismissed due to dissatisfaction with his programming and "other issues." Regardless of his personal difficulties, it could not be denied that he had left a good orchestra in Indianapolis, and certainly he had created a decent summer orchestra in San Diego. In Indianapolis, his successor, Izler Solomon, built on Sevitzky's foundation and created an even finer ensemble. In subsequent years, Solomon became a favorite guest conductor in San Diego and was the choice of many to succeed Earl Murray. However, by then he had become a fixture in Indianapolis and would not consider leaving there.

Sevitzky moved to Florida after leaving Indianapolis, and he conducted several local orchestras there. However, he never achieved the level of success he met in Indianapolis — or, for that matter, in San Diego. He reconstituted the orchestra here and hired a number of fine new players, a few of whom remained long-term members of the San Diego Symphony. Personality aside, he was stimulating and inventive, and he started the San Diego Symphony back onto its development track. The 1949 Symphony Association was daring in its attempt to find a "name" conductor, and the risk was well taken. Dr. G. Burch Mehlin had led the way in taking that risk, and in pushing hard to re-establish summer symphony concerts here. Like so many other San Diego musical pioneers, he should be remembered as an especially energetic, longstanding board member of the Symphony Association who labored in a symphony-less town to "put it all together" again after World War II.

CHAPTER VI

The Two Philharmonics

The San Diego Symphony Orchestra was not the only orchestra presenting symphonic concerts in San Diego, although it appears that they had the summers all to themselves. Only rarely did any other significant classical musical group present anything like a "season" in the Balboa Park Bowl. In the winter seasons, however, touring orchestras would come to town on occasion and would usually play in one of the larger downtown theaters such as the Spreckels, the Savoy or the Orpheum. Frederick Stock's Chicago Symphony played in San Diego a couple of times during the 1920s, as did the St. Louis Symphony, then under the direction of Rudolf Ganz. Walter Damrosch's New York Symphony toured nationally nearly every year until its late 1920s merger with the New York Philharmonic. Under Mengelberg and Toscanini, the newly melded orchestra stayed home most of the time and was rarely seen west of Chicago. Damrosch's tours, however, had been especially valuable because of his insistence that youth and children's concerts would be given as well as the more formal programs for adults.

Marcelli's vaunted San Diego High School Orchestra gave occasional concerts during the school year in the Russ Auditorium after it opened in 1927. Two other orchestras, however, became significant contributors to San Diego's musical scene. First and foremost was the Los Angeles Philharmonic Orchestra. Now it is known to the trade familiarly as the "LA Phil," but in the past it was called by its elegantly full title, "The Philharmonic Orchestra of Los Angeles." Another Philharmonic was the short-lived San Diego Philharmonic Orchestra. In its brief existence of only a few years it had great import in that it represented the first attempts by San Diegans to institute a normal, subscribed, winter season of indoor symphony concerts.

The Los Angeles Philharmonic had been founded in 1919. Although it was not the first permanent symphony orchestra to be organized on the west coast (that honor belonged to the San Jose Symphony, only recently the victim of bankruptcy in the severe economic recession affecting the Silicon Valley), in southern California it was to assume primacy. The first conductor, Henry Rothwell, was brought to the west coast from St. Paul, Minnesota, where he had led that city's orchestra. Rothwell had worked for a time as an assistant to Gustav Mahler in New York. According to an article in the July, 2003 *Opera News* by Lance Bowling, the Los Angeles Philharmonic was founded by a wealthy Angeleno, William Andrews Clark, Jr. Heir to a copper fortune, Clark was estimated to have spent three million dollars on the Orchestra over the fifteen years following its establishment. There had been a Los Angeles Symphony, founded in 1910, but its financial backing and artistic control were weak. Trained as a violinist, Clark tried from the outset to make the Philharmonic a first-rate group.

Another article about the Los Angeles Philharmonic's history, by Mark Swed, music critic for the *Los Angeles Times*, was published in the *Los Angeles Times Magazine* on August 31, 2003. Swed described the orchestra as, originally, "a rich man's toy." According to Swed, "William Andrews Clark plunked down $200,000 of his copper-baron father's money to hire first-chair players from the East Coast, and steal the rest of the players from the foundering Los Angeles Symphony. Culturally sophisticated, civic-minded and plenty quirky...he was eager for Los Angeles to catch up with Boston, New York, Philadelphia...all of which had major orchestras." Continuing, Swed wrote, "It was his band. He sometimes liked to sit with the second violins and even conduct on occasion — to the dismay of his music directors." Swed also wrote that it was Clark's dream to hire Rachmaninoff as the Los Angeles music director, but he had to settle for Rothwell. Swed described Rothwell as "...capable, if unimaginative."

For a few years, the Philharmonic played its downtown Los Angeles concerts in a large auditorium shared with a Baptist congregation. Then it moved to a larger hall shared with a Methodist Congregation. On days other than Sundays the hall was known as the Philharmonic Auditorium. It remained the orchestra's home until the Los Angeles Music Center was constructed in the early 1960s. Now, of course, Frank Gehry's new hall is the main concert facility in Los Angeles.

Only two years after its founding, the Los Angeles Philharmonic began its annual series of concerts in San Diego as well as in Santa Barbara and Riverside. Rothwell conducted the opening San Diego program at the Spreckels Theatre on December 29, 1921. The soloist was a soprano, Alice Gentle. The *San Diego Union*, announcing the concert in an article the day before, pointed out that the orchestra would be staffed by, "ninety picked musicians." Size has always seemed to count here. In subsequent years, even when the personnel of the San Diego Symphony was enlarged to full symphonic strength, it was often perceived by many as the little orchestra compared to the big Los Angeles Philharmonic. Size was not the only perceived difference. The list of musicians who led the Philharmonic, and especially many of the very eminent soloists who came to San Diego to play with them in their "run-out" concerts, were other factors.

Rothwell led the Philharmonic until his sudden death in 1927, and then Georg Schneevoigt, a Finnish conductor, was hired. In his article, Swed quoted an official 1963 Philharmonic history in describing Schneevoigt as, "flaccid, paunchy, phlegmatic, plodding, and with little or no sense of direction so far as discipline was concerned…" He lasted two seasons and then was replaced by a total opposite, the dynamic, colorful associate conductor of the Philadelphia Orchestra, Artur Rodzinski. Rodzinski had been working with another even more colorful conductor in Philadelphia, Leopold Stokowski, and had developed a reputation as a temperamental disciplinarian. His talents in that direction were soon in evidence in Los Angeles, and the orchestra developed into a first class ensemble. Rodzinski enlarged the orchestra's annual San Diego season to six concerts from the original four, but in his final, 1932-33 season the number of concerts were pared to five. After that, only four per year were given for eleven years. The depression would not allow for more, and during the first years of World War II the logistical and security problems could not be overcome.

Rodzinski's artistic success in Los Angeles attracted the management of the Cleveland Orchestra, whose leader until then had been Nicolai Sokoloff, so prominent in San Diego's musical scene later in the 1930s. Rodzinski created a superb instrument in Cleveland and eventually moved to New York as that Philharmonic's music director. In Los Angeles, meanwhile, Rodzinski had been succeeded by the great Otto Klemperer who had just fled Nazi Germany as a refugee. His earlier conversion from Judaism to Catholicism had not helped him there.

According to the Bowling article in *Opera News*, Clark was still the power behind the Los Angeles Philharmonic when Klemperer came. Bowling wrote, "Klemperer found Los Angeles bizarre. Clark invited the conductor to stay as a houseguest in his mansion…but when Klemperer discovered that Clark had several strange habits — including arriving for breakfast naked and appearing inebriated and naked in Klemperer's bedroom — the conductor checked into a hotel…" Despite such behavior, Klemperer apparently found Clark less fearsome than the Nazis, and he stayed to lead the Philharmonic to considerable national prominence. Swed opined, "[Klemperer's]…six years here put the Philharmonic on the map"

Clark died during Klemperer's second season, and with him died a generous bankroll, sorely needed during the great depression. After the death of Clark in 1934, an organized sponsoring organization was urgently needed to take his place. Harvey Mudd, the eminent engineer/philanthropist, worked hard to save the orchestra. He personally guaranteed Klemperer's salary for the next three years. The newly developed sponsoring organization running the orchestra in Los Angeles was aptly named the Southern California Symphony Society, and the tradition of run-out concerts to cities throughout southern California was continued.

Klemperer led the orchestra's four Savoy Theater concerts in San Diego during his first two seasons. Then, when he left for a time to guest conduct in non-German Europe, Jose Iturbi and Pierre Monteux shared the podium. Klemperer developed increasing aberrations during his last couple of Los Angeles seasons. It was eventually discovered that he had a brain tumor that was subsequently removed in 1939 at the Cleveland Clinic. At least, that is what I had been told in medical school by my professor of neurosurgery who said that he had assisted in that operation. Interestingly, in his *Los Angeles Times* article, Swed states that Klemperer was operated upon in Boston, where he had been incorrectly diagnosed as having a tumor, and that he was known to have been manic-depressive. Swed wrote about numerous Klemperer scandals, including his relationship with the wife of another conductor, his haunting of risqué Hollywood clubs, his spendthrift habits and occasional violent episodes. Diagnosis aside, Klemperer demonstrated that great conductors do not always equate with stability in other areas. Nonetheless, the Los Angeles Philharmonic survived.

The tumor had impaired his hearing, according to my professor, and he became severely depressed. For a number of years after his operation he was unable to conduct anywhere in the United States due to the rumors that he was mentally ill, and right after the war he sought refuge in Europe where he slowly regained his reputation. He did not return to the Philharmonic until the summer of 1953, when he conducted the Beethoven Ninth Symphony at Hollywood Bowl, marking the Bowl's one-thousandth concert.

Albert Coates led the Philharmonic in most of its post-Klemperer, four-per-season Savoy Theatre concerts here, although Bruno Walter and Igor Stravinsky also served as guests. The roster of guest conductors continued through the 1942-43 season when the Orchestra moved to the Russ Auditorium. There, the season was conducted by John Barbirolli, Leopold Stokowski, Bruno Walter and William Steinberg. The next season marked the beginning of Alfred Wallenstein's long tenure as music director. Swed described Wallenstein as, "...a respectable but not exciting conductor, he maintained a decent level of orchestral professionalism." In his second year, he increased the number of San Diego concerts to five, and featured such distinguished soloists as Jascha Heifetz, Yehudi Menuhin and Artur Schnabel. In 1946-47, there were six concerts. That number remained the rule through the nearly four subsequent decades of the Philharmonic's series here.

It was in the mid-1950s that significant backing was provided to the Philharmonic on an over-all community level, due to the hard work of Dorothy Buffum Chandler, the newspaper heiress. She developed plans to underwrite the construction of the Los Angeles Music Center where, she felt, the Philharmonic might find a good home. Stimulated by her Los Angeles activity, an active group of San Diegans worked increasingly hard to sponsor the appearances of the Los Angeles Philharmonic in Russ Auditorium and, after many years and its eventual opening, in the Civic Theatre. There was no internecine warfare in San Diego during those early years between the organizations sponsoring the Los Angeles Philharmonic and the San Diego Symphony because they never played against each other during the same seasons. The San Diego Symphony, even after its reorganization in the later 1940s, was always a summer orchestra, and the Los Angeles Philharmonic was always disbanded after its winter seasons due to the musicians' twenty-four week contracts. In the summer, many of its musicians played in the Hollywood Bowl. Eventually the Los Angeles Philharmonic developed into an orchestra that played throughout the year and continued its summer Bowl seasons. But the Hollywood Bowl was 135 miles from San Diego and there was no competition.

Later, after the San Diego Symphony established its winter seasons, the local Los Angeles Philharmonic sponsoring group and the San Diego Symphony Orchestra Association became warring factions, tragically for the city and its musical growth. Society wars developed, as well as the perception that the Philharmonic's support was mainly La Jolla-based, whereas the San Diego Symphony's was San Diego-based. That became a firm, albeit erroneous idea in the minds of many observers. The level of mutual hostility became intense. All attempts to bring the parties together or, for example, have the San Diego Symphony Orchestra sponsor appearances by the Los Angeles Philharmonic as part of the Symphony's own winter series of concerts, came to naught. The amount of money wasted on competing series was remarkable, and attendance suffered at the San Diego Symphony concerts. In contrast, the more glamorous Los Angeles Philharmonic, with its stellar list of conductors, guest conductors and soloists, attracted near-capacity crowds to Russ Auditorium and the Civic Theatre.

The glamour level of the Philharmonic increased after Wallenstein's departure in the mid-1950s when Edouard van Beinum, the conductor of the famed Amsterdam Concertgebouw Orchestra, became the Philharmonic's music director. Illness cut his tenure short after only a few years, and the Philharmonic selected Georg Solti as his successor. However, he soon became disenchanted when the Philharmonic management (actually, Mrs. Chandler) hired Zubin Mehta as a guest conductor without any of Solti's input or knowledge. Solti left in a huff before he began his term as music director, and Mehta was immediately hired as his successor.

Young, handsome, dynamic, and extraordinarily charismatic, Mehta led the Philharmonic into its glory years despite some critical complaints about his interpretations. Many appeared to believe that the performances reflected too much Viennese *Schlamperei* that may have been inculcated into him during his training in Austria. Toscanini had taught American audiences and critics to prefer tighter ensemble and precision than was often not evident in Mehta's *Mitteleuropa* style. San Diegans loved Mehta nonetheless, and less and less money seemed to be available for the continually struggling San Diego Symphony. It was extraordinarily difficult to compete with Mehta and his orchestra. However, competition was what the San Diego Symphony Orchestra Association had as its inflexible theme, often leading to disastrous results in the 1970s and '80s when financial losses led to early closure of its planned seasons.

Because the Los Angeles audiences also loved Mehta, he stayed on as Music Director for a record-setting seventeen years, until he decided to accept the offer that the august New York Philharmonic made to him. Mehta had done a number of things to increase the playing quality of what he had taken over as a very good orchestra. Among those factors was his recruiting a number of very fine violins for the orchestra in order to sweeten the sounds of the string section. Mehta's charm and charisma induced a number of collectors to lend their prized instruments to the Philharmonic. Swed wrote in the *Los Angeles Times Magazine*, "He was often accused of being a superficial showman, all glamour and no grit. He got reams of bad press, especially from this newspaper, and not all of it was undeserved. But in retrospect, Mehta, more than anyone else, gave the Philharmonic its personality and paved the way for its future." All in all, he had built the orchestra to a high enough level during his tenure that Carlo Maria Giulini, a universally revered conductor, agreed to take Mehta's place.

Giulini had become iconic as a conductor at Milan's *la Scala* Opera, and in Vienna, Berlin and, especially, Chicago. He served as principal guest conductor in Chicago under the musical directorship of Georg Solti whose departure from Los Angeles years before had originally allowed Mehta to take the Los Angeles podium. During the several years of Giulini's directorship, the Philharmonic continued its successful series of Civic Theatre concerts in San Diego although a number of attendees groused about the elderly maestro's relative lack of charisma. Musically, however, he was all anyone could wish for, and the reviews of his programs were generally ecstatic. He received frequent standing ovations, long before standing ovations appeared to become a standard, cliché response for almost any kind of completed performance.

Toward the end of his tenure with the Philharmonic, however, Giulini was obviously suffering with physical as well as emotional problems. His wife was also ill, and she determined that she should remain in their native Italy. The music began to suffer with Giulini, and tempos began to get increasingly slow. After he left the Philharmonic, Giulini returned to Italy and concertized only in

Europe. His recordings from that time demonstrate the slowness of his readings, especially when compared to his earlier recorded interpretations.

Upon the departure of Carlo Maria Giulini, Andre Previn was named as music director, but after a couple of years he became embroiled in a power struggle with the Philharmonic's notably autocratic general director, Ernest Fleischmann. Having little stomach for the combat, Previn left after Fleischmann, on his own, invited Esa-Pekka Salonen to be the Philharmonic's principal guest conductor and to take the orchestra on a tour to Japan in the summer of 1989. Fleischmann did to Previn what Dorothy Chandler had done to Solti.

Salonen had made a real hit as a guest conductor during Previn's reign. His youthful charisma won the hearts of his listeners and of the orchestra as well, and he became its next (and current) conductor. Actually, according to Swed, Fleischmann wanted Simon Rattle to succeed Previn, but Rattle did not want to leave his own orchestra in Birmingham, England. He came to the Philharmonic as a guest on several occasions, but Salonen became the Philharmonic's guide, and he has achieved remarkable success.

The Philharmonic had come to achieve an enviable position among the Country's symphony orchestras. With the San Francisco Symphony, it ranks as the finest ensemble west of St. Louis and has toured throughout the world to great acclaim. Unfortunately for its San Diego audience, it now plays here only sporadically (and only for single concerts) when it appears as part of a series sponsored by other organizations. The Philharmonic abandoned its longstanding run-out series to San Diego, Santa Barbara and Riverside in the late 1980s. Financial stresses were increasing as the orchestra provided more fare at home and on extensive tours, combined with ever-increasing salaries for its increasingly top-flight musicians. There had also been considerable problems trying to book concert dates in the Civic Theatre, where the local orchestra had contractual priorities. Although this was trumpeted as a major reason for the Philharmonic's leaving San Diego, they had cut down their appearances here significantly even after the San Diego orchestra moved to the Fox Theatre, thereby allowing much more free time for the Civic Theatre bookings.

The list of conductors brought to town by the Los Angeles Philharmonic was a distinguished one, and they provided a high level of musical sophistication. Not only the Philharmonic's music directors contributed but also the guest conductors. Those in the early years have already been mentioned, but in later years such distinguished leaders as Pierre Boulez, James Levine, Lawrence Foster, Michael Tilson Thomas, Oliver Knussen, John Williams and others provided considerable stimulation.

The importance of the Los Angeles Philharmonic in San Diego's musical life from the 1920s through the 1980s cannot be over-emphasized. Always a good orchestra, it gradually developed into a great one. It provided a level of play-ing that the fledgling, struggling San Diego Symphony could match only rarely, at least until the more halcyon earlier days of David Atherton's directorship. However, many of the other orchestras in the United States after the so-called "Big Five" could not match its level of performances, either. That performance level was a goal that the backers of the San Diego Symphony would strive for, although for the most part the record shows that the local backers had backed it more with moral encouragement than with the mandatory strong financial aid required to reach greatness.

The Los Angeles Philharmonic never saw itself as a competitor to the San Diego Symphony. Its management often announced its hope that its presentations here should increase the motivation of the San Diego public to press for compa-rable performances by a local orchestra. The situation was similar, for example, in Chicago and Milwaukee, where the latter city's orchestra was shut down for a number of years. The Chicago orchestra played ten concerts a year there. Finally, the Milwaukee Symphony was reorganized and the Chicago Symphony stopped going there regularly. It is a pattern seen routinely throughout the country when two cities, one large and one smaller, are close geographically.

The music presented by the Philharmonic in its annual concert series here, as well as the high quality of its performances, did eventually serve to stimulate local hunger for more such music from a local orchestra. That stimulation was essential if ever the dream of a full-time symphony orchestra in San Diego was to come to fruition. Instead of being a competitor, the Los Angeles Philharmonic must be seen as a promoter of live music in San Diego.

The Los Angeles Philharmonic gave its concerts in San Diego during the winter season when, before 1959, the San Diego Symphony did not play. After the Symphony was reorganized following the end of World War II, a group of musicians and music listeners began to promote the idea that the local orchestra should be heard in the winter as well as in the summer. The San Diego Symphony Orchestra Association had its hands full at the time, struggling to stay afloat during those first years of the reorganized ensemble. Thus, another sponsoring group was founded, the San Diego Philharmonic Society. Their purpose was to mount a hoped-for season of concerts played by the San Diego Philharmonic Orchestra. The players would be mainly those musicians who played under the rubric of the San Diego Symphony Orchestra during the summer seasons. This was the second of the "Two Philharmonics" that provided considerable impetus to the development of home grown music making in San Diego. Despite its relatively short life, the San Diego Philharmonic paved the way for future winter seasons to be played by the better-established San Diego Symphony Orchestra. It certainly deserves mention in any history of the San Diego Symphony.

The 1950-51 season of the San Diego Philharmonic was its first. At the time, Fabien Sevitzky was the conductor of the summer concerts of the Symphony. Although there is no information whether or not he was contacted to conduct the San Diego Philharmonic, he was obviously unavailable to assume the responsibility of a winter season here due to his obligations in Indianapolis. Another conductor had to be found. This turned out to be Leslie Hodge.

He was always referred to in the press and in the programs of the San Diego Philharmonic as Dr. Leslie Hodge. The source of his doctorate is unknown. I was unable to find any reference to it in any of the press or program materials available to me. The title was hardly unusual among conductors at the time, and many of them used it in different ways. As an example, Toscanini's associate conductor of the NBC Symphony Orchestra was always referred to as Dr. Frank Black, and the title was printed as so in the Orchestra's program booklets. Ben Grauer, the NBC announcer, always announced him as such. In Philip Hart's biography of Fritz Reiner (Northwestern University Press, Chicago, 1994), he writes about the famed conductor (pp 81-82): "Reiner received honorary doctorates from the University of Pennsylvania in Philadelphia in 1940 and the following year from the University of Pittsburgh…Both Reiners set great store by these degrees, as well as those Fritz later received from Northwestern University and Loyola University. He and Carlotta insisted upon his being addressed as Doctor Fritz Reiner. With his musicians and other professionals, he was no longer Maestro or Meister, but Doctor Reiner. In Reiner, who took such pride in being an American, this insistence on the honorific betrayed a vanity rooted in insecurity."

Hart knew Reiner well, so he had a right to that opinion. I never met Hodge, but it is apparent that the honorific was equally important to him (as well as it was to a future San Diego concertmaster ten years later). Dr. Hodge's first mention in the San Diego press was on February 26, 1950. An article announced then that he was to conduct the second of three spring programs performed at Russ Auditorium by another group that lasted an even shorter time than the San Diego Philharmonic, the San Diego Sinfonietta. The Sinfonietta was created by a local musician, John Metzger, who organized a community Board of Directors with Robert Sanders as president; E. T. Austin, vice-president; Hunter Muir, treasurer; and Edward S. Hope, Paul Jones, Mrs. Duke Lovell, Ray J. Miller, Dr. Alex Zimmerman, and Metzger as board members.

Metzger had been in contact with Hodge, who at the time was Music Director of The Orquesta Sinfonica de Guadalajara, in Mexico. Hodge had founded that orchestra and was giving concerts there regularly with some success. Metzger arranged to exchange podiums with Hodge for one concert, so he went to Guadalajara when Hodge came to conduct the Sinfonietta here, thus saving considerable expense for guest conductor fees for each orchestra.

Australian by birth and having completed most of his education there, Hodge was initially a protégé of the great Australian pianist and composer, Percy Grainger, with whom he often played in duo-piano recitals. At seventeen, he began conducting choral groups. Eventually he came to the United States where he studied conducting in San Francisco under Alfred Hertz. He began his conducting career leading federal symphonies in Sacramento, the San Francisco Bay Area, and in Portland, Oregon, before enlisting into the Navy in San Diego. He participated in four invasions in Italy, decoded enemy communications and eventually attained the rank of lieutenant commander. It was after his discharge from the Navy that he moved to Guadalajara. He married a very bright and attractive woman, Luz, who had dual Mexican and American citizenship. She was able to further her husband's career in Mexico via her extensive social and political contacts. Hodge became well known as an arranger as well as a conductor, with a famous volume of transcriptions of Australian aboriginal songs, subsequently recorded commercially. His gift for transcribing and orchestrating was to be exhibited further during his subsequent programs with the San Diego Philharmonic.

The Sinfonietta's life span was short due to the ubiquitous financial pressures always affecting the orchestra business, especially in a community that had no tradition of winter concerts other than by visiting orchestras, such as the Los Angeles Philharmonic. However, several members of the defunct Sinfonietta's board of directors determined to try again, this time with a far more aggressive posture and goal. After the collapse of the Sinfonietta in the spring of 1950, Hodge was contacted by the new board and accepted the post of music director of the new San Diego Philharmonic Orchestra.

The president of the board of the San Diego Philharmonic was the same Dr. Alex Zimmerman who had served on the predecessor board of the deceased San Diego Sinfonietta. A tireless worker for more and better music in San Diego, Dr. Zimmerman was the Director of Music Education in the San Diego City Schools. David Pain, who served as attorney for the new Philharmonic board, described Dr. Zimmerman as an incredible teacher. Pain related a Kiwanis Club meeting at which Dr. Zimmerman was the featured presenter. Dr. Zimmerman had brought a bag full of toy instruments that he distributed to the Kiwanians and, after only a half-hour of rudimentary instruction, he had them playing Leopold Mozart's "Toy Symphony." Pain said that he was absolutely astonished at Zimmerman's capacity to enthuse his audience and get everyone to participate joyfully — and musically — in the spontaneous performance. He thinks that it was probably that episode that stimulated his decision to serve the San Diego Philharmonic and review their articles of incorporation.

On August 25, 1950, the San Diego Philharmonic board announced a twenty-week winter season at the Russ Auditorium. Hodge was then thirty-six years old. An orchestra of seventy-two players was formed, and the list of most of the musicians was familiar to anyone scanning the personnel list of the summer symphony. The concertmaster was Daniel Lewis, later to become famous as a guest conductor of the Los Angeles Philharmonic as well as a noted teacher of conducting at USC. The late Leo Hamilton, who served as tympanist for Hodge as well as for the summer orchestra, spoke of Hodge bringing in several new musicians to San Diego for the Philharmonic, and said that they helped to "beef up" the sonority. They were, of course, from Los Angeles, where a large pool of studio musicians was always readily available. The union problem was not significant, according to Hamilton, who commented that it was not hard then for the newcomers to join the San Diego local. One of the percussionists (as well as manager of the business office) was Fred Plank, father of current San Diego Symphony drummer, Jim Plank.

A half-dozen subscription concerts were given at the Russ during the Philharmonic's initial season, beginning on November 28, 1950, with Jacob Lateiner as the piano soloist. Hodge's programming gifts soon became apparent; the first "Pop" concert followed soon after with an all Gershwin program. A series of youth concerts was also prepared, attracting considerable community approbation. The San Diego Council of Churches contacted Hodge and underwrote a special performance of Mendelssohn's oratorio, "Elijah," at Balboa Bowl in October, 1951. The renowned baritone, John Charles Thomas, was the soloist.

The birth of the San Diego Philharmonic Orchestra attracted the attention of the national press, including *Newsweek*. In its December 11, 1950, issue, the magazine wrote optimistically about the orchestra's future.

> "Last week, for the first time in its history, San Diego, California, had a full-time professional aggregation of its own. Called the San Diego Philharmonic Orchestra to distinguish it from the city's summertime San Diego Symphony...the organization was built up largely through the efforts of the musicians themselves...Pessimists felt that San Diego was no town for a permanent symphony. The summer series has had a hard enough time to keep going, and the Los Angeles Philharmonic visits...four times each winter. But if its first concert last week was any indication, the San Diego Philharmonic should be able to get through its first season successfully, for the Russ Auditorium, which seats 2,400, was crowded with an enthusiastically applauding audience of 2,200..."

For her previously noted 1962 San Diego State College master's thesis on the history of the San Diego Symphony, Mildred Lyman Tracy researched the

files of the San Diego County Board of Supervisors. She was able to find the
supervisors' response to a letter written to them by Dr. Zimmerman, dated
March 19, 1951. Zimmerman noted in his letter that the Philharmonic was a
great success, including the facts that the youth concerts were enthusiastically
received by the community, and that the orchestra was the second in the United
States to present a television concert. Zimmerman requested a grant of five thousand dollars and received twenty-five hundred. The next year, on March 17, 1952,
Zimmerman requested a grant of seventy-five hundred dollars and received five
thousand. In March, 1953, he requested another seventy-five hundred dollars,
and again five thousand dollars was granted. The orchestra was thereby barely
able to keep its collective head above water.

The San Diego Philharmonic board had strained to find the financial wherewithal to pay for the first season. They were able to make it with only a small
deficit, and the second season (1951-52) was announced with fanfare. Attendance
was generally good, and by the time of the second season the Russ was increasingly
filled. On April 11, 1951, an article in the *San Diego Union* quoted Drs. Hodge
and Zimmerman as being extremely proud of the success of the Philharmonic
over the initial, 1950-51 season that had just finished. They emphasized the
enthusiasm of their near-capacity audiences (at least near the end of the sea-

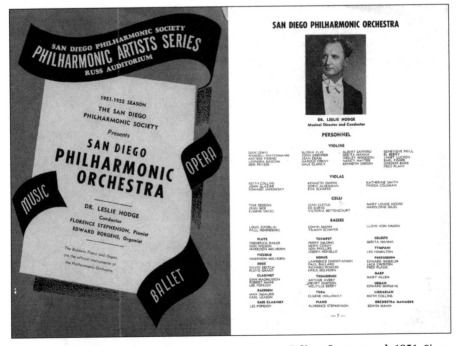

San Diego Philharmonic Orchestra program cover & list of personnel, 1951. *Photo courtesy San Diego Historical Society.*

son). As always, though, ticket receipts did not pay for all of the costs of the orchestra.

The concerts were, in fact, quite successful, musically and attendance-wise. One notable concert of the second season was given on December 2, 1951, when the orchestra played Mussorgsky's *Pictures at an Exhibition* in an orchestral version by Hodge instead of the more frequently played versions by Ravel or Stokowski. The meaty program opened with Wagner's Prelude to *Die Meistersinger*, and continued with Beethoven's Fifth Symphony. The next concert, on January 22, 1952, opened with Rossini's *William Tell* Overture and progressed

This Orchestra Is Yours

DEAR FRIENDS:

Tonight marks the opening of the second year of San Diego's first winter season resident orchestra. We are happy to welcome you on this momentous occasion.

When Dr. Leslie Hodge mounted the podium just one year ago, many of San Diego's finest citizens were skeptical about the life of the newly-formed San Diego Philharmonic orchestra. The culmination of that first brilliant season, however, marked the completion of one of the greatest pages in the musical history of our city. With each passing concert citizens who were quick to sense real cultural merit rallied to the cause of the Philharmonic and the season 1950-51 will always be remembered as the year of San Diego's great musical growth. Civic and business leaders, merchants and professional men began to realize that in music as in other things, San Diego had a home product that was worthy of the support and loyalty of all true San Diegans.

Responsible for this musical growth was the brilliant musicianship and humanitarian spirit of Dr. Leslie Hodge. He knew the important psychology of starting at the level of the musicians and the music lovers of the city. He took us as we were and started to build the foundations for our own orchestra. With each passing concert great strides were in evidence, both in the individual abilities of our musicians and in the toute ensemble of the orchestra. All of this was accomplished, too, by using the world's best music literature in the best of good taste.

Another outstanding achievement of the past year was the series of concerts for young people correlated to the public and parochial classrooms of the greater San Diego area. Here, in the making, was the assurance of a better musical day for San Diego in the years that lie ahead. How fortunate for San Diego that the man who wrote the first program materials for the Standard Hour—the oldest school broadcast in America—was none other than our own Dr. Hodge (then the protege of the late Dr. Alfred Hertz). For here was a man skilled in the difficult art of providing a series of children's concerts with lasting benefits.

As the second season opens, then, we urge all fair-minded and thinking citizens to rally to the support of our own San Diego orchestra. For years we have enjoyed the fine concerts provided us by the Los Angeles orchestra. These concerts will always be an inspiration to music lovers and musicians in San Diego. San Diego has become a full-grown city, however, and must have its own orchestra in addition to the fine concerts provided by Los Angeles. Therefore, we earnestly solicit your contributions and support. FOR THIS ORCHESTRA IS YOURS!

Respectfully,

President, San Diego
Philharmonic Society

Photo courtesy San Diego Historical Society.

with a series of operatic arias sung by Vera Jean Vary. The orchestra then played Liszt's *Les Preludes* and the Sibelius First Symphony. San Diego's long-time clarinetist, the late Dan Magnusson, received special billing in the program as solo clarinetist in the Sibelius.

The second season continued with six more subscription programs, including performances of Liszt's *A Faust Symphony*, and the west coast premiere of Felix Borowski's Organ Concerto. The new concertmaster, Gerald Vinci, played the Sibelius Violin Concerto, and Treble Clef, the women's chorus of San Diego State College, joined the orchestra in a performance of Debussy's rarely heard cantata, *The Blessed Damozel*. A characteristic review of the preceding evening's concert by Constance Herreshoff in the April 28, 1952 *San Diego Union* seems to damn with faint praise and apologies. Herreshoff wrote, "The orchestra played better than anyone had a right to expect, considering the limited rehearsal time...." She also noted the, ".....harmony of spirit between the conductor and musicians, both in performance and interpretation..."

Hodge returned to conduct in Guadalajara in the summer, following the close of each of his San Diego Philharmonic seasons. He had also taken over the management of the Price Box Office, the former booking agency for what had been known as the Master Artists Series. Under Hodge, the agency was to operate as the Philharmonic Box Office, and the Philharmonic was to sponsor appearances by a number of outstanding artists in recital. The artists came and were great successes, but the expenses continued to mount over and above the gate receipts. An organization separate from the San Diego Symphony Orchestra Association found it difficult to compete for the few dollars that were available as contributions, especially when the summer orchestra had such a long tradition. Apparently, Hodge saw the handwriting on the wall regarding likely financial problems here, and late in April, 1952 he accepted the position in Phoenix as music director of the symphony orchestra there, beginning in fall, 1952.

James Britten, the distinguished San Diego critic, wrote in *San Diego Magazine* in April, 1952, "Gentlemanly Leslie Hodge, a protégé of San Francisco's late Alfred Hertz, was well-liked by the union men here. His band fell apart when a sufficient budget could not be raised — in no small part because of society page war then in merry progress..." The development of society page wars in San Diego was burgeoning and would continue for years, always to the unwitting end of considerable harm to each of the organizations backed by each society faction.

Hodge had developed a good reputation in the southwest after a couple of seasons in San Diego. He had been invited to conduct the Doctors' Symphony of Los Angeles in the spring of 1952 and scored a considerable success there, shortly before he left San Diego for Phoenix. The *San Diego Union* reported on November 23, 1952, that the Phoenix audience gave Hodge a standing ovation at the end of his first concert as Music Director there. He stayed there for several years until financial difficulties there, too, forced curtailment of that orchestra's activities.

Hodge spent some years in Europe, according to an article in the December 17, 1967, issue of the *San Diego Union*. In Germany, he had guest conducted the *Gurzenich* Orchestra in Cologne, as well as the Hamburg Radio Symphony. The *Union* article mainly reported his return to San Diego where he and his wife had kept their La Jolla home. Luz Hodge had remained a La Jolla favorite. She had often returned to San Diego during her husband's absence and promoted Mexican-American activities that became quite popular. It was said in the December, 1967, article that he planned to teach, and he began a teaching career here that lasted for eighteen years. He also performed frequently as a pianist for groups at the La Jolla Athenaeum and elsewhere. He was killed in December, 1988, when his car collided with a truck stopped on Interstate Five near Sorrento Valley. He was seventy-five years old. At the time of his death, according to the obituary in the December 13, 1988 *San Diego Union*, Hodge was planning a program of music by Franz Liszt for spring performance.

On August 26, 1952, a *San Diego Union* article announced the appointment of Werner Janssen as the new music director of the San Diego Philharmonic. Janssen was a fine musician and a good conductor who headquartered in Los Angeles after having been the conductor for several years of the Portland, Oregon Symphony Orchestra. In Los Angeles, however, he had little chance of performing with the Los Angeles Philharmonic. Alfred Wallenstein, then music director there, would brook no local competition. Nonetheless, Janssen's career proceeded apace due to the fact that he had married Ann Harding, then a celebrated and very popular movie star. Her connections (and considerable bankroll) allowed him to form the Janssen Symphony of Los Angeles, manned by fine studio and free-lance musicians. He performed concerts with his own orchestra, often featuring rarely heard music. His wife even bought him and his orchestra a recording contract with RCA Victor. That infuriated Wallenstein and the Philharmonic musicians who had no recording contract with any company. Several Janssen Symphony recordings were issued by RCA, usually to pretty good reviews. Early in his career as director of his own orchestra, he brought his musicians in the later 1940s to San Diego where they played on the deck of the aircraft carrier, *Kearsarge*. All in all, he seemed a natural to succeed Hodge here.

Janssen brought a number of outstanding Los Angeles musicians with him to help staff the San Diego Philharmonic, and the performances were generally very well received. Israel Baker was his concertmaster (with Daniel Lewis alongside) and George Neikrug became principal cellist. Vladimir Drucker became principal trumpet and, all in all, according to Leo Hamilton, the personnel were generally at a considerably higher level than before. Salaries were higher, of course, for these imported players. Expenses rose to the extent that it was impossible to continue with a complete second season under Janssen. The board, under the Presidency of Ray Fox, requested another grant from the County Board of Supervisors, but this time there was nothing forthcoming. The last concert that season was conducted by Marcelli, as a fund-raiser.

In 1954, a real estate broker, Burling M. Stump, became the Philharmonic Board's president, with retired Navy Captain H. E. Le Barron as vice-president. A season of four concerts was planned, and a grant for a thousand dollars was given by the Board of Supervisors for a Columbia Masterworks recording by the orchestra, under Janssen, of music by the Brazilian master, Heitor Villa-Lobos. Insofar as I am aware, that recording was never made. After increasing financial pressures, the board finally gave up and entered into discussions with the San Diego Symphony Orchestra Association, hoping for amalgamation.

George Scott, the retail merchant, arranged a meeting of both orchestra boards in May, 1955. With the considerable aid of Captain Le Barron, a successful merger was accomplished. Agreements were reached for the Symphony to absorb the Philharmonic but not the imported players. Most of the rest of the local players were already San Diego Symphony members. Five members of the Philharmonic Board were to sit on the Symphony board, and two would serve on the executive committee. Janssen stayed home in Los Angeles.

The San Diego Philharmonic was a force of considerable influence in the development of symphonic music in San Diego. Although its life was brief, it provided a foretaste of a winter season to a community that had never before conceived of such a phenomenon. Symphonic music was a summer festival in San Diego. Winter had been a time for recitals and the Los Angeles Philharmonic. But the boards of both the San Diego Symphony and the San Diego Philharmonic were increasingly aware that a full-time, year-round orchestra was what was needed in a growing community if the concept of symphonic music was to become a permanent focus. Just a few years after the absorption of the Philharmonic, the San Diego Symphony Orchestra Association began to experiment with the idea of a couple of concerts in the winter at Russ Auditorium. History had shown that the risk was great. The need, though, was even greater, and eventually it was fulfilled.

CHAPTER VII

Robert Shaw: Home Town Boy Makes Very Good

In retrospect, it appears as if Robert Shaw had been destined from birth to become the music director of the San Diego Symphony Orchestra. Long before he first ascended the podium here, news reports of his successes were always accompanied by local pride in his origins and his noteworthy San Diego family. These tended to make him into a household name in his home town. As an example, as early as October 10, 1939, a *San Diego Union* social note reported that the son of the Reverend and Mrs. Shirley Shaw of San Diego had married Maxine Farley in a ceremony presided over by the Reverend Shaw at the Old Central Christian Church in New York City. The former Miss Farley was the daughter of an Indiana Congressman. The article noted that the groom was the Director of the Fred Waring Glee Club.

Three years later, on April 26, 1953, another *San Diego Union* article referred to Robert Shaw as, "…the most successful of choral conductors, whose newly-organized Collegiate Chorale will sing in concert in Carnegie Hall under Leopold Stokowski…" Numerous subsequent articles about Shaw always referred to him as the son of Reverend and Mrs. Shaw as they noted his repeated, increasing success as the New York and Los Angeles choral conductor who had been selected by Arturo Toscanini to lead the chorus in the Italian maestro's opera broadcasts.

Robert Shaw's family was intensely musical. His father, the Reverend Shirley Shaw, was Pastor of the University Christian Church in Hillcrest. His mother, Nelle, sang in the church choir as lead soprano, and his sister, Hollace Shaw, became a noted concert soprano. Young Robert attended San Diego Schools before matriculating at Pomona College. He worked his way through college by wrapping newly baked bread in a bakery and by waiting on tables. Although he originally wanted to follow his father into the ministry, his ambitions veered strongly toward music when he began to conduct the college glee club. Fred Waring heard the group and took Shaw with him to New York.

Shaw was awarded a Guggenheim Foundation Fellowship in 1944 to study conducting. His rapid rise to success followed, and in 1946 a new post was created for him at the Julliard School, Director of Choral Music. Soon afterwards

A young Robert Shaw. *Photo courtesy Mildred Lyman Tracy Thesis.*

he organized a professional choir at the Collegiate Church in New York City, and eventually he took it on tour as the Collegiate Chorale. He gave his first San Diego concert with the Chorale in November, 1951. The concert had been announced in the *San Diego Union* on November 18, as always with references to Shaw's San Diego background. The November 26 *San Diego Union* review of that concert by Constance Herreshoff began, "Not so many years ago, Robert Shaw was a schoolboy here in San Diego…" She continued, "It was a case of home town boy making good in a big way when he conducted his chorale and concert orchestra in their first concert here…"

When Sevitzky's contract was not renewed for the 1953 summer season, it almost seemed inevitable that the home town hero should stand on the home town podium. Edith Cushing, then Society Editor of the *San Diego Union,* wrote on June 10, 1953, "San Diego will welcome one of its favorite sons, Robert L. Shaw, at a gala public reception in the House of Hospitality Auditorium…He is one of the country's outstanding conductors…" She went on to note that Robert Shaw's mother was then living in San Mateo, California. "Her late husband, Reverend Shaw, had been on the board of the Summer Symphony, so it seems particularly fitting that his son should one day conduct the orchestra…"

Like Hodge and Janssen with their San Diego Philharmonic, Shaw also reached into Los Angeles for a number of musicians to bolster the local orchestra. A fine violinist, Werner Torkanowsky, became his concertmaster for the first season. Considerable enthusiasm greeted all six of the concerts that summer. Attendance increased past the average 2,400 characteristic of Sevitzky's seasons. Shaw's average attendance in his first season was nearly 2,800. A very large crowd came for the final concert, Beethoven's *Missa Solemnis*, with the San Diego chorus augmented by Roger Wagner's Chorale from Los Angeles. The average was nearly as high in his second season, featuring such choral/orchestral master-works (but hardly expected to be crowd-pleasers) as Stravinsky's *Oedipus Rex* and Haydn's oratorio, *The Creation*. Difficult music or no, the crowds came and were pleased by the performances, if not unanimously by Stravinsky's dissonances or Haydn's lengths. The six concerts of the 1955 season also drew large crowds averaging over 2,800 per concert. The lowest figures were for the opening pro-gram featuring a solo performance by Shaw's new concertmaster, Robert Gerle, and a concert featuring the music of contemporary composer/conductor, Lukas Foss. More than 4,000 attendees heard the final concert, a performance of the great Berlioz Requiem. Fewer attended an extra, fund-raising concert conducted by the celebrated Ferde Grofé.

Mildred Lyman Tracy's 1962 San Diego State College master's thesis pro-vides a rave article about Shaw and the San Diego Symphony from *Time Magazine*, August 1, 1955.

> "Old patrons of the San Diego Symphony could hardly believe their eyes: 4,000 of their fellow townsmen streamed into Balboa Park's Ford Bowl for the city's largest symphonic turnout in many a season. Then they could hardly believe their ears. The San Diego Symphony played its way through a difficult program of concertos with pianist Rudolf Serkin, and played beautifully. Critics, customers and pianist Serkin all agreed: the orchestra had come of age. So had the conductor; at 39, Robert Shaw had made the difficult transition from a brilliant leader of voices to a topnotch director of musicians.
>
> "In 1953, symphony in San Diego was in the doldrums, and hating it, and conductor Shaw was riding the high tide of success, and hating it, too. Restless, volatile, Bob Shaw felt that he had come as far as he could with Manhattan's famed Collegiate Chorale, the Robert Shaw Chorale and the smaller voice groups that ballooned him from a $35-a-week arranger for Fred Waring to a creative, sensitive stylist who could make some $75,000 a year. Shaw was looking for an orchestra to work and learn with. When San Diego issued the call, he lost no time in saying yes.
>
> "During his first two seasons, the musicians treated this stocky, new conductor as a kind of musical Boy Scout, frequently were noisy in rehearsals and harried him with unim-portant questions. But this year they defer to his authority

with respectful silence, passing their questions up through the concertmaster. Shaw, at home with the instruments as never before, is using a baton for the first time. 'I'm beginning to feel the orchestra in my fingers now,' he said last week. 'My fingers taste the sound; my ears taste the sound. I can't explain it — I just am closer...'

"For Shaw, this first permanent conducting is a combination training-ground and experiment in audience acceptance. Instead of programming the light music usually served up to hot weather audiences, he is putting San Diegans through a stiff summer course.

"Shaw is able and willing to pay for his experiment, is plowing back all his salary and some $3,000 more into the orchestra to get the talent and programming that he wants. But how long Shaw's San Diego phase will last nobody knows..."

It lasted a couple of more years, although the Symphony Association and the community had expected and hoped that it would have lasted longer. Despite Shaw's proclivities extending into the realms of more difficult music, everybody loved him. Although the *Time* article had commented that the musicians, especially in Shaw's first couple of seasons, had looked down upon him as inexperienced, Leo Hamilton disagreed with that when I interviewed him. The veteran drummer reported that only a few musicians made negative comments. He and most of his colleagues felt that Shaw knew his business. Besides, he added, the Los Angeles "ringers" he had brought to town certainly respected him and followed his wishes completely. As he told me, "You have to understand, the San Diego Symphony was only beginning to develop professionalism." Hamilton elaborated by describing the kind of attitude that indicated that the maestro's leads would be followed perfectly or at least discussed respectfully if there was disagreement or misunderstanding.

Henry Kolar, who began his long experience as a violinist in the San Diego Symphony under Shaw, thought he was, "wonderful." Kolar mentioned that Shaw, himself, considered that his San Diego post was "on the job training," but, again according to Kolar, he was so intensely musical that the experienced players in the orchestra forgave him everything. The inexperienced players needed a little more. Paul Anderson came to the San Diego Symphony as first cellist in 1955, after playing in the Chicago Civic Orchestra, the Grant Park Symphony Orchestra and the St. Louis Symphony, where he served for six years. He commented that he had played under some of the world's greatest conductors before coming to San Diego, where he had a teaching position waiting for him at the

State University. His opinion of Shaw was that he was a superb musician and, without question, the finest choral conductor he had ever known. As an orchestra conductor, he was not as great, but he worked hard. "I never heard much carping." Shaw often requested help from his musicians about bowing, etc., but his general approach was collegial and the musicians responded in kind.

No doubt, Shaw practiced his orchestral conducting in San Diego, and he could have been considered functioning in on-the-job-training. However, his innate musicianship and sensitivity had already been extensively developed, and the readings of the music he programmed were all thought to be exemplary by critical listeners. Shaw used his choral background to excellent, constructive purposes when he organized the San Diego State College Choral Workshop, an annual summer program that drew budding choristers and chorus directors from throughout the country. The co-director was Julius Herford with whom Shaw had worked in New York.

On October 17, 1957, in a valedictory *San Diego Union* article about the retiring Music Director, Constance Herreshoff wrote about a number of contributions made by Shaw in the direction of increasing community musical activities. She noted the development of "Inside Music" programs begun in 1956, featuring orchestra members and choral workshop performers in smaller-scaled performances. Chamber music concerts were given at the Fine Arts Gallery by orchestra musicians. Children's concerts were given during the summer seasons in Escondido and Oceanside as well as in San Diego. In 1956, the San Diego Civic Youth Orchestra was organized, trained and conducted by Daniel Lewis.

Robert Shaw conducting Jeanne d'Arc au Bucher by Authur Honegger; the San Diego Symphony, with chorus, at Ford Bowl, 1954. *Photo courtesy American Federation of Musicians, San Diego Local.*

Lewis had become Shaw's Assistant Conductor during the 1956 summer season. That began his own distinguished conducting career as well as the remarkable career he eventually made as a teacher of orchestral studies and conducting at the University of Southern California.

Robert Shaw's devotion to the development of his orchestra and to music generally in San Diego could not be denied. He continued paying sums out of his own pocket for specific soloists or for extra rehearsals for especially difficult pieces, notably those pieces with chorus and vocal soloists. The community returned his devotion with increasing, enthusiastic attendance. Shaw began the 1956 season soon after returning to the United States following what was described in the *San Diego Union* on June 21, 1956 as a "sensational," eleven-week tour of Europe with the Robert Shaw Chorale. For the opening of the 1956 season, Shaw presented the Beethoven Ninth Symphony. In her *San Diego Union* review on July 19, 1956, Constance Herreshoff wrote, "An enthusiastic audience welcomed Robert Shaw last night in Balboa Park Bowl...The big-scale program indicative of the conductor's ambition and courage was climaxed by one of the greatest symphonic works, Beethoven's Ninth Symphony...There was a prolonged ovation for Shaw and all participants...The Summer Festival Chorus of San Diego State College had been prepared by Leonard Moore, a choir director from the north. This chorus sang with a victorious sprit and remarkably well..."

The Choral Workshop Chorus participated in the season's final concert, a presentation of the Verdi Requiem. The Beethoven Ninth drew a paid attendance of 3,874, and the Verdi Requiem 3,387. Only a performance featuring the Dave Brubeck Quartet drew more (4,135). The average attendance in 1956 was 3,359.

The 1956 season, however, was preceded by some news that represented a significant omen for Shaw and San Diego. Shaw had accepted a position offered by George Szell to become his assistant in Cleveland, an opportunity no budding maestro could consider refusing. Under Szell, the Cleveland Orchestra was beginning to reach its peak as one of the greatest orchestras in the world. It seemed evident that Shaw's days in San Diego would be numbered.

The *San Diego Union* of June 24, 1957, announced that Robert Shaw had arrived in San Diego to begin his fifth season as music director. The average paid attendance that season was over 3,000, with the highest at a concert featuring the pop-singing group, the Hi-Los. Close behind was a concert featuring Isaac Stern as violin soloist. The choral works given that summer included the German Requiem by Brahms, and *les Noces* by Stravinsky. After that season was concluded, Shaw asked the Association to be granted a leave of absence for the 1959 season. The *Union* article said that the reasons for the request were his heavy recording commitments with his chorale as well as his contract to concertize with them throughout the country.

The leave of absence was granted in 1957 for 1959. Another *Union* article, on March 9, 1958, announced Shaw's plans to direct here that summer. However, just a month later he was released completely from his San Diego Symphony contract, ostensibly for reasons of health. According to Mildred Lyman Tracy's 1962 master's thesis, Shaw was suffering from nervous exhaustion. "His duties as associate conductor of the Cleveland Symphony, his recording commitments in New York City, his participation in the Alaska Festival of Music held yearly in Anchorage since 1956 — all contributed to the necessity for him to curtail the many activities he had undertaken..."

Despite that news, Shaw and the Symphony Association proceeded with long-discussed plans to present at least a trial winter concert. Shaw would be unable to conduct it due to his new Cleveland commitments, so the program was to be conducted by Jose' Iturbi. His sister, Amparo Iturbi, would be featured as piano soloist. The Iturbis were very popular due to their motion picture appearances, and Jose' had also been the successful conductor of the Rochester Philharmonic Orchestra. Two presentations were given. The first, at Russ Auditorium, was on March 3, 1957, and a repeat performance was given in Oceanside three weeks later. Neither drew well but Shaw and the Symphony Association decided that they would try again. The next season, during the spring of 1958, Andres Segovia was the soloist. The orchestra was under the baton of Erno Daniel, then the conductor of the Wichita Falls Symphony Orchestra, and later music director of the Santa Barbara Symphony. That concert drew a good audience and the Association was encouraged to try a few more.

A series of three concerts was given during the late winter and spring of 1959, and all the tickets were sold out in advance due to the fact that Van Cliburn, then at the very height of his worldwide fame, was one of the soloists. Maurice Abravanel, conductor of the Utah Symphony, led the first of that winter's concerts, with Paul Badura-Skoda as piano soloist. John Barnett, assistant conductor of the Los Angeles Philharmonic, conducted the Cliburn program, and George Barati of the Honolulu Symphony conducted the orchestra, with Igor Gorin as the baritone soloist on April 26, 1959.

It was obvious that, on the scale of prestige, the music directorship of the San Diego Symphony Orchestra provided nothing like the other activities that were beginning to crowd Shaw's schedule. It also appears that the San Diego public were not angered by what might be seen as a slight. They continued to love Bob Shaw, as, appropriately, one of their own who was making good over and over, and they took enormous pride in his accomplishments. They also were quite grateful for the high level of musical performances he had caused the

Symphony to reach here. They were sorry to lose him but they understood the dynamics involved.

The year after his resignation, however, he must have recovered well from his nervous exhaustion because he was exceptionally busy. In January, 1959, he conducted the Boston Symphony Orchestra in Boston and in Carnegie Hall. The next month, according to a February 7, 1959 article in the *San Diego Union*, he left to take the Chorale on a strenuous bus tour of the United States, giving six performances a week of the Bach B Minor Mass! During all this time, he continued working with and studying under Szell in Cleveland and conducting that orchestra there and on tour.

All in all, it is remarkable what Shaw accomplished here in the half-dozen seasons he was in San Diego. He excited an enlarging audience and left them with memories of fine performances. He really meant what he wrote for the *San Diego Union* on July 8, 1956 as his "Credo: Take the Best. Play it Perfectly."

> "What justifies an 'Operation Midsummer Symphonies,' its conductor and audience, to dare these heights of musical creativity…[as exemplified by the works of Haydn, Mozart and Beethoven]…? If memory is correct, it was Leigh Mallory who replied to the similar question concerning the assault on Mount Everest, 'Because it is there.'
>
> "…The fear is the fear of mediocrity - its dullness and infectiousness. Warmed-over composition invites shoddy performances and bored listening. Nothing will drive this orchestra and its growing audience from Balboa Park Bowl so quickly as the programming premise that one need to bring to these concerts only his union card or price of admission…It is absolutely necessary, then, for instance, that a community engage to produce and attend a Beethoven Ninth Symphony. Only the foolish, immodest or ignorant would expect it to burst forth in final and flawless perfection. But that its own self-discipline, vision and nobility should not mature an orchestra or leave its mark upon an audience would be by far the greater miracle…"

Shaw brought his own "self-discipline, vision and nobility" to town at just the right time and enabled San Diego's music-making to take an enormous step forward. When he finally returned to San Diego many years later as principal guest conductor while Yoav Talmi was music director, he was greeted appropriately as a longstanding, extraordinarily valued friend as well as one of the world's foremost musicians.

Shaw died from a stroke at the age of eighty-two on January 26, 1999, in New Haven, Connecticut, where he had gone to see a play that was his youngest son's senior acting and directing project at the Yale School of Drama. At the time, he had become the laureate conductor of the Atlanta Symphony Orchestra, which he led from 1967 to considerable acclaim. Many honors came his and the orchestra's way, including fourteen Grammys for the orchestra and the Presidential Medal of Arts for him. A man with few, if any enemies in a very difficult, often back biting profession, he was universally, deservedly mourned. In San Diego, his boyhood home and the home of the orchestra he had worked so hard to develop in its earlier years, he was mourned even more personally.

San Diego's 1958 summer season had to be planned without the guidance of Robert Shaw. Without Shaw, no Los Angeles "ringers" came down to play in the orchestra. Robert Gerle had left when Shaw left, and Joe Kirshbaum resumed the concertmaster's chair that he had held long before when he had played under Marcelli. The Choral Arts Workshop continued at San Diego State College under the sole direction of Julius Herford who had started it with Shaw. Roger Wagner, who led the Los Angeles Roger Wagner Chorale, came down to conduct two choral concerts with the Symphony. He then began to direct the Choral Workshop for its final two summers, and appeared with the orchestra and chorus in each of those seasons. The Symphony Association was able to hire John Barnett to conduct the first two concerts of the season.

Until then, John Barnett had been the associate conductor of the Los Angeles Philharmonic under Alfred Wallenstein. He had worked hard there, conducting many of the Philharmonic's youth concerts, tour and run-out concerts (including several in San Diego, beginning in 1951) and Hollywood Bowl programs. He had studied in the United States as well as in Europe before the War. He served in the military in World War II, and upon his discharge in 1946 he was the recipient of Columbia University's Alice B. Ditson Award.

When hired by the San Diego Symphony for his two concerts in 1958, he had just assumed the position in New York as director of the National Orchestral Association. Maurice Abravanel returned to San Diego to conduct two programs, and Daniel Lewis conducted a concert featuring the Dave Brubeck group. Barnett was named musical director and conductor for the summer of 1959, and conducted all the concerts but one. That was conducted by Roger Wagner when the Choral Workshop Chorus and the Symphony performed Orff's *Carmina Burana*. The next year Wagner conducted the final summer Choral concert in a program he often described as, "The loudest concert ever given!" It consisted of Sir William Walton's Cantata, *Belshazzar's Feast*, with the assistance of the local Marine and Navy bands, and a repeat of Orff's *Carmina Burana*. But by then, the Symphony's great leap forward into a year-round schedule had been made, and a new music director was its first, full-time conductor.

CHAPTER VIII

Earl Bernard Murray

I was in the audience at the Russ Auditorium that November night in 1959 when Earl Murray began his tenure as the first year-round music director of the San Diego Symphony. At the time I was serving as an active duty physician at the old Naval Hospital, where I was able to hear most of the rehearsal sounds of the summer orchestra from Balboa Bowl, just across Park Boulevard. For the sake of objectivity, I should point out that I had just come from Chicago, where I was used to hearing what was becoming the nation's finest symphony orchestra under the strict regimen of Fritz Reiner. What I heard from the Balboa Park Bowl was not encouraging to these jaded ears, and when I attended a few of the summer evening concerts I was not positively impressed.

What did impress me, however, were the newspaper articles I read that summer, announcing the hiring of a new, young conductor from San Francisco who would lead the San Diego Symphony into a full, year-round series of concert programs. The young man had been the assistant to Pierre Monteux, a world-renowned conductor spoken of with reverence. That was encouraging.

At my request, the Special Services Officer at the Naval Hospital was pleased to purchase several sets of tickets for the new winter season and, despite some lingering trepidation, my regular attendance at San Diego Symphony Orchestra concerts began. Murray opened his first concert with the Hamilton Harty arrangement of Handel's *Royal Fireworks Music*. When it ended, I turned to my wife and said, "I don't know who this guy is or how much they're paying him, but I think they should give him a raise. The orchestra started together and ended together, and in between for most of the time they played together..." That was a considerable improvement over what I had heard over the summer, and it represented enormous promise.

A profile of Earl Murray was written by Natalie Best for the October 5, 1959, *San Diego Union*. Murray came from a musical family. His father had been a bandmaster and had spent some time in San Diego conducting the Navy Band here. A native San Franciscan, Murray had attended the University of California at Berkeley where he began to study law. Music, however, drew him, and he determined that it would be his profession. A trumpeter, he had played under Monteux

Earl Bernard Murray. *Photo courtesy San Diego Symphony.*

in the San Francisco Symphony for several years, during which time he was the orchestra's youngest member. Monteux took the young man under his wing and Murray became the elder statesman's protégé. He learned his conducting skills from Monteux who encouraged him greatly. Aside from becoming the San Francisco orchestra's assistant, then associate conductor, he served as music director for the San Francisco Ballet during the 1952 season. Eventually, guest-conducting appearances became available. Murray led the Boston "Pops" on the Esplanade, the New York City Ballet, and the Denver and Utah Symphony Orchestras. In 1958, Murray toured Latin America, conducting a number of the symphony orchestras in the major cities. The San Diego Symphony Orchestra Association, headed then by Dr. G. Burch Mehlin, conducted a search for a new music director. Murray, highly recommended by Monteux, was the choice.

From the very beginning, Philip Klauber was of great help to me in preparing this history. He was active in the San Diego Symphony Association when Murray was hired, and remembered that a conductor selection committee had been formed to find a new music director. He was not on it, and he did not recall who had been members other than Dr. Mehlin. Nonetheless, I asked him why John Barnett had not been chosen because, after all, he had conducted the 1959 summer season and had also appeared here before. Klauber replied that it was felt that he simply had little drama or excitement associated with his name, but that Earl Murray did. Interestingly, when I asked Paul Anderson, the orchestra's first cellist in those years, about the passing over of Barnett as music director, he agreed with Klauber. Anderson's comment was, "Barnett just wasn't inspiring, but he was very competent."

Although neither Phil Klauber nor Paul Anderson mentioned it, the fact that Barnett had just left the post of assistant conductor in Los Angeles might well have placed the image of the San Diego Symphony Orchestra into a kind of satellite or branch status, at least in the perceptions of some of the board members. The social wars in San Diego between the San Diego and Los Angeles orchestra backers were just beginning to heat up. Moreover, the entire community was suffering even more overtly than now from a self-image that was, at best, second class when compared with the colossus to the northwest. Printed signs were beginning to be seen around town, "We don't give a damn *how* they do it in Los Angeles!"

Murray had been popular in San Francisco and had achieved a good following there. When his San Diego appointment was announced, an editorial in the *San Francisco News* on July 25, 1959, was headed, "San Diego's Gain." The editorial read in part, "The San Francisco musical scene is losing a good man in thirty-three-year-old Earl Murray, who has put new sparkle into the symphony's youth concerts. But we can only congratulate him — and San Diego — on his appointment as that city's first permanent symphony conductor…" Prior to coming to San Diego to open his initial season here, Murray conducted the San Francisco Ballet in Stravinsky's *Danses Concertantes* when it appeared as part of a San Francisco Opera double bill with Strauss's *Ariadne auf Naxos*. The review in the *San Francisco Chronicle* by Alfred Frankenstein lauded Murray. He wrote, "…One must observe that this performance marked, if I am not mistaken, the first time that a San Francisco conductor has appeared with the San Francisco Opera Company. Now that Earl Murray has emerged from the limbo of the San Francisco Symphony's assistant conductorship to take over orchestras in San Diego and Monterey, his career will develop in keeping with his gifts, and his lively, skillful, neatly turned direction of *Dances Concertantes* with the Opera Company signalizes the beginning of important things with his name on them…"

Murray was given a one-year contract by the San Diego Association, with a two-year option to follow. His first season was successful, and the option was taken up. He had conducted all four concerts presented as the 1959-60 season in the Russ Auditorium. Soloists included the basso, Jerome Hines, who sang Wagner scenes; the pianist, Jorge Demus; and the violinist, Isaac Stern. The final concert of the season on March 22, 1960, was all orchestral. It was repeated three nights later in Tijuana when Murray took the orchestra there to play in the *Teatro Reforma*.

The next month, Murray returned to the San Francisco Symphony as guest conductor for a pair of subscription concerts. The reviews were exceedingly favorable. The headline in Jack Loughner's review in the *San Francisco Call-Bulletin* read, "Murray Returns — Symphony Shines." In the April 8, 1960, *San*

Francisco Examiner, Alexander Fried reviewed Murray's concert, pointing out that the young conductor made the orchestra sound, "immediately keener, less fleshy," when compared to the sound heard the prior week under the guest baton of Bernard Haitink. Fried praised the ensemble and also reported his impression that Murray must have stimulated a good feeling within the orchestra so that the principals played with excellent tone and security. The noted critic, Alfred Frankenstein, in his April 8, 1960, review in the *San Francisco Chronicle*, wrote that Murray had made a "huge hit" with his performance of Carl Ruggles' difficult, granitic tone poem, *Of Men and Mountains*. Frankenstein concluded his review as follows. "Murray was actually engaged for this week's concert while he was still in San Francisco, and this circumstance suggests that things may be getting better so far as the recognition of San Francisco's gifted people are concerned."

Monteux retired from the San Francisco Symphony that year, and Murray was never invited back to conduct the orchestra, despite the rave reviews. The new conductors in San Francisco, Enrique Jorda and, subsequently, Josef Krips, wanted no part of a Monteux heritage.

The *San Diego Union's* music critic, Alan Kriegsman, wrote about Murray and the San Diego Symphony on September 11, 1960, before the opening concert of Murray's second season here. In his article he stated, "...It ought to be noted firmly that the San Diego Symphony's progress over the past few years has been considerable. Some of its fruits have been an expanded winter season, a new, young, energetic, full-time conductor, a new, enterprising manager, and the completion of the most successful summer season in the history of the organization...Credit for these accomplishments belong obviously to the entire San Diego Symphony Association and all its supporters, but more especially to the one key figure whose arrival on the scene coincides with the beginning of the march upward, Conductor Earl Bernard Murray..."

Kriegsman concluded his essay by pointing out, "...[The Symphony must]...find ways and means of inducing business and affluent individuals to make contributions on a much vaster scale than ever before, commensurate with those in other cities..." This truism is obviously as relevant today as it was in 1960. Not following Kriegsman's dictum led to several disasters in later years that seriously damaged the Symphony's stability. Funding aside from the grosses from ticket admissions was extraordinarily inadequate. The concept that a symphony orchestra functions as a non-profit organization was anathema to a number of members. Deficits were always barely grudgingly made up.

In June, 2002, I interviewed J. Dallas Clark, who had been president of the Symphony Association during the 1960s, and very active for several years before and after as well. His first recollection of his presidency, he said, was begging the audiences for money from the stage during intermissions. "The board *never*

Earl Bernard Murray and the San Diego Symphony at the Russ Auditorium. *Photo courtesy Mildred Lyman Tracy Thesis.*

raised enough money. I always had a terrible time with the board. They never gave a thing! I always preached three W's to them - Work, Wisdom and Wealth. I told them they had to have at least two out of three. Then we became known as the graveyard of managers. I blame that on the boards. They never gave any cooperation."

Research into the patterns of giving by the board and executive committee members of those years reveals that few reached the highest level of donors. As an example, during the 1969-70 season, of all the Executive Committee members, only Mr. and Mrs. Abe Ratner, Mr. and Mrs. Fred Goss, Mr. and Mrs. Arthur Johnson and Mr. and Mrs. Fred Rohr reached the so-called "Sponsor" level ($10,000). I was a vice-president of the board then, and an executive committee member. My few hundred dollars was considered a generous annual donation. No executive committee member was listed as a "Benefactor" ($5,000) or "Donor" ($2,500), the levels between the "Sponsors" and my level, the "Patrons." Some other executive committee members were also in that category. Others were even lower, in the "Sustaining Member" and "Associate Member" categories.

Late in the 1960s, a couple of newly influential San Diegans became steady contributors to the Symphony. They usually appeared at the last moment to "save the Symphony" by contributing just enough to keep it going, or else to reduce a large deficit to what was hoped would be a manageable amount. Bob Peterson and Richard Silberman were relatively young, newly rich San Diegans, somewhat disestablishmentarian if not overtly anti-establishmentarian in their outlook. They had founded a successful fast-food operation that was subsequently purchased by the Ralston-Purina Corporation of St. Louis. That city had a long history of symphony activity that the two men enjoyed when they went to the Midwest for their board meetings. Mrs. Silberman was a good pianist and a music-lover. Their usual, last minute salvations did not teach the Association that they had better improve their own fund-raising activities. Instead, they actually became dependent upon these last-ditch heroics.

The 1960s were also an era in which grants were made available by foundations as well as by the federal government for arts organizations. I had joined the San Diego Symphony Association Board of Directors during the 1963-64 season. I learned quickly that most but definitely not all of my colleagues on the board were extremely conservative people who would allow no federal money to come into their organization's treasury. They feared federal intervention would follow, and besides, the entire situation smacked of socialism in their eyes. That attitude, in general, mirrored the community's at that time.

Foundation money was another affair, though, and the Association accepted with alacrity a Ford Foundation grant of five hundred thousand dollars. That needed to be matched by a similar sum contributed by the community by July 1, 1971. The whole was to be held sacrosanct in perpetuity as the basis for an endowment fund for the orchestra, although the Foundation also threw in an extra $100,000 as an outright gift for operating expenses. Philip Klauber, president of the Association during the 1960s, recalled for me the difficulty met by the Association when the members tried to raise the necessary matching funds, but in the end they were successful. Unfortunately, nothing significant was ever added to the initial matched pot to enrich the endowment Eventually the entire enterprise was killed when, in later years, in the era of other music directors, the board cashed in the entire amount to maintain the running expenses of the orchestra, despite the illegality of that move.

In those days, the board depended mainly upon the managers to raise funds over and above the usual social events that garnered some money, and also to figure out some manner in which the organization could continue despite the b.oard's own recalcitrance. The "new, enterprising manager" about whom Kriegsman spoke in his September, 1960 article was Freeman Moeser. He replaced Alexander Haas, who had served as manager for several preceding seasons. Moeser, however, lasted only a single season. In 1961-62, Robert McIntyre was the manager, only to be replaced for the following season by Ralph O'Connor. Eva Irving was also hired that year as assistant to the manager; she proved to be a stabilizing influence throughout her service in the office because managers came and left so frequently. San Diego became known in symphony circles as the graveyard of managers. Managers would leave when they realized that they were unable to move the board to extend the orchestra season or to raise more money. If they would not leave on their own then they would be fired because of their conflicts with the unwilling board. In the 1964-65 season, William L. Denton began his tenure as manager, and he stayed for a much longer time than any of his predecessors, although the cash flow position of the Association never eased.

Earl Bernard Murray's popularity in San Diego was considerable during the first part of his seven seasons here. Personable, charming and extraordinarily articulate, he cut a wide swath through the community, always attempting to broaden the very limited outreach of the orchestra. He put the orchestra on television for the first time. A kinescope of that program is available at the San Diego State University Special Collections and Archives, at the Malcolm Love Library. It demonstrates unqualifiedly his attractive approach to a TV audience. As season followed season he attempted to enlarge the orchestra's repertoire as well as extending the number of subscription concerts performed during the year. The Tuesday evening Russ audiences were generally large and enthusiastic. It was not until several years later and under a different music director that the San Diego Symphony began to experiment with paired concerts.

In general, the orchestra responded positively to Murray's direction, although Henry Kolar, Murray's first concertmaster, referred to him as, "A pedantic little fellow." In contrast, Paul Anderson, Murray's first cellist, felt better about him. Anderson said that Murray had a good stick technique and, in a very positive sense, worked very hard with the orchestra. "He had to work with what he had here." Critical listeners could hear a relatively consistent level of improvement in the playing, especially in a tightening of the ensemble.

The personnel remained generally constant except for some of the principals. The major change was Murray's bringing in a new concertmaster from Rochester, Robert Emile. Like Leslie Hodge of yore, he was consistently referred to in the programs as Dr. Robert Emile, although to everyone who knew him he was "Bud." A very good violinist, he was an even better teacher. The undernourished violin section began to sound a little better, although several violinists continued to manifest problems with intonation. Murray and Emile needed to compromise often because, although they were aware of the faulty tuners, they were unable to get rid of them. Murray was able, very gradually, to add some string players to the orchestra but was unable to get rid of those who were problematic. There was certainly no money for the kind of far more experienced, better string players who would have made a significant difference in the sound.

Emile also served as assistant conductor. There was no question about the fact that he really wanted to be the principal conductor, and at times his efforts in that direction became obvious. He forged a reputation as a manipulative troublemaker, and a number of the musicians developed marked dislikes toward him. As concertmaster, however, he served a very positive purpose. More important, he formed the San Diego Symphonic Chorale, the predecessor of today's Master Chorale. The chorus provided some very good programs with the orchestra.

The orchestra's wind sections could always be counted on to produce some cracking sounds and faulty intonation during each concert. The principal oboe was a consistent problem for several seasons, even though different people subsequently sat in that seat year after year. Horns were also problematic. Despite all of these difficulties, some of the performances reached remarkably proficient levels. A recording available at San Diego State has several pieces on it from Murray's final concert here, including a fine performance of Ravel's very demanding Second Suite from *Daphnis et Chloe*. Despite the somewhat dim sonics, the quality of the performance can easily be determined.

As a student and protégé of Pierre Monteux, it was to be expected that Murray would shine in the French repertoire. In fact, his readings of the French classics were exemplary. Some of the other performances, however, reflected a lower level of interpretation. A good example is another recording available at State of the opening of the San Diego Civic Theatre in January, 1965. Before the intermission (and after the interminable welcoming, self-congratulatory speeches), Murray conducted the orchestra in Berlioz's Overture to *Benvenuto Cellini*. Again, despite the constricted sonics, the orchestra's fine performance could be well appreciated, as could the accompaniments to arias and duets sung by Dorothy Kirsten and Brian Sullivan. However, after the intermission Murray led the orchestra in Brahms' First Symphony. It may have been the fastest Brahms First on record. It is possible that it was necessary to speed the performance up because the hour was late — again, the fault of those earlier speeches. The Musicians' Union justifiably frowned on orchestras being on stage for hour after hour, and overtime fees were not available. Murray's mentor, Monteux, played the Brahms symphonies at relatively crisp tempi, but never like that performance.

When I interviewed Jim Plank, a long-time percussionist in the orchestra, he spoke about Murray as a conductor. Spontaneously, he, too, commented about Murray's facility with the French repertoire as differentiated from his less successful readings of the classic or romantic Central European composers. Plank related his own closeness to a small group of the leading figures in the orchestra during that era, including Fritz Baker (principal flute), Dan Magnusson (principal clarinet), Paul Anderson (principal cello) and Leo Hamilton (tympanist). "I was still really not much more than a student then, and I looked up to these people who were experienced and really seemed to know what to do. They also liked Murray's French music more than anything else he conducted…"

A number of Murray performances were memorable, even of the non-French variety. Perhaps the most notable was a concert reading of Bartok's great opera, *Bluebeard's Castle*. Beverly Wolff and Peter Harrower sang, both from the New York City Opera. The Berlioz Requiem was another outstanding performance, given in the Golden Hall with an augmented orchestra and extra brass on either side of the hall. Murray extended the concert year of the orchestra by experimenting with three so-called Promenade concerts in Golden Hall after the end of the 1965 summer Balboa Park season. Each of these programs was devoted to the music of a different country. Tables were set up on the floor of the hall and light refreshments were served by a hired caterer. Their popularity was limited, however, and the audiences they attracted did not pay enough, so no more of those programs were ever planned. Those were the days in which San Diego was only beginning to get used to the idea that symphony concerts could become part of a routine attendance experience, even if they were not restricted to the summer in Balboa Park Bowl.

The summer concerts continued to be successful and generally well attended throughout the Murray era. Murray had a light touch when it was appropriate, and he programmed Rodgers and Hammerstein, Lerner and Loewe, and ballet evenings. More substantial symphonic fare was also played with some outstanding soloists, including Gary Graffman, Claudio Arrau, Leon Fleisher and Mischa Elman. The lighter evenings played to crowds over four thousand, while the more symphonic programs averaged about twenty five hundred. Arthur Fiedler came in the summer of 1961 and drew over four thousand, but he was overshadowed that season by Andre Previn who drew over forty seven hundred when he guest conducted and played the piano. Previn did not return but Fiedler became a seasonal fixture.

Despite some of his successes and despite the generally improved quality of the orchestra's playing, it was becoming apparent that Murray was approaching the end of his San Diego tenure after the 1965 summer season and especially after the economic failure of the Promenade series. I sat on the board beginning the year before and moved to the executive committee during the 1964-65 season. I knew more about music and the symphonic literature than most of my committee colleagues but, shamefully, I was equally ignorant of the business aspects of building and running an orchestra. Even more, the concept of fund-raising was totally foreign to me, and I, too, depended on the manager to take those matters into his hands. It was obvious that some board members had shared a feeling for a couple of seasons that it was time to get a new conductor who could build on what Murray had created, and who could lead the orchestra into major status.

Major status turned out to be an over-used catch phrase. The American Symphony Orchestra League classified orchestras on the basis of their budgets. In those years, any orchestra with a budget of over a million dollars was considered major. When Murray first ascended the San Diego podium the annual budget for the orchestra was $150,000.00, an amount that increased to nearly $170,000.00 by the time of Murray's final season. The gossip was that a new face might lead the San Diego Symphony into that Major League Promised Land. The tenor of the Association's thinking was, as always, that it was up to the conductor to accomplish that task, or to the manager. It always seemed that it was never up to the board.

This was obviously unfair to Murray, who recognized that the process of building an orchestra took a long time. It took longer — if at all, in fact — if money was not forthcoming to attract better players, and there was none. The board of directors in those years collectively represented the classic San Diego syndrome, emphasizing that musicians would love to come here and live in this gorgeous place with this marvelous climate. I would argue; I knew at least that much about business! My response to that oft-spoken San Diego watchword was that they would indeed love to live here but would enjoy even more being able to afford to live here — and eat here as well. Of course, I had no idea how to obtain enough money to get them properly fed.

Murray, whose job depended upon the board's good will, was more passive and only shrugged his shoulders. A couple of board members (or their husbands) who owned large businesses would provide a few jobs for some of the players. The Ratner family was outstanding in that regard. In no way was playing in the San Diego Symphony Orchestra of those years a full-time job. Rehearsals were held at night in the Musicians' Union Hall, with only a dress rehearsal the evening before the concert in the hall in which the concert would be presented. The progress made by the San Diego Symphony Orchestra and the San Diego Symphony Association since the Schryock era could not be ignored. However, it was painfully obvious that many of the difficulties extending back into the Schryock years continued their resistant ways.

Murray told me shortly before his departure that he was proudest of having taken the San Diego Symphony Orchestra into the Civic Theatre as their new home. He was deeply involved in some of the planning for the new structure and was generally very pleased at the way it turned out, although he was also frustrated by some of its defects. He felt that the shell built for orchestral concerts was sonically unflattering to the orchestra, and he arranged to have some of the diamond patterns on the rear of the shell cut out so as to minimize the sound of the brasses that tended to overpower the strings. He did not believe that it was possible for the strings to sound out more due to the limited number of players as well as their limited quality. He was also disappointed that he was unable to place the orchestra near the extended lip of the stage made possible by raising the orchestra pit. The Fire Marshal refused to allow that because, as he said, the orchestra needed to be seated upstage of the asbestos curtain for safety reasons. This led to a weakening of the sound of the violins because the ceiling of the shell "leaked" sound into the stage loft. The ceiling had been constructed in such a manner that it was too high. It "floated" over the upright side and back walls of the shell. Murray had vainly hoped that a forward-seated orchestra would sound into the acoustical clouds that formed the ceiling of the hall and provide a better body of sound.

Frustration with the Civic Theatre, however, provided only the lesser portion of the frustrations Murray felt during the 1964-65 season. Marital problems began to develop at home, and occasionally bitter battles developed. These arose during the time that Murray obviously required more rather than less support from his wife, due to the rumors that his contract would not be renewed. The *coup de grace* occurred when a freak accident at home left Murray severely injured. He was seated in a lounge chair that had an adjustable slant and back. Murray's hand caught in the controls beneath the chair and the chair toppled over with him in it and also with a finger in it that was amputated traumatically by the metal control. He wound up in a hospital with a fractured femur as well as the traumatic amputation.

The eminent Mexican composer-conductor, Carlos Chavez, had guest-conducted the concert the week before Murray's accident. An emergency meeting of the executive committee was convened to determine what should be done. Bud Emile wanted to conduct in Murray's place. However, as I pointed out in the meeting, Rimsky-Korsakoff's *Sheherazade* was programmed for that concert, and no one other than Bud would be able to play the fantastically difficult violin solos in that work. Everyone agreed, including Bud (albeit grudgingly), and Carlos Chavez was called back from Mexico City to lead the orchestra again. My relationship with Bud Emile regretfully changed from that moment on to a far less open and friendly one.

Murray's recovery progressed without complication. He was determined to return to the podium to lead the orchestra in the remaining concerts of what he feared might be his last season. At the start of the next scheduled concert, he was wheeled out onto the stage and lifted in his wheelchair onto the podium, facing the orchestra. The audience stood and applauded, and so did the orchestra. Murray turned his chair around to face the audience and, after everyone sat down, he addressed them, "So, what's new with *you?*" The concert was a reasonable success but everyone knew that Murray's days were numbered. The collective guilt feelings of the board were relieved somewhat when the conductor began to stand again and lead the orchestra in the standard manner. They no longer felt, as one board member told me, as if they were thinking about kicking out a cripple.

The final concert of the season was a performance of the Beethoven Ninth Symphony with vocal soloists and the Symphonic Chorale. The previous concert had featured the world premiere of the piano concerto by a Los Angeles musician,

Morris Hutchens Ruger. Donna Clitsome, a San Diego favorite, was the soloist. The performance was reviewed on May 7, 1965, by Alan Kriegsman in the *San Diego Union*. The performance was praised, and Murray was especially praised for promoting a premiere. However, the work itself was felt to be warmed-over Rachmaninoff. That program also featured Debussy's *La Mer*. Kriegsman noted that in that performance the "Symphony scaled new heights" via a "unified, convincing interpretation…" Again, French music proved to be Murray's forte.

The Beethoven Ninth, acme of the symphonic literature, might have been programmed by Murray for the end of that season because of his dread that he would not be here for the following year. Were that situation to have been true, Murray would have gone out with a musically appropriate bang. In any event, he stayed for one more year. The review of the performance of the Ninth seemed to describe most adequately the over-all state of symphonic music-making in San Diego at that time. On April 21, 1965, Alan Kriegsman's *San Diego Union* review was headlined, "Symphony Hits Peak in Beethoven." Kriegsman wrote, "The limitations of the San Diego Symphony Orchestra took their inevitable toll, but in the face of the Orchestra's larger musical duty [i. e., presenting the Ninth to begin with] this can be easily dismissed…As for Murray, he has now led for us all the Beethoven Symphonies but one. These interpretations have been among his most impressive…"

Perhaps symbolically, Murray opened his final, 1965-66 season with the same work with which he had opened his initial concert here six years before, Handel's *Royal Fireworks Music*. The season continued without significant problems, and it ended on May 5 with a rather unbalanced program. Before the May 5 intermission, the San Diego Symphony Chorus joined the orchestra in a series of excerpts from Handel's oratorio, *Judas Maccabeus*. During the intermission, then-Symphony Association president Philip Klauber took the stage and, calling Murray out, lauded him as a fine conductor who did fine work for the orchestra and the community, praising him for his seven years of devotion and extending the hope that he would return soon as a guest conductor. The audience and the orchestra stood and applauded. After the intermission, Murray conducted the orchestra and chorus in Debussy's *Noctournes* and Ravel's Second Suite from *Daphnis et Chloe*.

Notably, on the preceding Sunday, the Arts section of the *San Diego Union* provided a small article about the forthcoming, final San Diego Symphony concert of the season with a headline, "Murray's Finale: A Choral Concert." The entire article was boxed into a small space in the middle of a page-wide article headlined, "Six Symphony Visitors: Will One Sign a Lease?" The larger article by Beverly Beyette described the next season of "auditions" for guest conductors, one of whom might become the next music director — a much more newsworthy subject.

Donald Dierks, the then-new music reviewer for the *San Diego Union*, reviewed Murray's finale in the issue of May 6, 1966. Dierks's approach was not as charitable as Kriegsman, his predecessor, who had decamped for a larger arena in Washington, D. C. Where Kriegsman always appeared to temper his more severe comments with at least faint praise, Dierks was much more objective and, as his career here over many years revealed, always called the shots as he heard them. The Handel oratorio performance was referred to as tepid. He was far more positive about the performances of the French music. "In this repertoire, the orchestra's playing was distinguished by the particular beauty of the string tone...The general orchestral effect was one of refinement, and rewarding to hear..."

As always, when it came to French music, Murray was his mentor's prize pupil, but season-long programming calls for much other music as well. It was not as if Murray led the other music ineffectively. It was simply that his love for French music was revealed far more in his performances. He must have demanded more from the orchestra then, possibly resulting in the relative impression that he may have been somewhat limited as a conductor of other music. At his final curtain call, he was greeted by a *tusch*. A *tusch* is a fanfare, a spontaneous custom among central European orchestras when the bands were particularly impressed with the stellar quality of the performer, conductor or performance. The orchestra and audience rose and provided a prolonged ovation. Unfortunately characteristic of Murray's career here, the *tusch* was not spontaneous. Murray left with an ovation that he, himself, had to arrange.

He deserved better. He never received it anywhere. Although he kept insisting that he was going to Britain to guest conduct, this never panned out, nor did many other conducting opportunities come later other than some performances with the San Francisco Ballet Orchestra, the Monterey Symphony and the Salt Lake City Ballet. For a time he was associate conductor of the Dallas Symphony Orchestra when his good friend, Anshel Brusilow, was their music director. Shortly before that orchestra stopped playing for a time due to their own financial debacles, they toured the southwest and played a concert here. Murray was with them, and at dinner after the afternoon concert he was his usual, chipper, charming self. Insofar as I am aware, he never returned to San Diego after that. Mainly, he stayed in San Francisco and did — what? Rumors occasionally flitted down to San Diego that visitors to the Bay Area had seen Murray driving a cab there.

In March, 2003, Philip Klauber sent me a copy of an obituary from the *San Francisco Chronicle* dated a year before, March 5, 2002. A San Francisco friend had meant to send it to him sooner but it had fallen into the cracks. The obituary noted that Murray had died at seventy-six in a hospital in San Francisco, of esophageal cancer. He had remarried. His widow was Joan Murray, Music Director for a San Francisco area youth orchestra. The obituary was rather extended and related some details about Murray's early life as a musician in San Francisco. In his later years, according to the newspaper, he was in semi-retirement.

As archivist, I wrote a column for the Symphony program booklet about the loss of our first, full-time music director. However, it was not printed then. Welton Jones, former Editor of the Arts Section of the *San Diego Union*, sent the column to the local newspaper, but probably as old news they, too, determined not to publish it. It appears sorrowfully characteristic of Earl Murray's contacts with San Diego that his death went unnoticed here until a year later, and that it was never noted in any local media. Eventually, after months, the article was printed in the *Archivist's Corner* column in the program booklet of the Symphony.

He deserved better.

CHAPTER IX

1966-67: The First Audition Season

A season of guest conductors was planned for the year after Earl Bernard Murray's "resignation" as conductor of the San Diego Symphony Orchestra. This was the first of several seasons of guest conductors in San Diego following the departures of relatively longstanding musical directors. The practice remains generally used throughout the orchestra world. A number of *maestri* would be invited to lead the needy orchestra, and a decision would be made to hire one by virtue of his (until recently, always his) ability to mobilize or galvanize the orchestra into playing better, his personality and capacity to mesh socially with the community, and his plans for programming and otherwise increasing the audience for the orchestra.

Sometimes a delegation of players might be asked for their opinions as well as those of the board. In 1966-67 no formal representation by the orchestra entered the selection process, although informally there were a lot of questions and answers. The executive committee of the board served as a committee of the whole, functioning as the *ad hoc* search/selection committee. The candidates were usually selected by studying the lists of available conductors sent to the orchestra by the conductors' managers. Sometimes a conductor with a permanent position in a leading orchestra might have a recommendation, usually of one of his students, or an assistant.

Guest conductor years are always interesting to the audience and are generally newsworthy. The contest of who will achieve the desired position always attracts increased interest in the orchestra. For the orchestra, itself, however, it can have mixed effects. The varying personalities and, above all, the varying technical capacities of the different conductors auditioning their wares can result in losses of ensemble as well as deterioration in the general quality of playing. On the other hand, the presence of an experienced conductor who really imposes a strong professional will on a previously demoralized group of musicians can be a very exciting situation. All of the conductors in the 1966-67 guest conductor parade were well-experienced and, with a single exception, motivated to come to San Diego as music director. They all had the professional capacity to impress the orchestra so that it played reasonably well for each of them. The level of playing did not diminish appreciably and, in fact, sometimes an increased quality of what was heard demonstrated a higher degree of stimulation among the musicians.

Very gradually, Earl Murray had been able to increase the size of the orchestra by increasing the number of string players. When he began his tenure the orchestra had twenty-five violinists, and eight each of violists and cellists. There were seven basses. In 1966-67 the string sections had increased to thirty-one violins, ten each of violas and celli, and nine basses. The wind players were generally unchanged; new principals cost more money than the Association was willing to spend. Triple woodwinds were consistent through Murray's years and after, but the horns were increased from a quartet to five, and the trumpets from three to four. The orchestra had enlarged to over ninety players. The sound was, of course, richer and the new conductors had more to play with. The guests were all pleased with the orchestra. They all had good words to say about it, or at least about its potential. In private, however, there were some criticisms of some of the string players (the same ones as before), and especially of some of the woodwind principals. However, everyone seemed pleased with the brass section despite occasional squalling by the horns and a regrettable nervous tendency of the trumpets to crack when they would begin to play.

The 1966 summer season was planned and conducted by John Green, who had previously been a summer guest in San Diego. He was popular with the audiences and had a capacity to program both popular and light classical music. He was respected by the orchestra, as he always was wherever he conducted. Musicians nearly everywhere always hoped that, as music director of MGM Studios, he might find some members suitable for studio work, with a very great increase in income. They always played well for him. He hired no one from San Diego to play at MGM.

The distinguished Mexican composer-conductor, Carlos Chavez, opened the 1966-67 winter season. He had conducted here twice during the 1964-65 season, the second time as a substitute for the injured Earl Murray. Chavez very badly wanted to be the music director here. He and I had become quite friendly over the several years during which he had guest-conducted here. Therefore, I had no hesitation in asking him frankly why he, of all the candidates, wanted this music directorship. After all, he was a world-famous and world-honored musician who had guest-conducted all of the best orchestras in the world. He had recently been recording in Europe and in Mexico, where he had founded the Orquesta Sinfónica de México, but due to the politics inherent in institutions such as these he no longer conducted it. I asked him fairly bluntly why he wanted to stick his hand into the financial and social hornet's nest represented by the San Diego Symphony when he could otherwise rest on his many laurels. Why in the world, I asked, does he want this struggling orchestra? His answer was a brief thesis about conductors. He replied, "Because I could help it in its struggle. I could make it better. I have done it before and can do it again. You have to understand, Mel, that all conductors want their own orchestra. As a psychiatrist, you understand about the ego. The orchestra is an extension of the ego of the conductor. Guest conducting, where a person can not make changes or teach very much, is a lifelong vacation but it doesn't take the place of having an orchestra of my own."

San Diego had the advantage of being near Mexico and his home. Everyone on the executive committee recognized his extraordinary capacities and respected his reputation. Several members also recognized his value as a person who might attract a wealthy Tijuana audience to San Diego Symphony concerts. Some others, in contrast, were adamant in their refusal to consider a Mexican as permanent conductor. They also minimized any genuine Tijuana contributions that could be counted on. The polite rationale for refusing Chavez the post was that he was too old.

Zoltan Rozsnyai was the second guest that season. He was hired to direct two concerts, one early in the season and the next much later. The second concert would be the great Verdi Requiem with chorus and vocal soloists, as well as added brass. He was the conductor of the Utica Symphony in New York, a small orchestra that he had built for several years into a group he was able to take to Carnegie Hall for a benefit concert.

Rozsnyai had fled his native Hungary when the Russians invaded in 1956. He had an aura of being a cold war warrior who had carried his small daughter on his shoulders as they walked to the border to escape the Communists. In 1966, this was quite a plus in arch-conservative San Diego. Rozsnyai and his family made it to Germany where he founded the refugee orchestra, the Philharmonia Hungarica, with which he toured western Europe and the United States to some acclaim. He left Germany to come to the United States at the invitation of Antal Dorati of the Minneapolis Symphony Orchestra (now the Minnesota Orchestra). Following his well-reviewed guest conducting there and in Calgary, Canada, he became Leonard Bernstein's assistant in 1961, with the New York Philharmonic, before taking up the baton with his own orchestra in Utica, as well as assuming the post of conductor of the Cleveland Philharmonic, that city's second orchestra. In addition, he composed several scores for motion pictures.

Rozsnyai had also become the "house conductor" for Columbia Records. He conducted the so-called Columbia Symphony Orchestra in accompaniments to the great organist, E. Power Biggs, for various organ concerti by Handel, Haydn and Mozart. Interestingly, he also conducted the eponymous Columbia orchestra in the first recording ever made of Carl Ruggles' *Of Men and Mountains*.

Coincidentally, that was the work led by Earl Murray when he was finally able to conduct the San Francisco Symphony to such great acclaim in a subscription concert following the completion of his first season here.

Rozsnyai's first concert was a reasonable success, especially in his conducting the accompaniment to Malcolm Frager's playing of Bartok's Third Piano Concerto. Bartok had been one of Rozsnyai's teachers at the Franz Liszt Conservatory in Budapest, and Rozsnyai revered him. Later in the season Rozsnyai scored a major triumph with the performance of the Verdi Requiem. Some board members at rehearsals noted how he worked the celli over and over before he was satisfied with their unanimity and collective intonation in their famously difficult entry for the *Offertorium* section. He placed his extra brass in the loges on both sides of the Civic Theatre, creating a dramatic effect. It was felt that he had sufficient imagination and energy to stimulate the orchestra and the audience.

Louis Lane, George Szell's associate conductor with the Cleveland Orchestra, conducted two programs. No one questioned his remarkable talent, and he made the orchestra play rather well. The ensemble was remarkably tight under his baton. However, many of the people who got to know him during his several weeks here, including a number of orchestra members, questioned his personality. They found him relatively unlikeable. He seemed to be too glib at times, according to one board member, and many of the musicians found him patronizing. A great deal of this negative criticism obviously covered over the feelings of homophobia that were apparent among the critics. San Diego was not yet ready for a gay conductor in 1966.

Izler Solomon, music director of the Indianapolis Symphony Orchestra, conducted two programs. Seemingly, he became everyone's favorite candidate. The orchestra loved him and he achieved excellent results with them. However, by the time he appeared here he turned out to be not a candidate at all. He did not want to leave Indianapolis, which he had built for the previous dozen years into one of the best orchestras in the country. He had followed a former San Diego summer music director, Fabien Sevitzky, to that orchestra. Solomon had become very dejected, however, over the labor difficulties there that had closed down the orchestra for a time, and he sought guest conducting appointments. By the time he conducted in San Diego the problems in Indianapolis were being worked out, and he made no secret of his wish to return to his own podium. Had he not, the board would have snapped him up in a minute.

Akeo Watanabe was the conductor of the Japan Philharmonic Orchestra. He had conducted that orchestra on tour in San Diego two years before and had made a very favorable impression. He had since become increasingly active in the United States, especially during the Aspen Festival. His recordings of contemporary music as well as all the Sibelius symphonies had been praised. In San Diego, his concert was taped for rebroadcast by the Voice of America. It contained a short, contemporary Japanese piece but the rest of the program was very listener-friendly: the Bruch Violin Concerto with Joseph Fuchs, and the Brahms First Symphony. All were well played. The orchestra responded well and so did the audience, but the board was simply not ready to consider a Japanese conductor twenty years after the end of the war.

The last guest of the 1966-67 season was Igor Buketoff, a very experienced conductor who had actually made more of a reputation as a music educator and as a promoter of contemporary music by his organization of the World Music Bank than he had as a conductor. However, he was at the time the music director of the Fort Wayne, Indiana Symphony Orchestra, and had enjoyed a long career as the conductor of the children's concerts of the New York Philharmonic. Jovial, with a quick wit, and very personable, he made an excellent impression on the audience and the board, especially with his conducting of the Rachmaninoff Second Symphony.

Several other conductors were added to the list of those nominated as potential candidates, even though they had not been invited to guest conduct in the 1966-67 season. Andre Previn had been quite successful in his guest appearance several summers before. He and I had corresponded informally about the possibility of his getting interested in a position here. He responded enthusiastically that he would certainly enjoy being music director of the San Diego Symphony Orchestra. This was at the time of his cutting back at MGM, where he had scored a number of movies and had conducted their orchestra, winning an Academy Award for his efforts. It was, however, prior to his developing a reputation as a symphonic conductor with eventual welcome, successful, repeated guest appearances and recordings with world-famous orchestras in this country and in Europe. The general impression of the board about him in 1966 was that he was, "too Hollywood," and not a serious enough musician.

Another name I very tentatively put forth was that of a musician who definitely was serious, Leopold Stokowski. He had left the music directorship of the Houston Symphony and was guest conducting regularly in New York and Chicago. However, he had recently been divorced by Gloria Vanderbilt, who had moved to Los Angeles with their two sons. Stokowski very much wanted a west coast post so that he could be near his adolescent sons, but Mehta's Los Angeles Philharmonic was unavailable. The idea of Stokowski was justifiably too big for the San Diego board, but the rationale for their refusal to consider him was, like Chavez, he was too old. No other names were put forth by anyone on the board or by the manager.

Franz Waxman was initially interested in assuming the San Diego podium. He contacted the board on his own and came down from Los Angeles for a luncheon meeting with the executive committee. He was a famous, Oscar-winning composer of film music, but he also had organized and led the Los Angeles Music Festivals for a number of years. Soon after his interview here, he decided that he was not as interested as he thought. He withdrew his name because he had been able to find funds to continue the Los Angeles Festival.

Another conductor who presented himself at a meeting of the executive committee was Stefan Bauer-Mengelberg. Personable and articulate, he had less conducting experience than the conductors who were to guest conduct that year. However, he was something of a polymath, with an extensive background in and an enormous reservoir of knowledge about many subjects, including highly arcane mathematics and philosophy. His musical background was also impressive, as was his name. He was a nephew of the great Dutch conductor, Willem Mengelberg, whose reputation had been badly tarred by his collaboration with the Germans after Holland was invaded. Guilt by association reared its ugly head among several of the board members, as well as doubts about his ability to serve as a music director of any orchestra because of his limited conducting experience. However, Simon Reznikoff, later to be an Association president, kept repeating his impression that the man was some kind of genius, and that it might be worthwhile to have a genius in residence. In any event, he was not invited to conduct here.

Buketoff became a serious candidate among the board members, along with Zoltan Rozsnyai. However, the cold war heroics of Zoltan Rozsnyai seemed to tip the scales. Also, a number of positive musical impressions about him were gained by the board, over and above the remarkable performance of the Verdi Requiem. In that vast project he had worked successfully in close cooperation with Bud Emile, the orchestra's concertmaster, who was also the director of the Symphonic Chorale. Kenneth Owens, successor to Dr. Alex Zimmerman as Director of Music Education in the San Diego City Schools (and a violist in the orchestra and a board member), raved about Rozsnyai's ability to sit down at the piano and play any of the symphonic pieces he and Owens had been talking about at the time. Rozsnyai was able to promote an atmosphere of excitement and enthusiasm, and this stimulated the board. The contract was signed, the announcement was made, and, at forty-one, Zoltan Rozsnyai began to plan his first regular season here.

CHAPTER X

The First Hungarian, Zoltan Rozsnyai

I t took almost no time for Zoltan Rozsnyai to make himself at home in San Diego. Rozsnyai's family had remained in Germany, where he had organized and led the Philharmonia Hungarica. Although they visited him when he worked in New York City, Cleveland and Utica, they had never established residency in the United States. However, when he began his tenure in San Diego, he was joined here by his wife and pre-adolescent daughter, as well as by his wife's mother. The family lived in a tract house in Pacific Beach and added a large German shepherd to their ranks. They all adored San Diego, especially the outdoor activities that were so much a part of San Diego life. Rozsnyai had been a yachtsman in Hungary and had even served on that country's Olympic sailing team. Friends with sailboats were treasures to him as well as to the rest of the family.

Flying had also been one of his Hungarian activities, and a rumor soon spread that he had been a flying cadet for the Luftwaffe during World War II. He denied that, but Rozsnyai and his family remained generally silent about their activities during the war, although they were never shy about speaking about the terrors of the Communists and the Russians who finally invaded Hungary. On the other hand, he would protest that he did not want to be perceived as a freedom fighter who carried his daughter on his back to freedom. Instead, he insisted, he was only a musician.

Indeed, he was a fine musician when he wanted to apply himself to music. His background was impeccable, with studies at and diplomas from the Franz Liszt Conservatory in Budapest, and with such teachers as Leo Weiner, Kodaly and Erno von Dohnanyi. He conducted a great deal in Hungary, usually in smaller cities, but he had also conducted a great deal in Budapest, in symphony and in opera. Although obviously a conductor of considerable training and background, Rozsnyai's performances in San Diego, and the audiences' experiences as well, were at the mercy of his widely varying degrees of application to his music. Easily distractible, and with a too frequent tendency to sacrifice musical preparation for activities that he saw as fun for himself, his record as conductor here was, at best, spotty. When he was good he was often much more than adequate, but

Zoltan Rozsnayai. *Photo courtesy San Diego Symphony.*

when he was not — again, often based upon a drop in interest or concentration — sloppiness was often the result. As time went on during his San Diego career, the bad clearly outweighed the good.

Rozsnyai's first concert as music director demonstrated an attempt to impress that was clearly, considerably beyond the reach of the orchestra. The opening number was Brahms' *Academic Festival Overture*. Near the beginning, the trumpets enter, playing a little mock chorale based on a student tune. The anxiety of the occasion reared its ugly head. They cracked on the first note, and the rest of the performance was shaky throughout the orchestra. Rozsnyai followed that piece with one of the most difficult in the contemporary repertoire, Bartok's *Concerto for Orchestra*, and after the intermission the orchestra played Beethoven's "Eroica" Symphony. The concert was too long and far too difficult for the 1967 orchestra, and some listeners as well as many musicians began to wonder about the new conductor's judgment.

His knowledge of the standard symphonic repertoire was more than adequate, but there were many aspects of American, Spanish and English music that he knew little of. Once, I suggested that he program Vaughan-Williams' very popular *English Folk Song Suite* for a Christmas concert. I had to play a recording of it for him so that he could consider it. The performance could be described only as dreary, with an almost total absence of the crispness necessary for success in that music. One program was scheduled for recording by the Voice of America for beaming to Spain. I suggested some music by Turina, but he knew nothing of that composer, including his existence. When Sir Edward Elgar's elderly daughter visited in San Diego and was scheduled to attend a concert that featured the Mahler Second Symphony, Rozsnyai was unfamiliar with the fact that Elgar had written five *Pomp and Circumstance* Marches, not just one, and that he could program a less hackneyed one quickly for the occasion.

Gratefully, he was a quick study and could assume adequate control over a new work. When it was necessary for him to be very professional, he could rise to that occasion, and often did so. In that same Voice of America program, the world premiere was to be given of Morton Gould's Concerto for Four Guitars. The concert celebrated San Diego's two hundredth anniversary. It featured the original Romeros' Guitar Quartet, not the later generation. As the composer confided to me, he was unaware that the father of the group, although a consummate natural musician and a superb guitarist, could not read music and played instead by ear. The concerto was made even more complex by Gould's directions that the guitarists were to stroll on and off the stage as they played. During the dress rehearsal the father continually missed cues, musically and choreographically. Gould was becoming frantic because he was going to conduct a performance of the concerto with the Romeros the following week at the Hollywood Bowl. "I'm terrified the old guy'll fall into the reflecting pool," he whispered. But Rozsnyai took over, coached the father and the other three as well, maintained his equanimity, rehearsed them again and, according to Gould, provided one of the best demonstrations of true professionalism that he had ever seen.

The orchestra had violently mixed feelings about Rozsnyai from the outset. His appearances during the audition season, before he was hired as conductor here, were praised by most of the orchestra members. Most of them approved of his selection, and they continued to like him for a time during his initial season as Musical Director. Millicent Froelich, who had begun to play in the San Diego Symphony under Rozsnyai, described him as, "Jolly in rehearsals, but very inefficient." Many of the musicians enjoyed him as a person at first, but had little respect for his conducting abilities. This feeling developed early in his tenure when he tried to teach the orchestra that Mozart and Haydn symphonies were to be played via a formula taught in Vienna that created strict mathematical relationships between their movements. Usually, dull, plodding Mozart was the result. Little Haydn was played. Some Mozart, however, turned out to be marvelous — especially when Lili Kraus came to play with the orchestra. She was, of course, famous for her Mozart playing which was anything but dainty. It was strong and, above all, propulsive, causing Rozsnyai to keep up well and maintain uncharacteristically brisk tempi. At her first appearance here, she played two concerti. She was so popular with both audience and orchestra that she was invited back for another all-Mozart program the next year.

In one particular way, the experience with Lili Kraus was characteristic. Rozsnyai was an excellent accompanist/collaborator, especially when the soloists were of a caliber as high as Lili Kraus. Some of his best performances were his accompaniments to such artists as Claudio Arrau, Michael Rabin, Peter Frankl and Mischa Dichter. Although it certainly could not be considered an accompaniment, Rozsnyai's conducting of a January, 1969, concert presentation of Gluck's *Orpheus and Eurydice*, to some ears may have been his finest work here. Donald Dierks, the music critic for the *San Diego Union*, wrote in his review that he was so taken by the music and the performance that he was going to return for the repeat performance!

The board passed a $323,000 budget for the 1967-68 season, a considerable jump from the last Murray season. COMBO, short for a planned community-wide, combined arts giving program, had been instituted a couple of years before. A large number of San Diego arts organizations were covered under that blanket, but the Symphony was always among the larger beneficiaries. Originally, the funds were to be used only for capital expenditures. The Symphony's portable shell was purchased with COMBO funds and is still in use today, especially for the summer concerts. After a couple of years, however, the funds began to be used by all beneficiaries for operating expenses and prevented independent attempts to find their own funds. This led to some skepticism on the part of some board members because of the necessity to share the city-wide collected pot with others. Necessarily, they correctly believed, they could expect little, if any success from the Symphony's own fund-raising efforts. "I gave at COMBO," was heard all too frequently, and contributed funds (including COMBO) provided less and less of the orchestra's needs. COMBO lasted until about the mid-1980s, with less and less enthusiastic participation by the arts organizations and the general public.

In another move that would have affected the organization's finances, the manager, William Denton, formed an umbrella organization that merged the business and promotional operations of the Symphony and San Diego Opera, which had just begun to mount its own seasons a few years before. The artistic leadership of each organization would remain separate. That was a short-lived arrangement, however, due to Denton's leaving.

At Rozsnyai's urging, the subscription concerts were paired beginning in his first season. The audiences, however, rarely if ever filled the hall for both nights, much less for either night. Generally, they numbered less than twenty-five hundred. The image of the orchestra remained no better than second-class compared to the regularly visiting Los Angeles Philharmonic. Many attempts were made to increase the audience numbers but they generally stayed the same. The 1960s were years during which grants from foundations and from the federal government remained readily available. The resistance of some influential board members remained staunchly against federal grants, just as they had during Earl Murray's regime. During one executive committee meeting, I proposed that we apply for a grant from one of the local foundations that would underwrite attendance by disadvantaged minorities from Southeast San Diego. A hue and cry went up from several members, "You want *them* here?" I replied that I would settle for any bodies to fill the empty seats, especially since the financial situation of the orchestra was so precarious. The matter was promptly dropped.

Rozsnyai not only enlarged the season by pairing the subscription concerts, he also enlarged the orchestra. He began auditioning local players before beginning his initial season, and he also invited several players from distant places to join the orchestra. Notable among these were the Feld Quartet, from Ball State University in Muncie, Indiana. Otto Feld became assistant concertmaster, and his wife became one of the first violinists. Rebecca and Glenn Campbell joined the viola and cello sections, respectively. Like Rozsnyai, Otto Feld had been trained in Budapest, and he was aware of Rozsnyai (who was four years older) as, "... a brilliant pianist, whose playing was well-known all over the Liszt Conservatory." Also like Rozsnyai, Feld fled Hungary when the Russians came in 1956. He was able to make it to Vienna. His background as a violinist in the Budapest Philharmonic led him to the Vienna Philharmonic, where he played for several years. When Rozsnyai began organizing the Philharmonia Hungarica, he contacted Feld in Vienna and asked him to join. Feld played in that orchestra for over two years. That was his first experience with Rozsnyai as a conductor, and he shook his head sadly as he commented, "He was like that then, too. His was a marvelous talent but he had no personal organization — then, too." He also noted that Rozsnyai was, even then, a womanizer. "He never grew up."

Every musician I interviewed for this history referred to Rozsnyai in the same general terms. Paul Anderson, the long-time first cellist in the orchestra, seemed to summarize everyone's impression when he described Rozsnyai: "He was an enormously gifted man who was quite lazy."

Other stalwarts-to-be brought into the orchestra during Rozsnyai's tenure included violinists Eileen Wingard and Millicent Froehlich, as well as harpist Sheila Sterling Kornbluth. For the 1969-70 season the orchestra had as its first cellist Milos Sadlo, a recent emigrant to the United States from Prague where for many years he had been the principal cellist of the great Czech Philharmonic Orchestra. Sadlo was due to begin his contract with Indiana University so he was unable to stay for more than a single season, but he worked hard and well with the celli. A stereotape recording is available in the SDSU Historical Archives of his fine performance of the Dvorak Cello Concerto, with the orchestra under Rozsnyai.

All of these and a number of other musicians enriched the orchestra a great deal, but many people believed that the new musician who made the most difference in the playing of the orchestra was Donald Hyder, who became principal oboe. A student of Ray Still, the great principal oboe of the Chicago Symphony, Hyder's work affected all the wind players to a considerable degree. Intonation problems among the winds had always been a problem. Hyder's arrival made an immediate impression on the wind players, and their tuning became much more precise. Hyder's work might best be appreciated by listening to the recording of the orchestra's performance of Rossini's Overture, *la Gazza Ladra*, also available at San Diego State. Donald Dierks wrote in his *San Diego Union* review of that concert of January 25, 1968, that he found the ensemble "astonishing" in the overture, and said that the concert was "...the best in two seasons." The major work on that program was the Mahler Fourth Symphony, also available on recording at SDSU.

Rozsnyai had instituted the practice of recording all the subscription concerts, and I helped with that project. Some of those reel-to-reel stereotapes, including those mentioned above, may be found in the San Diego State Special Collections and University Archives. They may provide a good idea of the quality of the orchestra's playing during Rozsnyai's best performances, although the lesser quality playing can also be heard on some. Rozsnyai had special sympathies for Mahler's music, and the performance of the Fourth Symphony, cited above, as well as the performance of Mahler's Second, "Resurrection" Symphony, demonstrated them. Janet Baker was another favorite soloist. She sang the role of Orpheus in the performance of the Gluck opera, noted above, with Carol Neblett as Eurydice and Mary Costa as Amor. That recording, too, is available at San Diego State. Baker returned several times during Rozsnyai's tenure, each time to sing Mahler or Berlioz songs with the orchestra. Unfortunately, no tapes have survived of those performances.

Richard Strauss was another composer for which Rozsnyai demonstrated an affinity. He conducted the tone poem, *Also Sprach Zarathustra* in its first performance here, as well as the Suite from *Der Rosenkavalier*. Interestingly, he programmed relatively little Hungarian music. Rozsnyai expressed the fear that his audience might get tired of it (and him) if he played too much music by Hungarian composers. But Kodaly's *Galanta Dances* and Suite from *Hary Janos* were very well received. The review by Donald Dierks in the March 29, 1968 *San Diego Union* noted that the playing achieved, "...a level of performance not previously heard." Erno Daniel, who had been one of Rozsnyai's piano teachers in Budapest, had come to play Liszt with the orchestra on that same occasion, and the performances were excellent. Daniel had guest conducted the orchestra a number of years before and he was struck by the remarkable change he heard in its performances. Recordings of all of these can be found at San Diego State.

The artistic progress of the orchestra, however, remained a see-saw, as elaborated by Donald Dierks in his article in the April 21, 1968, issue of the *San*

Diego Union headlined, "Symphony Season, Good, Bad." According to Dierks, the most important advance made during Rozsnyai's first season was his insistence on playing subscription concerts in pairs instead of singly, "...equal in persuasion to having obtained a larger unsecured loan from a conservative, flinty-eyed banker..." Dierks' criticisms included programming errors, such as trying to play music that was, at the time, beyond the orchestra's capabilities. When the music programmed was within, "reasonable technical limits, the orchestra played quite well." Such problem pieces as Stravinsky's *Petrouchka*, the Bartok *Concerto for Orchestra*, Respighi's *Feste Romane*, and the Brahms Third Symphony were singled out in the article.

The major responsibility for this was, of course, Rozsnyai's. Other, more external situations were to blame for the see-saw as well, such as the chronic financial problems and the resultant concerns among all the musicians that their payroll would not be met — as it had not on several occasions. Morale was generally low throughout the ranks. Increased dissatisfaction with their conductor on the part of the musicians was simply another major part of that problem. As one told me, "You just couldn't trust him. He'd get lost at times in performances. He'd flail around and we'd have to continue playing as together as we could."

Aside from that aspect, the increased number of concerts and the contracts with the new musicians added considerably to the Association's financial burdens that compounded the dread felt by most of the orchestra that it was likely that they would not get paid. The frequent pleas to "Save the Symphony" became increasingly tiresome to the community.

Nonetheless, at times everyone came through and occasional performances were excellent. Rozsnyai's first summer season was rated a success, with attendance averaging a third higher than the average attendance at Civic Theatre

Zoltan Rozsnayai and the San Diego Symphony in the San Diego Civic Theatre.
Photo courtesy San Diego Historical Society.

concerts. The first and last summer concerts that year were sellouts. The tradition of concert going in the summer was still stronger than adapting to a winter subscription schedule. The summer concerts had been moved that year to the amphitheatre at San Diego State University, where landing airplanes were not a distraction or out-and-out disturbance, as they had become at the Balboa Park Bowl. The amphitheatre had been re-named the University's Open-Air Theatre, and had been considerably refurbished with the aid of a considerable financial contribution by Mr. And Mrs. Arthur Johnson. The devoted Arthur Johnson served on the executive committee and later became Association president during extremely critical times. The refurbishing of the amphitheatre consisted mainly of new seats and a new lighting system. Rozsnyai commented to Carol Olten for her July 7, 1968, *San Diego Union* article, "The stage is bigger than the Civic Theatre's and it's all covered in wood."

Bill Denton had resigned as manager in April, 1968. Three months later the board approved the hiring of Alan McCracken, formerly the manager of the Columbus, Ohio Symphony. McCracken came into a chaotic financial situation. The orchestra's musicians' union contract with the Symphony Association expired on November 4, 1968. The players demanded twenty dollars per service instead of the $15.50 they had been receiving as their base scale rate per service. The 1968-69 season opened in the face of that crisis.

The opening concert near the end of October featured a fine performance of the Beethoven G-Major Piano Concerto, with Peter Frankl as soloist. Donald Dierks' review noted an improved ensemble and better acoustics. Rozsnyai had arranged for remodeling of the Civic Theatre shell during the summer break. The portions cut out earlier under Murray's direction were restored and, perhaps even more important, the ceiling was cut down so that it fit into the shell instead of floating above it. This allowed far more sound to be projected into the hall.

The musicians refused to sign any extension of their contract and refused to play under the terms of the expired contract. Arthur Johnson, who had become president of the Association the previous spring, canceled the concerts remaining after the well-received first pair. Donald Dierks, in his November 17, 1968, *San Diego Union* article headlined, "Canceling Symphony Season Deals City Incalculable Loss," provided a concise summary of the financial imbroglio. According to Dierks, "Considering the serious consequences of a city without an orchestra and the blow to the civic image, $49,150 seems a small amount, indeed." The $49,150 figure represented the total expenditure increase for the season (based solely upon the base scale rate, which actually would have been exceeded by a significant number of the musicians) to the Symphony Association under the terms asked by the orchestra. In those days, however, getting an extra $50,000 seemed like a Herculean task, especially when the larger community showed relatively little interest.

Millicent Froehlich, a violinist who later played a significant role in developing an agreed-upon contract for the orchestra, noted that the morale of most of the musicians was at rock bottom. They were sick of Rozsnyai, his instability and his undependability. That reached a low point when he failed to show up for a rehearsal. He was in Los Angeles at the time with a lady friend. Another violinist, Eileen Wingard, was more charitable as she charged that lapse to a mistake in his schedule caused by all of the missteps then characteristic of management. As another example of those missteps, Millicent Froehlich related that the musicians were handed their next individual contract offers from the administration in envelopes addressed incorrectly, so that everyone then knew what everyone else had been offered! If there had been dissension within the orchestra's ranks before, it can only be imagined now how it exploded after that!

Eventually the musicians made another offer, a temporary compromise, accepted by the Symphony Association, and the concert series was resumed on December 5 and 6, 1968, with the Modern Jazz Quartet as featured soloists. Millicent Froehlich noted that the problem was that the board and the musicians' union always had an adversarial relationship, but that, "...the musicians would have always been agreeable to lots of things if only they felt appreciated. They never felt that."

Alan McCracken resigned as manager during the financial crisis, claiming personal reasons. By February 15, 1969, Johnson was predicting a deficit of over a hundred-thousand dollars by the end of the fiscal year. William Phillips was named the new manager a week later. Pleas were made to City and County administrations, and extensive fund drives were begun. They achieved some success because by the end of that fiscal year the deficit was only $6,800. Some high spots were notable during that difficult season, including the Voice of America-recorded concert featuring the Gould Concerto for Four Guitars, described earlier.

Lili Krauss returned in the spring of 1970 and played two more Mozart piano concerti to considerable acclaim. Misha Dichter and the orchestra played the Brahms First Piano Concerto in February, 1970, and Michael Rabin played the Brahms Violin Concerto during that same month. These were exceptionally good performances. Recordings of these and other music of that troubled season are preserved at SDSU.

Before the beginning of the 1969-70 season, Welton Jones wrote in the September 21, 1969 *San Diego Union* that the Symphony Association had prepared a budget of over $388,000, and also projected an income of $341,000. He noted the Symphony Association's pleas to music lovers to come forth with needed funds. An editorial in the *San Diego Union* decried the Symphony's poor public support and inadequate attendance. In contrast, an article by Lew Scarr in the *San Diego Union* of November 2, 1969, profiled several of the orchestra's players, and commented that most observers were saying that the San Diego Symphony orchestra was better than ever. The players profiled were Sheila Sterling Kornbluth (harp), Anthony and Peter Swanson (violin and clarinet), Donald Hyder (oboe), and "Papa" Frank Sokol (bass). The first three remained in the orchestra for many years. Unfortunately, Donald Hyder left during that season due to a series of domestic difficulties. His was a grievous loss.

Arthur Johnson announced that unless twenty or twenty-five thousand dollars in new ticket sales and new donations were found, "We won't get all the way through the winter season." The financial crisis continued unabated. The City Council was asked for an emergency grant of $50,000. At that point, the Association was $105,000 in the red. One change, characteristically too little and too late, was the revision of the by-laws of the Women's Committee. Now membership meant that each woman was to purchase a season ticket, "or else ten dollars in scrip redeemable for tickets." During the 1968-69 season, 285 out of 1,800 members had season tickets.

The new president, Robert Sullivan, was away during the first part of the 1969-70 season. The executive committee (including me) floundered and also argued a great deal among themselves. I can attest that the stress level in the Executive Committee was dreadful. The decision was made that the orchestra would cease operating after the December 13 children's concert. In response, the orchestra voted to give its own Christmas concert under Emile's direction on December 11 and 12, featuring Zina Schiff as violin soloist. In response to the orchestra's move the board announced, "The San Diego Symphony will continue. It has only stopped for breath," according the *San Diego Union* of December 9, 1969. The board also stated its decision to plan a 1970-71 season. A week later, the board turned down an "impossible" proposal by the musicians. Finally, the impasse was bridged when the musicians allowed the Association to hire them on a concert-to-concert basis, without a master contract. The winter season resumed with a pair of concerts on January 22 and 23, 1970. In the pair of concerts on April 9 and 10, 1970, the orchestra played Haydn's "Farewell" Symphony, and, as Haydn had directed, each member whose part was over closed his or her score and tiptoed off the stage. Although it had been programmed far earlier for performance then, it certainly made for an effective editorial comment on the times.

Arthur Johnson remained close to Rozsnyai during all of these difficulties, even after his presidency terminated. He truly loved the orchestra and gave a great deal of his time and emotions to it, as well as money. He even underwrote a special commercial recording to be made in late 1970 by the orchestra under Rozsnyai. Professional recording engineers set this up in the top floor of the California-Western Law School Building where chamber concerts had frequently been given. The acoustics were wonderful there. The orchestra recorded Wagner's Prelude to *Die Meistersinger*, Beethoven's *Coriolan* Overture, and the Schubert "Unfinished" Symphony. The whole was published as an LP disc (STPL 517.100) by Vox Records, again with Johnson's underwriting. The stereo sound is exemplary and the performances are quite polished. Rozsnyai was stimulated during the project and the orchestra sounded first-rate. A compact disc copy of that record is available at SDSU.

Rozsnyai was given a one-year renewal of his contract at a salary of $22,500. In April, 1970, the Association announced that they were going to plan for a 1970-71 season of ten pairs of subscription concerts, with four children's concerts. The orchestra would have eighty-five members and the minimum scale would be $21.50 per service. On April 23, 1970, Donald Dierk's *San Diego Union* column was aptly titled, "Where Does the Symphony Go From Here?" He wrote about the frequent changes in managers that had so adversely affected the orchestra's administration. Now, Philip Whitacre, a San Diegan who had been assistant manager of the Syracuse Symphony, had been appointed. On the other hand, attendance during the makeshift 1969-70 season represented an all-time high. But soon afterwards the concerts of May 21 and 22 were cancelled. There was simply no money to fund them. The deficit was forty-five thousand dollars.

The tension in the executive committee became intolerable. Arguments became louder and feelings rode high. I left, resigning my position as vice-president because I simply was unable to stand the constant fighting over plans or lack of them. Too much sleep was lost, and too many bellyaches were developing. The drain was too much, and I feared that my contacts with my patients would suffer. It was hard to leave then because my good friend Simon Reznikoff was to become president. He needed to be able to count on as many people as he could. To this day I feel considerable guilt and shame about leaving but there was really little else I could do. Certainly, there was little enough constructive that I could do for the orchestra.

The situation that had continued to deteriorate over the prior two years had worsened for another reason. As if there had not been enough trouble, Rozsnyai had been injured. During the longer than usual layoffs, he had developed a deepening relationship with an American Airlines stewardess whom he had met on a trip to New York. His marriage had been suffering due to a number of factors including the stresses of his job here, and he began to meet the young woman increasingly frequently. One afternoon, while waiting to meet her in a strip shopping center in Laguna Beach, a car careered out of control in the parking lot, ran over the sidewalk curb and struck Rozsnyai in the hip and thigh, pinning him against the brick wall of the store behind him. He was taken to the hospital in Laguna Beach where his leg was operated upon, and he stayed there for several weeks. He was bound and determined, however, to conduct his next scheduled concert, so a repeat of the Earl Murray orthopedic performance was made by another conductor in a cast. Rozsnyai came out on crutches, ascended the podium, handed his crutches to the concertmaster and sat in a rehearsal chair to conduct. The gossip about the scandalous relationship was not helpful to him, however, and certainly not to the Symphony.

The 1970-71 season limped on, just like its conductor. In March, 1971, it was announced that the matching funds for the Ford Foundation grant were short by a hundred thousand dollars. The grant needed to be matched by the end of that June. Meanwhile, Bill Phillips had been fired and a new manager, John Willett, from San Diego's Starlight Opera, had been hired. Rozsnyai stood up for Phillips, saying to the board and the press that the problems were not of Phillips' making but rather the board's. One must wonder about the sense of rage he must have been feeling, combined with disappointment and frustration. The same feelings were being felt by the board, though, directed at Rozsnyai, and this eruption did nothing to smooth things over.

In my interview with her, Eileen Wingard expressed some sympathy toward Rozsnyai, indicating her opinion that he always was trying to do too much, running the office in the absence or even presence of the managers, running the USIU Music schedule and conducting its orchestra, and composing for films and TV, as well as conducting the San Diego Symphony. In March, 1971, Rozsnyai resigned, but then announced his supposed agreement to stay on until June, 1972. Willett resigned later in March, 1971. The situation became increasingly complex and conflicted when Simon Reznikoff, the Association president, announced that Rozsnyai would not be staying after the end of the current, 1970-71 season. Fifty-three members of the orchestra had signed a petition threatening to resign if Rozsnyai stayed.

Lee Adams was hired as acting manager, and Rozsnyai gave his final performances here on April 29 and 30, 1971. The Beethoven Ninth Symphony was played, surprisingly fairly well considering all the circumstances. Adams resigned on May 10, and two weeks later Thomas Halverstadt became Association president. Somehow, funds were found to make up the shortfall affecting the Ford Foundation. The first good news announced by the Symphony in a very long time was that the grant had been matched in the nick of time, and the money was theirs. A conductor selection committee was formed, headed by King Durkee, Director of Education for the Copley Newspapers and an Executive Committee member.

In the spring of 2003 when I interviewed him for this history, King Durkee expressed his opinion that Rozsnyai was, "…axed after the dropped season, cruelly." Because Rozsnyai was fired late in the year, Durkee called Zubin Mehta in Los Angeles and met him for an emergency luncheon consultation. Mehta suggested several names but none were available. "We had no money at all." Durkee then called the head of Columbia Artists, who was very helpful in finding guest conductors. He also called Arthur Fiedler, who agreed to conduct one concert but then had to cancel. Rafael Druian, the retired concertmaster of George Szell's Cleveland Orchestra, then living in La Jolla, suggested Andre Kostelanetz, who came to help but not to be considered for the post of music director. Durkee also recalled hiring Neville Marriner from Columbia Artists, and he cancelled just a few days before he was to rehearse the orchestra. "I had to hire the assistant conductor of the National Symphony, who had never conducted the Brahms Second or the Mahler songs to be heard on the program. But it went well."

After his final concert, Rozsnyai and his wife separated and eventually divorced. His wife, an architect, moved to Los Angeles where she remarried and continues to practice with several firms. His daughter, grown by then, moved back to Budapest. Zoltan Rozsnyai, however, remained in San Diego. He remained Head of the School of Performing Arts Music Department at United States International University, where he had been contracted as far back as late 1967. Among his other duties there, he conducted their student orchestra, whose concertmistress he eventually married. He had met her much earlier, during his tenure as conductor of the Philharmonia Hungarica. She had been a guest violin soloist. Occasionally, he had some guest conducting dates in South America. Peter Eros, his successor as Music Director, had known him as a student and conductor in Budapest and elsewhere in Europe, as well as here. Eros told me that he had arranged for those dates for Rozsnyai that he, himself, was unable to fulfill.

I saw Rozsnyai only very occasionally after I left the symphony's executive comittee. We had been quite close during my time serving on the board, but my leaving understandably adversely affected our relationship, although he always remained friendly. I asked him why he did not return to Europe and resume contacts with the Philharmonia Hungarica, after he had made some low-budget recordings with them. He gave some rationalizations but, as I learned later, they wanted no further part of him. Moreover, his reputation was such that decent artist management would not touch him.

His sudden death in September, 1990, from a heart attack was front-page news in the San Diego papers. The Latin Rite funeral was very well attended at Holy Cross Cemetery. Peter Eros returned to town to conduct Rozsnyai's student orchestra and a small student chorus in excerpts from the Mozart Requiem as part of the service.

The Rozsnyai story is a sad one. His fate — and the fate of the orchestra — was dependent upon his unfortunate, markedly immature character. Rozsnyai needed a strong stimulus to push the immaturity out of the way and to make way for the professionalism that he was otherwise able to demonstrate at times. However, even if he would have worked consistently hard and well during his tenure here, the Association's financial situation based upon the inability of the board to remedy it would have led to the same catastrophes that sometimes were blamed solely upon him.

CHAPTER XI

The Second Hungarian: Peter Eros

In his interview with me, King Durkee told me that, although he had been named chairman of the new conductor selection committee, he had nothing to do with the hiring of Peter Eros as the next music director, nor did any of the other committee members. When I asked him how, then, Eros was selected, Durkee replied that he hadn't any idea. He commented that Eros did not come from Columbia Artists, as had most of the other guest conductors considered for that audition season. "Someone — I don't recall who — told Mike Gonzales about Peter, and they brought him over themselves from Amsterdam. They assigned him two concerts. And he worked cheap!" (Upon reviewing the first draft of this chapter, Eros commented that $6,000 per pair of concerts was not working cheaply!)

Interestingly, much later, when I interviewed Yoav Talmi about his own music directorship history with the San Diego Symphony Orchestra, he also commented that he had no idea why Peter Eros came to San Diego. Talmi described Eros collegially as a real "comer" in Europe, and his fame was increasing greatly when Talmi was leading his own first orchestra in Arnhem, Holland. Talmi knew of Eros' work at Salzburg and with the Amsterdam *Concertgebouw* Orchestra, and he felt that Eros had a fine future ahead of him in Europe. Talmi pointed out that he could understand Eros coming to a more significant, well-funded American orchestra — that was the dream of most young European conductors, but why he came to San Diego remained a mystery to him.

Peter Eros came to visit his family in San Diego over the Christmas holidays in 2003, during which he was kind enough to set up a date with me in order to provide some more personal material for this history. When I told him about Talmi's comments, he agreed that he did, indeed, have a burgeoning European career, but that he had been brought to the United States by George Szell. Szell had guest conducted the Amsterdam orchestra frequently, and he was impressed by Eros. In 1963, he invited the young assistant conductor to come to Cleveland and to work with him as a resident conductor with his own great orchestra. "Szell pushed the United States as the ideal place for young people because there was so much opportunity here, with lots of good guest conducting positions." Eros stayed with Szell for a year and then returned to his post in Amsterdam, from which he had taken a temporary leave, and remained there until 1966. Then he began the rounds of guest conducting engagements throughout Europe and Great Britain.

He developed a good relationship with Columbia Concerts Management. The Mexico City orchestra invited him as a guest conductor in 1971, and after his concerts there Eros stopped to visit with a San Francisco friend, Walton Wickett. Eros described him as a wealthy, extremely influential person who simply picked up the phone and called his friend, Michael Ibs Gonzales, then president of the San Diego Symphony Orchestra Association. Gonzales wrote to Amsterdam, requesting information and recommendations, and he also suggested that Eros come to San Diego to speak with King Durkee. Eros contacted most of the influential musicians he had met in this country, and all — especially Szell — recommended that he not have anything to do with the San Diego orchestra because of its dreadful history. Despite those admonitions, Eros met with Durkee's committee and was offered two concerts as guest conductor to open the forthcoming season but, as Durkee had noted, not the music directorship.

I questioned Eros about his not having listened to Szell and the others. He replied that he had, indeed, listened, but he came as a guest conductor, not as music director. He found that he liked the city, liked California, thought this was a good place to live and to rear his children, "and I liked the challenge of the orchestra." Durkee's comments about not having selected Eros as music director, but only as a guest conductor, were accurate. Due to the excellent impression made by Eros from his guest conducting appearances here, Tom Halverstadt, the new president, determined that he was the man for the job. He and Florence Goss, then still a power in the association, bypassed the conductor selection committee and offered Eros the post. Eros spoke of having received a "mandate" from them, "...to elevate the orchestra and to do something about this cesspool..."

The 1971-72 season consisted of eight pairs of subscription concerts, all to be directed by guest conductors, some of whom were supposed to be in the running for the music directorship. Michael Zearott had been named acting music advisor for the guest conductor season. An obviously talented, young Los Angeles musician with some guest-conducting experience, he was retained to help program the season and to audition necessary personnel replacements in the orchestra. As he told Donald Dierks in the latter's *San Diego Union* column, he had heard forty-five applicants for vacancies in all the string sections, trombones, trumpets and oboes. A number of musicians who had formerly played with the San Diego Symphony had left due to the financial insecurity as well as their difficulties and disappointments with Zoltan Rozsnyai. Zearott himself had never heard the San Diego orchestra. He did not conduct that season but was given one set of concerts to lead the following year.

Peter Eros was invited to conduct the first two pairs in 1971-72. He was followed by Andre Kostelanetz, Donald Johanos, Harry Newstone and Bud Emile. James Levine, then just beginning his conducting career, had also been contracted but he cancelled, ostensibly due to illness. James de Priest took his place. Kostelanetz obviously was not a candidate, but the others (except for Levine and de Priest) hoped for consideration. Donald Johanos had guest conducted in San Diego during the series of experimental winter concerts given by the orchestra at Russ Auditorium. He was the assistant to William Steinberg at the Pittsburgh Symphony, and before that he had led the Dallas Symphony Orchestra. Harry Newstone, an English expatriate, was conductor of the Sacramento Symphony. Bud Emile, who had gained some good conducting experience here, also vied strongly for the job. He needed as much experience as he had gained for the concert he eventually conducted to conclude the season because the announced soloist, Horacio Gutierrez, had suffered a finger injury and was unable to play. Emile's success in dealing with an unrehearsed substitute pianist, and his further success in the orchestral portions of the program cast him in a good light as a credible candidate. The reviews of his concert were the best of the season, but Eros had already stolen the inside track. The audition season of 1971-72 drew a fifty-five percent increase in subscribers and Civic Theatre attendance. Seventeen new musicians joined the orchestra.

More good news was the signing of a new, three-year contract with the Musicians' Local 325 that guaranteed no further labor disputes for that time. The contract called for the Symphony Association to provide 5-1/2 percent raises for each of the years of the duration of the contract. It also increased the number of services for the orchestra from ninety-two during 1971-72 to 104 he following year, and to 112 the season after that. Phil Whitacre, the symphony manager at the time, had worked closely with the committee from the orchestra personnel, which included Peter Swanson, Millicent Froehlich, David Greeno, Ray Dymott and Alfiere Pierno. The Association's team consisted of James Smith, Oliver Peters, William Stephens, Judge Bruce Iredale, and Thomas Halverstadt, the Association president. The contract also provided for a sabbatical for all orchestra members without danger of losing their positions or seniority after their having played for seven years. The contract also allowed for increased participation and authority by a committee of orchestra members when auditioning new members. Everyone was very pleased with the new contract, and a new, refreshing feeling of ease was apparent among all parties who remembered the chaos of 1968. All that was needed was the raising of enough funds to pay for everything.

Peter Eros, like his predecessor, Zoltan Rozsnyai, was a Hungarian refugee, trained in piano, composition and conducting at the Franz Liszt Academy in Budapest. Born in 1932, he had left Hungary at the same time as Rozsnyai, in 1956, and found conducting positions in Europe. Before 1956, however, he had worked for several years as a coach and *repetiteur* for several opera companies in Hungary, including the State Opera in Budapest. He had also begun to develop a career as a symphony conductor as well. At times, he was assistant to Klemperer and Fricsay at festivals in Salzburg, Bayreuth and the Netherlands. According to *Who's Who in American Music*, edited by Jacques Cattell Press (R. R. Bowden, NY, 1985), after a number of guest conducting positions, he became chief conductor of the Malmo, Sweden orchestra between 1965-68. He had moved there from Amsterdam where he had been an assistant conductor of its famed *Concertgebouw* Orchestra under Eugen Jochum and then Bernard Haitink. In Britain, he had guest conducted the Royal and Liverpool Philharmonics, as well as the Scottish National Orchestra. On the continent he had guest conducted the Vienna Symphony Orchestra, as well as the orchestras of Hamburg, Stuttgart, Oslo and Helsinki. His first contact in the United States was as an assistant to George Szell (after whom he named his elder son) in Cleveland, and then as a guest conductor of the Denver Symphony, which he led again as a guest during the 1971-72 season. He also guest conducted the symphony orchestras of Chicago, Indianapolis, St. Louis and San Francisco. Outside of the USA, he conducted in Mexico City and Rio de Janeiro, as well as in Madrid and Goteborg, Sweden.

Earlier, when I interviewed Otto Feld, he told me that it had actually been Rozsnyai who recommended Eros as his successor. Eros, with a wide smile, totally denied that, saying that his predecessor, whom he had known well, had nothing to do with recommending or hiring him in San Diego. Feld's impression of Eros was that he was, "...totally different from Zoltan. He was completely focused and always prepared." That critical evaluation was generally the same as the evaluation of most of the orchestra musicians whom I interviewed. Eros was named permanent guest conductor of the San Diego Symphony following his opening concert of the 1971-72 season. Some complained that he was named too soon but, again according to a Donald Dierks *San Diego Union* column, "A good man is hard to find at any price." Most of the orchestra liked Eros for most of his San Diego tenure. According to Eileen Wingard, "He spoke clearly in rehearsals. He knew how to rehearse efficiently. He was witty and made us laugh." Millicent Froehlich agreed, saying, "He was really pleasant with the orchestra for the most part. He had a wry sense of humor. He also hosted some events for the musicians at his home." Jim Plank described Eros as, "A real orchestra builder. I really liked him as a conductor. We played some really interesting music. You could trust much more what was coming from the stick, and could really play out..."

After his first pair of concerts in 1971, Eros was profiled by Donald Dierks in a *San Diego Union* column of November 7. Dierks wrote at the outset, "[He].. is an uncomplicated man. His interests off the podium are much the same as they are on it — his hobbies are the same as his work: music…" After describing Eros' predilection for participating as a chamber music pianist and quoting him as stating, "I can play anything that is put before me with a pretty high degree of accuracy," Dierks went on to comment, "From some people, such a statement might seem immodest, but with Eros it was uttered with a kind of unaffected simplicity that one uses in relating some other personal fact such as, 'I am 5 feet, 4 inches tall,' which Eros is…"

Eros's short stature eventually became a point of some notoriety when it was said to have affected some relationships between him, some orchestra members and some soloists. According to orchestra gossip — characteristically always plentiful and too often, like this, quite malicious — Eros tried never to hire soloists who were taller than he was unless they were pianists, who would, of course, play sitting down. He was said, according to the same gossip, to have hired his first concertmaster, Harold Wolf, because of his height. However, it turned out that he was not that good a violinist, and Eros fired him soon afterwards.

Dierks also provided another Eros quote in his November, 1971, article. "I am not running for the job and I don't want to speculate about any permanent connection with San Diego. I want to give two good concerts, and what happens afterwards is something I am not even thinking about…..Look, I am a contented man. I have known my wife since I was 8 years old and she was 4, and we are happy and comfortable in Holland. I am financially secure, busy and am considered a success in my profession. This is enough, so I don't need to speculate. When I receive offers I consider them, but between times I am a satisfied, uncomplicated man in my present busy life."

Later that same month, he was named permanent guest conductor and music advisor, assuming Zearott's previously announced position. He returned to San Diego in November, 1972, accompanied by his wife and two young sons, after a series of guest conducting dates in South Africa, and in New York at the Mostly Mozart Festival where his reviews were very good. He had just been named as the San Diego Symphony's next music director. On November 19, 1972, Donald Dierks' *San Diego Union* column was headed, "Symphony's Eros Looks Far Into the Future." Dierks referred to Eros's three-year contract with the orchestra that was to begin the following season. That meant that he was to be in San Diego for at least four years. During the immediate 1972-73 season, he would direct more concerts than he had the prior year, but there were still other guest conductors who had been contracted. In his interview with Dierks, Eros commented that he wanted to make the orchestra fully professional and wanted the musicians to earn fully professional fees. Eros concluded, "What the Symphony Association has in me now is a dreamer with great dreams, but also a dreamer with a grasp of reality."

Eros set about planning a season of twelve pairs of subscription concerts. The budget for his first season as music director (1973-74) was set at more than a million dollars. At last, the fabled major status had been achieved! On December 27, 1973, the *Los Angeles Free Press* published a lengthy article by Don Ray about the San Diego Symphony Orchestra, its new major status and its new music director. The headline referred to the "San Diego Philharmonic," but much of the rest of the article seemed reasonably valid. Ray wrote about Eros as a man who, "…reunited rival elements in the community, raised morale, provided the administration with level headed aid, gained the respect of his players and generally proved himself to be the man of the hour and all-around good guy. Ticket sales have soared, the players now smile and chat before a concert, and there is an air of cheerful prosperity at board meetings."

There was no question about his being the man of the hour, although his being an "all around good guy" was questioned by some. Despite his wry wit, Eros's personality was often abrasive. Sometimes his sense of humor seemed in short supply within him and from him, both when he was in contact with musicians and non-musicians as well. Paul Anderson, who had retired as the San Diego Symphony's first cellist several years before Eros came on the San Diego scene, sometimes played as a substitute musician under his baton. Anderson made no bones about his opinion of the man. "He was a good musician but not a nice man. He could be cruel. I was the first chair in Eros's La Jolla Chamber Orchestra and learned how sarcastic he could be…" Nonetheless, Anderson acknowledged, "The orchestra grew under Eros, and even much more under Atherton, who was the pinnacle."

Eros himself noted, "Not everybody in the community, on the board or in the orchestra liked me, and not all the critics liked me. I had some fights with people on a pretty personal level." One problem was broached early in his tenure when he announced to the orchestra that one of his official first steps was to move to daytime rehearsals. He knew that this would cause him to lose about 15-20 percent of the orchestra musicians who could not make that change due to their necessary daytime jobs. "But this was needed if we were going to professionalize the orchestra." Eros gave the musicians three years to make the determination if they could change to daytime rehearsals. "I didn't give them an immediate ultimatum, and it took three years to solve. Immediately, I developed a group of enemies. Those who didn't want to change complained to the board and to the media, and they started rumor campaigns." The other major problem about which he complained was the fact that the Association, "…made seven management changes in my eight years."

As differentiated from the often-slipshod practices and distractibility of his predecessor as music director, Eros was nothing if not completely focused. He made sure that ensemble was as tight as it could be, and that crispness in attacks was routine. Zoltan Rozsnyai had told me that he had modeled his own conducting approach on the image of Wilhelm Furtwaengler. That great conductor sometimes neglected controlled attacks and often played at relatively slow tempi. It was obvious that those aspects were not the secret of Furtwaengler's deservedly enormous reputation and success, but they were the unfortunate traits, among others, that marked Rozsnyai. Eros, on the other hand, adored Toscanini and, of course, Szell. He adopted many of their attitudes regarding precision and tempo. In fact, he was criticized by many for playing everything too fast, often creating an atmosphere of superficiality instead of deeper meaning.

In his *Los Angeles Free Press* article quoted above in part, Don Ray described Eros's conducting technique as follows. "Visually, Eros is small of stature and rather slim. He approaches the podium with a seriousness of purpose that borders on the pugnacious, conducts with a spastic flamboyance that would make Bernstein blush, and is passionately proud of the players in his orchestra, as revealed in the way he brings attention to talented instrumentalists who have distinguished themselves. Although he thrashes about, his gestures are nevertheless articulate and the players know exactly what he wants."

Ray reviewed the concert he had heard, emphasizing Eros's control in the Schumann Fourth Symphony, "...one of the few works in the repertoire that must be brought to life by the conductor...His orchestral music somehow requires an identity to breathe life into it, and for the most part Eros did this well." Continuing, Ray commented, "In the slow movement, there were melancholy passages of touching eloquence, the strings achieving an elegance of phrasing worthy of the Philadelphia strings. Alas, it all went up in smoke when Eros succumbed to the temptation to extract that last extra bit of excitement by exaggerating the tempo of the last movement. It broke the expressive tonality that had been achieved to that point; it caused the players to scurry through passages faster than they were obviously expecting to take it, and ultimately it seemed cheap." He concluded by saying, " As satisfying as much of the evening was, I'm afraid that million dollar budget rises up before my eyes and I am compelled to report that I did not hear a million dollar orchestra; a hundred thousand, yes. A million, no..."

Two guest conductors in the 1973-74 season distinguished themselves, Yoshimi Takeda and Isaac Karabtchevsky. Takeda was the Conductor of the Albuquerque Symphony, and Karabtchevsky was music director of the Rio de Janeiro Municipal Orchestra, which Eros had guest-conducted previously.

Karabtchevsky was a favorite of the musicians and received an inscribed silver tray from the orchestra following his second concert with them. Eileen Wingard made a touching and gratifying presentation to the conductor on stage.

The orchestra began a routine of concerts in outlying communities as far away as Riverside and San Bernardino, as well as appearances in North County communities such as Oceanside, Fallbrook and Escondido. A North County newspaper, *The Sentinel*, published a review by their critic, R. Appel, of the December 13, 1973 concert. He described the near-capacity house and the general level of enjoyment of the concert, but also described, "…the dynamic, sometimes too intense, yet showy baton of Peter Eros…" This seemed to be a consistent theme among most of the local reviewers throughout Eros's tenure here. On the other hand, the orchestra performed the Bartok *Concerto for Orchestra* on February 14, 1974, and Donald Dierks raved about the performance in his *San Diego Union* review. He described, "…an exciting rhythmic drive and dramatic thrust that the orchestra had been able to achieve only rarely in the past…"

For the first several years of Eros's direction, the audiences were generally larger and more enthusiastic than they had ever been in the past for the winter subscription concerts. By and large, the concerts were well reviewed. Nonetheless, money was always tight, and season after season there were drastic attempts on the part of the Association to raise more funds and to reduce, if not eliminate the annual deficits of well over a hundred thousand dollars, very significant sums in those days. These deficits, of course, mounted up via accumulation over the years. The board was finally pushed to contribute more heavily, and a collective goal of $250,000 *per annum* was set for them. In 1979, that goal was raised to $300,000. The only exception to years of constant deficits was at the end of the fiscal year in June, 1975, when the association ended in the black, at least insofar as its operating expenses were concerned.

Eros spoke to me with pride about the growth of the audiences during the years he was here, despite the ongoing management problems. "In 1975, I started bringing in better soloists, people I had known and worked with in Cleveland and in Europe…" He specifically mentioned Rubenstein, Menuhin and others of that ilk. "Then the La Jolla Chamber Orchestra came after me. Its board invited me to become their music director." Eros discussed this with the Symphony Association board, and it was determined that there would not be any conflict of interest, especially because all of the members of the La Jolla Chamber orchestra were symphony people. "I was there for five years and there was always cooperation, but then Donald Dierks kept writing that this made me 'emperor of music' in this community, and began writing worse reviews of my concerts. But I enjoyed every minute of it…"

Eros also mentioned that he had some personal difficulties with one of the successor Association presidents following Halverstadt (who had always been very supportive and friendly), as well as with some of the board members. Between that and the development of continuing, worsening reviews by Donald Dierks (made for reasons which Eros insisted were personal, about which he was loath to discuss), "the atmosphere began to become increasingly unpleasant." Another problem developed when some of the younger musicians wanted him to fire some of the older musicians who had given long and usually good service to the orchestra. Eros told me that he wanted to do this gradually and, as much as possible, naturally over a period of time. Divisions developed within the orchestra.

In the October, 1977 issue of *San Diego Magazine*, William Sullivan's monthly music column was headed, "The Politics of Culture: Feed a Combo and Starve a Symphony." The San Diego Symphony had withdrawn in 1976 from COMBO, the combined giving for the arts organization that provided some, but never enough, funds for the beleaguered orchestra. As described in an earlier chapter, COMBO was organized initially to provide funds for capital expenditures for the arts organizations in San Diego. For the Symphony, it provided a portable shell that continues to be used for summer outdoor concerts. But the thrust of COMBO's giving changed after a couple of years, when it determined that the funds it provided were to be used for ongoing operating expenses. The expenses of the Symphony continued to increase but the income did not ever keep pace, and COMBO's grants were always too small to cover the deficits. The Symphony board determined that independent fund-raising would provide more, and they were correct, at least in theory.

In the fall of 1976, Danny Kaye came to preside over a benefit concert. It helped a little. The Symphony closed its 1976-77 season with a deficit of $446,000, twice what it had been the prior year. In 1978, all the music critics in town sent a jointly-signed letter to the San Diego City Council. The Council had ceased providing grants to the orchestra because it felt that by doing so they would undermine the effectiveness of COMBO, whose backers had far more political clout. The critics' letter pleaded for the Council to resume its grant to the Symphony, but it was met with stony negativism. A winter Pops season of three concerts was prepared in for the spring of 1978, with such stars as Benny Goodman and Henry Mancini. The hope was that these programs would attract more cash but the attendance was disappointing.

Early in January, 1979, the Irvine Foundation provided a grant of two hundred thousand dollars to spark the 1979 fund drive. It helped, too, but the public's response was again disappointing. The image of the San Diego Symphony Orchestra stuck in their perceptions as a constantly struggling organization that could never seem to lift itself successfully enough by its own or the community's bootstraps. The community became increasingly disenchanted and the attendance showed it more and more. Nonetheless, in September, 1976, despite a deficit of nearly $163,000, Eros was given another three-year contract.

As tough as times always remained, however, there were notable musical advances. The personnel of the orchestra were generally enriched by Eros, who hired a number of excellent players. The orchestra was enlarged to ninety-five players. Eileen Wingard pointed out that Eros always prepared well, and the orchestra played better. "I found him inspiring as a leader." She mentioned also that there were, as there would always be in orchestras, a couple of first chair musicians who wanted to get rid of him and were the ringleaders of dissenters. One of these, Peter Rofé, eventually moved to a position in the Los Angeles Philharmonic, albeit much later, after the reign of the subsequent music director. The other major dissenter was the flutist, Damian Bursill-Hall, who stayed in the orchestra through the tenures of two succeeding music directors. However, according to a number of other musicians, he continued to make repeated, negative and disruptive comments during rehearsals, etc., until the 1995 bankruptcy when he went to Pittsburgh and their first chair.

An assistant conductor was hired — not Bud Emile, who had served in that position before. Eros had fired him not only as assistant conductor but as concertmaster as well during the 1973-74 season. The real reason for that act will continue to remain a mystery. Millicent Froehlich insisted to me that the break with Emile was due to a misunderstanding on Eros's part about something Emile had said in rehearsal. "I was sitting right there. Bud didn't say what Eros thought he did..." Nonetheless, Eros took considerable umbrage. Froehlich went on to describe Eros as defensive in general and especially insecure with Emile in his chair, with the concertmaster's many orchestra and board friends as well as his reputation with the Chorale. More important, it was related by a number of musicians as well as by Eros himself that it was never a secret that Emile had always wanted Eros's job. The concertmaster had wanted to own the San Diego Symphony podium even before Rozsnyai had been hired. When he was allowed to conduct, he received pretty good reviews for the results, and everyone liked his work with the Symphonic Chorale. However, that never seemed to satisfy his ambitions, and he remained a figure of dissention within the orchestra.

Orchestra gossip had long implied that Emile had always been a troublesome sort, especially because he wielded power over the orchestra by determining and selecting who would be made available for extra jobs. Emile filed a lawsuit upon finally being fired, and hard feelings were felt throughout the ranks of the musicians who, characteristically, were divided in their opinions. The lawsuit was arbitrated. Emile lost the arbitration and eventually left for the University of Nebraska and the Lincoln, Nebraska Symphony. According to Millicent

Froehlich, that imbroglio severely wounded Eros's relationship with the orchestra. He became even more defensive, she said, and the butt of even more jokes
because of the new, short, replacement concertmaster whom he subsequently
fired.

The next concertmaster, Tony Lucia, came with his wife. Both had been
experienced, valued members of the Saint Louis Symphony. Eros met and
courted them during his sessions as a guest conductor with that orchestra. Theirs
was a troubled stay, however, based upon Tony Lucia's illness. He eventually left
after several lengthy hospitalizations and medical leaves, although his wife stayed
for a time as principal oboist.

Charles Ketcham,. hired as Assistant Conductor in 1973, proved a valuable asset. He had served for the prior three years as assistant conductor of
Portugal's famed Gulbenkian Orchestra. Inexperienced as a choral conductor,
he nonetheless readily took over the Symphonic Chorale that eventually became
the San Diego Master Chorale, with an administration totally separate from
the Symphony. After one season, he was promoted to associate conductor of
the orchestra and was granted some subscription concerts. He was well liked
by the musicians, the choristers and the audience, and the reviews of his performances were generally praiseful. In March, 1978, Ketcham conducted the
orchestra in its first performance ever of Stravinsky's *Rite of Spring*. Sullivan, in
San Diego Magazine, called the performance, "sensitive, careful, efficient," but
warned against anyone trying to compare it against the recordings by the New
York Philharmonic under either Bernstein or Boulez.

Ketcham conducted many of the summer concerts at the San Diego State
Amphitheatre. As always, the summer concerts were generally successful and
drew good audiences. Two concerts in the 1978 summer season were especially notable for disparate reviews. The July 8 review in the *San Diego Union*
by Donald Dierks was critical of Ketcham's interpretation of Strauss's Suite
from *Der Rosenkavalier*, although he praised the performance of the "Symphonic
Picture" of Gershwin's *Porgy and Bess*. In contrast, two reviews of the 1978 season's final concert of August 18 were raves. In the *San Diego Union*, Kenneth
Herman described the purely orchestral portion as brilliant, and Louise Nelson,
in the *Star-News* of August 24, was in complete agreement. She described the
Pines of Rome performance as one of "extraordinary range and subtlety, ending
the evening in a blaze of glory."

William Sullivan's music column in the March, 1978, *San Diego Magazine*
noted that every January the San Diego Symphony Orchestra starts to sound
better. January, 1978, was described as, "A very rewarding month for symphony
patrons. In two bang-up concerts, Peter Eros and the orchestra did as much as
anyone could ask them to do… To top it off, the symphony board announced a

1978-79 season of sixteen triple concerts at the Civic Theatre." The article did not editorialize about or even mention the concept of a sixteen triple concert season in the face of gross financial problems, constantly compounded by a constantly compounding deficit.

The January 12, 1978, issue of the *San Diego Reader* featured a column by Paul Krueger, "City Lights," in which he reported on a San Diego State master's thesis by David Estes, a former horn player in the San Diego Symphony Orchestra. Estes had mailed the abstract of his thesis, with a covering letter, to over two hundred persons he deemed as influential in the community. He also hand-delivered copies of the entire thesis to the mayor, the opera office, COMBO and to various reporters. In his thesis, Estes documented the frequency and extent of public funding of the orchestra over the years since its founding. The nubbin of the covering letter as well as the thesis was that the symphony's present financial crisis was sufficiently deep as to presage the demise of the orchestra by March, 1978. According to Krueger, "Specifically, Estes claims the organization's operating deficit, which he claims now stands in excess of $600,000, will soon outstrip its total assets and drive it to bankruptcy. He also notes that part of a million-dollar endowment, designed to be used for its interest-drawing capabilities only, has been spent to pay bills..."

Krueger noted that Dick Bass, then-general manager of the symphony, argued that Estes' predictions are, "...way off base from a chronological point of view." The board was upset at the public airing of the difficulties, although some felt that it might be helpful in stimulating donations. Krueger also commented on the firing by Bass of his assistant, Marion Bremner, a six-year veteran of the staff. That move was also upsetting to many of the board members who were preparing for another appeal to the City Council for money. Prior appeals had been denied, and this one was felt not to have much of a better chance of success. Krueger noted, "...and another group has begun preparation for the inevitable: a general reduction of the symphony season."

The 1977 Estes thesis, "Community Influence in San Diego Performing Arts Organizations: An Institutional Building Approach," went much farther afield than Krueger's brief comments provided in the *Reader*. Krueger emphasized the accusatory aspects of the piece, but in the original Estes was far more analytic than accusatory in tone. In his introduction, Estes noted, "The low level of C. E. O. representation from major employers and large corporations provides an indication of what seems to be a lack of commitment by business leaders to performing arts institutions in San Diego." With a nod to the losses of many large local businesses and possible donors, Estes wrote that the adverse effects from the loss of aerospace firms and their contracts in the later 1960s and 1970s caused art groups, over and above the Symphony, "...to become compelled to respond by seeking other sources of support..." or by maximizing what might be gained from the remaining business sources. Estes pointed out, quite accurately, that in San Diego the power structure had changed during those years from business, military and wealthy old line San Diegans to public officials, with the election of a strong mayor, Pete Wilson. Although the new mayor proved himself a good, constant friend to the symphony, Estes continued, "The leadership of the city has been in flux since 1969. Jim Copley has died, and C. Arnholt Smith and John Allessio have been discredited. Many of the second level leaders died during the 1966-76 period..." and although some new leaders were emerging they were still trying to establish themselves.

Estes also wrote, "The Symphony has seemed to lack a continuing heritage or an historically valid power base within the community. This vacuum resulted from the lack of proportional representation in leadership posts or some other clearly defined criteria for the assignment of these positions." According to Estes, "The post-1969 members were largely without the resources, influence or knowledge of the community necessary to support an expanded role for the orchestra."

I can attest to that from my own experience, and add to it that before 1969 the situation was quite similar. I was asked to join the board in the early 1960s, a result of my having sent a couple of letters to Florence Goss suggesting a few things and criticizing a few more. It was far too soon after I had moved here and had established a private psychiatric practice. My only criteria for membership were my knowledge of music and the orchestral literature by virtue of my rich Chicago experiences and my fairly extensive musical background, as well as my penchant for giving unasked-for opinions. With no community clout and with no financial resources comparable to the level that should have been demanded of the board members, I had as much business being on the board (and even less being on the executive committee) as the man in the moon. However, the essential weakness of the board was demonstrated by its allowing people like me to be on it. During my half-dozen years on it, the power continued to be invested in the old-line San Diegans who continued the same inadequate methods of trying to raise funds and run an orchestra with questionable management. I confess that it is only in retrospect that I recognize how foolhardy and self-defeating that was.

Estes's conclusions from his research were as follows.

"The data presented in the thesis indicated that the San Diego Symphony's organizational and financial problems derive from three characteristics of the board: (1) the low level of economic, social and political influence among the members; (2) instability or rapid turnover of the members; and (3) the dominance of earlier members through 1973-74." The comments in the Krueger article about the profligate spending and lack of financial stability related to these conclusions.

As time went on and the community's disappointment continued with the constant struggles manifested by the Symphony Association, the audiences thinned even more, and the financial stresses became worse. As in the latter part of the Rozsnyai era, season-ticket holders were chary of renewing their seats for fear that the symphony would go under and that they would be left with meaningless tickets. Robert Christian became the next manager, succeeding Dick Bass, and was eventually replaced by Michael Maxwell.

My 2003-4 communications with Peter Eros resulted in the conductor's sending me the list of the managers who served the Association during his tenure. In the order that he remembered them, they were: Phil Whitacre, Bob Christian, Marion Bremner, Richard Bass, Bob Christian (again), Richard Bass (again), Michael Maxwell and Bill Denton. As he pointed out in an e-mail to me, the order in which he recalled them may not be the actual order in which they served, "...but there they were, all of them! This cavalacade of ambitious but rather lazy executives (Phil Whitacre was not lazy) did not make my work any easier..." It is possible that Peter Eros suffered more from San Diego's being the "graveyard of symphony managers" more than any of the other conductors, but each maestro had his own share of difficulties with the administration.

A prescient article by William Sullivan in the November, 1979 *San Diego Magazine* again brought to light, as had Estes's thesis, the disastrous practice that would eventually lead to disastrous effects. "Something must be done to reverse the deficit that threatens to wipe out the orchestra's nest egg, a one million dollar Ford Foundation grant obtained several years ago and which has been kept in the bank and borrowed against in deficit seasons. And there have been plenty..."

The threat of possible repetitions of concert cancellations and losses of paychecks, such as had existed during the Rozsnyai era, was a sword of Damocles over the heads of the musicians, and the levels of tension within the orchestra gradually increased. Increasing negative feelings about Eros began to be apparent among the musicians and the audience as well. The reviews of his performances, though, continued to be generally favorable — frequently, however, with the same caveats about his lack of expressiveness sacrificed to fast tempos and over-loud dynamics. As an example, Donald Dierks reviewed the concert of January 11, 1979 in the *San Diego Union*, and wrote about the performance of the Schumann "Rhenish" Symphony, "...a grateful work to play —melodious, rich in sonorities and dramatically expansive. These qualities the orchestra grasped well, and the performance was consistently even and sure-handed. Intonation was secure, attacks precise and the tone quality, in general, had warmth and richness. Would that the interpretive concept had reached a level comparable to the instrumental per-formance standard…[T]he first movement of the symphony had a frantic quality that was cheaply dramatic, but not appropriately heroic and noble…" Continuing, Dierks wrote, "In the outer movements…the conception was unnecessarily overwrought and uncomfortably driven…"

Other examples of the up-and-down comments about Eros's readings with the orchestra appeared in successive issues of *San Diego*

Peter Eros. *Photo courtesy San Diego Symphony.*

Magazine. In the February, 1979 issue, reviewing a December, 1978 concert, William Sullivan wrote about, "one of the dullest performances of Schubert's Fifth Symphony I have ever heard…The interpretation had no sunshine." On the other hand, reviewing the concert of January 25, 1979, in the March, 1979, *San Diego Magazine*, Sullivan wrote, "It was impossible not to have been swept along by the quality of the playing, under Peter Eros, heard in the Kodaly 'Peacock' Variations, the Beethoven 'Empero' Concerto and the Shostakovitch 'Happy' Symphony Number Nine." In his magazine columns, Sullivan had more room to expand than the daily newspaper reviewers, but they all expressed the same opinions about Eros. They all praised his work with the orchestra and noted how much he had improved it. However, as Sullivan wrote in the June, 1978 *San Diego Magazine*, "I wish that Peter Eros would accept the mood of the evening and relax up there on the podium, not conducting too fast and perhaps pausing a little more than usual to allow the crowd to express its admiration and appreciation…"

In contrast, one of Eros's finest evenings was his conducting of a special concert performance of Verdi's great opera, *Otello*, featuring James McCracken in the title role and Cornel MacNeil as Iago. It took place in the Civic Theatre on

June 1, 1973, at the end of his first full season as music director. His *tempi* were well judged, allowing for considerable, needed excitement but also providing wonderfully flexible, sensitive underpinning of the vocalists' needs and expressions. Eros's predecessor, Zoltan Rozsnyai, was in the audience. He came up to me after the performance and expressed considerable praise for Eros's conducting and his over all reading of the score. When I went backstage to congratulate Eros, I told him that he really should conduct opera more because of the remarkable capacity he demonstrated of that flexibility. He smiled and said that this was not the first time anyone had told him that. Unfortunately, he conducted no other opera performance in San Diego, although there were a few compositions that were quasi-operatic in nature and form. But as far as the standard symphonic repertoire was concerned, the same critical complaints about too rapid tempi and rigidity in his symphonic readings continued.

One of the other quasi-operas conducted here by Eros was a concert presentation of a very rarely heard piece by a generally unknown Hungarian-American composer, Gabriel von Wayditch. Titled *Jesus Before Herod*, the piece was given during the 1978-79 season with the financial help of the von Wayditch Foundation, of which Eros was a member. Eros himself described the piece to me as , "...a symphonic poem with some voices." The work was recorded, also via a grant from the Foundation, and appeared on a Musical Heritage Society stereo disc. The performance was excellent, but the music and libretto were generally considered to be near hopeless by critics. In the June, 1979, *San Diego Magazine*, William Sullivan wrote that the idea of presenting the work, "...puts only another question mark beside the already much-questioned musical sense and judgment of Peter Eros, who brought it about." Nonetheless, the recording (currently in the San Diego Symphony Archives at the San Diego State University Library's Special Collections) attests to the excellence of the orchestra trained so diligently and effectively by Eros.

Another especially remarkable performance by Eros and the orchestra was somewhat close to operatic. The 1977-78 season closed with Berlioz's *The Damnation of Faust*, with vocal soloists and chorus. On May 5, 1978, Andrea Herman reviewed it in the *San Diego Evening Tribune*, and she began her column as follows. "When the San Diego Symphony played the last note of Berlioz's "The Damnation of Faust," last night in the Civic Theatre, there was a silence of wonderment and reverent joy. No need to search through a vocabulary of superlatives. Anything expressing praise will do. From 'amazing' to 'inspiring.' Peter Eros conducted with a master's hand..." That kind of praise was exceptional. However, Eros ended the season with a framed civic proclamation calling the day of the concert his day, and Charles Ketcham led the orchestra in a fanfare in his honor. The only negative aspect of the evening was the relatively sparse audience, symptomatic of the way that the attendance was going generally during those later years of the Eros era.

The 1978-79 season was announced as comprising sixteen pairs of concerts. Due to the growing financial problems, there was only one guest conductor. Eros and Ketcham directed the bulk of the performances. A January 26, 1979, article in the *San Diego Evening Tribune* by Andrea Herman was headlined, "Ketcham To Lose Position." The article reported that beginning with the fall of 1979, Ketcham would conduct one set of concerts during the subscription season in the capacity of guest conductor. He would also continue to direct the Young People's Concerts. A symphony spokesman was quoted as saying that there were no plans to fill the position of associate conductor until 1980 because all the subscription concerts would be conducted by Eros or guest conductors. The spokesman went on to describe a possibility of bringing in a new assistant conductor with "junior status," who will "learn the ropes and cover for the music director should he become ill…"

The article was transparent insofar as covering some likely underlying reasons. It cost the Association too much money to keep Ketcham in his usual job when the financial situation continued getting increasingly tight. Besides, according to local gossip from inside and outside the orchestra, the increasingly critically beleaguered, defensive Eros (as they described him) was beginning to perceive the always-personable Ketcham, a community favorite, as a personal threat. Eros has told me, on the other hand, that he had always been very friendly with Ketcham, and that he remains a good friend. He wrote to me, "I was actually promoting Charles's career far longer than my San Diego tenure lasted. Together with Pete Wilson, he was my most loyal and trusted friend there. We are still friends and sometimes talk on the phone. I am very sorry that he did not continue pursuing a career in conducting after his job as assistant conductor in Utah, but instead went into the computer business…"

Three days later, another Andrea Herman article in the *Evening Tribune* was headlined, "Eros Asks Aide to Stay On." Eros was quoted, "I don't know whether Charles Ketcham would like to keep his title of associate conductor; however, I have asked him to stay on with the symphony for the next season, which will be my last year as music director…Mr. Ketcham's merits during his tenure in our community are obvious. His fine winter and summer concerts, the building of the symphony chorale, and his nationwide respected Young People's program made him highly respected by the community…The president of the board of directors is aware of my wish to have Mr. Ketcham re-engaged, and I know that negotiations are going on at this time…" A large photo of Charles Ketcham topped the article; there was no photo of Eros.

It appeared quite possible that Eros, in his declining years here, needed to protest too much, to uphold his image as the "good guy" noted in earlier articles, and to demonstrate unqualifiedly that the Ketcham situation was not of his making. My understanding of Eros' leaving after the next season was the result of a genuinely mutual understanding between the conductor and the Symphony Association. Eros was no longer a draw, nor was he any longer the community's fair-haired boy.

Late in 1978, Eros had his contract as music director extended by the board for only one year, for the 1979-80 season. Eros conducted nine sets of concerts during that season, after which he was given the honorary title of Conductor Laureate. He had planned only that portion of the season involving his own concerts. The new manager, Michael Maxwell, did the rest. Six guest conductors, none of whom had ever appeared with the orchestra before, assumed the podium for the remainder, except for the concert for which Charles Ketcham had already been contracted. Eros would also conduct two special benefit concerts featuring Mstislav Rostropovich and Isaac Stern as soloists. The benefit concerts were much needed because the coffers were continually going down. Maxwell, the manager since fall, 1978, had programmed an expensive season for 1979-80, with a budget of $180,000 for soloists and guest conductors.

Andrea Herman's article in the January 26, 1979, *Evening Tribune* refers to Maxwell's concept of, "The Giant Years." She wrote,

> "There are only a handful of managers in this country who have Maxwell's contact clout. Having been at the business helm of the prosperous Cleveland Orchestra for 10 years, he has accumulated a roster of awe-inspiring artists whom he can tap for support. Now, it seems, Maxwell is calling in this support. Well, a portion of it. (Leinsdorf, he says, he's saving for another year). His motive might sound self-serving at first. To properly impress the music establishment with his first season as manager. (He's been the sole architect.) But Maxwell strongly believes that by importing a succession of international conductors and soloists, the orchestra will climb right up there into the company of '...the 12 best. Those giant years — we shall enter them this next decade,' he said. Maxwell's thinking is simple. He believes that it's impossible to raise the orchestra from its present stature without 'names'..."

The Ketcham situation had also been changed, at least insofar as his title was concerned. Ketcham had been named resident conductor for the 1979-80 season. In announcing that, according to a news article in the March 2, 1979, *Evening Tribune*, Maxwell stated, "It is abundantly clear by now that we are looking for a new permanent conductor and that he will certainly want to pick his own associate or assistant conductor." When asked about the change in name, Maxwell said, "Charles felt that associate conductor would no longer be appropriate, and we agreed...Residency indicates an ongoing attachment but that he is in transition because he's preparing to launch his career on a national basis: to establish himself elsewhere..." As it turned out, after the 1980 summer season, Ketcham moved to Salt Lake City.

Donald Dierks, in his *San Diego Union* review of Ketcham's March 1, 1979, concert, referred to it as possibly the season's best. It featured the Berlioz *Symphonie Fantastique*. Dierks commented specifically about one section of the orchestra, "And the string basses, which one recalls only a few seasons ago played like a bunch of cobblers, on this occasion displayed consistent finesse and musicality." The soloist for the evening was the orchestra's new first flutist, Damian Bursill-Hall, promoted to principal by Eros (despite his problems with him) in one of his last major contributions to the orchestra. On the day of that Ketcham concert, Eros announced his own guest conducting contracts in Hungary, his first return to his native land since leaving it in the mid-1950s. Eros had guest conducted elsewhere during his tenure in San Diego, generally successfully, perhaps most notably in Australia. He went there for seven years in a row to conduct several concerts each year with Orchestras in Melbourne and Perth, as well as with several other Australian Broadcasting Corporation orchestras.

The summer seasons in 1979 and 1980 were the most ambitious ever programmed for the orchestra. The July and August regularly scheduled concerts were expanded by presenting added performances throughout the county, at La Costa, Southwestern College in Chula Vista, Rancho Bernardo and Ramona as well as at UCSD. The expansion of the summer program was made possible by a $250,000 grant from the Irvine Foundation.

All told, under the Eros reign (and that of Maxwell), the orchestra's performances increased from thirty-six a year to eighty-two! The 1979-80 subscription season was also the most expansive and expensive the orchestra had ever presented — again, in the face of continuing financial stresses. The number of triple concerts was enlarged to eighteen instead of sixteen and, as Maxwell had promised, "names" were prominent in the schedule as soloists and guest conductors. The guest conductors included Roberto Benzi, music director of *l'Orchestre de Bordeaux-Acquitaine*; David Atherton of the Royal Opera, Covent Garden, as well as founding director of the London Sinfonietta; Aldo Ceccato, director of the Hamburg Philharmonic and former music director of the Detroit Symphony; Emil Tchakarov, conductor of the Sofia Philharmonic; Stanislaw Skrowaczevski, music director of the Minnesota Orchestra; and Erich Bergel, chief conductor of the BBC Welsh Orchestra.

The budget became quite strained from the outset. The Symphony Association had embarked on a series of *Radiothon* fund-raisers a few years before. In his article about the 1979 *Radiothon* in the April 1, 1979, *San Diego Union*, Donald Dierks was prescient in his first paragraph. "Pressure is the name of the game. This year's San Diego Symphony *Radiothon '79* is expected — needs — to be more successful than *Radiothon '78*. It is crucial that this major fund-raising event keep pace with the expanded activities of the orchestra…" It did not, similar to its predecessors. COMBO was still active then, and it was expected that a fifth of the Symphony's budget ($250,000) would be contributed by COMBO. The COMBO allocation also fell short.

Many years later, at lunch with Henry Fogel in Chicago (he was then president and C. E. O. of the Chicago Symphony Orchestra Association, and soon would take the helm of the American Symphony Orchestra League), he told me of his experiences over several years in San Diego as guest master of ceremonies for some of the *Radiothons*. He was severely critical, pointing out that the goals to be reached were far too small, and that the San Diego Symphony boards with whom he worked did little on their own to increase the sorely needed funds for the orchestra. The letter written by Helen Marquardt, Producer of the 1979 *Radiothon*, announcing its catalogue, pointed out that the 1978 *Radiothon* raised $87,000, "primarily due to the active support of so many residents and merchants." Fogel believed that at least twice that should have been set as a goal for a community like San Diego, and that with better and earlier public relations ploys it could have been reached. Fogel commented that the San Diego board was inadequate in that it had too few genuine community business leaders. "It had some of their wives, but where were the C. E. O.s themselves?"

During the final years of the Eros era, another important issue began to be raised. Its first appearance seemed to be in a *Los Angeles Times* (San Diego Edition) article by William Sullivan, headlined, "Fox Theatre: Home for the Symphony?" Sullivan wrote, "Michael Maxwell, the Symphony Assn's general manager, admits he is 'serious about the exploration' of the possibility." The article also noted that a Symphony board member paid the expenses of famed acoustical consultant, Christopher Jaffe, to come to San Diego and sit in the theatre during orchestra rehearsals. Jaffe pronounced the venue as, "a very fine environment for symphonic presentation," and pointed out that the greatest need was for better reflecting surfaces around the orchestra on the stage.

Donald Dierks picked up the thread in his *San Diego Union* article of July 8, 1979. He wrote mainly about the need for more performing spaces due to the likely increase in symphony and opera schedules that would create insoluble conflicts in the schedule of the Civic Theatre. "The only real solution to the coming scheduling crunch is a second theater, and the only second theater in town now that could serve, with some redecorating and remodeling, is the Fox." It was believed that it would take no less than $500,000 to bring the theater up to minimum standards for the symphony. The Fox had been closed for several years but, unlike a couple of other downtown movie/vaudeville palaces, it had not been torn down. Until the opening of the Civic Theatre, it served as the home to the visiting San Francisco Opera. The reconstruction of the Fox is a part of the chapter devoted to the successor music director to Peter Eros, but it is significant that the movement toward that end began during the 1970s. Much of the impetus came from Michael Maxwell, who always seemed to think big — sadly, usually too big for the San Diego board and for the San Diego audiences of his time.

William Sullivan's column in the January, 1979 issue of *San Diego Magazine* was headlined, "Eros, A Long Goodbye." Sullivan referred to the announcement that Eros would have fewer appearances during the forthcoming 1979-80 season, and that his latest contract was only for one season instead of the usual three. Sullivan wrote, "Over the last six years, my feelings about Eros have remained essentially the same. He has been a marvelous music master for the musicians of the orchestra. But I believe his ability as an interpreter is limited. Excitement with Eros is limited to passages which are either fast or loud or both, and that leaves a style of music that is predictable, shallow, dull and not the stuff which makes up good box office. The music wrought by Eros from his musicians has not been the sort to warrant rave reviews, nor has his professional deportment been anything to provoke our scorn. Peter Eros got his musicians to fiddle and blow and otherwise execute the basics," but in terms of creating moving music, Sullivan believed that there was little there.

Sullivan pointed out that the San Diego Symphony was an excellent orchestra, with winds that play with distinction. He specifically mentioned flutist Damian Bursill-Hall and principal horn Jerry Folsom in that regard. The orchestra has attained a level of competence, he said, that, "...sometimes overshadows that of some of the presumably more mature European orchestras which have drifted through San Diego...He eliminated poor players and motivated the better ones to try harder and to exert their leadership. Eros got them better wages and arranged for daytime rehearsals...He gave them something to look and feel proud about...

"The stumbling block...[for the San Diego Symphony]...to an even deeper maturity would seem to be the same music director who has brought the orchestra to where it is today...Mr. Eros does not seem to be able to get free of making every concert sound like a musical exercise, albeit a very advanced one...[His] chief drawback is his lack of luster as an interpreter..." Sullivan concluded, "This is not to say that the maestro deserves our scorn or our resentment. On the balance scale of his contributions to San Diego, the positive aspects are ahead of the negative...Mr. Eros moves on with his head held high."

Peter Eros did indeed leave with his head up. Aside from the above praises given to him by Sullivan (and other of the community's music critics, as well as by many of the orchestra's musicians), it should also be noted that he was the only San Diego Symphony Orchestra music director (at least thus far) after Earl Bernard Murray who led the orchestra through a series of uninterrupted, non-cancelled seasons completed as planned. By any San Diego measure, this represents a quantum of success in this city that cannot be disputed. His predecessor and both of his successors were unable to maintain uninterrupted seasons due to financial failures, although those debacles cannot be placed on their shoulders as much as on those of the boards and the managers. Eros kept the orchestra together (and not only in terms of ensemble) through times that were treacherous and often very near the abyss in terms of financial catastrophe. Maxwell was fired before Eros left, and the seemingly constant rotation of managers appeared bound to continue. As Eros told me with considerable vehemence, "Seven managers in nine years!" The orchestra was aware of all of that, but Eros, in his capacity of leader, maintained a high standard.

From San Diego he moved to Baltimore, where he became head of orchestra studies at the famed, venerable Peabody Conservatory. After several years (and a divorce), he returned to Europe where, in 1982, he became the music director of Denmark's Aalborg Symphony, where he stayed for seven years, and also guest conducted frequently. In Europe, he led the Scottish National Orchestra, the Bournemouth Symphony and the Stockholm Royal Opera, as well as giving concerts in Holland, Germany and Scandinavia. He had three tours to Australia and two to South Africa.

While vacationing in Budapest to visit friends, however, he had a serious heart attack. He realized that he would have problems traveling and touring, so he moved to Seattle where he remains conductor of the University of Washington Orchestra and a professor in the Department of Music. Occasionally, he continues to guest conduct, and plans are said to be afoot to invite him to return as a guest with the San Diego Symphony. In more recent years, he has conducted the Seattle Symphony and the University of Washington Opera Theatre, as well as the Bournemouth Symphony Orchestra in England, and the Scottish National Orchestra. He enjoys his student musicians enormously and derives terrific satisfaction from what he refers to as their exceptional level of performing. As he told me with a broad smile, "Waving my arms around keeps me alive."

CHAPTER XII

David Atherton: Triumph and Tragedy

A more auspicious roster of guest conductors than had ever been presented before by the San Diego Symphony was listed for their "audition season" following the announcement of Peter Eros' departure as Music Director. The names were relatively famous, and the reputations, at least as judged by their recording contracts and other orchestras they had conducted, were of the first order. Aside, however, from the performances by David Atherton, as well as by Charles Ketcham — and by Peter Eros in his final appearance, the reviews were, at best, tepid.

Jonathan Saville summed up the season in his April 17, 1980 column in the *San Diego Reader*. He commented that the guests, "...gave us a good deal more variety on the podium than we have heard and seen in recent years. Whether they actually gave us better music-making is another question...Several of the guest conductors — Roberto Benzi, Aldo Ceccato, and Erich Bergel — showed themselves to be dreary *routiniers*, and the orchestra sounded far less impressive under their direction than it has, in recent years, under the leadership of Eros." Kenneth Schermerhorn and Stanislaw Skrowaczewski also disappointed the reviewers. Mainly, the reviews emphasized the lack of significant musical profile in the performances, although for the most part the orchestra would play reasonably well for all the guests.

Earlier that season, in a column headed, "Two Batons," in the January 24, 1980 *San Diego Reader*, Saville concluded his comparison of the performances by Atherton and Ceccato by announcing, "Authoritative rumor has it that Aldo Ceccato has already been selected as the next music director of the San Diego Symphony, to succeed Peter Eros. At the moment, my judgment is that if this rumor proves to be true, the news does not bode well for the future of the symphony and of San Diego musical life."

Saville continued on April 17, 1980, in the *Reader*, "Looking back on the season, I realize that of the guest conductors, only David Atherton gave me real pleasure, and only David Atherton demonstrated that the San Diego Symphony is capable of truly first-rate playing. Atherton's performances of the Beethoven First Symphony and Nielsen's 'Inextinguishable' remain fresh and pleasing in

David Atherton. *Photo courtesy San Diego Symphony.*

my memory while many of the other concerts are scurrying away into oblivion."

Saville's opinions about Atherton's debut with the San Diego Symphony were, by and large, echoed by the reviewers of the two major San Diego dailies. The January 11, 1980, columns in the *San Diego Union* and the *San Diego Evening Tribune*, by Donald Dierks and Andrea Herman, respectively, praised Atherton's guest conducting performance, especially that of the Nielsen Fourth Symphony, "Inextinguishable." Dierks liked the preceding Beethoven a little better than Herman did. Herman noted, "Even technically the performance ...[of the Beethoven]...was far from smooth, but this was not the principal matter. The symphony was played with musical automation." In his column in the March, 1980, *San Diego Magazine*, William Sullivan commented that Atherton's work in the Nielsen symphony was "breath-taking," although he, like Herman, was displeased with the Beethoven.

The Times-Advocate, in San Diego's north county, ran a feature article about Atherton as early as January 10, 1980, indicating the conductor's leading position in the race for the local podium. Atherton was thirty-five years old when he made his debut here, and had recently been appointed as principal conductor and musical advisor of England's famed Royal Liverpool Philharmonic Orchestra. While a very bright music student at Cambridge, he attracted the attention of Georg Solti, who heard him conduct a student orchestra there. Solti gave him a trial at the Royal Opera House, Covent Garden, where he conducted two Verdi operas with considerable success. Atherton eventually spent twelve years there as resident conductor, conducting over 150 performances with the company, including a very successful tour to *la Scala,* Milan. Subsequently, he organized the London Sinfonietta, a twentieth century music ensemble of twenty core players that often becomes a little larger if the music demands it. The Sinfonietta was extremely successful and had toured England, the continent and the United States to great acclaim. They made many recordings of contemporary music, including some best sellers. The Sinfonietta's recording of works by Kurt Weill was awarded the *Grand Prix du Disque* in 1977. Atherton also guest conducted a number of English orchestras and recorded with them as well. Other guest appearances had been with orchestras in Holland, Germany, Scandinavia and the USA. Most of his reviews were very enthusiastic.

Musical headlines were made when Atherton organized a Stravinsky Festival in London to mark the tenth anniversary of the great composer's death. The Festival drew participants and listeners from all over the world. The Sinfonietta, the London Symphony, the Royal Opera and the Royal Ballet all took part. Arranging for these disparate, independent groups to program collectively and to dovetail their schedules certainly demonstrated a remarkable organizational capacity in the young maestro, and people were beginning to get increasingly impressed.

Music was always important to him, even as a child, although soccer, tennis and hockey were close rivals for his attention. Atherton's mother was an amateur singer, but his father was a professional musician, a piano/organ teacher, and eventually conductor of an orchestra in Blackpool, England. Young David began piano studies at age four, and clarinet at seven. At Cambridge, with his friend and classmate, Andrew Davis, he organized performing groups and found himself conducting them. Then Solti came to watch and listen.

Later, during his music directorship here, Andrea Herman wrote a somewhat more gushing profile of Atherton for the 1982-83 season's publication, *Symphony Today*. The article began, "David Atherton, San Diego Symphony's conductor, has abandoned the fanciful thinking of a young man. He spends enormous personal energy trying to overcome his impatience with low artistic quality and a lethargic public who suffer from a cultural myopia…Immediately discernible to almost all: his energizing self-confidence, his natty clothes, his courtly manners, the way his words fall orderly and reasonably and grammatically — and his frankness…"

His plans, according to Herman, were to spend a quarter of his time in San Diego, with the rest taken up by Liverpool and increasing guest conducting invitations. The San Francisco and Metropolitan Operas, among others, had asked him repeatedly to conduct operas by Benjamin Britten. Atherton dismissed the idea that spending only a quarter of his time here would compromise his work as music director and in building the orchestra. Herman quoted him, "In 1982, people have different aspirations. Jet travel and communication are such that one can more adequately do the job without necessarily being present." He enlarged on that theme by pointing out that if too much time is spent in one place, "You become too familiar. You become too much a part of the furniture…too easily available to all rather than having your time productively used." In her article,

Herman noted that Atherton's point of view was that the twenty-five percent of the time he spends in San Diego could more than equal the productivity of others spending double that time!

Atherton did not move to San Diego with his family, who, perhaps fatefully, remained in their London home. Herman wrote, "He's determined not to dismiss his family. 'If I have three weeks in San Diego I won't go back and immediately do three weeks in Liverpool. I'll make sure I have at least a week with the family. It may include recordings or whatever, but at least I'll be home.'" There were three small children, and a wife who was said to be absolutely adored. Herman reported, "There seems to be no one Atherton admires more than his wife. She's no ordinary woman, he tells you, and he muses poetically. 'She's marvelous when it comes to bringing up the children. It's not with nannies, either. And she doesn't gallivant around the world - even though before the children were born she came everywhere with me. Hong Kong, Korea, Japan, Russia...'"

The 1980-81 season proceeded with guest conductors, but the list did not include Atherton. Bergel and Ceccato returned, and the others were Michael Palmer, Kazuyoshi Akiyama, John Green, Gaetano Delogu and Sir Charles Groves. Some were better received than others, but none developed the sense of excitement created by Atherton in his previous season's appearance. Toward the end of 1980, Atherton was signed as the new music director, even before all the guests were heard. Maxwell had left as manager in the midst of the seemingly constant financial crises, and Atherton's tenure began with the return of William Denton as General Manager. Plans for twenty weeks of concerts were announced for the 1981-82 season, with Atherton conducting ten, including a Sibelius cycle.

The season began with an omen, an acute, severe cash flow problem that threatened the salaries paid to the orchestra. Paul Krueger, in the October 8, 1981 San Diego Reader, reported, "Twenty-five-dollar donations and a $250,000 loan will allow the San Diego Symphony to open its winter season, but the road to financial bailout has been littered with wounded egos, flared tempers and unsold tickets." Krueger elaborated, "...[F]ormer symphony development director Milo Clark had chosen...a series of newspaper ads designed to generate much-needed donations. The ads...made no mention of the symphony's dismal financial state, and were thus vetoed by the symphony's board members who felt a stronger appeal was needed. Before the board members could review and reject Clark's idea, he managed to place the ad in the September 24 edition of the San Diego Daily Transcript. The full-page ad, donated by the paper, yielded two contributions totaling forty-five dollars. The symphony board, on the advice of Union-Tribune advertising managers, decided on a gutsier appeal — an ad showing a semicircle of empty chairs under the headline, 'Without Your Help,

In Less Than a Week We'll Lose Our Symphony.' Run in the Sunday, September 27 *Union*, that appeal led to more than $30,000 as of last week. Clark, whose previous business experience included a stint as owner of a knickknack shop, the Yab-Yum store in Mission Beach, quit after the incident..."

Krueger continued by reporting the failure of another symphony fund-raiser, a benefit showing of the Isaac Stern film, "From Mao to Mozart." Finally, he wrote extensively in that article about William Denton's tiff with a *Los Angeles Times* reporter who questioned him about the idea of taking a pay cut during the symphony's crunch. The previous July, Denton had received a twelve percent raise. Denton told Krueger, regarding the hypothetical pay cut, "We probably should have...it would have been a nice thing to do. But if...[the cash short-age]...has ruined the musicians' morale, I didn't want it to ruin the staff's too."

A 1983 San Diego State University Business School master's thesis by Mark J. Lusvardi was titled, "A Marketing Study of the San Diego Symphony Orchestra." It dealt in great part with the continuing, deepening financial stresses afflicting the Symphony during the early Atherton years. However, instead of analyzing the problems as emanating from board weakness as Estes had done a half-dozen years before, Lusvardi focused on the marketing failures of the Association. It should be pointed out initially that those were the days prior to the hiring of a marketing or development specialist by the Association. All of those facets were held to be parts of the manager's job. Although there had been some mar-keting people in the symphony adnministration, there was really no organized marketing department until Nancy Smith Hafner became the first Director of a separate Department of Marketing and Public Relations for the San Diego Symphony Orchestra Association in March, 1986. Before, she had functioned mainly as public relations officer of the Association. In effect, without damn-ing the board, Lusvardi certainly stigmatized it indirectly as much as Estes had directly in 1977.

Lusvardi began, "Today, the San Diego Symphony Orchestra is one of thirty-three major orchestras in the United States. Under the direction of its new conductor, David Atherton, the Symphony is attempting to reposition itself to appeal not only to the more mature person, but also to the twenty-five to forty-four-year-old audience. Atherton has attempted to mix classical standard music with modern compositions in an attempt to attract a younger audience...Ticket revenues make up about 52 percent of all income...The 1981 winter season has averaged only 58.2 percent paid attendance at the concerts...This represented a loss of nearly $16,000 in foregone revenues each time the Symphony played."

Lusvardi developed a questionnaire that he mailed to every fourth home in selected communities in the San Diego area where it was thought symphony-goers might live. The communities included La Jolla, Del Cerro/College area,

La Mesa/Mount Helix, and Point Loma. The responses allowed him to develop some strong ideas about the marketing of the local orchestra.

"When asked to name any performing arts organization which came to mind (unaided recall) "the Symphony" received the most overall mentions." However, further analysis led to the recognition that, specifically, the San Diego Symphony Orchestra, as an individual entity, was only in third place, preceded in order by "The Opera" and "The Ballet." The San Diego Symphony as an entity was tied with the Old Globe Theatre.

Further research revealed that half the sample had received a 1981-82 season brochure, but that twice as many subscribers had received one as did the respondents from the general, non-subscribing public. Moreover, 2/3 of the total sample looked at the brochure, but many had little or no recollection of its contents. Lusvardi's figures indicated that 26 percent of the brochure's recipients did not attend the Symphony's concerts because the prices were felt to be too high. However, his research also indicated that the "...ticket prices as related to anticipated concert attendance show that the demand does not fall off substantially when prices are raised above $15 to either $18 or $20. On the other hand, there is a marked increase in demand at the lower prices (lower than $10) for those individuals who are price sensitive."

Specifically about the marketing, Lusvardi concluded, "There is a lack of overall continuity in the San Diego Symphony Orchestra's marketing strategy...borne out by the incongruities of the newspaper ads as related to the brochure..." Most respondents to the questionnaires saw both the ads and the brochures but could not recall the message of either,

The basic message of Lusvardi's thesis reflects in considerable part that of the earlier thesis by Estes. That is, that Estes's stodgy, weak, perhaps stultified symphony board did not aggressively market the orchestra. They did not increase the prices even a little, which Lusvardi said would not have hurt the attendance. Nor did they attract lower-priced patrons who would fill the seats by outreach moves to areas where new audiences could be developed. It must be remembered that each of these master's theses were written following long-term financial stresses (read: crises) that adversely affected the likely continuity as well as the artistic growth of the orchestra. Unfortunately, the major significances of the money crunches were not recognized early enough, and the financial deficits continued to mount.

Regardless of the money problems, the orchestra under David Atherton became a far better instrument than it had ever been. The reviews in the daily newspapers and other media were generally very complimentary toward the conductor. Atherton was perceived as the catalyst stimulating the San Diego Symphony Orchestra in its progress toward developing into a truly fine ensemble, if not a great one. His programming was fairly adventurous, although sometimes it was not seen in a completely positive light. As an example, Atherton liked to present cycles of music by a single composer over several successive concerts within the symphony series. In his first year, he conducted a Sibelius festival, loved by the critics but not enjoyed as much by the audiences. Subsequently, he programmed Brahms, Beethoven and Tchaikovsky festivals, the latter, of course, becoming the popular favorite. In his February 3, 1981 column in the *San Diego Reader*, Jonathan Saville expressed disappointment at the Brahms Festival. His comments made it clear that that composer was definitely not his favorite to begin with, but then he continued, "When Maestro Atherton left to conduct elsewhere, we were deprived of the one element that might have made the Brahms series more than tolerable: the vital excitement of listening to one brilliant musical mind in confrontation with another. How much better the Sibelius series last year was managed, ...[with]... Maestro Atherton our confident cicerone through all of them..."

Otto Feld, who had been assistant concertmaster under Rozsnyai and Eros, and who was to be demoted after a single season with Atherton, also opined that the orchestra played much better under Atherton. He also told me that he thought that Atherton was positively brilliant in modern music, but that his readings of the standard repertory pieces were not of the same standard. Moreover, Feld believed that Atherton's friends from England, whom he brought over to guest conduct, were mainly poor conductors. Feld recalled that Atherton's personal difficulties with the musicians started about six or eight months after he came as music director. The musicians made several complaints about him to the board but there was never any response.

Another source of programming controversy appears to reflect a hangover from the conductor's days as Music Director of the London Sinfonietta. In San Diego, Atherton programmed a number of works for small orchestra, often presenting them as the entire first half of a concert that, only after the intermission, presented the full orchestra. Many of the subscribers resented that practice, feeling that they were being cheated out of hearing what they had paid for, that is, a full symphony orchestral program.

Donald Dierks noted that Atherton had planned a varied season for 1983-84, and wrote in a highly anticipatory vein about it in his *San Diego Union* column of February 11, 1983. "For next season, Atherton will focus attention on Maurice Ravel by playing all of the composer's original orchestral works in two November programs." Dierks wrote that Atherton would conduct half of the season's programs. The orchestra's just-hired associate conductor, Richard Hickox, would conduct several programs, including a special Christmastime performance of Handel's *Messiah*. Hickox had been well known to Atherton before his selection as associate conductor here, via his own growing conducting career in his native England where he had been especially successful in choral concerts. Hickox remained with the orchestra through several of the Atherton years, and he gained considerable experience in San Diego. After he left to return to England, his reputation grew, and he developed into a very busy performing and recording conductor. The other conductors announced as guests during the 1983-84 season were Paavo Berglund, David Zinman, Rainer Miedel, James Paul and Oliver Knussen, another English musician previously well known to Atherton. Matthew Garbutt, who had taken over the task of conducting the summer "Pops" programs, was also given a 1983-84 concert.

In 1982, there had been no summer season. The Symphony had cancelled it due to the increasing financial crunch that had been characteristic of the Association for the prior half-dozen or more years, about which much has been written elsewhere here. As Lanie Jones stated in her February 4, 1983 column in the *Los Angeles Times* (San Diego edition), "About this time last year, the San Diego Symphony Ass'n. was pleading poverty. It cancelled its popular summer season and told its 70 musicians to find other work, all to avert an expected $535,000 summer season deficit and possible bankruptcy. Jones quoted Atherton as stating, "We won't do Patti Page backed by the San Diego Symphony, which actually doesn't build an audience...We will present the orchestra...Turn it into an evening with the orchestra. And if there happens to be a soloist here or there, the focus is the orchestra..." Garbutt was named resident conductor for the summer "Pops" series. Quite popular with the summer audiences, he has remained in that position off and on to the present day.

The "Pops" Association was given its own board of directors, separate from that of the Symphony Association, but was to use the Symphony's staff and, of course, the Symphony's musicians who were performing the summer concerts under the terms of their 1982-83 contracts with the Symphony Association. M. B. "Det" Merryman was the new "Pops" president; Louis Cumming was the president of the Symphony Association.

The 1983 summer season did not make enough money for the orchestra to provide financial security for the Association, although it was deemed successful. Merryman noted in an October, 1983, news article that, in the last (1981) summer season, the orchestra lost $485,000 in expenses over income. "Last year, the summer program was cancelled because of another projected loss of $485,000...But this year, we had a surplus of $2,000 over expenses for the ten weeks. We took a fixed loss and turned it into a break even situation..." The "Pops" group was planning its next summer season at a new, (said to be) permanent location, Hospitality Point at Mission Bay.

Andrea Herman wrote in the October 6, 1983 *San Diego Evening Tribune* that symphony president Lou Cumming expressed enormous disappointment in the community's response for funds to match the $325,000 pledged to the Symphony Association by the James Irvine Foundation. Spring, 1984, was the deadline for matching funds, but there was little hope that they would be made available from contributions. Generously, the Irvine Foundation instead pledged that it would match all funds generated by the Symphony through new subscription sales, up to $325,000. The subscription base for the concerts had improved from fifty-five to sixty percent renewals when that was announced, but not enough was eventually generated to save the grant.

In the midst of the seemingly constant sense of financial disaster affecting the Symphony, Atherton's contract was renewed in the spring of 1986, through the fall of 1989. His first contract had been for four years, from 1980 through the end of the 1983-84 season. According to an unsigned article in the April, 1985, *San Diego Magazine* (but probably by John Willett), "By his own admission still not satisfied with many aspects of the association's operations, he was loath to renew his affiliation thereafter except in short increments. Two single-season extensions ensued, which carried Atherton's commitment to the fall of 1986..."

The article continued, "Had a more attractive post or other causes beckoned Atherton away at this point, it could have proved an enormous problem for the association. Atherton's musical and artistic contributions to the orchestra since 1980 have been great. His popularity with audiences, musicians and the press has become uncontested." Willett's comments about Atherton's relationship with the musicians indicate that he was not then aware of the developing resentment felt by most of the orchestra toward their music director. Willett's article continued, "Atherton and the SDSO have become synonymous; it is almost impossible any more in the public mind to conceive of one without the other... The product, the music, is all that matters in the end. Atherton's accomplishments with the orchestra have been the single most important of all the association's accomplishments in recent years. That this exciting upward trend is now assured for the foreseeable future may well be the most germane of all developments affecting the cultural life of this city for months and years to come."

The article also noted that changes had been made in the administration of the Symphony Association. "Financial problems are being turned around. New top-level management is brought in. board members renew and deepen their involvement in massive capital development and Fox restoration fund drives..." All of the local press was not only enthusiastic about Atherton's conducting. They also praised his administrative, community leadership, especially insofar as his role was concerned in moving the base of the orchestra from the Civic Theatre to the Fox Theatre, which was scheduled to become the new Symphony Hall.

In March, 1984, the San Diego Symphony Orchestra Association purchased the Fox Theatre.

"Det" Merryman had succeeded Lou Cumming and was the Association president at the time of the re-opening of the restored Fox Theatre/Symphony Hall on November 2, 1985. In the souvenir program book for opening night, he prepared a narrative of the purchase and the complex negotiations that preceded that historic evening. He dedicated the evening and the entire 1985-86 season to Blaine Quick, a Symphony board member, "...appointed as a committee of one," to develop the successful plan that would allow the orchestra to settle into its own, new home. As Merryman pointed out, "Some might say the plan was audacious." They would be right, but no one can argue with success.

The plan called for the purchase not only of the Fox Theatre, but of the entire Fox block. The Association posted a small deposit and had 120 days to raise the down payment. Merryman related that five symphony board members "...stepped up and fronted the deposit, and we were on our way." Continuing, Merryman wrote, "Four months later, the symphony completed a deal with Charlton Raynd Development Company. They assumed the symphony position in escrow in exchange for a long-term lease on the theatre and perpetual participation in the rent structure of a 400,000 square-foot, mixed use office complex. In December of 1984, the developer agreed to donate a 40 percent interest in the theatre to the Symphony." The month prior to the November 2, 1985 opening, the Symphony Association, "...completed a bargain sale contract for the remaining 60 percent. Symphony Hall is ours!" In sum and substance, the Association bought the block and sold it all, except for the theatre, to Charlton Raynd.

Merryman extolled a number of other people who were instrumental in allowing the project to proceed successfully. He named attorney Bob Caplan, who served as the project lawyer. Hal Stephens and Mission Federal Credit Union refinanced the block. That allowed construction financing to be granted. Herbert Solomon, later to become Association president, and Irwin Jacobs, later to become the symphony's angel, put together the construction financing. Ballard Smith assumed control of the $6,500,000 capital campaign and gathered an energetic group of San Diegans around him.

Atherton led the orchestra for the opening night concert, but the program was severely criticized by all the town's music critics for demeaning the orchestra, for whom the hall had been purchased. Only the first part featured the orchestra playing symphonic repertory. The superb flutist, James Galway, was soloist. After that, Oscar Peterson, the great jazz pianist, appeared, followed by Diahann Carroll, Hal Linden, Joel Gray, Ben Vereen and Toni Tenille — all top-flight popular stars but with no relationship to the orchestra or its performances. The attendees (other than the music critics) enjoyed it all, but they did not fill the house.

The theatre looked gorgeous. It had been totally renovated. The major worry centered about the air conditioning, which everyone hoped would not be too loud and disturb the concentration of either the orchestra or the audience. The experience of Sherwood Hall was on everyone's mind. In that auditorium of the La Jolla Contemporary Arts Museum, where many chamber concerts and recitals were given, the air conditioner could not be used. It had been placed directly beneath the stage and created considerable, very distracting noise. San Diego music lovers had been sensitized. The acoustics of the renovated Symphony Hall had been supervised by the renowned acoustical team of Artec Consultants. Studies of the hall's acoustics had proceeded apace since 1978, when it had been determined that the theatre was ideal for live, unamplified performances. After the opening, many felt that the hall was hyper-resonant, "too loud," as some commented.

In March, 1984, the orchestra had played a pension fund concert at the Fox, under the direction of Skitch Henderson. Jonathan Saville reviewed the concert in the March 22, 1984, issue of the *San Diego Reader*. After damning the conducting of Skitch Henderson, he wrote, "The sound of the orchestra, with no greater alteration to the theatre than the installation of a temporary shell on stage, was stunningly rich, clear, close, full and resonant from virtually every section of the house. I moved around quite a bit and did not find any seat to be acoustically unsatisfactory. The front rows of the balcony offer magnificent sound, along with a close-up view of the musicians and luxuriously spacious leather-upholstered seats. From the very top of the balcony, in spite of the much greater distance from the stage, the orchestral sound is (if anything) louder and richer, as it picks up more of the hall's warm resonances. Downstairs, the front section provides a beautifully integrated and balanced sound. Even the seats under the balcony are remarkably good…"

The hall's "warm resonances" remained problematic for many listeners, however, at least until the alteration of some of the acoustical problems. But as most of the music critics wrote, too much resonance is never a problem in halls because it can be (and mostly was) fixed relatively easily with dampening materials strategically applied. On the other hand, a lack of resonance, such as in the ambience of the Civic Theatre, is much harder to repair, as was the relative lack of bass response from the Civic Theatre stage. Atherton was preoccupied with the Fox Theatre stage, and he wanted the orchestra to be placed as far downstage as possible so that they could sound out directly into the hall. However, this tended to crowd the musicians and made for uncomfortable positioning. Moreover, it was alleged by some of the musicians with whom I spoke that Atherton insisted upon a beaded curtain as a background for the orchestra instead of the more usually-affixed shell. A shell would focus and push the sound outward. The beaded curtain, especially without a ceiling above the orchestra, reflected no sound.

I have also been given other, conflicting information about the recommendation for the curtain. One party close to Atherton has insisted that Russell Johnson, of Artec Consultants, developed that idea, and that Atherton originally had thought it meritless. Nonetheless, it was accepted. Communication with Artec in New York City confirmed that the beaded curtain was their unfortunate idea. Renowned acousticians made many mistakes in many towns during the concert hall building boom of the 1970s and 1980s. Subsequent adjustments were frequently required, often of significant proportions. For example, there is no reason not to assume that San Diego's hall might turn out with acoustics at least as difficult as New York's Philharmonic Auditorium at Lincoln Center (now known as Avery Fisher Hall, modified and remodeled twice by renowned acousticians and still a problematic space for listening). It was only in the next decade that Symphony Hall's acoustics were really fixed.

Later in Atherton's tenure, more trouble developed over that beaded curtain because orchestra musicians were sometimes seen walking backstage behind it during performances. This irritated the conductor, who issued a directive that all musicians must remain downstairs, below the stage, when they are not playing. As a result, the musicians only developed more antagonism toward the music director whom they described as increasingly autocratic because there was little space below the stage for them to gather, with little light and ventilation. Apparently, it had not been made known to the players that Atherton agreed with them in that regard, believing and stating his opinion that the backstage facilities for the musicians were terrible. They still are, but plans are afoot for some remodeling.

In June, 1986, the orchestra traveled back to the Civic Theatre for a pair of free concerts open to all San Diegans, as a gesture of appreciation to all who helped the Symphony get over the severe cash flow crunch of the preceding season. Jonathan Saville, in the *San Diego Reader* of June 26, 1986, opined that the orchestra sounded, "...(from the first row of the mezzanine) less richly resonant but far clearer and better balanced than it has been sounding in its new home, Symphony Hall." During the reign of the next music director, a real shell was provided to the orchestra in Symphony Hall, and eventually a new wood floor was laid on the stage. These modifications improved both the resonance and the focus and clarity of the sound throughout the hall. As that music director, Yoav Talmi, put it, "Now we're playing in a concert hall, not a theatre..."

Earlier in 1986, Andrew Porter, the distinguished music critic of the *New*

Yorker Magazine, had visited San Diego and heard a symphony concert in the then-new Symphony Hall. In his words, quoted from his February 10, 1986, *New Yorker* article, "Like many other picture palaces, this Fox is a curious and attractive mixture of gimcrack pretension and real grandeur — an evocation in plaster of what the old craftsmen carved in stone...But it is a building that disposes listeners to pleasure as they enter it, and promises them something unusual, lifted above the daily round." He continued about the acoustics, "I sat in the first of its two balconies and found the results pleasing. Ideally, I would ask for slightly longer reverberation, for chords to go ringing on for just a moment after the singers and players sounding them have stopped. But the sounds that reached me were true. The hall's profusion of balustrades, bosses, and bas-reliefs, pilasters, coffering insures a proper dispersal of timbres throughout the range."

Porter's comments provide definite contrast to those who found the Fox too resonant in those early days of its use as a concert hall. Insofar as the orchestra and the concert were concerned, Porter wrote, "This was a Stravinsky double-bill: the Mass...and 'The Soldier's Tale'...The conductor was Michael Lankester, conductor-in-residence of the Pittsburgh Symphony. He gave an excellently poised account of the Mass, combining lapidary strength with elegant phrasing. The San Diego Master Chorale sang surely...'The Soldier's Tale' was given in a crisp, clear production, directed by Jack O'Brien...Andres Cardenes, the orchestra's concertmaster, was trim in the important violin part, and all the instrumentalists were expert, Peter Rofé playing a strikingly melodious double bass."

After the first season at the redone Symphony Hall, extensive modifications were needed for the seating in the balcony. The view of the orchestra, and especially of the conductor and soloist was limited due to the angle of the balcony as well as the forward position of the orchestra on the stage. The seats in the Grand Tier, in the front of the balcony, were all elevated six inches, and that allowed for a fuller view of the downstage area. The modifications were expensive, but eventually they pleased the audience who sat in the hall's priciest seats.

The balcony modifications became a *cause celebre* among the orchestra musicians, who resented the expenditure when they, themselves, were unable to obtain any raises. In fact, that reconstruction work was done during the period when the musicians were locked out and not playing as the San Diego Symphony Orchestra. The debut of the newly raised seats was delayed considerably because the 1986 season did not open as scheduled in October, 1986. It had been, in fact, indefinitely postponed due to a labor dispute based on the longstanding dissatisfaction of the musicians with their pay scale. They felt that the expenses of the Symphony Hall purchase and modifications drained funds that should have gone to them. They complained that they had worked for salaries that had been much too low far too long. No one disputed the meagerness of their salaries, but the Association almost went bankrupt early in 1986 and claimed that it had no money for raises. As it turned out, the money for the balcony modifications had come from one anonymous individual who had extended a line of credit to the Association solely for capital expenditures.

By the time of the 1985 opening of the hall, the orchestra had a fine, new concertmaster, Andres Cardenes, complimented so well above by Andrew Porter. The change this time was not due to any dissatisfaction with the prior concertmaster. Tragically, it resulted from the untimely cancer death in his thirties of William Henry, who had sat in the first chair since the Eros era. Other changes in the orchestra were due to Atherton's judgments about the musicians, and they sometimes led to increases in union grievances or to other personnel disputes. For example, Otto Feld, who had been assistant concertmaster since the Rozsnyai era, was demoted to a chair in the second violins. Feld believed that his age was a principal reason for this, although he insisted that his playing was unaffected by his years.

Charles McLeod, the long-time principal clarinet, was also demoted. His age came into question, too, although his playing was often praised in the concert reviews. He and Otto Feld were only two of a significant number of musicians, each over fifty years old, who were demoted or who were asked to resign. These actions did nothing to endear Atherton to most of the orchestra musicians who were already upset by what they saw as the conductor's increasingly dismissive attitude on the podium and off. The musicians developed a bill of particulars about Atherton that was presented to the board as well as to union officials. It set forth a number of claims, some of which have been alleged by people close to Atherton to be exaggerated. Again, it should be noted that I had been informed by Nancy Bojanic, Atherton's longtime associate and good friend, that the conductor would not allow himself to be interviewed personally for this history.

James Plank summarized the seesaw of Atherton's career in San Diego as follows. "When he came in, he was like a panacea. The orchestra made real strides. Where we ended up six years later was with a conductor who had built a fine ensemble but who then completely lost his relationship with the orchestra. It was not only his general, hostile attitude toward the musicians that did this; his affair with one of our first violinists really poisoned the atmosphere and split the orchestra..." Although other musicians have told me that Atherton changed from demanding, as he was early in his San Diego career, to increasingly impatient and critical after the first season, Plank opined that Atherton may not actually have changed as much as the musicians' tolerance of his behavior. Other musicians as well, who played under him during the '80s, have told me that he began as a strict taskmaster, but that this approach was felt by all to be beneficial and, in fact, necessary. The orchestra members, themselves, recognized their improvement and took increased pride in their performances. During our interview, for example, Plank and I reminisced about one exceptionally fine performance given by the orchestra under Atherton of Rachmaninoff's *Symphonic Dances*, a notoriously difficult piece that was brought off with remarkable polish and *élan*. Plank credited Atherton's strict podium manner for that well-remembered performance.

Later, however, according to Plank and others, Atherton's strictness was said to have become laced with insults and demeaning comments from the podium that began to tear apart the original fabric of collegiality and mutual respect that characterized the first Atherton season. Nancy Hafner Laturno Bojanic has told me that, as Development and Public Relations Director of the Association at the time of Atherton's tenure, she was to sit next to him during any and all public appearances, during which she would kick him beneath the table if he started to say something bad. He was often wont to do that, even in meetings with the press and public. Patience and tact were not the conductor's strong suits, at least during those trying times.

Combined with the chronic, justifiable anger the musicians felt over their low pay, the deterioration of the conductor's relationship with the orchestra led to a complex of issues that caused considerable dissention. When the orchestra went back to work briefly after the 1985-86 labor dispute, the playing continued to demonstrate the increased professional sheen that had been previously characteristic of the orchestra, but the attitude was severely damaged. That attitude was picked up by an especially sensitive critic, Martin Bernheimer, of the *Los Angeles Times*, who reviewed the orchestra's pair of concerts at the Hollywood Bowl on August 22 and 23, 1986. Bernheimer knew about the problems. His final comment, "They played; what else could they do?" spoke volumes. The Hollywood Bowl program had been contracted early in the 1985-86 season, when the orchestra was playing well and was not quite as emotionally upset.

The premiere season in Symphony Hall was greeted with acclaim by all the music critics, but it was not hard to see that trouble might be brewing regarding the Association's finances. As an example, reviewing the November 21, 1985, concert in the next day's *San Diego Union,* Donald Dierks began, "It is easy to have enthusiasm for the San Diego Symphony season just under way. The orchestra, under its conductor, David Atherton, is playing unusually well and seems to be settling into its new quarters, Symphony Hall, very well. And, if the audience last night for the orchestra's all-Beethoven concert is any indication of things to come, attendance will be picking up as people adjust to a new concert hall and a new geography. The house was not full, but it was of respectable size. One can hope that everyone there — press excluded, of course, had paid for their tickets..." In an attempt to attract more patrons, Atherton had planned a special series of five programs, each featuring the music of a single composer. It did not work. The audiences dwindled to far less than respectable sizes. The financial situation had hit a stone wall.

In February, the Association announced that it would enter Chapter 11 bankruptcy proceedings unless an infusion of two million dollars would be made available almost immediately. "Det" Merryman announced that nothing less would help. There were 1.7 million dollars in accumulated deficits, and about two hundred thousand dollars more was necessary to offset the expenses of the present season. Cash flow had been reduced to zero. The *San Diego Evening Tribune*, on March 6, 1986, published a story by Jane Clifford, a staff writer, that detailed the Association's debts. The accumulated deficit stood then at $1.93 million, while contributions to help offset it had reached only $1.6 million. Bank and board loans totaled nearly a million dollars, and Symphony Hall liabilities totaled $4.783 million. The only major asset held by the Association was Symphony Hall, valued at $6.0 million, and that did not reach the debt level of more than $6.5 million.

In the April, 1986, *San Diego Magazine*, John Willett reported that anonymous donors pledged $900,000 toward total debt retirement, and Muriel Gluck pledged another $250,000. "Community support exploded. Musicians and staff worked without pay for the final two concerts...Citizen contributions flowed: $205,000 in two hours of KUSI-TV's March 6 telethon alone..."Willett named the Judson Grosvenor family, Dr. and Mrs. Roger Revelle and the Copley interests as contributors to the final "big money infusion."

The March 9, 1986 *San Diego Union* article by Mary Hellman (with input by Donald Dierks and Lori Weisberg) was optimistic because the deficit had supposedly been paid off by the emergency fund-raising, and the orchestra played the Beethoven Fifth Symphony as a gesture of victory. Bankruptcy had been staved off. The payroll was to be met but the union sought an injunction against the symphony to restore the musicians' full salaries. "Sources close to the union say that the musicians intend to stick to their demands for full annual pay and, after a review of the symphony's finances, may press for changes in operations and staff..." The article continued, "In 1981-82, in the aftermath of an equally severe financial crisis, the symphony board stripped its president of power, and gave a four-member board committee authority over daily operations. That committee eventually forced the resignation of the symphony's manager. Sources close to the symphony board say there is growing dissatisfaction with the current president, M. B. 'Det' Merryman, and that, even before the financial woes became public, there were calls for his resignation. He has been criticized for his handling of the crisis. Union leaders, on the other hand, are focusing their ire on Bass."The column referred to the orchestra's new manager, Dick Bass, who had received much praise for assuming considerable control over the seemingly successful fundraising.

Just a few days later, another *Evening Tribune* article noted that the symphony board had changed its mind about pay cuts and would reinstate the proposed four-weeks that were going to be cut from the orchestra's payroll. The Association defended its original plan to make the cuts, even after they rescinded them, as fiscally responsible. In contrast, Greg Berton, spokesman for the orchestra musicians, said, "Belt-tightening is not the answer to fiscal responsibility...[The answer] is bringing in more money and tapping into that segment of the business community that remains unconvinced as to their fiscal responsibility..."

The discord between musicians and Association continued even louder when, on March 12, 1986, the management reversed its position given a couple of days before and, instead, presented its plan to impose a ten percent pay cut that would be retroactive to the beginning of the season. The pay cut would be arranged, as decided before, by canceling ten percent of the season. According to Hilliard Harper's *Los Angeles Times* article of March 12, 1986, "The musicians responded with loud hissing before a rehearsal Tuesday morning when a letter was read from symphony management suggesting that negotiations on the pay cut begin." The article noted that Atherton had just heard the news himself, and was "disgusted" by it. He immediately cancelled the rehearsal.

The all-Mozart concerts for that weekend were given, nonetheless. Donald Dierks reviewed them in the March 14, 1986, *San Diego Union,* in an article headlined, "Symphony performance reflects unkind cut." Dierks referred to the general level of performance as "workmanlike," and not up to the polish or expressiveness he had become used to from the orchestra and Atherton. "The final work on the program was the Symphony No. 40 in G Minor, and here Atherton and the orchestra tried to lift themselves from their expressive doldrums, and they almost succeeded. One has to admire them for trying, wounded as they are."

On March 21, 1986, Richard Bass projected a deficit of $820 thousand for the end of the 1985-86 season, despite all of the earlier fund-raising that had supposedly saved the symphony. Soon afterwards, he left.

John Willett wrote a lengthy column on the 1985-86 crunch in the following month's *San Diego Magazine.* He began, "The San Diego Symphony Orchestra's financial problems are not solved. They are miles of money and years of public attitude change from being solved...The two million-plus that was crash-generated was nothing but a big Band-Aid. It did nothing but pull the symphony's feet from the fire temporarily. It did not more than help ensure the completion of the 1985-86 season while supposedly retiring the plaguing $1.7 million debt — and that depended on whether all the pledged funds become birds in the hand." Continuing, Willett wrote that the two million, "…did nothing toward providing for the symphony's long-term needs, its continuing and continuous requirements for significant annual contributions to meet operating costs while at the same time establishing substantial endowment funds…[It] left untended the low blood pressure, anemia, malnutrition and osteoporosis from which the organization has suffered for so long and from which it is ultimately doomed to die a lingering death unless things are done differently in the future…"

Willett noted that the attitude of the populace in general is apathetic, and that the spectrum of financial support is very narrow in relation to its potential base. Willett scoffed at the notion that San Diego as a branch office town lacked sufficient clout to get more from the home offices or, for that matter, the branch offices. He called that, "The corporate cop-out." In contrast, the positive attitude of a number of local office and even distant home office corporations was remarkable, he noted, during the recent fund-raising drive, and must be repeated annually.

Headlines and more news and opinion articles were to come when the entire 1986-87 season had to be cancelled — not all at once, but three weeks at a time at first, and then totally. The union contract with the orchestra had expired on August 31, 1986. The musicians had rejected the new contract offered them by the Association that, according to the Association's October 13, 1986, press release signed by its president, Herbert Solomon, "…embodied the best terms and conditions the Symphony Association could reasonably offer…" Solomon pointed out that the musicians were paid a minimum of $21,250 in the 1985-86 season, representing a 25 percent increase over the 1984-85 minimum. Because many of the musicians were paid more than the minimum wage, the average wage during the 1985-86 season was more than $26,000. Solomon continued,

> "As you are well aware, the Symphony nearly went bankrupt earlier this year. We must begin to break the recurring cycle of spending more than we earn. In seeking the financial stability necessary for the survival of the Symphony, we have reduced our annual operating budget from $7.5 million to $6.5 million. Only 40 percent of the necessary reductions will be a result of the cutback in musicians' salaries. For the coming year we have asked the musicians to take a 7.8 percent cut in earnings, resulting in reducing the minimum salary to $19,600. This would be increased by 13.6 percent over the second and third years of our proposed agreement, ultimately exceeding the 1985-86 salary. The remaining 60 percent of our cost reductions include a 25 percent decrease in the size of our

administrative staff and substantial cuts in administrative and
concert production costs..."

The musicians refused the new terms. The Association had no more to
offer, so the season opening was postponed at first, and eventually cancelled
completely on November 10, 1986. In effect, the orchestra was locked out.
The work stoppage during the 1986-87 season brought forth a huge expression
of rage against the Association by the orchestra members, with special attacks
against "Det" Merryman and his successor, Herbert Solomon. Merryman's plea
that the two million dollars that had been needed to be raised would guarantee
the continuation of the 1986-87 season was a prime target, for the season did
not continue even after it had been raised. It was not until March, 1987, that the
orchestra reassembled in Symphony Hall to proceed with the season after nearly
two months of silence. They had been told in February that there was no money
at all to cover their paychecks. The "Pops" was under a separate management,
albeit as an arm of the Association. It was the "Pops" that went to Hollywood
Bowl with Atherton later that summer.

The *San Diego Union's* editorial of November 7, 1986, mourned in advance
the absence of the coming symphony season, although only six weeks had been
cancelled by then. The newspaper sympathized with the musicians, whom they
described as justifiably suspicious of management, and long-suffering by being
underpaid, but the *Union's* major favor seemed to be with the Association and
its president, Herbert Solomon. The editorial noted, "Not least among the symphony's valuable assets is Herb Solomon himself. That this distinguished attorney
is devoting almost all his time to the symphony these days is reason enough to
believe in its future..."

From the opposing viewpoint, an article in the February 3, 1987 *San Diego
Newsline*, a markedly anti-establishmentarian publication that referred to itself
in considerable understatement as a "Journal of Opinion," was by-lined Floria
Duncan. That was a name described in the editor's note as a *nom de plume* of one
of the locked out musicians. "Floria Duncan" related the tale of Atherton dis-
missing out of hand a Los Angeles high school band that had been contracted by
the Hollywood Bowl to play the accessory brass music for the Tchaikovsky *1812
Overture* during the San Diego ensemble's concert there. When he heard the band
in rehearsal, he refused to work with them. Therefore, there was no added brass,
although it and the band had been publicized. She also related, with emphasis,
Solomon's pointing out that the Association could not afford to pay the premiums on the musicians' instruments when they became due, in December, 1985,
although, "...the premiums had come out of our own pockets, and again (like in
February) the Association hadn't sent them in! It was called embezzlement..."

The author of the "Floria Duncan" article in the *Newsline* most unfortunately — and significantly — let her rage run away with her to the extent that it clouded her judgment, and apparently the judgment of the editor of the paper as well, who really should have known better. In her so-called diary (the format in which she wrote her article), the section dated October 13, 1986, stated, "The Association responds by canceling three weeks of the winter season — Herb Solomon's *Yom Kippur* gift to the orchestra?" The author apparently had other issues with Mr. Solomon over and above the problems affecting the orchestra.

In his interview with me in November, 2003, Solomon said that the budget of the Association, "…reflected what was given. The main item was the salaries for the musicians, and then the money for guest artists. The breakdown came from the fact that expenses simply exceeded the income. The problem was that the musicians were underpaid by any absolute or relative standard, and they wanted more money. We simply didn't have it. I became Association president after 'Det' Merryman, and inherited a massive deficit. The previous fund-raising didn't take care of it. We reached an impasse in our labor negotiations because we had no money to raise their salaries."

Referring to the music director, Solomon noted, "Any expenses he created made no difference." Solomon restored fiscal stability for the Association in the three years in which he served as president. He raised money and finally cleared the deficit. "We operated then on a balanced budget." When I asked him how he did this, he told me that he, "…expanded the universe of people who were asked to contribute, and I asked for more money than ever before. I went to businesses, banks and everywhere else I could…Finally we entered into new negotiations with the musicians and reached an agreement with them, but it was for fewer services and less money than they had sought." Solomon also pointed out that the manager of the orchestra, Dick Bass, resigned soon after he became president. "For a long time, I was acting as C. E. O. and general manager. Finally we hired Wes Brustad."

During the lockout, the musicians of the orchestra banded together to present a self-generated series of concerts. They did not refer to themselves as the San Diego Symphony Orchestra but, rather, as "The Musicians of the San Diego Symphony." They hired a few guest conductors, and locals Matt Garbutt and Thomas Nee also conducted. The San Diego Philharmonic Association was formed to promote concerts by the group and to try to provide some underwriting and other financial and public relations support. Lewis Silverberg, a prominent San Diego lawyer, headed the organization, which, it must be pointed out, was a new, *ad hoc* organization with no relationship at all to the old San Diego Philharmonic of the early 1950s that eventually merged into the Symphony Association. Silverberg emphasized that the organization was a temporary stop-gap and was not intended to take the place of the Symphony Association. It was there only to help the beleaguered and increasingly hungry musicians until times got better.

Times did not really get better until much later. The musicians played a few concerts as an orchestra, and a number of chamber concerts throughout the area. The chairman of the orchestra committee, Greg Berton, a bassist, wrote an article that was published in the October 17, 1986 *San Diego Union*. He was quoted as stating that contract negotiations were being "…held hostage by the tyrannical demands of an overpaid and, at least locally, highly over-rated music director …Maestro Atherton has repeatedly demonstrated his disregard for our lives and careers, most recently by refusing to relent in his desire for a completely lopsided power base…"

Berton meant that all power was in the hands of the music director and none at all in the hands of the musicians. Moreover, Berton noted that the power of the music director was apparently stronger than that of the Association because Atherton always got what he wanted. For example, the Association had leased a late model car for Atherton and replaced it after the car failed due to (it was alleged) Atherton's failure to maintain it routinely. The Association then replaced the car for the leasing firm and paid the bill originally sent to Atherton.

It must be pointed out that Atherton did not join in a media battle with the very angry musicians, whose complaints about the music director were literally shouted out. The maestro made few statements to the media during this entire situation, and none defending his position against all the allegations leveled by the musicians.

Atherton's salary in his new, three-year contract was reputed to be $237,000 for 1986-87, and $275,000 and $315,000 in the last two years. However, on his part, Atherton agreed to forego the salary increase he had been guaranteed for the 1986-87 season under the terms of his new contract. Moreover, prior to the never-performed 1987-88 season, upon his resignation, Atherton did not ask for any of the money due him under the terms of his contract. Meanwhile, during the summer of 1986, until the contract with the musicians expired on August 31, the musicians had been given only one paycheck but continued to play — including the Hollywood Bowl concert. Further, Atherton had also written a check for thirty thousand dollars, for funds to be distributed to the orchestra.

Sam Denov was a retired percussionist of the Chicago Symphony Orchestra who came to live in Escondido. He wrote an interesting letter to the editor in the February 4, 1987 *San Diego Union* in which he, too, noted the remarkable powers wielded by Atherton. He contrasted those powers against the supposed tyrannies of Toscanini and Reiner, with whom he had been very professionally familiar. Atherton sought control, he wrote, not only over the musicians but also over the marketing of the symphony as well as its programming. Denov commented, "Admittedly, these are areas that turned away more potential ticket buyers than any symphony orchestra can afford to lose." Denov pointed out his own background as "Founder and former Chairman of the International Conference of Symphony and Opera Musicians," which often caused him to serve as, "...a mediator who met with musicians and conductors whose relationships have been strained. Invariably, the only conductors that insisted upon having extraordinary powers were those who could not earn the respect of their musicians through their own artistic merits and personality..."

In contrast, Valerie Scher, music critic for the *San Diego Evening Tribune*, had written in that newspaper's March 5, 1986 edition, "...[M]usic director David Atherton has championed the orchestra's cause on radio and television, on the pages of newspapers and the podium of Symphony Hall." The Association had threatened to enter bankruptcy proceedings a few days before unless the community could raise over a million dollars, and, in response, according to Scher, Atherton, "...has shattered the traditional image of the hoity-toity maestro, aloof from the public and too lofty for money matters. By responding to the crisis with articulate assurance, and the intensity that marks his conducting, Atherton has become the symphony's most dynamic spokesman..." In her article, Scher emphasized how Atherton praised his musicians, saying that their morale was "incredibly high," despite their not having been paid for three weeks. Neither had Atherton. "What they are going through is enough to...bring tears to one's eyes," he told Scher. Atherton also commented, "The terrible irony is that we missed payroll within weeks of my arrival in 1981, and if we go under we will have missed payroll within weeks of my leaving."

The rage of the musicians against Atherton was increasingly ferocious and seemingly unstoppable, despite the impression one might gain from Valerie Scher's *Evening Tribune* article. A committee of San Diego Symphony musicians had corresponded with musicians in the Royal Liverpool Philharmonic, who, according to the local musicians, revealed that they, too, had major problems with Atherton and did not want him to remain as conductor. Atherton had been engaged as a guest conductor by the Los Angeles Philharmonic, whose members put up a backstage notice that behavior such as the conductor was known to have manifested in San Diego would not be tolerated in Los Angeles.

The San Diego musicians drew up a "Partial List of Abuses" committed by Atherton, similar to the earlier list presented to the union and to the board, but this time it was publicized. The list referred in part to Atherton's personal behavior and alleged intemperate remarks. Some of the many complaints in the list may be referred to here as examples. A child made noise during an El Cajon concert. Atherton stopped the orchestra in the midst of the music and told the parents to, "Take that child back to Mexico, or wherever you came from!" Referring to the entire orchestra, Atherton once commented, "It's a housewives' orchestra. Only fifteen people are qualified to play in it." One musician who had been outspoken for musicians' rights was told when she went to the podium to check on a score, "Get out of here, you fat cow!" In his own words, according to the musicians' grievances list, Atherton noted, "I go after the weak players to toughen them up."

Despite the grossly deteriorating relationship between orchestra and conductor, the performances in San Diego, at least before the crash of the 1985-86 season, continued to be greeted for the most part with critical enthusiasm. As an example, in a summarizing article in the October, 1985, *San Diego Magazine*, John Willett wrote, "If the essence of the San Diego Symphony Orchestra's 1985 performances could have been bottled like wine, we would have corked and stored a vintage year." Combined with praise for Andres Cardenes, the new, twenty-eight-year-old concertmaster, was an announcement of the hiring of a new assistant conductor, David Commanday. Richard Hickox had returned to London and a subsequent burgeoning career there, although his departure may well have been hastened by the serial financial crises of the orchestra. Commanday was the son of Robert Commanday, the distinguished music critic of the *San Francisco Chronicle*. Unfortunately, little chance was available to appraise his work due to the work stoppage.

The next month, Willett's *San Diego Magazine* column was headed, "The Symphony's Rolling: No More Blues in the Night." In retrospect, talk about miscalculation! Willett recounted the great assets of the orchestra, including Cardenes and Commanday, as well as the new principals and assistant principals he felt were upgrading the entire ensemble. Specific mention was made of Cynthia Phelps, who became acting principal violist. Now, following her leaving here for the Minnesota Orchestra's first viola chair, she is the possessor of that chair in the New York Philharmonic. She returns often to this city as a distinguished and welcome guest.

Shortly before the opening of the 1986-87 season, the Association made a final offer to the musicians of $18,933 per season, on a proposed 1986-87 budget of 6.5 million dollars, which it did not yet have. The musicians refused that offer and the season collapsed three weeks at a time. On January 12, 1987, the Association announced that as of that date it would cease operating its present orchestra. A week before that, there had been more talk of an impending bankruptcy, but the board wished to avoid that recourse. This conclusion to the financial crisis was viewed appropriately with alarm by many in the community who had grown weary of the repetitive crises that had characterized the history of the orchestra. The *San Diego Union* of January 13, 1987, ran a headline,

"San Diego Loses its Symphony," and many pages were devoted to the long and difficult story.

"Lessons in How to Destroy a Symphony in Order to Save It" was the title of a page-wide commentary by Wayne Cornelius, printed in the January 14, 1987 *San Diego Union*. Cornelius pulled no punches regarding his contemptuous attitude toward the board and management of the Symphony Association. "It would be difficult to think of another major orchestra in the United States that has been more ill-served by its management over the years than the San Diego Symphony. This adds up to a stunning failure of civic leadership, ironically coinciding with an era of unprecedented improvement in the...performance standards and artistic leadership...Under an internationally renowned music director and a marvelous new prize-winning concertmaster, the orchestra in its last season was continuing to make...major strides..."

When he wrote this, Cornelius was Gildred Professor of Political Science at UCSD. In spite of his academic credentials, I must argue just a bit with one of his theses. I have no argument at all with his condemnation of the boards extending back many years, including the years I served as a member of the board. I also agree heartily with his condemnation of the management inadequacies that had led the San Diego Symphony to become known as the graveyard of managers. But Cornelius went on to state, "In retrospect, the most spectacular imprudent action taken by the Symphony Association in recent years was not the much-maligned labor contract that expired last August, but the decision to purchase and elaborately refurbish the former Fox Theatre, *before* the symphony's finances could be stabilized, *before* its base of contributors could be broadened, and *before* its audience could be expanded to generate an adequate level of earned income." The italics are by Cornelius.

I agree with Cornelius that the purchase of the Fox was a terrific gamble by the Association. On the other hand, in my opinion, that gamble had to be taken. The Civic Theatre was getting to be more of a liability to the orchestra than a blessing. It was never their home. They could not even rehearse there except on the evenings prior to the concerts. The theatre's schedule was getting increasingly tight. Dates for good soloists that had to be made several years in advance by the orchestra were hard to come by due to the theatre's management needing to take any and all bookings that they could get. In those days, more traveling shows came through town, and the Civic Theatre was the favored place to present them. The opera also needed increasing amounts of time. All told, time crunches were becoming as common as financial crunches.

When the announcement was made that the Association was purchasing the Fox, I called Lou Cumming (whom I had not known before) and met him for lunch because I was very stimulated by the promise of that move. To me, it meant permanence. If the Association owned its own house, that meant that there would always be a place for the orchestra and its audience, even though at the time of that luncheon the labor problems were horrendous. In contributing funds to the purchase of the theatre, I felt that I was contributing to something that would be a prize asset for an organization that desperately needed one. Cornelius may have his points when he disparages the timing, but irons must be struck while hot. Who knew when and if the theatre would be available later? Deals must be made when property is available — and reasonable. Moreover, the fund-raising for the purchase of the theatre was a separate project from the fund-raising to relieve the orchestra's terrible financial situation. Donors for the purchase of a physical property asset were certainly more motivated to give than if they had been asked only to contribute to the operating deficits. It was a necessary move, as I saw it, and as I continue to see it. Certainly, listening to the orchestra — and guest orchestras — in Symphony Hall, especially now that a shell has been placed on the stage, and now that a beautiful, new wooden floor has been installed, demonstrates that it provides a far more resonant, bass-rich, generally "live" audition than at the Civic Theatre, which remains a sterling opera house.

The theatre had to be refurbished. It was quite run-down, and no management, no matter how inadequate, could expect people to come there unless the hall was made more comfortable and inviting. On the other hand, I have no argument at all with either the musicians or Cornelius when they cite the ridiculous, expensive, beaded curtain, still erroneously said by them to have been decided upon by Atherton, that allowed sound to be dispersed to the backstage and into the fly rafters. That money could and should have been invested at that time in a shell, which was not supplied until much later by one of Irwin and Joan Jacobs' generous grants. At least Cornelius grants that, "The opportunity to own its own hall at a fraction of the cost of building a new one was undoubtedly an attractive one."

Cornelius opined that the orchestra would be alive in January, 1987, if they had stayed at the Civic Theatre. I fear that this must be erroneous because there was absolutely no money to keep them there any more than to send them on a European tour. Cornelius is correct when he states that the elimination of the 1986-87 season cut off the flow of state and local public grant income, private donations and ticket sale income. However, those funds had always been inadequate, and it appears as if the orchestra would only have gone into crisis a little later that season with those funds. In fact, Herbert Solomon, upon his assumption of the presidency, went around unafraid and unashamed to buttonhole many who had given too little or nothing at all before, and he gradually eliminated the terrible cumulative deficit that had been a previously unsolvable burden to the organization. He has been criticized for not bringing back the orchestra before he had collected enough funds but many perceive that as a prudent move. His point of view is that he offered the orchestra musicians what he could afford after the deficit had been cleared, and to offer more (no matter how much they and he knew they deserved more) was to invite a repetition of the struggle that the orchestra had gone through for years. It would only create another cumulative deficit and invite more crises down the line.

Many other very critical op-ed columns appeared in the *Union-Tribune* about the handling of the symphony crisis, including one signed by the Orchestra Committee (Greg Berton, Arlen Fast, Rebekah Campbell, Randall Brinton and Warren Gref), printed on January 30,. Their anger is a given here, and quite understandable, when they wrote, "…The ultimate irony has transpired. The board remains in possession of a glowing new hall while the musicians and the public are locked out of the facility bought with their sweat and contributions — San Diego's version of the neutron bomb — forsaking life (the musicians who play in the symphony and those who come to hear them), but leaving the building standing." They were grateful for her attention and her efforts, but the musicians criticized the Mayor's recommendation for compulsory arbitration. The arbitrator would have been William McGill, appointed by the mayor. Via her plan, he also would become the *de facto* head of a new symphony management team, and because of that the musicians thought that the deck would be stacked against them.

Some of the musicians believed that the Association had deliberately set out to destroy the season because of the possible problems based upon the construction of Symphony Towers next door to Symphony Hall. The *Los Angeles Times'* Hilliard Harper, on November 12, 1986, wrote about that accusation and disputed it strongly, pointing out that the musicians had unanimously refused the Association's money offer, and the Association's acceptance of changes in audition and firing procedures. Harper wrote, referring to the raising of the grand tier seats, "If the board did not plan to keep the hall open this season, why did it spend $500 thousand on improving sight lines this year? If no season were planned, why did the Symphony Towers contractor arrange with the Fire Marshal for approval for fire exits for concerts? And why is the La Jolla Chamber Music Society still planning to present the first of five concerts in the hall this season?"

The struggle went on and on, and in the meantime the only band in town presenting a regular season was the visiting Los Angeles Philharmonic, which had cut its own series considerably. The conductors who appeared on their podium at the Civic Theatre all spoke about their sincere wishes that the problem affecting our symphony would be solved and that the orchestra should be revived in a healthy manner. Unfortunately, that was to take some time, and resulted in continued bitterness. When George Solti brought his Chicago Symphony to San Diego on the day after the announcement of the disbanding of the San Diego Symphony, he announced from the stage that he would come to conduct it if the San Diego Symphony went back to work. Unfortunately, no one seemed to hold him to that promise.

I believe that much bitterness has stayed in the collected feelings of many of the participants of the 1980s symphony wars, and even of the observers. Trust and confidence in the San Diego Symphony has never been a hallmark of its community acceptance, and the 1986-87 lockout was, perhaps, the most significant source to that time of accenting and continuing those lacks. The organization must always continue to combat that problem.

Meanwhile, Atherton's day in San Diego was long past due to the lockout and season cancellation, as well as by the terrible level of dissention centered about him. He resigned with two years left on his contract. He continued guest conducting — in the United States principally at the Met and San Francisco Opera. He did not return to England to assume a music directorship there, although he retained his post for a time as principal guest conductor of the BBC Symphony Orchestra there, and even resumed for a time his association with the London Sinfonietta, which he had founded twenty-two years before. Mainly, he remained a San Diego resident, with a Scripps Ranch home. Wealthy Hong Kong eventually beckoned, and he became music director of their developing orchestra for several years, even bringing them to Escondido for a touring concert. He also used his continuing San Diego connections to organize and conduct annual Mainly Mozart concerts at various local venues. These have been quite successful, financially and artistically. No one I have talked with has indicated any knowledge of his attending any San Diego Symphony Orchestra concerts since the orchestra reorganized after his directorship, although plans call for his being one of the guest conductors for the 2006-07 season, conducting an all-Mozart program.

Further insight into the Atherton era was provided by the very helpful and articulate former concertmaster of the orchestra, Andres Cardenes. He telephoned me in response to my request for an interview, and we spoke at some length on December 19, 2003. By and large, although he recognized the conductor's personality created difficulties with the musicians, he was defensive about but generally supportive of Atherton. Musically, especially, Atherton was described as brilliant, and as a disciplinarian — "Well, the results spoke for themselves. The orchestra played better than it had before."

Cardenes had been concertmaster of the Utah Symphony, where he was not particularly happy. When Atherton came to guest conduct, they talked.

"Atherton knew I was looking for something else, " and said that he was interested in hiring Cardenes as his own concertmaster. That eventually happened, although not before Cardenes came to San Diego to listen to the orchestra under Atherton. "I was really impressed with Atherton and by the orchestra and its discipline." Cardenes knew the reputation of the San Diego Symphony as a recurrently crisis-ridden ensemble with a long history of labor and management problems. However, Atherton assured him that those days were in the past, and that they were making great music in a more secure situation then. "I did notice a feeling of unrest within the orchestra when I came to play with them," and he also commented that he saw how much anger many of the musicians manifested regarding Atherton's discipline practices. "It was the way he disciplined…" Cardenes spoke about conductors like Atherton who were exceptionally tough on themselves and on the musicians in their quest for perfection. Even over the phone I could picture him shrugging his shoulders as he commented that toughness on the podium could be expected by experienced symphony players who had often played under better conductors. "It's your job as a symphony musician to play the way the conductor is trying to get you to play. It's what you do!"

In retrospect, Cardenes believes that he saw more and more the residuals of the past problems of the musicians and the orchestra compounding their responses to Atherton, as well as to the management. "There was lots of old, dirty laundry, and a long history of lots of bad feelings. Atherton was largely the recipient of this, too." Cardenes believed that the "…loudest screamers were people who really had no place else to go. When David resigned, I left, Jerry Folsom left, Cynthia Phelps left — we all had careers that we wanted to advance and we knew we could. The people who stayed felt stuck here because they feared that could not go anywhere else." He left about a month after Atherton's resignation. "I left mainly because I saw that there was not any artistic decision-making, just 'good riddance.' To me, that meant that the problems were going to continue and that the orchestra was going nowhere." Cardenes said that when he left San Diego, he had no wish to play in any other symphony orchestra. He had been turned off to orchestral playing. Instead, he continued playing chamber music and solo performances, and taught at the University of Michigan. However, Pittsburgh had wanted him as concertmaster for some time, and he finally gave in and went. He is very happy there. "Our orchestra has its problems. They all do, but we're making great music."

Continuing, he commented about both the musicians and the management, "The San Diego Symphony is the prime example of them versus us. Confrontation and divisiveness were the hallmarks of the way they operated, and they always shot themselves in the foot." Regarding Atherton himself, Cardenes opined, "David was not the easiest of men." He described Atherton's attitude as "character de-building," i. e., his process of dealing with the (often) same, inadequate players who kept causing the orchestra to rehearse the same passages over and over. "Those people were simply not doing their jobs…I guess I'd call him grating, not rude…"

In hindsight, if all the players in the San Diego Symphony had been of Cardenes's caliber, one must wonder if the attitude Atherton expressed toward his players would have been as it actually was here. It appears that the same kind of "us versus them" mentality described by Cardenes may have operated between the podium and the stands, as well as between the stands and management. One need only remember, however, the complaints from the Liverpool and Los Angeles Philharmonics about Atherton as a conductor, as well as the type of "character de-building" remarks he made to some of the musicians, as noted in their bill of details. Another however — and this is a big however — it is a tough job to build an orchestra and to instill not only discipline but stronger professionalism as well. Some great podium magicians, e. g., Bruno Walter and Pierre Monteux, did it with love and collegiality. Atherton had his own system. Unfortunately, it proved a difficult one to implement on a long-term basis and to allow a continued constructive relationship with the musicians..

On November 30, 1990, James Steinberg's column in the *San Diego Union* was, for the most part, a review of his interview in Hong Kong with David Atherton, when the conductor looked back at his earlier years in San Diego with varied points of view. Atherton commented, in that interview, that one of the most important facets of his music directorship of the Hong Kong Philharmonic was his sole authority to hire and fire musicians. In San Diego, of course, he was viewed as a tyrant by many of his players because of that same insistence. Steinberg noted that Atherton was still a strong critic of the situation that exists with unionized American orchestras, where auditions are often "blind," and a committee, including orchestra musicians as well as the conductor, collectively makes the hiring decisions. By the time of the San Diego Symphony's 1986 demise, Atherton's insistence that he alone be allowed to hire and fire was a "sore point" (Steinberg's relatively polite, mild term) during contract negotiations.

Atherton also reviewed his feelings about the financial debacle of the 1980s. He commented that the situation leading to the Symphony's collapse — bigger budgets, and the money spent in acquiring and renovating Symphony Hall — was, "…very unfortunate — a tragic miscalculation. At the time, the orchestra was really developing into something…The orchestra came within six weeks of making it all work, literally — and we'd really made some artistic strides… A decimation took place. The best people had no alternative but to walk away from it…"

In Hong Kong, according to the interview, the financial aspects of paying for the orchestra are handled differently than in the USA. "In San Diego, I had to spend all my waking hours raising the money. I remember the words, 'fiscal responsibility.' If you cut and cut and cut, you eventually reach the point where you break even, but at the same time you destroy the product... [In Hong Kong], you just concentrate on the music..."

Atherton continued, "Altogether in America, there is too much emphasis on box office. Some people have the attitude that you have to pander to popular taste. My attitude is that you have to have a quality product, and if you do that people are going to trust what you're doing and come..." Insofar as the role of the music director, Atherton expressed some strong opinions. "[He is]...a strange sort of figure. He's not a member of the orchestra or the board or of management. He doesn't have a vote, doesn't attend negotiations, doesn't attend union meetings. He doesn't have a voice..." Continuing, he opined that the result in San Diego in the later 1980s was, "...an orchestra blown out of the water by a combination of mismanagement, bungled union deals, demands from players that were unrealistic. I wasn't in on the negotiations, I made no public comments, I wasn't involved in the decision that the players be locked out..." Atherton's complaints about the system and mismanagement may have a strong margin of truth, but it appears that his attitudes remain unchanged. In no way did the Steinberg interview bring forth any acknowledgement by the conductor that he may have been his own worst enemy in a losing situation.

Regardless of the inglorious end to his music directorship here, and to the highly stressful effects of the crisis on the orchestra musicians, Atherton's tenure here must be considered at least an artistic success. The orchestra had never played anywhere near as well before, despite the increasing resentment felt toward him by most of the musicians. He sowed the seeds of his own destruction via his hostile and demeaning attitude toward his players that, with other allegations as well as difficult behavior, tore the orchestra apart. In his case, the financial crises were simply additions to the personal tensions that had adversely affected the relationship between music director and orchestra for several years. But even had Atherton been the world's best-loved maestro, he would not have had a chance of continuing with the orchestra during the cash flow desert and the labor dispute that followed. It would take the considerable efforts of the next music director to restore collegiality and good feelings between podium and players.

A significant comment by that next music director about his predecessor might be an appropriate way to end this otherwise sad chapter. In our November, 2003, interview, Yoav Talmi pointed out to me that, before he came to San Diego, he knew how much the orchestra resented Atherton. However, Talmi continued, Atherton had left him an orchestra that was very well disciplined, and polished far better than the other orchestra that had offered him more money — even after the significant interruption of their playing due to the lockout. "I came here because of the quality of the San Diego orchestra, and I owe that to Atherton." Kind words about one conductor from another are not often heard. They deserve repetition here. Atherton certainly deserves to hear them.

CHAPTER XIII

Back to Playing Music — Again

I t is most appropriate to have this chapter begin with an extensive quote from Herbert Solomon, the Association president who maintained his office through the terrible days of the work stoppage brought on by the 1980s financial debacle. The following is from his message to the Symphony patrons presented in the program booklet for the opening concert of the 1987-88 season, given auspiciously and courageously on Friday the 13, in November, 1987.

Solomon wrote, "…We — directors, staff, musicians, patrons and donors — have all learned much from the challenges of the past year. I am convinced that as a result of that experience our community now has a stronger and much more stable symphony.

"During the past year the Symphony has accomplished a number of significant steps designed to chart a new direction. 1. We raised $1.25 million in start-up funds last summer so that the orchestra could begin its winter season with no overdue obligations and no accumulated deficit for the first time in more than seven years; 2. We entered into a new two-year agreement with our musicians calling for increased weekly compensation in exchange for a substantially reduced season, achieving savings of $1 million during this season alone; 3. We adopted a balanced budget of $5.7 million, which is 25 percent less than actual 1985-86 expenditures; 4. We engaged as executive director Wesley O. Brustad, whose extraordinary professional skill and talent has been instrumental in many of these and other recent achievements; 5. We restructured the board of directors so that the daily operation of the orchestra is by the professional staff, allowing the board to concentrate on setting policy, raising money and providing for effective fiscal management; 6. We instituted a number of innovative concert series designed to involve wider audiences, and adjusted the major classical subscription series to include more of the traditional symphonic compositions; 7. We reduced the capital debt for the purchase and renovation of our magnificent Symphony Hall to $3 million after deducting remaining Hall contribution pledges; 8. We increased our endowment fund from a mere $13,000 to approximately $400,000; 9. We recently elected 18 outstanding new board members who, along with members elected during the preceding year and the nucleus of committed longer-term board members, provide the knowledge, experience and commitment necessary to provide the Symphony with the effective leadership it requires; and 10. We are engaged in future planning for appropriate artistic objectives and the financial requirements to achieve them.

The Mayor and City Council joined in the congratulations by proclaiming November 8 to 14, 1987, as "Welcome Back, San Diego Symphony Week." The proclamation also encouraged all San Diegans to support the orchestra through attendance and financial gifts. In the program booklet for the opening concert, Herbert Glass, a distinguished, nationally recognized music critic, wrote about the orchestra's difficult recent history and the present situation. He pointed out, "...Prospects are, if not precisely bright, then at least hopeful. With Wesley Brustad at the helm...there is considerable reason for optimism. The fourty-four-year-old Brustad has earned the reputation of a 'turnaround man' for ailing orchestras, credited with reviving both the Spokane Symphony...and the Los Angeles Chamber Orchestra..."

Glass also noted, "In rebuilding, one of the obvious question marks would normally be performing personnel. Yet, surprisingly, the orchestra will be basically the same ensemble that won so much praise when it was conducted by Britisher David Atherton who, pessimistic about the Symphony's future, departed earlier this year — before the revival of the orchestra's hopes. He is unlikely to return..."

In a lengthy June 2, 1987, *San Diego Union* article, several months before the 1987-88 season opening, Donald Dierks reviewed the prospects for the orchestra's future a little less glossily than Solomon would do in his article, or Glass in his. Dierks began by pointing out, "...the orchestra on stage is likely to be far different from the finely tuned ensemble of the 1985-86 season. Idle now for an entire season, it surely will be some time before the ensemble can recover its former technical edge and emotional balance. Add to that the loss of three excellent principals...plus a few other players who will not be available, and the costs of the labor dispute that silenced the orchestra take on real artistic significance..."

Andres Cardenes had left, eventually to become the concertmaster of the

Pittsburgh Symphony, and Jerry Folsom, principal horn, left for the Los Angeles Philharmonic where he soon became co-principal. Peter Rofé also joined the Los Angeles orchestra as co-principal bass. Karen Dirks and Igor Gruppman became acting co-concertmasters in San Diego. Dirks later changed her instrument and eventually led the viola section. Gruppman subsequently became concertmaster. John Lorge, who had been assistant principal horn, became acting principal and, subsequently, principal horn. The string section was reduced, however, to twenty-three violins, and nine each of violas and celli. There were seven basses. The reduction was principally due to the departure of temporary or acting musicians who had not been fully contracted during the 1985-86 season.

Dierks continued, "During the 1985-86 season, each subscription program was repeated four times at Symphony Hall, generally to audiences that filled less than one-quarter of the hall. That situation was psychologically discouraging for audiences and the orchestra...In the coming season...each program will be played only twice, and sometimes only once. The hall is likely to be fuller than in the past, and that is desirable; but orchestral improvement is directly connected with the amount of rehearsal and performance time logged...."

In his article, Dierks also commented on the orchestra's new salary schedule.

> "Of the 32 weeks of annual employment promised in the first year of the new, two-year contract, 19 weeks will be given over to subscription concerts, 12 weeks to a Summer Pops series, and one to paid vacation. Also in the first year, principal players will receive only $30 more a week than the basic $575 paid orchestra members. The importance of these figures is the effect they can have on the artistic quality of the orchestra. The former contract called for a minimum weekly pay of $470 for forty-five weeks of employment, but only 18 members of the 61 players under contract worked for the minimum scale. The rest had negotiated better salaries, with some principals said to be earning salaries two to three times above scale. It is likely that these players will be looking to move to other orchestras as positions become available. A maximum possible wage of $19,260 is not close to being competitive with salaries of other major symphonies. In the second year of the contract, the terms are somewhat better: players are guaranteed 37 weeks of employment at $625 per week, with an additional $40 for principals. But such wages will not attract top players here from other orchestras or keep key personnel already

in the orchestra. Brustad said that he intended to schedule all symphony concerts around…opera productions in order to allow the symphony players who played in the opera orchestra to earn extra money…"

Despite some of the less than enthusiastic premises of his article, Dierks concluded, "But at least there is hope. Come November, the orchestra will be back on stage at Symphony Hall doing what an orchestra should be doing — making music." That part of his prediction came true, thankfully in spades.

There was, of course, no musical director. Brustad had arranged for Fabio Mechetti to serve as resident conductor in the absence of a musical director. Mechetti was a native of Brazil who came to the United States to study at Julliard, where he earned his master's degree in conducting in 1984. Brustad knew Mechetti well as the former assistant conductor of the Spokane Symphony, where his children's concerts programming won the National Endowment for the Arts award in 1985 for best educational programming in the United States. Mechetti left Spokane to become the Exxon/Arts Endowment Conductor of the National Symphony Orchestra in Washington, D. C., where he led the orchestra in many concerts. He had also guest-conducted the Rochester Philharmonic Orchestra, as well as smaller orchestras in Boise, Idaho, and Arlington, Virginia.

Mechetti was scheduled to conduct all the San Diego Young People's concerts, several other special concerts and a pair of the regular classical concert series. Fourteen pairs of "Ovation Series" concerts were scheduled, a reduction from the 1985-86 season's scheduled eighteen. Each pair was to be under the direction of a single guest conductor, some of whom were to be considered as candidates for the San Diego musical directorship.

Aside from Mechetti, the conductors scheduled were Lawrence Leighton-Smith, music director of the Louisville Symphony; Daniel Lewis, Director of Conducting Studies at the University of Southern California, and an old friend of the San Diego orchestra, which he had once, long before, served as concertmaster; Bernhard Klee, conductor of several European orchestras; Maxim Shostakovich, son of the eminent composer, and the conductor of the New Orleans Symphony; Sixten Ehrling, a noted Swedish conductor; Andrew Litton, an assistant conductor in Washington with the National Symphony, and soon to become director of the Dallas Symphony; Hugh Wolff, conductor of the New Jersey Symphony; Gerhard Zimmerman, conductor of the North Carolina Symphony as well as the Canton, Ohio, orchestra; Guido-Ajmone-Marsan, music director of the Essen, Germany, opera; Yoel Levi, a busy guest conductor with many orchestras, who would soon take over the Atlanta Symphony from an ailing Robert Shaw; Gunther Schiller, a famed composer-conductor and music educator; and Theo Alcantara, conductor of the Phoenix Symphony, and familiar to San Diegans for his work with the local opera company. One other scheduled guest conductor, Yoav Talmi, was so unknown to most of the patrons as well as to the administration that his name was misspelled in the program booklet for the opening concert of the season.

Lawrence Leighton-Smith conducted the opening concert of the revived orchestra, according to Donald Dierks, "...before a capacity audience of well-wishers eager to show their support for the musicians and their enthusiasm for the occasion. The evening was something like a get-together for a friend who has recovered from a very serious illness..." The critic did not like the performances very much, however, although he understood the tentativeness of the playing as part of the residue of the long layoff. The next concert was conducted by Daniel Lewis, and Dierks reviewed it much more positively than he had the earlier performance. The orchestra played Beethoven's "Eroica" Symphony, and Dierks noted, "The performance was crisp and tight in the outer movements, and appropriately brooding and funereal in the second movement...[M]uch more often than not the reading did credit to both conductor and orchestra," so it was becoming apparent that things were progressing.

However, Valerie Scher, in the November 30, 1987, *Evening Tribune*, began her review of a concert of four of Bach's Brandenburg Concerti, conducted by Mechetti, announcing, "Barely three weeks into its new season and the San Diego Symphony is experiencing the same old attendance problems. Yesterday afternoon's presentation...filled only 600 to 800 of the 2,200 or so seats in Symphony Hall..." The next concert was conducted by Yoav Talmi. It was his debut with the orchestra. The December 5, 1987, *San Diego Union* review by Donald Dierks began,

> "At Symphony Hall last night, there were times, not many, but reassuring times, nonetheless, when the San Diego Symphony sounded something like its old self, like the way it played before failed contract negotiations shut it down for 18 months. Under Yoav Talmi, a young Israeli conductor who seems well on his way to establishing a prominent career, the concert got off to a reasonably promising start. Not that one could get very excited about Jean Sibelius's folksy and rather trite 'Karelia' Suite, Opus 11...This suite does not have any depth of musical thought to speak of, so Talmi's interpretation of it could not go any farther than its inherent message of Finnish nostalgia. Still, he did manage to set good tempos, bring out colors and employ an expressive range of dynamics..." The orches-

tra's major contribution to the evening was the Dvorak Eighth Symphony, the performance of which Dierks felt was not up to good standards due to the layoff. "The strings sounded thin and ragged, often the result of playing out of tune and without unified bowing. Bad intonation is always shocking in a professional orchestra, but sloppy bowing violates elementary ensemble discipline…Yet, with this said, and letting a few disturbing examples stand for many, there were flashes of former days. As for Talmi's conducting, it could be admired unreservedly for its technical command and expressive content."

The audience was the major issue in Dierks' next review, when he began, in the January 15, 1988, *San Diego Union* review, "If all the San Diegans who pay lip service to the importance of a symphony orchestra would attend a couple of concerts each season, we would not be in danger of losing the San Diego Symphony — for good..,.[M]ake no mistake, if box-office revenues do not increase, there is bound to be another accumulated deficit at the end of the season that could make this the last season that America's finest city will have an orchestra. The situation is a serious one…"

The conductor of that and the next series of programs was Bernhard Klee, who made a splendid impression on the orchestra, critics and audience. Dierks made an interesting, highly critical observation of Klee, however, worth repeating here. "One thing about Klee the conductor — that has nothing to do with his conducting — I found him annoying. After the concertos, this week and last, he remained on the podium applauding the soloist through all the curtain calls. Even if the audience didn't want to applaud any more, it could hardly stop until Klee chose to leave the stage. And it's silly for conductors and players to applaud a soloist, as if the soloist were the whole show. They, after all, had important parts of their own to play, so the impression is left that they are applauding themselves." Despite this caveat, Klee became an early front-runner for the position of next music director in San Diego. In her own review in the *Evening Tribune* of January 23, 1988, Valerie Scher began, "If Bernhard Klee's name isn't already on the San Diego Symphony's list of candidates for the post of music director, it should be." Later that year, Maestro Klee announced that he was not a candidate, although he returned to guest conduct during the next season..

Maxim Shostakovich was the next guest conductor. David Gregson wrote the January 29, 1988, *San Diego Union* review of his concert, summarizing it with, "The orchestra's various sections responded to the conductor with some fine playing, all the strings sounding better than at almost any time within recent memory." The eminent Swedish conductor, Sixten Ehrling followed. In his

February 6, 1988, *San Diego Union* review, Donald Dierks noted, "...an extraordinarily fine performance of the Sibelius Symphony No. 1 in E minor...[I]t would hardly be an exaggeration to say that the performance was stunning..." And so it went, with guesses and guests.

On March 8, 1988, in the *Evening Tribune*, Valerie Scher reported the names of thirteen conductors confirmed as "the list" by Symphony officials, and complained that no familiar names and no established stars were among them. She named Andrew Litton, Guido Ajmone-Marsan, Yoav Talmi (who had just brought his Israel Chamber Orchestra to the East County Performing Arts Center for a very well-received tour concert), Okku Kamu, Hermann Michael, Donato Renzetti, Reinhard Peters, Gustav Kuhn, Walter Weller, Leopold Hager, Christof Perick, Klaus Peter Seibel and Janos Furst. Only some of them, however, had been scheduled to guest conduct the orchestra during the 1987-88 and 1988-89 seasons. Those who were not scheduled were going to be interviewed as well as observed in Europe during a tour taken by Wes Brustad and Dr. Warren Kessler, chairman of the conductor selection committee.

In March, the two flew to Europe and, equipped with color photos of Symphony Hall and tapes of some of the orchestra's performances, visited ten cities. The Association paid the $11,000 airfare for both, according to Valerie Scher's June 24, 1988 *Evening Tribune* story. Brustad's expenses were also paid by the Association; Kessler paid his own daily expenses. According to Kessler, the trip was "...mandatory. Not only did we meet with all the guys on our list and some major agents, we told them that the San Diego Symphony is alive and strong. They didn't realize the tremendous strides we've made since we were silent for a season..." In her article, Scher also noted that the decline of the American dollar has led to the symphony being able to buy less in terms of conducting talent, "And snobbery persists, especially among the more established European maestros."

The announcement of "the list" led directly to the resignation of Fabio Mechetti as resident conductor and musical advisor of the San Diego Symphony Orchestra. "There's no hard feelings," he was quoted as saying. "It's just a question of professional different paths." His own path was simply not chosen to be the same path of the expected candidates for the music directorship. He had applied for the position but was advised that he was not going to be considered. His name, however, should be remembered with some good feelings by San Diego Symphony listeners. He had organized and supervised auditions, filled some vacancies and had worked with the orchestra in rehearsals and youth concerts, as well as in one pair of subscription concerts.

Despite the dire warnings provided earlier by Donald Dierks about the expected lack of musicians to play in the orchestra due to the low salary schedule, the February, 1988 auditions had attracted more than a hundred players from around the country. Principals selected (some of whom remained with the orchestra even after the financial debacle and subsequent bankruptcy of the later 1990s, included Heather Buchman, principal trombone, and Calvin Price, principal trumpet, as well as Nick Grant, who became assistant concertmaster (seated next to Igor Gruppman, then acting concertmaster, who subsequently became concertmaster). Mechetti eventually became associate conductor of the Syracuse Symphony Orchestra.

Murry Sidlin took Fabio Mechetti's place as leader of the youth concerts, and eventually developed an extensive program of special, family-oriented, popular classic-type programs that have remained successful to this day. A graduate of Baltimore's Peabody Conservatory, he developed a successful series of children's concerts with the Baltimore Symphony and with Washington, D. C.'s National Symphony. He also organized and hosted a prize-winning TV series for children, premiered in 1977, "Music is…" He soon became a popular favorite in San Diego, as well as maintaining a post for a number of years as resident conductor in Portland, Oregon.

The parade of guest conductor/possible candidates continued with Hugh Wolff, lauded for the musicality of his performances but criticized heavily for the excessive physicality of his conducting, found by the critics to be distracting. As Valerie Scher noted in the March 25, 1988, *Evening Tribune*, "As a conductor, Wolff has become ever more demonstrative. Physically, that is. The lanky, red-haired Harvard graduate…bends, twists, jabs and bounces. Some gestures are pure Leonard Bernstein; others belong in Jane Fonda's workouts…"

Gerhard Zimmerman was rather peremptorily dismissed by the critics in April, 1988. Later that month Guido Ajmone-Marsan received fairly good, but not particularly enthusiastic reviews Yoel Levi, later to take a different podium as Atlanta's music director, led Stravinsky's Symphony in Three Movements. In his April 22, 1988 review in the *San Diego Union*, Donald Dierks referred to a "…moderately good, but not a fine reading." David Gregson gave a poor review to Gunther Schuller, more widely-known as a composer and music educator than as a conductor. "In brief, Schuller's conducting was just plain dull." Theo Alcantara led the orchestra in its final subscription pair of the season, and both Donald Dierks and Valerie Scher were rather dismissive in their May 21, 1988 reviews. To quote Scher, "His florid and rather nervously athletic conducting style" made him a distraction to watch, "…something that could be partially forgiven if better results had been produced…"

Meanwhile, back at the Symphony's offices, Lynn Harrell, the eminent cellist, had been named on May 12 as music advisor to the Symphony Association. He was set to choose repertory, guest conductors and soloists (at least, those not already contracted), and participate in auditioning new players. Harrell, in fact, supervised the selection of Igor Gruppman as sole concertmaster, and was also influential in the subsequent hiring of Eric Kim as first cellist. It was understood that Harrell was not in the running for the position of music director. However, his open-ended contract would allow him to maintain his position until a new music director would be chosen. In addition to his widespread, active concert schedule, Harrell was continuing to serve as artistic administrator of the Los Angeles Philharmonic Institute, a six-week summer program for future symphony musicians.

During all of the season's excitement centering about a selection of a music director, as well as the very presence of the San Diego Symphony Orchestra on stage again, little was publicized about the financial status of the Association. The budget had called for a sixty percent attendance during the subscription series, and that was at least approached. The *Radiothon*, held in May, 1988, was a disaster. The goal had been set at $80,000, but it grossed only $43,000. After expenses, the Association netted only $15,000. The previous *Radiothon* had been held in 1986, and that raised only $52,000, less than half of the 1985 total of more than $130,000. Clearly, considerable suspicion about the financial stability of the Association clouded the minds of many possible donors. Meanwhile, Brustad announced plans for the forthcoming 1988-89 season, enlarged to thirty-seven weeks from the 1987-88 season's thirty-two. The increase was inherent in the orchestra's labor contract with the musicians. The winter season was set to last four weeks longer than the 1987-88 season. Most significant was the budget, proposed at about $7 million, a rise from the 1987-88 season's $5.7 million. That, according to Brustad, was admitted to be, "A real stretch."

"Contrary to speculation, innuendo, gossip and everything else, I am happy to tell you our management is not in upheaval," was Brustad's optimistic, major statement. "We are not in administrative chaos...or on the verge of financial collapse. As a matter of fact, I think things are looking pretty good." The targeted goal of $2 million in contributions was on its way, he said, because $1.6 million had already been raised. The 1988 summer "Pops" series had already generated over $550,000 in ticket revenue.

The summer programs were generally far lighter than they had been in the past, with mainly pop star soloists and little actual playing by the Symphony, other than from the prepared "charts" to accompany the solo singers or musicians. Mission Bay's Hospitality Point was a favored location by many, although the take-off pattern from Lindbergh Field was a distraction — albeit considerably less of one than Balboa Park Bowl had provided.

"The San Diego Symphony's pops season is usually a money maker that helps underwrite the rest of the year's programming, but this summer it is running in the red." So began a July 20, 1988, *San Diego Union* article by Christopher Reynolds. Figures were given that indicated that the season had attracted only 26,735 listeners during its first third, whereas in 1986 there had been 44,735 seats sold by the same time. Wes Brustad was unable to provide any reason for the downturn The pops income was showing only about sixty percent of the estimated figures. In her article in the *Evening Tribune* the following night, Valerie Scher was critical of Brustad's pops programming, that has, "…switched to slick, pre-packaged acts such as the Dukes of Dixieland, The McLain Family Band and Rita Moreno. Though he says, 'the fan mail is unbelievable — people are having a great time' — statistics suggest that patrons are reluctant to accept the new emphasis."

In the end, the 1988 pops season ended $500,000 short of the set goal of $1.6 million. According to Valerie Scher, in the September 8, 1988, *Evening Tribune*, "What makes the red ink unsettling is that it recalls the bad, old days. The 1982 summer pops season was cancelled rather than risk running a deficit to the tune of $535,000. The series was reborn in 1983 at Mission Bay's Hospitality Point in the hope (largely unfulfilled) that it would break even, if not make at least a little money for the orchestra." In her opinion, the last pops concert was the best, due in great part to the conducting and emceeing of Murry Sidlin. David Gregson, who also reviewed that concert for the September 8, 1988, *San Diego Union*, was also excited about Sidlin. He began, "Are you sitting down? Are you ready for a San Diego Symphony SummerPops concert that was actually very good? At times even excellent? Imagine a young Leonard Bernstein, with all that fire and intellect, but without all the self-aggrandizement and overdone podium theatrics…That man is Murry Sidlin, a stunning young conductor…who has just now catapulted the SummerPops far beyond its usual level of mediocrity." SummerPops, spelled in that manner, had become the new logo for the series, but it had not helped a great deal.

A week later, all of the fears associated with the financial situation were eased. Christopher Reynolds' September 14, 1988, *San Diego Union* article was headlined, "Donations Put Symphony in the Black: Private Gifts Balance Ticket Sales Shortfalls." The gifts deserved headlines. Herb Solomon, who had been made board chairman (a newly created position) after his term was completed as president (Elsie Weston took his place as president), announced, "Our number one objective was to establish financial stability. This…demonstrates that considerable progress has been made." The key donors in the successful fund-raising campaign were Ellen Revelle and Judson Grosvenor, both board members, as well as Helen K. Copley, publisher of the *San Diego Union* and *Evening Tribune*. Solomon and Wes Brustad noted that the campaign began in earnest in August. A key donation was a joint $250,000 challenge grant by Grosvenor and Revelle, and that quickly led to pledges from a number of others, including Mrs. Copley, who contributed $100,000. The James S. Copley Foundation put up another $100,000. Moreover, aside from Grosvenor and Revelle, the entire board provided about $800,000 of their own or their firms' money. The budget was balanced.

Throughout the summer and early fall of 1988, Valerie Scher continued running a series of columns maintaining considerable interest and suspense about the race for the San Diego podium. She described the Association's secrecy about their choices and considerations, but she revealed that the salary of the conductor designate, whoever he would be, would be in the neighborhood of $200,000 annually. Yoav Talmi, one of the favorites for the job, was given considerable space in her columns because, as she noted, he was the only candidate willing to speak freely about his wish for the job and his ideas about it.

"My discussions with the symphony are still at the general level, " he said. "Wes has checked about my willingness, my general ideas, my view of what could be done…" As Scher described him, "Compact and curly-haired, with a musical assurance at once suave and expressive, Talmi is a Julliard graduate who has conducted everything from the Los Angeles Chamber Orchestra to the Berlin Philharmonic (once replacing an ailing maestro on only a few hours notice.)" She described the conductor's tilt away from living in Israel to the United States. She also asked him his goals as a San Diego maestro. "This won't sound very original," he replied, "But I'd like the orchestra to be really good. Have it work with wonderful guest conductors and soloists. Have it tour and make records. Then it could be a source of pride, a treasure for San Diego…"

Christof Perick was also given considerable column space, as was Hermann Michael. However, neither of these were actually interviewed. As for Leopold Hager, only his blurb in the program brochure was quoted, describing him as, "…one of the most internationally renowned conductors of our time," which, according to Scher, "will doubtless make many concertgoers wonder why they've never heard of him…" Scher noted that one highly regarded European guest conductor destroyed his chances here by going out to lunch and returning fifteen minutes late for a rehearsal. Another candidate was described as speaking English so poorly that it was always necessary for him to be accompanied by a translator. "Nor are conductors' personal lives immune to scrutiny. Problems with drugs, alcohol, potentially embarrassing romantic entanglements — all come under consideration. 'Every day I get a call about somebody — I sometimes feel like I'm running a detective agency,' Brustad says with a chuckle. 'We need to know if they do weird things in the night. Character and stability are factors along with musical abilities…'"

The 1988-89 season opened on October 14, 1988, with Leopold Hager on the podium. In the next day's *San Diego Union*, Donald Dierks described the orchestra's playing of a Mozart symphony under Hager as, "Admirable. The string tone was as refined as it has ever been at its best…" He also praised Hager's post-intermission conducting of the Tchaikovsky Fourth Symphony. In contrast, Scher, in the *Evening Tribune*, said, "Hager is undeniably proficient, blessed with admirable energy and a formidable memory. He's just not very interesting."

Christof Perick, who conducted the second pair of concerts, was also praised warmly by Dierks, as was Talmi, who conducted the third set. In the October 29, 1988 *Evening Tribune*, Valerie Scher was far more expressive in her praise of the Israeli conductor. "His abilities on the podium were much in evidence last night in a French and German program that found him animated and expressive, with an interpretative conviction that often inspired the orchestra." Bernhard Klee returned for a pair of concerts, but he had already distanced himself from the competition. Kees Bakels conducted de Falla and Saint-Saens and, according to Dierks, made a hit.

At the beginning of 1989, Christopher Reynolds wrote a *San Diego Union* article that reviewed what had been described by Mayor Susan Golding as, "The Year of the Arts." In that January 1, 1989, column, he quoted Wes Brustad. "It certainly has been a pretty good year, so let's give her credit. Why not? It certainly raised everybody's consciousness level." Regarding his own organization, Brustad related, "It went terrific. Nobody thought we'd make it. Not only did we make it, we ended the year with a modest surplus. And in our orchestra we started with fifteen vacancies, and are now down to seven. We've made incredible artistic progress and incredible financial progress."

The first San Diego Symphony program of the year also received up-beat comments from David Gregson in his January 6, 1989 *Union* review. Hermann Michael conducted Bartok's Concerto for Orchestra, and it was described as, "… a fine performance." The underside was another reference to poor attendance. Full houses, however, were at Robert Shaw's renditions of the Beethoven Ninth Symphony. In the January 14, 1989, *San Diego Union*, Donald Dierks wrote, "The orchestra's response to his leadership was positive. The musicians played with precision and finesse. The woodwinds and brass have seldom sounded better, and the string choir turned in one of its best performances this season." Talmi returned to lead the orchestra's January 26 and 27, 1989, performances. Valerie Scher, reviewing the concert in the *Evening Tribune*, described the concert as, "…dinner music without the dinner." She felt that the program lacked beef, and commented that the conductor had led, "…a similarly quirky program here in October…Is this a trend, or what? Let us hope not…" The January program presented a Rossini overture, the Mendelssohn "Italian" Symphony, a Rameau ballet suite, and the Ravel Suites Nos. 1 and 2 from *Daphnis et Chloe*. Scher opined,

"Aside from his peculiarities in programming, Talmi is an appealing candidate for San Diego Symphony music director. Exacting yet expressive, he exhibits a winning enthusiasm for the music he performs, no matter how superficial it may be. The orchestra responds well to him, as it did last night…"

Talmi returned in March, following several appearances by Russian or Russian émigré conductors who had been invited as part of a Russian Arts Festival, sponsored by several of the city's arts organizations. In the March 20, 1989, *San Diego Union*, David Gregson reviewed the Talmi performance of the Dvorak "New World" Symphony, comparing it to the famed Toscanini recording. Although he noted that Talmi did not eradicate memories of Toscanini, his reading had plenty of drama, and the orchestra played well and evenly throughout all its sections. "Under Talmi, the symphony admirably met all challenges in a highly pleasing, vigorously paced performance." In contrast, the concert conducted by Hans Graf, another candidate, was found to be exceedingly boring, according to David Gregson, in the April 8, 1989, *Union.*

With the way the reviews were going, as well as the leaked gossip from musicians and symphony staff, it came as no real surprise that Yoav Talmi was selected to become music director. The announcement was made on April 25, 1989, three days prior to his forty-sixth birthday. He spoke with Valerie Scher via telephone from his home in Israel, and told her, "I am very, very happy. Some of the financial offers I received from other orchestras were better than the one from San Diego. But over the last year and a half I have developed a warm relationship with the musicians and management in San Diego. I do love this orchestra. It has wonderful potential. And the city is a wonderful place to work and live." He was given a three-year contract at an undisclosed salary, beginning with the 1990-91 season. His plan was to conduct ten pairs of concerts initially, and then gradually increase that number.

Talmi said, "I knew from my first visit that I would be considered for a permanent appointment. I was led to believe that I was a strong candidate, but it was only in the last two weeks that we got down to serious negotiations." He has scheduled himself to conduct the opening concerts of the 1989-90 series, and has programmed the Mahler Fifth Symphony for those evenings. He will conduct only three other subscription weeks during that season, while music director designate. He believes that being in front of the orchestra for ten weeks after becoming the actual music director is enough, especially if he devotes several more weeks here to administrative work. "It is a delicate matter to know just how much time to spend with an orchestra, but for me something about fifteen weeks seems about right. Some conductors of American orchestras may not agree with me, but it may be that they give too much time, and their musicia may get bored. Of course, the total commitment of George Szell in Cleve' and Eugene Ormandy in Philadelphia are exceptions." Talmi's comments make an interesting contrast to the schedule planned by his predecessor when his contract was signed. Atherton determined to spend even less time in San Diego, but insisted that his limited expenditure of time here would provide great results because of the manner in which he would manage his time and energies.

That difference was only one of the major differences between Talmi and his predecessor. In the community, it seemed as if a sigh of relief was palpable, if not audible. The *San Diego Union* editorialized about the Symphony's choice in its April 30, 1989, issue.

> "The appointment of Israeli conductor Yoav Talmi as director of the San Diego Symphony Orchestra is the culmination of a musical renaissance in this city. And we have another confirmation of the leadership of Herbert J. Solomon, Chairman of the symphony's board of directors, during the orchestra's continuing recovery from financial ruin.

> "...[T]he orchestra opened its 1988-89 season with its account books in the black, thanks to the generous support of San Diegans who contributed $2.4 million to the budget. Of that amount, one third was donated by the symphony's board of directors.

> "In its search for a music director, the symphony wisely sought the opinions of the orchestra's musicians, who completed survey forms after every performance by a guest conductor. The 46 year-old Israeli maestro rated tops with musicians as well as with management. Maestro Talmi's outstanding record proclaims his achievements...During his three-year tenure with the San Diego Symphony Orchestra, he will retain his post as music director of the New Israeli Opera.

> "He will inherit well-trained, disciplined musicians who are capable of greater achievements. In Mr. Talmi's words, 'This is an orchestra that...can really go places.' Undoubtedly it will."

CHAPTER XIV

The Talmi Era: From "The Golden Age" to Shattering Silence

Yoav Talmi was conductor of the Israel Chamber Orchestra. He had begun to tour widely with them, as well as to record with them on the prestigious DGG label. He also led the New Israel Opera in Tel Aviv. Born and reared in Israel, Talmi was a graduate of the Rubin Music Academy in Tel Aviv, as well as the Julliard School in New York. There, he studied composition further, as well as conducting with Jean Morel and others. After spending some more time at Juilliard teaching harmony and theory, following his receipt of an M. A. with distinction, he became Jorge Mester's assistant conductor for the Louisville Philharmonic. Part of his duties there were run-out concerts to small Kentucky communities, one of which was named London. Talmi said, "I sent a cable to my parents in Israel — something like, 'Just made highly successful debut in London...'"

He won the Koussevitzky Prize in Conducting at Tanglewood in 1969, and subsequently returned to a burgeoning guest conducting career in Europe. In 1973, he won the Rupert Conducting Competition in London. Talmi became the music director of the Gelders Orchestra in Arnhem, Holland, in 1974, and stayed in that position for six years. He also served as principal guest conductor of the Munich Philharmonic before assuming his position in 1984 as music director of the Israel Chamber Orchestra and, in 1985, of the New Israeli Opera as well.

He guest-conducted the Berlin Philharmonic and the Amsterdam *Concertgebouw* Orchestras, as well as the French National Orchestra, and the Tokyo and Vienna Symphony Orchestras. In North America he guest conducted the Detroit, St. Louis, Houston, Dallas, Indianapolis, Seattle and Vancouver Symphonies, as well as the New York Chamber Symphony, the Los Angeles Chamber Orchestra and the Ottawa National Arts Center Orchestra. He also conducted many European radio symphony orchestras and appeared at the Aspen, Waterloo, Helsinki and Israel Festivals. Aside from the DGG recordings noted above, he recorded the completed version of the Bruckner Ninth Symphony for Chandos Records,

Yoav Talmi. *Photo courtesy San Diego Symphony.*

with the Oslo Philharmonic Orchestra, for which he was awarded the *Grand Prix du Disque* in 1987.

Following his initial guest appearance in San Diego, he was named music director designate of the orchestra in 1989, and conducted his first season as music director in 1990-91. He was forty-six years old, married to a distinguished concert flutist, Er'ella Talmi, with whom he often gave joint recitals, and a father to two college age children. The family set up housekeeping in a Hillcrest condominium.

When he returned after a several year absence to guest-conduct the San Diego Symphony in October/November, 2003, Talmi and I were able to talk at length about his experiences as music director with the orchestra. I asked him my standard question asked of every available ex-music director, "Why in the world did you decide to come here, with all the difficult history that you must have known about the orchestra and the management?" He responded, "The San Diego Symphony Orchestra provided an opportunity to a conductor who had something to give. I came as a guest in 1987 and did the Dvorak Eighth Symphony. I was a candidate, along with Ling, Hans Graf and Christof Perick. I wanted a USA position. I had left Arnhem and Munich four years before in order to return to Israel. We did great things with the Israel Chamber Orchestra. We toured, recorded and did well. I became a candidate in Indianapolis, Phoenix and San Diego. Phoenix offered me more money and more perks, but I took San Diego because it was a much better orchestra. I knew I'd be able to go places with it. The rapport with the players was great. There was just a great attitude..."

In summary, Talmi commented, "It was all wonderful until the financial problems started. Ellen Revelle was a savior at times, giving hundreds of thousands of dollars. But the musicians hated the board, and I was always in the middle."

Talmi opened his initial season as music director designate on October 19, 1989. In the next day's *San Diego Union*, Donald Dierks gave the entire evening one of the most favorable reviews he had ever provided. He began, "With recently appointed music-director designate Yoav Talmi on the podium, the San Diego Symphony opened its Ovation Series. The orchestra, the conductor, the soloist and the program all proved to be highly deserving of that appellation, for it was an exquisite evening. From the onset, Talmi had full command of the orchestra…"

In a subsequent *San Diego Union* column of November 4, 1989, Dierks reported that Yoav Talmi had been conducting in Oslo over the previous week. He wrote that, "Positive responses to Yoav Talmi, the conductor designate of the San Diego Symphony, have been pervasive here. But here is not the only place. In Oslo, Norway, Idar Karevold, writing in the daily *Aftenposten* about a recent concert Talmi led there, said, 'Yoav Talmi unfolded as a masterly orchestral conductor. His insight into the material and his intense power to communicate, contributed in giving drive and lift to the Saint-Saens Third Symphony. The concert hall was full to capacity and the response of the public enormous…'" Dierks continued with another Oslo review, this time by the critic of the *Oslo Dagbladet*, who wrote, "Talmi has previously made himself noteworthy in the large format of Mahler and Bruckner, with qualities which could be heard in the Saint-Saens Symphony Number 3. But in Grieg's miniatures, he showed how no task is too small not to be a starting point for remarkable music-making, when the conductor is great enough."

Christian Hertzog, in the December 7, 1990, *Evening Tribune*, reviewed a Talmi program. Headlined, "Symphony Sounds Sensational," Hertzog began his review, "The San Diego Symphony concert last night probably left many regular patrons wondering just what Yoav Talmi and the musicians have done to sound so good… Whatever the answer, the San Diego Symphony is playing as well as it did during its glory years under David Atherton. The musicians appear to be comfortable with, and responsive to Talmi's musical judgments. The most marked feature of Talmi's approach to scores is his sense of long-term pacing. Without sacrificing details, Talmi conveys the broad sweep of a piece, admirably rendering large-scale formal structures as clearly as possible…"

A few days later, the *San Diego Union* reported that the distinguished Norwegian composer, Arne Nordheim, had attended a concert of the Oslo Philharmonic Orchestra, guest-conducted by Talmi, who had become a frequent visitor on that podium. After the concert, Nordheim contacted the orchestra's management and insisted that Talmi, and only Talmi, should conduct the Oslo orchestra in the first CD recording of two of his most important, new works. One of them had been commissioned by the Amsterdam *Concertgebouw*

Orchestra, and the other was a new cello concerto commissioned by Mstislav Rostropovich. Talmi, at the time of the writing of the column, was guest conducting the New Japan Philharmonic Orchestra on a two-week tour of Japan. He was scheduled to return to Norway in January, 1991, to conduct the Bergen Symphony, and planned to set aside a few days to rehearse the Oslo orchestra in the pieces and record them. High times, indeed, for the new conductor of the San Diego Symphony and, judging from the reviews, for the San Diego orchestra as well.

The 1989-90 season was not only the debut season of Yoav Talmi as music director designate. It also offered an old friend, Robert Shaw, as principal guest conductor. When Talmi had been interviewed upon accepting the music directorship, he told Donald Dierks, "What will contribute greatly to leading the San Diego Symphony in directions I want it to take, will be the appointment of a permanent guest conductor who will conduct a number of weeks each season when I am not there. This will be a conductor in whom I have complete confidence — we must have completely similar artistic points of view." Dierks commented in that April 26, 1989, *San Diego Union* article that Talmi was not at liberty then to reveal the name of his choice as permanent guest conductor, but he said that negotiations were under way, and that an announcement could be made in several weeks. Shaw was a natural choice.

Robert Shaw, of course, had been extraordinarily influential in developing the San Diego Symphony in the 1950s, but he had not returned to conduct the orchestra after that, with the single exception of his guest appearance for the Beethoven Ninth a couple of years before, until his new appointment as principal guest. He had just announced his retirement as music director of the Atlanta Symphony, an orchestra he had honed beautifully. With it, he and they had won a large number of Grammy awards for their recorded performances. In Valerie Scher's *Evening Tribune* review of his January 13, 1989, Beethoven Ninth Symphony concert, she noted that, "Stocky and silver-haired at 72, Shaw has made inevitable concessions to age in his somewhat stiff conducting gestures, though none could doubt his authority. He's a *paterfamilias* on the podium, inspiring affection and respect..."

Although Shaw's chronic cardiac ailments would render his tenure far too short as principal guest conductor here, choosing him was inspired. It created an aura of renewed confidence in the orchestra's future, as well as in Talmi's judgment and his own self-confidence in choosing him. In his year-end review, published in the December 25, 1989, *San Diego Union*, Donald Dierks opined, "Their appointments will provide the continuity of artistic leadership any orchestra needs to reach and maintain high performance standards."

Another piece of news coinciding with Talmi's assumption of the San Diego podium was the assumption by Dr. Warren Kessler of the presidency of the Symphony Association. He was profiled in the *Evening Tribune* on February 7, 1990, by Nancy Scott Anderson, who noted, "Modest without being coy, he has spent almost a decade in symphony trenches, working during what he calls, 'the dark days when it wasn't real prestigious to be on the board…' In that era of season cancellations and financial ruin, he earned the respect of allies and adversaries for his finely wrought and subtly employed political skills…" He was unusual as a president of this Symphony Association in that classical music had been one of his great passions since his childhood, when he played piano and trombone. Kessler noted that, as a surgeon, he sometimes causes grief among the operating room personnel because he insists upon classical music being played there when he operates. Talmi and Kessler developed a close, personal relationship that allowed them to function well together.

Things obviously were looking up. In January, 1990, an anonymous gift of $2.5 million was given to the Symphony which, with the forgiveness of loans to the Symphony Association by a consortium of four banks, allowed the orchestra to settle all of its bills and to burn the mortgage on Symphony Hall. Three months later, the name of the anonymous donor was made public. It was Helen Copley, Chairman of Copley Press, Inc., and publisher of the two daily San Diego news-

papers. Her contribution was the largest ever to have been made to the orchestra to that time, and in her honor the orchestra's venue was re-named Copley Symphony Hall.

Another highlight for the orchestra was the fact that they started to record again for the first time since the recording of the dismal *Jesus and Herod*, conducted by Peter Eros in the 1970s. The only other, preceding commercial recording had been conducted by Rozsnyai in the late 1960s. Talmi told me, "I forced the issue of recordings to the board, even if it cost money. That was the best calling card we could have." He said that he had "shopped around" several recording companies to

Helen Copley. *UT Photo.*

see which might be interested in recording the San Diego Symphony Orchestra. The timing was not the best because the process of recording concert music in the United States was beginning to sour due to the recording companies' refusal to pay the high fees demanded by the musicians of the country's foremost orchestras. Besides, the compact disc revolution had allowed many of the larger, more prestigious firms to recycle their own backlog of older recordings. By reprocessing them digitally, and subsequently issuing them as compact discs with better, clearer sound than the older, analog, long-playing records, and with much more music on each of them, the recording companies made new fortunes from old sources.

In that unpropitious time, Talmi was nonetheless able to strike a deal with Intersound, the manufacturer of Pro Arte CDs, who were agreeable to record the kind of music that Talmi felt the orchestra should play. It is important to note that Talmi's negotiations for the recordings began even before his actual assumption of the music directorship. He was still only music director designate when the contract with Pro Arte was signed. The energy that he was directing into the organization, even from the outset, was remarkable, and the musicians responded well. The three digital CD's made for Pro Arte under Talmi's direction were the Symphony Number 3 by Reinhold Gliere (subtitled, "Ilya Moroumetz"), a disc of orchestral transcriptions of music by Brahms (several of the transcriptions were by Talmi), and some rarely heard works by Rachmaninoff. No recording company was going to let an unknown orchestra and conductor make new recordings of popular Tchaikovsky or Beethoven symphonies at that time, already recorded so many times with the greatest orchestras and conductors. Orchestras like the San Diego Symphony had to find a niche, and they succeeded under Talmi.

As Talmi related, "Pro Arte wanted classical repertoire, but one seldom recorded which may create some special interest. I then presented them with some six or seven ideas, from which we mutually agreed on three." The differing opinions between Talmi and Wes Brustad about the importance of these recordings eventually highlighted their more general differences over the role of a symphony orchestra in a community. The symphony orchestra as a repository and purveyor of classical music (Talmi) or, in contrast, as an increasingly pops-oriented organization (Brustad) that, it was felt, might make more money, were seemingly inflexible positions held by the two leaders of the organization. All was not going smoothly in the Symphony offices.

The first two recordings made for Pro Arte were led by Lalo Schifrin, the Argentinian musician who had made a remarkable career in Hollywood. Appropriately, he led the San Diego Symphony (called the San Diego Symphony Pops on the CD labels) in movie music. He conducted two CDs, one of background music from Hitchcock films and a second of marches from the movies.

Many of the marches had not been written originally for the films but had been appropriated for them, such as some Sousa pieces, anthems of the military services, and even Wagner's "Ride of the Valkyries." That last had been used in the film, "Apocalypse Now," about the Viet Nam conflict.

According to Talmi, "The idea to record with Lalo Schifrin came, of course, from Wes Brustad, who at this stage was pushing the orchestra toward the "Pops" side. Although I knew well the reputation of Mr. Schifrin as a film composer, I didn't know much about his ability as a conductor. Fearing that his recordings will not bring out the best of the orchestra, I insisted that his discs will not carry the name of the SDSO."

The Schifrin recordings were excellent. The music director did not need to worry on that score. The process was completely digital and the sound was exemplary, especially in the marches. The performances were first-rate, and the brass section shone. One march, "The Hymn of the Red Army," had been used in the film, "The Hunt for the Red October." The performance of that particular cut was notable for the striking effect by the trumpet section, imitating the nasal, narrow-bored instruments characteristic of Russian bands and orchestras. All in all, the marches were characterized by a sense of swing completely lacking in the recordings made by many famed symphony conductors who conducted them with their own orchestras. The only symphony orchestra performances of marches with comparable élan that I personally know (and I love and have collected much march music!) were led by Sir Adrian Boult — high praise, indeed.

In contrast, Preston Turegano, who reviewed the special concert of April 6, 1990, given by the orchestra under Schifrin before they actually recorded the pieces, was highly critical in his April 7 column in the *Evening Tribune*. His judgment was, "At the risk of being marched over by thousands of patrons who appeared to be delirious over the program,…this special single performance concert was excessive, a mess and often embarrassing…" Turegano objected to the orchestra's appealing to "…the lowest common entertainment denominator — movies. Could a recording of schmaltzy, loud and tiresome march music be what symphony music director-designate Yoav Talmi meant recently when he said the San Diego Symphony must build a devoted public and be exposed beyond San Diego?" Turegano, of course, was unaware at the time that the Schifrin recordings were the result of Brustad's arrangements, not of Talmi's.

Donald Dierks, in the April 7, 1990, *San Diego Union*, was less upset. He noted, "Lalo Schifrin, who has composed a few marches himself, and countless award-winning scores for television and films…seemed to be having a good time conducting, and for its part, the orchestra was responsive and played well for Schifrin…""Those Fabulous Hollywood Marches" turned out well as a recording

(Pro Arte CDD 504). I have heard it played over FM music stations in Chicago and Los Angeles as well as here.

Talmi related,

> "The musicians had agreed to put their radio money into a foundation fund to help pay for the recordings. Basically, the orchestra paid for the recordings we made for Pro Arte. Again, it was I who corresponded with Klaus Heymann, the founder and head of Naxos records, and convinced him to give the San Diego a chance to be the first American orchestra to record for Naxos. He then sent me the Naxos catalogue and asked me to see what was still missing in there. Unlike other companies, Heymann could not care less if other companies recorded things a hundred times. All he wanted was that the Naxos catalogue should include *everything* [emphasis Talmi's]! When I saw that they had only two rather old CDs of Berlioz, I jumped on it immediately. I suggested to him to record the entire Berlioz orchestral repertoire within a period of 5-6 years, and he agreed to record us, but at a very low fee. I threw my own fee into the foundation, and we made four discs."

The relationship between Talmi and Wes Brustad became increasingly strained as the apparent differences of opinion regarding the role and function of a symphony orchestra became greater. Their differences gradually extended into many areas other than issues surrounding the making of recordings.

By May 1, 1990, Dierks was able to report in the *San Diego Union* that the symphony receipts were up in comparison to preceding years. "Last season, the total attendance at winter concerts was 114,340. For the current season, with seven concerts still to be played, concert attendance stands at 115,203. Last season, to help make ends meet, symphony management estimated it needed ticket revenues of $1.3 million. This goal was missed by slightly more than $6,000. The ever-increasing goal for ticket revenues during the current season is $1.4 million. As of Thursday, ticket revenues were up by 14 percent and were only $20,000 shy of the hoped for mark." The next week, for Dierks' concert review in the May 7, 1990 *San Diego Union*, the headline read, "Yoav Talmi Earns his Warm Welcome." The reviewer noted that Talmi was apparently "...asking the orchestra to stretch itself, to go beyond what it might ordinarily do," for its playing of excerpts from Smetana's "The Bartered Bride." After the intermission, Tchaikovsky's "popular behemoth" (according to Dierks), the "Pathetique" Symphony, was played. The reviewer complimented the orchestra for the many beautifully played solos. Also, "What was much to be admired about Talmi's interpretation was its even-handedness. He did not overdramatize. He captured the romantic nature of the work without once resorting to simple, pandering sentiment. Some conductors cannot resist gilding this work's lily…"

Happy times seemed to be coming to the San Diego Symphony scene for a change. The 1990 summer concerts were also being reviewed fairly well. Much of that had to do with the fact that more "real music" was programmed than had been the rule in prior summers. The orchestra was more heavily billed, and the programs sometimes even included a whole symphony. As Donald Dierks noted in the June 29, 1990, *San Diego Union's* review, "After intermission, there were solid performances of the Brahms 'Academic Festival' Overture, and the Beethoven Fifth Symphony. If a complete symphony was ever programmed at a pop concert here before, it escapes memory." The complaints about the airplanes continued unabated, however, as did their flights over Hospitality point. Nonetheless, the people came and the series at least broke even.

Excitement was considerable for the opening night of the next season, Yoav Talmi's first as music director. He had written a special fanfare for the occasion, and arrayed his brasses in the balcony recesses on either side of the newly renamed Copley Symphony Hall. The main orchestral piece was the Brahms First Symphony. Donald Dierks, in his October 6, 1990, *San Diego Union* review, felt that, "… Talmi was asking more of the orchestra than it could give…That said, as Talmi and the orchestra get to know each other better, it seems certain that they will reach new levels of excellence and make beautiful music together." By the next set of concerts, things were better, except for the attendance. The headline for the Dierks review in the October 13, 1990, *San Diego Union*, was "Symphony Performs Superbly Before a Disturbingly Small Audience."

Two weeks later, Talmi led a performance of the Faure Requiem, the performance of which was said by Dierks (*San Diego Union*, October 22, 1990) to have been, "…a carefully sculpted one, with heartfelt dynamics and superb orchestral balances…" This was the first of a planned series of requiems conducted by Talmi, one per season, each of a markedly different character. On December 3, 1990, Dierks wrote in the *San Diego Union* about the orchestra's performance under Talmi of the Bruckner Seventh Symphony. The headline said it all. "Symphony Plays Splendid Bruckner No. 7: Musicians Respond Adeptly to Talmi's Focused Conducting." Talmi had said upon accepting the music directorship that he had special affection for and affinity to the music of Bruckner and Mahler, and expected to conduct much of it here.

The year's end article by Donald Dierks in the December 30, 1990, *San Diego Union* was optimistic, although he warned, "Being in the black and staying in the black…are two different things. To its credit, the symphony management has moved with unprecedented aggressiveness to increase its earned income…"

Even John Willett was beginning, albeit somewhat grudgingly, to issue greater praise for Talmi and the orchestra in his *San Diego Magazine* reviews. During the auditions seasons, he was, at best, lukewarm about the possibility of Talmi's possible selection as music director, all the while pushing hard for Bernhard Klee, even after it became known that that conductor no longer considered himself as a candidate. In the July, 1990, *San Diego Magazine*, reviewing the same performances of the whirlwind Overture and Dances from Smetana's "The Bartered Bride," noted above by Donald Dierks, Willett wrote, "I don't know just what the synergy is when Talmi and the SDSO strings get together these days, but the results are definitely gratifying — wonderful sound — coupled with attacks that were the strongest and most precise in memory..." Later, in the January, 1991, issue, Willett wrote about, "...the gentle, sympathetic and genuinely moving performance of the Faure' Requiem," and in the April, 1991, issue, about the performance of three musical settings of Shakespeare's "Romeo and Juliet," by Berlioz, Tchaikovsky and Prokofiev: "The strings shone so brightly that we forgot the triteness of the content."

The July, 1991, issue of the magazine, however, allowed Willett to re-assume the not-so-enthusiastic posture he had originally maintained. The occasion was an end-of-season review, headlined, "The Bottom Line on Our Musical Season." He began by describing the entire musical season as inconsistent, although in seeming contradiction he noted that the San Diego Symphony Orchestra was playing better than ever.

> "It seems now that Talmi was selected, in part, at least, because he could be something for everyone and counted upon to offend no one politically, musically or socially. This can be an insidiously dangerous philosophy upon which to base important decisions. You may recall that something-for-everyone thinking resulted in such things as the design of UCSD's Mandeville Auditorium and, before that, the camel. Talmi's relations with the orchestra management and board of directors seem to be a landscape of mutual admiration and limited, if any, friction. It has been reported from inside the orchestra that all goes smoothly there as well. Talmi remains as well liked by its members as he was when their representatives sat on the search committee that selected him as music director. The orchestra has grown somewhat under Talmi's guidance. The upper string sound and technical facility have improved markedly, although, in honesty, it must be said that this is a trend that has been ongoing for longer than just the season under scrutiny...The sound

has become cleaner and more encompassing. The ensemble
— unanimity of pitch, attack, articulation, volume — the consistency of effort and the blend within these sections approach
levels of perfection one might have considered unachievable
even a year or two ago..."

These comments make one wonder, "Well, then, what could be wrong? It
sounds OK to me." It is notable that Willett, in his comments about all going
well between Talmi and the management, did not make mention of the growing, increasingly difficult friction between the music director and the executive
director, noted above. What Willett did emphasize as problems were the defi-
ciencies in the lower strings, although it was possible, he said, that the problem
could be the basic acoustics of Copley Symphony Hall. He also criticized Talmi
for not listening to the orchestra from various parts of the hall, "...and he does
not spend enough time in the hall — when it's full of people and the orchestra is
performing — listening to what the patrons hear. How can he? He's off conducting in Switzerland or Norway or Israel when not on the podium here. This very
globe-girdling career that makes him unavailable to study his own orchestra is, of
course, in the best interest of that very orchestra's international reputation and
recognition. Damned if you do, etc..."

Willett praised Talmi's readings of the post-romantics, the Bruckners,
Mahlers and Glieres, while he opined that Talmi "...will inevitably play Mozart
too fast and will sacrifice the grace of its *galant* style in favor of any heated, direct,
emotional appeal." Willett also wrote, "The real contretemps that emerged
during the last season was that the orchestra seems to play better for truly talented visiting conductors than it does for its own, well-liked music director."
This is in direct contradiction to one of the leads of a Dierks *San Diego Union*
review during the 1990-91 season: "The boss is back," which led to a discussion
of how much better the orchestra plays under Talmi than anyone else, Robert
Shaw excepted. Willett concluded, "...Talmi is not genuinely exciting over the
distance. Observation indicates that his desires are never in doubt where the
orchestra is concerned, all well and good. But his podium personality is dry
and somewhat martial: he becomes boring after several viewings/hearings. He
becomes a filter instead of an open channel between orchestra and audience, the
two vital channels of the concert experience."

As a category, excitement was also rated highly as a necessity for every
conductor by Valerie Scher throughout her series of reviews of Talmi's tenure.
On occasion, she would contrast Talmi's approach on the podium to that of then-
recently deceased and lamented Leonard Bernstein. Although she often tended
to make fun of the latter's famous, often over-theatricalized podium calisthen-

ics, she obviously was moved more by conductors who were more emotionally demonstrative on the podium than Yoav Talmi. She did not consider Talmi as a very exciting or stimulating conductor — insofar as her own or the audience's appreciation of that trait was concerned. In direct contrast, however, the orchestra usually played well and she would praise the music itself and the performances. At times, when she as well as Willett would write about their concerns regarding relatively low attendance figures for the concerts, Talmi's lack of so-called sparkle would be considered the likely reason.

Talmi offered himself as a person who wished to make the orchestra feel the music more intensely and to inspire the musicians to make it and the excitement come out of them instead of from the podium. He wanted increased sensitivity in the playing and, like most conductors, did most of his teaching and his own emotional pleading with his musicians during rehearsals instead of acting it out during the concerts. The image, however, of the unexciting conductor as elaborated so often by both Willett and Scher clung to Talmi throughout his stay as music director. Practically every other critic, however, never mentioned that aspect; they simply wrote about the marked improvement in the orchestra and the beautiful readings that Talmi offered of the music he programmed.

The summer season of 1991 "Pops" concerts was held at a different venue, Marina Embarcadero Park South, opposite the Convention Center, quieter and with a great view of the illuminated city center. More seats were available and the public sometimes appeared to come in greater strength than it had to Hospitality Point. The programming was also less patronizing; more classical music was played. In fact, the season ended over Labor Day weekend with a performance of the Beethoven Ninth Symphony under Murry Sidlin's baton. In the September 7, 1991, *San Diego Union*, David Gregson panned the reading by the conductor as plodding, although, "…by the last movement, things seemed to jell." Bad weather did not help the Symphony's move to a better locale, however. A $200,000•loss was expected in ticket revenue for the twelve-week series after all the accounting was finished. However, the orchestra balanced its budget for the fiscal year that ended at the end of September, 1991. According to Wes Brustad, reported by James Steinberg in the November 5, 1991, *San Diego Union*, "A few key contributions enabled the symphony to post a $50,000 surplus on its $7.6 million budget." According to Steinberg, "Brustad credited board president Kessler and the other individual board members for helping to deliver almost $3.5 million in contributed income. He also cited an increase to 1,700 in the number of individuals and organizations contributing to the symphony, up from, 1,000 the year before."

More financial decisions also played in the spotlight as the musicians' contract expired and a new one was needed. For a change, a tentative contract was reached at the end of September, 1991, which made it likely that the forthcoming season would open without a break. The musicians had asked for a multi-year contract. The Association would grant only a single year, without an increase in the musicians' weekly base salary of $700. The Association also wanted to trim the season to thirty-four weeks from the prior season's thirty-eight weeks in an attempt to reduce the continuing operative deficit of $200,000. At least a tentative agreement allowed the rehearsals to start and the season to begin, even without signatures on the dotted line, which came within a few days. A related series of crises about contracts was revealed between the musicians and the San Diego Opera, which used an orchestra composed mainly of San Diego Symphony players. The scheduling conflicts that would and did necessarily result from the two organizations sometimes simultaneously pulling for the same musicians had grown, and they would continue to grow through the years.

The 1991-92 season was dedicated to the memory of UCSD's Nobelist, Roger Revelle, who, with his widow, had worked long and hard for the restitution of the orchestra during the late 1980s and beyond. Ellen Revelle continued her own philanthropy without interruption, and eventually the room used for social events off the upper lobby of Copley Symphony Hall was named in honor of the Revelles. The opening concert concluded with the Beethoven Fifth Symphony, a performance described by Valerie Scher in the October 5, 1991, *Evening Tribune*, as having, "…brisk tempos and a rhythmic vitality that encouraged the triumphal stride of this famous war horse."

The Symphony's recording of Gliere's "Ilya Moroumetz" Symphony was released soon after that, and received a good review in the *Los Angeles Times* as well as in *Fanfare,* a leading record reviewing magazine. In San Diego, both Valerie Scher and James Steinberg praised the recording in the daily papers. As Steinberg wrote in the November 19, 1991, *San Diego Union,* "The conclusion — first-rate in every way…Talmi and the orchestra have faithfully captured the grand sweep of this majestic work from its solemn opening to its dazzling finale. The playing is subtle and nuanced, and, when called for, bold and vigorous. The big surprise here is the San Diego brass, which in live performance has on occasion been guilty of some roughness around the edges; this time the players are all perfection, playing full and rich and very sure of themselves. The strings and woodwinds perform to their usual high standards."

Unfortunately, the San Diego performance was released at the same time as two other totally unexpected performances of the work recorded by better known orchestras and conductors on better known (and better-marketed) CD brands. That, of course, tended to minimize the splash of the fine San Diego recording with record buyers. During the 1991-92 season, recordings were made for Pro Arte of orchestral transcriptions of Brahms piano and chamber works. That recording received an outstanding review in *Fanfare*, especially of the Talmi transcription for full string orchestra of the great Brahms Sextet for Strings. After a time, music by Rachmaninoff followed onto the digital recording apparatus. After that recording, the relationship began between the San Diego Symphony Orchestra and Naxos records, and a Berlioz cycle began to be recorded. The first disc of that collaboration was a program of Berlioz overtures, described in *Fanfare* as "a romp," and greeted with enthusiasm elsewhere as well.

The 1991-92 season provided the occasion for another appearance by Robert Shaw on the San Diego podium. He was ill with heart disease, but he conducted the Beethoven *Missa Solemnis* with, as Valerie Scher wrote in the October 26, 1991 *Evening Tribune*, "undeniably authoritative presence, asserting the command of vocal music that has long distinguished his career." The season was also notable for a six-hour "Mozart Marathon," commemorating the 200th anniversary of the composer's early death, and featuring Talmi and the orchestra in wigs and other 18th century dress. Dennis Michel and John Lorge, principal bassoon and horn, respectively, shined in their concerti by the master. The season also led to some increased criticism of Talmi for talking too much on stage. As Valerie Scher wrote in her year-end review in the December 29, 1991, *Evening Tribune*, "Strictly speaking, this is what the program notes are for, and the chatter would be better left to popsmeister Murry Sidlin."

The January 9, 1992, issue of the *San Diego Reader* provided a remarkable review by Jonathan Saville. He attended the final concert of the orchestra's Mozart commemorative series. Saville sat near the stage, downstairs, for the performance of the "Jupiter" Symphony, and panned the reading and the performance. "The performance sounded gray and indifferent, weak and lackadaisical..." During the intermission, he climbed to the top of the balcony. "From that position, the orchestra and its conductor looked like miniature manikins on the other side of the world, but the moment the music started they all leaped into my lap, and at the first blast of chorus, trumpets and drums, I realized that I was in the presence of a conductor of stupendous strength and dynamism, and listening to a performance of the Requiem that ranked with the most dramatic, intense, and moving I had ever heard. This was no illusion, for Talmi sustained the powerful drive from first to last..."

January, 1992, also brought a little more change of heart to John Willett in that month's issue of *San Diego Magazine*. "It is humble pie time. Last month in this column, comment was made to the effect that Yoav Talmi was not exactly strong in the interpretation of the music of the era of Mozart and Beethoven. Then the orchestra under Talmi, with Peter Frankl as soloist, played Mozart's Concerto No. 15 in B Flat...No one could have asked for better." Because it was a concerto, with a strong soloist, as Willett noted, "…Talmi could not impose his will alone upon the piece. Frankl's technically facile and thoroughly musical reading may have gone far to shape the absolutely appropriate style and vibrancy of the performance. At this point, however, I will go all the way and give Talmi the benefit of the doubt and pull in my own horns…" The same concert also provided Talmi's reading of the Bruckner Ninth Symphony. Willett concluded his remarks about that: "It goes without saying that Talmi's interpretation was everything the specialist's should be: authoritative, emotionally commanding and superbly shaped structurally."

Preston Turegano reviewed the symphony's performance under Talmi in the February 1, 1992 *Evening Tribune*. He began, "Any one wondering if the San Diego Symphony has yet developed into a world-class ensemble should take note of the orchestra's extraordinary performance of Shostakovich's Symphony No. 5 last night…It is worthy to note that the symphony was taped for broadcast…What the orchestra should do is record the performance commercially as soon as possible…" In the midst of all the good feelings generated by great reviews (even by Scher and Willett, despite their caveats about excitement) and the balanced budget, the Association announced the forthcoming summer season, with varied, less expensive ticket packages and other ploys to stimulate better attendance at the Embarcadero Park site. The season would offer a mixture of music, from country-western to another performance of the Beethoven Ninth. A month later, the 1992-93 winter season was announced, reported in the March 13, 1992, *San Diego Union-Tribune* (the two papers had by now combined) by Preston Turegano. Shaw was scheduled for two programs and Talmi for eleven. There would be sixteen sets. "While classics …will serve as a traditional program base, the San Diego Symphony will attempt to broaden the tastes of its audiences with four world premieres, two west coast premieres and other contemporary works…" Scheduled choral programs featuring the San Diego Master Chorale were to be Orff's *Carmina Burana* for the season opener, Handel's "Messiah," Verdi's Requiem and Mendelssohn's "Elijah."

Paul Hodgins became a music critic for the *Union-Tribune* for a time, and his reviews of the orchestra's performances under Talmi were also generally quite positive. On March 30, 1992, he reported that the performance of the Brahms German Requiem, "…celebrated the work's profound beauty and only occasionally made us aware of its daunting demands." But at the beginning of the 1992-93 winter season, it was apparent that Valerie Scher had the job. In the December, 1992, *San Diego Magazine*, John Willett headlined his article, "Tough Love: A Hard-Nosed Prescription for the San Diego Symphony's Future." He wrote about the October, 1992, financial crisis of the San Diego Symphony, contrasting the emotion of that time with March, 1984, when the orchestra acquired the Fox Theater. At the same time, "David Atherton was driving the orchestra beyond its own expectations to what were sometimes dizzying heights of performance excellence. Whether you liked him or not or agreed about his programming, Atherton was never dull." About the October, 1992, recurrent financial crisis, Willett wrote, "...The San Diego Symphony announced that it had no cash flow. After an initial wail of begging that fell upon ears deafened by too many years of such lamentations, it began canceling concerts, cutting staff wages, and so forth. Slowly dying for years, the symphony will expire within the next eighteen months, I believe, if things continue as they are. World-class symphonic music will become unavailable in the sixth largest city in America."

Willett hit hard in his article at the manifold causes of that most recent of the repetitive crises that had befallen the orchestra. "First, we must acknowledge the political, historical and social changes that have taken place since 1982. The economic conditions that we insist on calling a recession, for example, will have enormous future impact, for America is undergoing a sea change in its economic and social structure....bound to affect the availability and distribution of discretionary income, among other things." Willett blasted the "...hoary old excuses that too long had been the refuge of the intellectually bankrupt and the imaginatively defunct," referring initially to the excuse that San Diego was not a home-office town where large corporations existed to spread their largesse. Other examples included the many cutbacks by government agencies and foundations, as well as the notion that, "In the long run, there's too much competition from the sunshine in San Diego..."

He contrasted the ideas of the "symphony fathers" with what he felt was really needed. He blamed the notion of a "major orchestra," with a too-large budget, as providing the tools for disaster. Also, "It isn't 100 year-old concert formats, it isn't all pleasant music from the 18th and 19th centuries, it isn't an emphasis on the symphony as a society function. What it *is* is what the up-and-coming concert community wants: totally new programming concepts, exciting musical direction, a concentrated concert calendar, and so on..." Only the San Diego Opera, he wrote, under Ian Campbell's direction, had learned from the past mistakes of his predecessors in attempting to do too much and eventually to break the organization. "The first element of the symphony's solution to declining concert population is a mercilessly realistic assessment of what the San Diego public wants and how much it will take...Tangential effects such as reduction of orchestra earnings cannot be considered. Once houses are full and tickets are hard to get, cautious expansion can begin again." Most important, Willett emphasized, "...the following as a point of departure in future planning: *There is no new audience for great music in San Diego...Education and the home have failed to prepare the next generation for the experience of great music...*"

Willett emphasized that last point by pointing out that the control of the country's money will be in the hands of the twenty-five- to forty-year-olds who have, "…(a) little or no education in or appreciation of great music and (b) no established track record of philanthropy or noblesse oblige…" Willett described that group as completely media-oriented and addicted to the star syndrome. "It does respond to more contemporary music and doesn't recognize traditional lines between classical and popular musical culture." Which, as might be expected, brought Willett back to the subject of the music director.

"A good beginning would be the replacement of … Yoav Talmi. He is a nice man, a diplomat and a talented but unexciting musician. He lacks name recognition in San Diego; the symphony has done nothing to change that condition. In reality, he is an absentee landlord for whom chasing his career around the international circuit is of far greater importance than the welfare of the musical life of San Diego. San Diego needs either a red-hot American *wunderkind* who can be hyped into a star or — preferably — an already established talent of broad accomplishments who is exciting in the concert hall, already has an international reputation but is at that point in his career where he wishes to become a genuine part of the community… Orchestra programming must be radically rethought. Talmi is programming for 19th century Europeans in a 21st century American city whose potential audience doesn't give a damn about Europe and cannot conceive — without help — of a time so distant as the 19th century."

From this angle, it seems as if Willett forgot to include, "And doesn't give a damn about great music," the baleful sequel to the deterioration of American education at home as well as in school, which Willett admirably decried in his article. Most observers of the American cultural scene had begun to focus on that aspect of the all-over crisis in American culture, referring to what soon became known as the "dumbing down" of America. Those observers might also have pointed out that "red-hot American *wunderkinds*" had more often than not failed to turn around the course of that lack of caring in many economically stretched cities. A major question remained unanswered by Willett: what will happen to the ongoing presentation of acknowledged masterful serious music if the uneducated audience is "given what it wants?" Finally, Willett objected to that which most American orchestras preach — the need for a home-town conductor whose presence is demanded on other podiums as well as his own, thereby giving increased grace to the home town band.

Willett's editorial had an italicized appendage, *"The views herein do not necessarily reflect the opinions of the publishers of San Diego Magazine."* Despite its dreadfully pessimistic, generally negativistic tone and, to these eyes, some misplaced reasoning, the article was important. It highlighted the severe problems affecting the San Diego Symphony Orchestra and many of its brethren ensembles across the country. The history of repetitive crises in San Diego certainly turned off a number of potential subscribers and listeners, much less donors, and the financial crisis continued. But so did the music.

1992 was the 500th anniversary of Columbus's first voyage of discovery to the New World. The San Diego Symphony participated in the commemoration by staging a brief tour into Mexico. They played a Columbus Day moonlit concert (thankfully, the predicted rain held off) at the base of one of the pyramids in *Chichen Itza*. Of course, as expected, numerous hardships developed, as well as failures of contracted technicians, etc. Nonetheless, the tour was described as a rousing success, and certainly provided remarkable stimulation for the musicians. It was televised throughout Mexico — and subsequently in San Diego, via videotape. Brustad and Talmi, both exhausted, survived, as did the orchestra, augmented by a large contingent of Mexico City percussionists for that program.

Just before the Mexican trip, in the October 2, 1992, *Union-Tribune*, Valerie Scher asked, "How does Talmi measure up?" She provided ten categories and graded him in each. They are as follows.

> 1. Recognition — negative: he is unknown to the public at large because of "…an image of lofty remoteness." 2. Conducting — very positive. 3. Touring — not yet, but scheduled to perform in Mexico on Columbus Day, at Chichen Itza. 4. Attendance — losing the battle of the box office. 5. Morale — "a healing presence." 6. Recordings — made but little noticed outside of San Diego. 7. Soloists and guest conductors — prestigious performers are rarely seen. 8. Repertoire — "Good, but probably not good enough to fill Copley Symphony Hall. There must be a way of making concerts appealing without selling out the orchestra's serious ambitions." 9. Orchestra — "A good regional ensemble. Missing, and missed, is the exciting excellence that characterized its finest achievements with the previous music director, David Atherton." 10. Musicians — "Talmi keeps hiring young instrumentalists. And they continue leaving, either because the symphony's disappointed in them or because they're disappointed by the pay scale and status…So, unless wages dramatically increase or Talmi finds other ways to compete, Symphony Hall's revolving doors will just keep spinning."

The symphony began 1993 by presenting another commemorative concert, this time honoring Dr. Martin Luther King, Jr. It was conducted by an African-American conductor, Thomas Wilkins, from the Richmond, VA, Symphony

Orchestra. The San Diego Community Chorus also participated, as well as the pianist, Leon Bates, who played Gershwin. The first subscription concert of the new year, however, was given on January 14. It opened with a performance of part of the finale from Rossini's Overture to "William Tell." The playing of that music was a gimmick used by the orchestra to demonstrate that money was needed, and also to demonstrate how much had been collected of the goal set for that project at $250,000. Every concert opened with the playing of just a bit more of the piece, calculated by determining the number of notes in the work. Eventually, the entire finale would be able to be played — to great applause — but early in January, 1993, the $250,000 had not yet been completely raised.

The subscription concert's more formal beginning was a performance of a work by Yoav Talmi, "Overture on Mexican Themes," written late in the 1960s when he was an associate conductor in Louisville. Valerie Scher commented about it in her January 15, 1993, *Union-Tribune* review. "It's like Ravel's *Rapsodie Espagnole* meets Copland's *El Salon Mexico* in the valley of experimentation." Later that month, another disc of the Pro Arte series was released, the series of transcriptions for orchestra of works by Brahms. One of the pieces was a revision by Talmi for full string orchestra of the great Brahms Sextet, and this particular work received a rave review in a *Fanfare* column.

Even the "William Tell" Overture gimmick did not help enough to allow Wes Brustad to stay in his position of executive director of the symphony. After three years, he resigned early in February. The announcement was a surprise, since he had been touted as a savior of several financially-strapped orchestras, and was working hard to try to save this one. He was also the highest paid arts executive in town, with a salary of $150,000 — more than the nearly $140,000 received annually by Yoav Talmi. Brustad's pet, the SummerPops, had perversely served to drag down the finances of the orchestra instead of bolstering them. The summer concerts had simply failed to draw, and the more than $900,000 deficit continued to be a sword of Damocles over the entire organization's head. Eventually, he took a job in Eugene, Oregon, as director of the Lane County Fairgrounds. That gave him more opportunity to exercise his love of popular and country music that far exceeded his love of (and knowledge of) classical music. Incidentally, it was soon after Brustad's resignation that the "William Tell" Overture's finale was finally played to the finish at a concert. The $50/note campaign raised $10,000 more than the $250,000 goal. The final success of that campaign was not considered to have anything to do with Brustad's leaving.

Without an executive director and without any deficit relief, the orchestra continued playing. It even made their third contracted recording for Pro Arte, this time of music by Rachmaninoff. That disc also included transcriptions of piano pieces, but these transcriptions were by Respighi, not Talmi. Talmi's cycle of performing the great requiems continued at the end of February with the Verdi, which received a fine review by Valerie Scher. However, the hall was only half-filled. Needed good news, other than the good reviews, came in the form of a $300,000 grant to the orchestra from the Anheuser-Busch Brewing Company of St. Louis. That gift was to be earmarked for music education. But this gift did not ease the need for the $2 million needed by the symphony to stay afloat for the season, and obviously had no effect on the deficit.

For the March 23, 1993, *Union-Tribune*, Valerie Scher wrote an article about the relatively large number of arts executives who had left their jobs over the past year, including the executive directors of the Seattle, Sacramento, Milwaukee and Dallas Symphony Orchestras, and the Florida Philharmonic. The article revealed that the Seattle orchestra's accumulated deficit was $3 million, that the Milwaukee orchestra's was over a million, and that the Sacramento orchestra had declared bankruptcy and folded. In Canada, the Vancouver Symphony was also a million dollars in the red, and its director had also left. Misery may love company, but the article did not make many of the San Diego readers feel any better or any more confident. It did highlight, however, the dreadful difficulties that the arts in general were having in contemporary America.

Meanwhile, the 1993 SummerPops were being planned. The announced goal of $600,000 to meet the expenses of a summer season was being met by a strenuous campaign, helped a little bit by the Port District's forgiveness of a few thousand dollars in damages created by the prior year's concerts. The season would consist of twelve weeks of concerts, but only ten would involve the orchestra's musicians. In order to minimize costs, some programs would be planned for three nights a week instead of the previous four or five. The Port Authority allowed the symphony to expand its programming by including rock performers and groups such as Duran Duran, Air Supply, Sade and Chicago. Warren Kessler, who, as president, also had to assume the temporary mantle (and duties) of the absent executive director, pointed out that there would be no heavy metal or rap acts that appeal primarily to teen-agers. But insofar as the other acts were concerned, according to the symphony president, "Clearly, our being able to present these non-orchestral events will allow us to increase income, which is so important to our existence."

In conjunction with Logan Heights community organizations, the symphony also began to collaborate on a neighborhood arts program designed to provide underprivileged children and their parents with musical instruments and lessons. Too, the Symphony announced that it would present a series of free outdoor concerts at malls and other public areas. The programs, to be conducted by Matt Garbutt, were described as previews of the forthcoming French Fortnight Festival, to be given as part of the subscription series at Copley Symphony

Hall near the season's end. In the midst of all of these plans, Lynn Hallbacka, the Symphony's general manager, also left on April 23. She, however, denied that the stresses of the financial situation had anything to do with that.

The night before that announcement, the symphony presented another subscription concert. That one featured the orchestra's excellent, young principal trombonist, Heather Buchman, who played the Concerto for Trombone by David Ott, which she had commissioned in 1990. Robert Shaw conducted, and the concert also included Tchaikovsky's Overture-Fantasia, "Romeo and Juliet," as well as the Beethoven Seventh Symphony. Shaw returned to lead the next set

Matthew Garbutt. *Photo courtesy San Diego Symphony.*

of programs as well, featuring infrequently heard Brahms choral works and the First Symphony. After returning home, Shaw wrote an open letter, printed in the *Union-Tribune* on May 16, 1993, in which he praised the orchestra to the skies. He even compared it favorably with other orchestras he had conducted frequently, including those in Toronto, Birmingham (England), Philadelphia and Cleveland. As he wrote, "…the San Diego orchestra played right along with them." Continuing, he noted, "It has a world-class music director, and players who continue to grow in soloistic capacities and ensemble expertise. Eventually — if there is an eventually — its performances will be enhanced by players as required by the gigantic symphonic scenarios of the last century. But, at the present and to a visitor, it appears to be as a "voice crying" — however beautifully — "in the wilderness."

Meanwhile, Yoav Talmi was touring as a guest conductor, notably in Russia where, as the first Israeli invited to conduct there, he led the St. Petersburg Philharmonic in a very well received program. He even had to succumb to audience pressure and conduct an encore. Back in San Diego, he prepared for the French Fortnight Festival. Yefim Bronfman was piano soloist in the Saint-Saens Second Concerto, and Talmi led scores by Bizet, Debussy and Ravel. Talmi celebrated his fiftieth birthday at the concert, and cakes were served in the lobby.

The final concert, also led by Talmi, featured the orchestra's principal clarinet-ist, Sheryl Renk, playing Debussy's First Rhapsody for Clarinet. Meanwhile, a new operations manager was hired, and it was anticipated that a new executive director would come aboard soon. At the same time, an agreement with the Port Authority allowed the symphony to expand the summer season to seven-teen weeks, the extra weeks being reserved for non-orchestral performances by popular artists and groups. The Port Authority also authorized the symphony to enlarge the seating capacity at Marina Embarcadero Park South to 5,200 seats for some programs. The first Pops orchestral program was slated for June 30.

The 1993-94 season was also announced, budgeted at $6.7 million. The season was described as a cut back version of the previous seasons, with few big-name soloists. Talmi was scheduled to conduct ten of the fifteen programs, and none of the guest conductors were household names. Joseph Silverstein, of the Utah Symphony, was probably the best known. The others were Mexico's Enrique Diemecke, Belgium's Ronald Zollman, and Poland's Grzegors Nowak. Shaw was not going to come but promised to return the following year. Tragically, he never made it. A number of works originally planned by Talmi were elimi-nated because they cost too much to produce. But there would be a two-week Tchaikovsky Festival as well as a commemorative program honoring the 150th anniversary of the birth of Edvard Grieg. And Talmi's opening concert for that season would feature the Beethoven Ninth Symphony as well as Stravinsky's Symphony in Three Movements.

Then the city dropped a bombshell. The TOT funding for the arts was severely cut. The symphony had been receiving nearly a half-million dollars in TOT funds, and this was to be cut in half. Kessler protested, as did the heads of all the major arts organizations, but to no avail. The good news was that Murry Sidlin was actively involved as music director of the SummerPops programs. He was to lead what everybody hoped would be a very attractive season that would draw customers and relieve the pressure. Sidlin, of course, had gained much popularity in San Diego.

Finally, on June 24, 1993, it was announced that a new executive direc-tor had been hired. The choice was Michael Tiknis, who was coming to San Diego from Buffalo, where he had been executive director of that city's noted Philharmonic Orchestra. After holding marketing positions with the San Antonio and Cincinnatti Symphony Orchestras, he had become executive director of the Virginia Symphony before assuming the Buffalo post. Preston Turegano quoted Warren Kessler in his June 24, 1995, Union-Tribune article. Kessler said that Tiknis was chosen, "...because of his really remarkable track record. He has done a fabulous job in Virginia and now in Buffalo, and possesses many skills that I think will make him an extraordinary executive director..." In Virginia, he increased subscriptions from 5,000 to 10,000, while the orchestra's earned income swelled from forty percent to sixty percent of budget. The Buffalo subscriber base also grew, from 9,000 to 12,000 people during Tiknis's tenure there. He also oversaw the elimination of that orchestra's multi-million dollar deficit, and increased its earned income from $1.9 million to the current $3.1 million — in a budget of $7.6 million. Kessler told me, "I was acting as CEO after Brustad left. There were constant battles to be fought. I felt that we needed someone with Tiknis's ebullience. Besides, he was a guy from the trenches. He had served orchestras like ours well, and they survived. Others were recommended to us, by the American Symphony orchestra League and elsewhere, but none of those people ever worked in a place like ours. They were the assistants to the execs of big-time orchestras, and they had no knowledge of the kinds of problems we had…"

During our 2003 interview, Talmi told me, "I warned Warren about Tiknis. I had heard of problems about him in Buffalo and elsewhere. But Warren insisted that I meet with him and find out about him on a personal basis, so I did, and I found that he was prepared like no one else I had ever known. He knew about all the problems we had with Brustad. He really sold himself. He knew and answered every argument I gave him. And until the very last minute, the musicians supported Tiknis, and so did I. He had worked very well with me. In fact, my own first clash with the orchestra was because I became critical of Michael. At the end, the orchestra's anger toward the board was vented on me…"

Tiknis came aboard like a house afire. He was reputedly very strong in the area of marketing, and the advertisements for the symphony programs developed a new, somewhat glitzy look. He presented himself well in public and gave talks before many civic groups, always working hard to attract increased interest. Unlike his predecessor, he was quite knowledgeable about the classical music scene and its performers, and he attempted to obtain the services of many of the more recognized players and singers for symphony performances.

The 1993-94 season opened with a better financial picture. Kessler had set a $2 million dollar fund-raising goal. It had not been reached, but despite that the Association was able to balance its 1992-93 budget, and even to end the fiscal year with a $300,000 surplus just before the new season started. The deficit had grown to $1,100,000, however, and the surplus was applied to it in an attempt to begin the process of reduction. Tiknis pointed out a manager's truism, "The deficit is certainly a problem, but what has become a greater problem is the cash-flow situation." Tragically, that was to become a prescient comment.

The Beethoven Ninth was played before a new acoustical shell for the orchestra that had been donated by Dr. and Mrs. Irwin Jacobs, long-time symphony patrons and large donors. The firm of Jaffe Holden Scarbrough Acoustics

Yoav Talmi conducting the San Diego Symphony in Copley Symphony Hall before the installation of the Jacobs Shell. *Photo courtesy San Diego Symphony.*

designed the shell. The infamous beaded curtain, wrongly attributed by many to Atherton, had been scrapped several years before. They also developed a very subtle electronic enhancement system to provide better orchestral sound under the balcony, formerly a relatively dead area. As Valerie Scher noted in her October 11, 1993, *Union-Tribune* review, "The improvement was audible…As one listened, it seemed that the orchestra was winning the acoustical war." As expected, John Willett also commented on the shell, although he waited to do so. In a February, 1994, *San Diego Magazine*, headlined, "Sonic Snags," he described the new acoustical system in the hall as a great success for the orchestra and its listeners. However, he complained, it did not work at all for small chamber groups. Talmi, himself, commented, "Now we're playing in a concert hall instead of a theatre…"

The season proceeded apace and the reviews were generally enthusiastic. 1993 ended with a Tchaikovsky Festival, highlighted by a performance of Talmi's orchestration of the Tchaikovsky chamber piece, *Souvenir de Florence*, to which dances were added for that performance. Talmi had commissioned the Malashock Dance Company to appear with the orchestra on the Copley Symphony Hall stage for that piece, and it was a resounding success.

In the same *San Diego Magazine* article cited above, Willett wrote, "The fact that I am passionately fond of Tchaikovsky's string sextet, *Souvenir de Florence*, was a great place to start. Then, when John Malashock choreographed a new arrangement of it made for the San Diego Symphony strings by music director Yoav Talmi, experiencing the result was something akin to having died and gone to heaven!" Willett also praised the orchestra's other Tchaikovsky performances, writing, "The orchestral works offered were superior from first to last. Talmi finally achieved near-perfect balances with the new sound system for the first time in the festival-opening Symphony No. 1, 'Winter Dreams'…This 'Winter Dreams' may have been the best I've ever heard. I attribute this primarily to a subtle interpretive tactic by Talmi. This approach seemed to say, 'Let's think of Tchaikovsky as great music first and Russian music second — if at all. Let's look first for the genius, the brilliance, the sweep, the joy in the music…Thus, Talmi and the orchestra achieved buoyant, translucent Tchaikovsky in which crafts-manship and strokes of genius were revealed like successive little miracles…"

Talmi left for guest conducting stints on foreign podiums after the Tchaikovsky Festival, so the first concerts of 1994 were conducted by Ronald Zollman. In the February 7, 1994, *Union-Tribune*, guest critic David Burge (former chairman of the Eastman School of Music Piano Department) reported on the music director's return. "Yoav Talmi's re-creation of Bruckner's Fourth Symphony had a unanimity of spirit and consistency of understanding that was powerfully persuasive…Talmi has molded the orchestra into an ensemble that follows his every wish. His tech-nical control is so complete and his musical conceptions so fully-formed that he can allow his players to express themselves with equal freedom and cohesiveness as soloists, as sections, and as a single large unit."

The 1994-95 season was announced by Tiknis early in February. The pro-jected budget for it was set at $7.1 million, $400,000 higher than the prior season. Yoav Talmi's contract as music director was also extended for three years, and it called for him to conduct in San Diego for at least twelve weeks per season. His salary, $118,400 at the time of the extension, would eventually rise to $148,000 by 1996-97. Talmi had also been receiving an added $20,000 for living expenses in San Diego as well as for travel expenses. The 1994 SummerPops was also announced. American Residential Mortgage Company contributed $150,000 as an underwriting gift for the summer programs, so the series bore that firm's sponsoring name. Qualcomm, Inc., Independence One Bank of California, and Solar Turbines also contributed to underwrite the series. A new stage would be provided, with new sound and light systems, the cost of which would be divided between the symphony and promoter Bill Silva. Nineteen orchestral programs would be presented over thirty-nine performance nights through a twelve-week season. In addition to the orchestral programs, sixteen non-orchestral evenings featuring popular music acts would also be given. The Pops ticket sales goal for the year was set at $1,150,000. Things seemed to be going well, and Tiknis's enthusiasm was contagious.

Talmi returned from more guest conducting to conduct the concert reviewed by Valerie Scher in the May 7, 1994, *Union-Tribune*. He had been away for more than two months following the Bruckner concert. "Hurrahs to Talmi and his program...Featuring principal violist Karen Dirks in Hindemith's *Trauermusik* and Israeli mezzo-soprano Dalia Schaechter in Mahler's "Songs of a Wayfarer," the lineup underscored the orchestra's strengths in ardently expressive terms." The next concert finally provided the music by former UCSD composer-in-residence Roger Reynolds that had been postponed from the year before. By the time of the concert, it was no longer a world premiere, as had been planned, but it was a welcome arrival at Copley Symphony Hall. On May 16, 1994, Valerie Scher wrote in the *Union-Tribune*, "Though the four movement piece has been performed before, it's difficult to imagine any group doing it any better than the San Diego Symphony under Yoav Talmi's guidance." Also on the program was the Cherubini Requiem, "...persuasively performed by the orchestra and the Master Chorale..."

The next day's *Union-Tribune* reported on the auditions being held for the post of assistant conductor for the orchestra. A young Californian, Jung-Ho Pak, described by Valerie Scher as, "...a batonless wonder," was eventually selected. Talmi was reported as stating, "All of us are happy with the choice that has been made. He has a more mature musicianship than the others, and so much willing-ness to learn. His conducting has vision, although it's sometimes difficult for a large orchestra to work with a conductor who doesn't use a baton..." Scher asked the music director if he would eventually convince Pak to, "...pick up a stick." Talmi laughed and said, "That we shall have to see about. It is something for him to decide, not me."

He never did use a baton, but the orchestra rapidly grew to love him, and had no problems following his direction. The audiences loved him, too, not only for his conducting and musical abilities, but also for his youthful charm and remarkable articulate capacities. Pak was the principal conductor of the Disney Young Persons' Symphony Orchestra, which performs annually on the Disney TV Channel. He also was director of the International Chamber Orchestra, based at the Idyllwild School of Music. Trained at USC under Daniel Lewis, Pak became music director of the University Symphony Orchestra in Berkeley, and of the Bay Area's Diablo Ballet Company. It appeared as if he worked especially well with students and young musicians.

The orchestra was also enriched by the hiring of a new principal cellist,

Brinton Smith. Despite his having been considered a genius in mathematics, allowing him to enter Arizona State University as a young adolescent, he also was sufficiently talented as a musician to have chaired the cello section of the Julliard Orchestra.

Tiknis, meanwhile, had continued inventing and using more marketing and public relations tools. Corporate sponsorship of individual subscription concerts were becoming more frequent events. In March, 1994, he presented the orchestra in a free, "thank you," Copley Symphony Hall program for subscribers, conducted by JoAnn Falletta. He developed a system of cut-rate tickets that worked in that it filled the hall more than it had been generally filled before. However, the increased attendance did not fill the larder enough. The financial problems continued, especially when the increased fees for the higher-paid soloists were considered. But Tiknis's enthusiasm and energy stimulated the board, and they were pleased at having him. They were exceedingly pleased by his work with the orchestra and the union, when he was able to establish a new, three-year contract with the musicians that promised to avoid any of the repeated labor disputes of recent history.

That contract, finalized and signed in early October, 1994, restored the wage cuts and work-week reductions that had been approved by the players during the 1992 financial crisis. The new contract called for an increase in the minimum scale to $835 the first year, and to $870 and $900 in subsequent years. The work year was set at thirty-six weeks for the 1994-95 season, thirty-seven weeks the following season and thirty-eight weeks during 1996-7. The musicians also gained, for the first time, benefits such as rotated vacations, long-term disability insurance, and more cost-effective medical and dental coverage. The orchestra committee praised the new contract. As Preston Turegano quoted Michael Tiknis in his October 7, 1994, *Union-Tribune* article, "The agreement will challenge the Association's ability to raise the money to meet the pact's provisions. But it's a challenge and we have to accept it, and I'm confident that we can rise to it." In retrospect, it is impossible not to wonder about the source of his confidence.

Turegano wrote that successfully negotiating a new contract with the musicians was considered to be Tiknis's most challenging task. But, he also noted, during his first year in San Diego, Tiknis "…dramatically increased ticket sales with innovative marketing strategies." Tiknis also was praised in the article for revamping the SummerPops that, until the 1994 summer season, had suffered four consecutive annual drops in attendance.

During the summer of 1994, Tiknis and Talmi instituted a separate, summer classical series to be played indoors, at Copley Symphony Hall. The soloists were all first-rate and exciting. They included Sarah Chang, Vladimir Feltsmann,

Andre Watts and Marilyn Horne. Jonathan Saville commented in the August 11, 1994, *San Diego Reader*: "The San Diego Symphony's Great Performer Series this summer is an effort to attract real music lovers, those to whom the outdoor Pops, with their mixture of very light classics and popular music, cannot satisfy serious musical appetites...The quality of the soloists has been high, as has the conducting; the orchestra is in fine shape, and is playing with commitment and even brilliance. The series is a welcome innovation..."

The house was packed for each of these (without papering or cut-rate seats), but the concerts were not paired, so more income could not be obtained. The receipts from the box office did not make up for the salaries, not only of the high-priced soloists but also of the orchestra and the guest conductors. Talmi conducted two concerts. George Cleve and Henry Lewis conducted the others. In Preston Turegano's August 8, 1994, *Union-Tribune* article, Tiknis was quoted as saying, "The summer classics series has changed the image of the San Diego Symphony in the community. People now expect to hear great performances with the orchestra." He characterized the public's response to the series as, "overwhelming."

Because of the success of that summer series, Tiknis devised a "Festival of Orchestras" for the fall of 1994. Dudley Moore, the comic actor and part-time pianist, would appear with the San Diego Symphony, and, in the same program, so would violinist Joshua Bell and cellist Nathaniel Rosen. Talmi would conduct that concert, featuring the Beethoven Triple Concerto. The guest orchestras were the English Chamber Orchestra, with Pinchas Zuckerman soloing and conducting, and Schlomo Mintz doing the same services for the Israel Chamber Orchestra. Grand Tier subscribers would be invited to post-concert receptions with the performers.

Valerie Scher reviewed the first year's performance of Michael Tiknis as Executive Director in her August 28, 1994, *Union-Tribune* article. Mainly, she liked him. She pointed out that he had forged a productive relationship with the music director and the musicians, that he had overseen the installation of the new shell contributed to Copley Symphony Hall by the Jacobs family, and that he had "sealed the recording deal with Naxos without the orchestra having to play the kind of tacky pops albums required by the orchestra's previous label, Pro Arte." Actually, of course, that had been "sealed" by Talmi before Tiknis came to San Diego. Scher also praised Tiknis for bringing the symphony to the new hall in Escondido, and for his over-all marketing skills. Further, according to Scher, he "...brightened the 1994 SummerPops," and also improved the quality of the food served at that venue. Tiknis was also praised for bringing Albert Rodewald into the program booklet as writer of the program notes, following the death of the former writer, Leonard Burkat

Murray Sidlin. *Photo courtesy San Diego Symphony.*

Scher's September 5, 1994, *Union-Tribune* review of a SummerPops program was informative. "Among the many improvements made to the San Diego Symphony's SummerPops programs this year, perhaps the most admirable has been the greater number of concerts devoted to classical music. The near-capacity crowd at the Embarcadero Friday night was happy proof that San Diegans will enthusiastically embrace such offerings…" She praised conductor Murry Sidlin, whose, "…presence throughout the summer has given the symphony a cohesion lacking in previous SummerPops seasons, where they faced a new conductor every program…"

The 1994-95 season opened on October 9, with the Mahler First Symphony and the colorful Nadia Salerno-Sonnenberg as violin soloist. Jonathan Saville reviewed the performance in the November 10, 1994, *San Diego Reader*. "I had come to the concert with a particular interest in hearing the violin soloist, the notorious Salerno-Sonnenberg. But, as it turned out, there was equal musical excitement in the Mahler performance, for Talmi conducted the work with impassioned heat and with a superbly nuanced sense of its vast emotional itinerary, and the orchestra played with such splendor and sensitivity that you would have thought you were listening to the Chicago Symphony." Moreover, in the violin concerto, "It is a tribute to the courtesy of Yoav Talmi and the responsiveness of the San Diego Symphony that the orchestral accompaniment…followed the soloist's eccentricities with such accuracy and suppleness; it must have been like mimicking the erratic twists and turns of a fish in rough water." It seemed as if the critics were giving up the complaint of Talmi's lack of creating musical excitement.

The next concert was notable for the apparance of Er'ella Talmi, the music director's wife, as soloist in Ellen Taafe Zwilich's Flute Concerto. She was warmly received. Valerie Scher wrote in the October 15, 1994, *Union-Tribune*, "With such talents, Talmi should conduct Talmi more often." Good press for the symphony continued, with Welton Jones writing in the October 23, 1994, *Union-Tribune*, that a "renaissance" of symphony successes "...has blossomed since Michael Tiknis took over as manager *(sic)* last year...If music director Yoav Talmi can be said to control the soul of the symphony, then Tiknis runs everything else..." In his article, however, Jones was careful to recall that the Association still carried a deficit of a million dollars. Regarding that issue, he quoted Tiknis: "We're waiting to hear on our application to the National Endowment for the Arts for a $200,000 challenge grant. For the first time, they're taking applications to reduce deficits. It would need a three-to-one match, which makes exactly $800,000..."

The season continued with an appearance on the podium by Maximiliano Valdez, from Tiknis's old Buffalo Philharmonic. Valerie Scher gave him a tepid review in the October 1, 1994, *Union-Tribune*, pointing out quite notably that, "...Valdez was often placid and emotionally remote...He made Yoav Talmi seem like the flamboyant successor to Leonard Bernstein..." The second disc for Naxos was recorded in mid-November, and Tiknis's new project, the new "Classic Encounters — the Rush Hour Series" debuted successfully in early December. Each of those programs was planned as an early evening, intermission-less, hour-long concert preceded by a social hour. Jung-Ho Pak conducted the series and made a hit with his small but enthusiastic, young, yuppie audiences. Later, Jonathan Saville got around to reviewing those relatively brief, socially-oriented programs in the May 11, 1995, *San Diego Reader*. "If the large contributors the symphony desperately needs have any doubts about whether the orchestra is worth financing, they should have heard this super performance..."

Things were humming. In his year-end summary in the December 25 *Union-Tribune*, Preston Turegano wrote that the "...second-best achievement in resurrection in the past 1,964 years" was the turnaround by the San Diego Symphony, spurred by Michael Tiknis's marketing savvy. But there was still that deficit, and Turegano also noted that the symphony continued to lag in contributed income.

1995 began with a splashy New Year's Eve blast at Copley Symphony Hall, musically presided over by the increasingly well-liked Jung-Ho Pak. However, despite the glamourous presence of Roberta Peters, the evening really starred a fake floor built over the orchestra level seats in the hall, with tables and chairs set upon it for the high-ticketed patrons to sip champagne and enjoy the buffet. The regular concert series began later in January with guest conductors Uri Segal and Jean-Claude Casadesus during Talmi's midwinter trip to other guest podiums. Tiknis then announced a repeat of the successful "Great Performers Series" given the prior summer inside the Copley Symphony Hall. In 1995, this series would feature Emanuel Ax, Andre Watts, Frederica von Stade and Jean-Pierre Rampal. Ax would appear in three concerts, playing all five Beethoven Piano Concertos under Talmi's baton, in Escondido's new hall. The other programs as well as the Ax performances were scheduled for downtown San Diego.

The 1994 series brought in ticket revenues of $215,000, and Tiknis projected earnings of $280,000 for the 1995 summer event. "San Diego has a healthy ego," he said. "People want world-class quality. That was the philosophy with which we began 'Great Performers'..."

Yoav Talmi's return to San Diego was acclaimed at his concert of February 3, 1995, by Pam Dixon, whose review was in the *Union-Tribune* three days later. She wrote, "Chalk it off to the 'maestro theory,' that the same orchestra can sound completely transformed as they play for different conductors, that the timbre of the San Diego Symphony sounds richer and darker when Talmi conducts it... This denser acoustic was evident even in Glinka's cheerful overture. Instead of Talmi encouraging a brassy glint to the rapidly ascending string passages, with darting movements he smoothed the sound to a cognac veneer..." The orchestra also performed the Gorecki Third Symphony on that occasion, a contemporary work that had achieved considerable popular success as a kind of "new age," seemingly monochromatic, pseudo-minimalist presentation of sadness. It was subtitled, "Symphony of Sorrowful Songs." Jonathan Saville wrote about the orchestra's performance in the February 23, 1995, *San Diego Reader*. "The local performance went a long way toward convincing me of this symphony's true power and majesty, much more than the recordings had managed to do. It was not only that Talmi conducted with searing intensity..."

A few days later, in the glow of those reviews, Talmi and Tiknis announced the 1995-96 season, including such guest stars as violinists Zukerman and Perlman, pianists Ax and Feltsmann, and even an appearance by famed actor Christopher Plummer. He would serve as narrator in Berlioz's "Lelio," to be recorded by Naxos. The season would hold sixteen sets of classical programs, with nine of them offering Sunday afternoon repeats.

Talmi waxed enthusiastic in Valerie Scher's February 7, 1995, column in the *Union-Tribune*. "I have always wanted musicians of this caliber here. Now it is possible. During the previous administration, I was always told that even if we sold out a concert with a Perlman or Zukerman, we would lose our shirts. But Michael Tiknis — who's a wizard at ticket sales — says we will fill the hall and earn money. And he has proved it…" "The wizard," himself, noted in the same column, "No orchestra in the country has had such dramatic increase in earned income. Before, there was real doubt that an audience could be built here. It obviously can…" As an incentive, the symphony programmed free bonus concerts for those who would renew their subscriptions by March 31, 1995. Jung-Ho Pak would conduct, with violinist Chee Yun as soloist.

In the midst of all this good news, Scher pointed out briefly that an $800,000 deficit still remained over the Association's head, and that fund-raising remained troublesome in what she described as the "recession-ravaged" San Diego economy. Tiknis acknowledged, "We're still having a great deal of difficulty with contributed revenue. That's definitely our biggest challenge." Months later, I interviewed Warren Kessler, and he contradicted that Tiknis remark. Kessler said that the problem with the San Diego Symphony had never really been in terms of contributed funds. "In terms of orchestras of that size, we were at least in the middle regarding contributions…" The much greater problem was the scarcity of earned income, which led to near-constant cash flow problems. He pointed out that even the board did not know how many of the attendees at the concerts were paid and how many were either discounted or, for that matter, overtly papered. "It's amazing what an executive director can do without the board having any idea…"

Despite the deficit and the fund-raising problems, the Association announced a new series of recitals to be held during the 1995-96 season under their sponsorship, presenting three outstanding soloists: pianist Alicia de Larrocha, soprano Kathleen Battle, and flutist James Galway. Tiknis visualized that series as an outgrowth of the earlier, successful "October Festival of Orchestras," which, he said, made money for the Association. Profits from the recital series would help, he said, to cover some of the $300,000 it takes annually to operate and maintain the symphony's home venue.

Soon after that, Tiknis announced (independently, according to Kessler, without input from the board and without earlier information to the board about the season) the 1995 SummerPops season, to begin on June 28 and continue through September 16. There would be twenty-one programs scheduled over thirty evenings at the Embarcadero Marina Park South and the California Center for the Arts in Escondido. Aside from appearances by the Boston "Pops" touring orchestra and the Asian Youth Orchestra, a concert performance of Bizet's "Carmen": would be given, as well as programs with Roberta Peters and Misha Dichter as soloists. Popular stars were listed as well, including Marvin Hamlisch and Burt Bacharach, Dianne Warwick, Maureen McGovern, Mel Torme, Johnny Mathis, Natalie Cole and John Denver. Thirteen other popular artists were also to be presented during the series, but those would be sponsored by Bill Silva

Presents. Tiknis said, "We're trying to give the kind of entertainment people would find at the Hollywood Bowl. We think this is world-class summer entertainment." The ticket sales goal was set at $2.4 million, a half-million dollars higher than the previous year's receipts. Partial underwriting for the summer season was in the form of a $200,000 grant from the Barona Band of Mission Indians in east San Diego County, operators of a highly successful casino on their reservation.

The 1995 summer season was, according to Kessler, the major factor leading to the demise of the orchestra. It had been planned solely by Tiknis, he said, who announced it late as a *fait d'accompli*. It cost far more than the symphony could possibly afford, with the line-up of big stars that he had signed ostensibly without the board's being aware of it until the announcement. The winter sales had been less than expected, Kessler said, so Tiknis needed to make that up, hopefully via the summerPops programs. Finally, the three-year contract with the musicians was also too expensive for the Association, but it, too, was a *fait d'accompli*. As he repeatedly pointed out to me, "You'd be amazed — executive directors can do these things..."

The financial struggles continued, as did the well received, highly praised music making. In the midst of all this, the city's Commission for Arts and Culture contributed $400,000 to the symphony. On April 11, 1995, Welton Jones, critic-at-large for the *Union-Tribune*, chastised the Commission for not completely rescuing the orchestra by paying off the deficit instead of what he described as docking them. Jones lectured the City Council, "First you bail it out, and *then* you insist, with all the clout of a major contributor, that the thing be fixed!" Cash flow was becoming increasingly scarce in the symphony's ledgers, and by April 28, 1995, Preston Turegano wrote in the *Union-Tribune* that the Association could barely make its payroll. Moreover, Michael Tiknis had told the board of directors that he would quit his $125,000 a year job at the end of August unless the crisis is resolved. "Making the orchestra's $240,000 a week payroll...is killing me. Because of it, I'm physically sick at times, and I have no commitment to the San Diego Symphony after my contract expires August 31st..."

Turegano reported that the symphony had already drained a $1.7 million line of credit secured the prior year, had already spent the $800,000 it had received as receipts for the 1995-96 winter concert subscription series, as well as the $250,000 receipts for the 1995 summer Pops series, scheduled to open in two months. The board responded by approving a six-month, $6 million fund-raising effort. Tiknis told Turegano, "It's my fervent desire to see this new campaign succeed because more than anything I want to remain with the orchestra, but the situation must be resolved...I have met with the executive committee and the full board and told them of serious problems I have continuing to manage this organization until substantial financial, specifically cash flow, problems are effectively addressed. I need to know when the crisis is going to end, and right now I'm not sure when that is, and that is giving me grave reservations about whether I should continue..." The seemingly ubiquitous cash flow problems had become even more intense over the prior year or two, based upon the new, universally hailed, three-year contract with the musicians, as well as the raises given to the administrative staff in October, 1994. The over-all lack of earned income, of course, was crucial.

Talmi also spoke with Turegano, saying, "I hope he will not leave. We need him, as before, if not more. He was the one who helped everyone realize that the San Diego Symphony is needed, and that the concert-going public is there for us. The threat of Michael leaving is so enormous that perhaps this will be an act that will make everyone realize the severity of the situation..." The new symphony president, Tom Morgan, previously chairman of the Greater San Diego Chamber of Commerce, echoed Talmi's wishes and concerns. He said that the new drive, "Symphony 2000," will retire $1 million in outstanding bank loans, eliminate an accumulated deficit of another $1 million, bring current $500,000 in accounts payable, establish a cash reserve fund of at least $1 million, and account for $2.5 million of the contributed income necessary to balance the operating budget for the then-current, 1994-95 season.

On May 3, 1995, the *Union-Tribune* editorialized, "By filling the concert hall, we have shown our enthusiastic support for the symphony as the cultural cornerstone of San Diego. Now the time has come to be just as enthusiastic about opening our checkbooks." The editorial did not recognize that the filled concert hall was frequently filled with papered, if not discounted attendees. The time was also coming, however, for the Republican National Convention to be held in San Diego in late summer, 1995, and the city's expenditures for that event would be spectacular. In terms of fund-raising, the symphony provided little competition.

Valerie Scher commented that the seats in Copley Symphony Hall were set with envelopes for contributions when Yoav Talmi next led the orchestra early in May. In her May 8, 1995, *Union-Tribune* review, she wrote, "...[O]f this there can be no doubt; the orchestra is eminently worth supporting. Reverberant proof was provided by the high performance quality of the evening's concert. The program...showed an orchestra of impressive strength and flexibility. An orchestra, moreover, that transcends the stress of financial uncertainty with gratifyingly accomplished playing. That was obvious in Brahms' Symphony No. 1, which capped the evening with music that was, by turns, brooding and stirring, tender and triumphant. If only the orchestra's victory over financial adversity could be as decisive." A couple of days later, Preston Turegano reported that Michael Tiknis had taken indefinite medical leave. "I'm home, I'm sick, I'm exhausted," he said. To add to the burdens, Tiknis also was facing a lawsuit filed the previous month by facilities manager Karen Anderson, accusing the executive director of physical and verbal abuse. On May 13, Tiknis resigned his position.

Welton Jones commented on May 16 in the *Union-Tribune*: "…Michael Tiknis will be accused of everything from the selling of too many tickets to the declining quality of oboe reeds. The truth is, though, that Tiknis did a better job than his many predecessors. His crime, perhaps, was optimism…So, goodbye, Michael Tiknis; hello, crisis as usual. What next?" Next was the next concert, a fine rehearsal for the orchestra's next scheduled recording for Naxos. The soloist was the famed violist, Rivka Golani, and the music was Berlioz's pseudo-concerto, "Harold in Italy." When the disc was finally released over a year later, it received fine reviews from several influential record review journals, including *Fanfare*, which noted that the performance and recording were at least the equal of, if not superior to a number of higher-priced CD's of the same music.

Before the May 19, 1995, final concert of that season, numerous media articles brimmed over with opinions and interviews about the orchestra, Talmi and Tiknis. All the comments about the orchestra and Talmi were indicative of the general impression that the ensemble was excellent and that Talmi had burnished it beautifully. No one, including Valerie Scher, was complaining any more about his lack of excitement on the podium. John Willett was no longer the music critic for *San Diego Magazine,* and even he had more than mellowed toward the music director before he retired. In the magazine's June, 1995, issue, David Gregson, who had taken his place, wrote, "I have only the highest praise for the San Diego Symphony Orchestra under Yoav Talmi's inspired leadership. His recent performance of Beethoven's 'Eroica' Symphony packed an emotional wallop. Every section of the orchestra played to a burnished perfection….I was not the only listener to leave Copley Symphony Hall utterly stunned…I have heralded the symphony's 'golden age,' but it is Talmi who most often finds the gold where others mine lesser ores…" Later, in a retrospective review in the June, 1997, *San Diego Magazine*, he would compare Talmi with his predecessor music director, "…David Atherton, the brilliantly gifted British conductor who, from 1980 to 1987, turned the San Diego Symphony into a really important orchestra…Later, another great musician, Yoav Talmi, would bring the symphony to world class status just before its catastrophic financial collapse. Sometimes we lose our heroes. Great artists mix awkwardly with politics and economics…"

On the other hand, Tiknis was treated ambivalently in the media. In Turegano's May 16, 1995, *Union-Tribune* column, the ex-executive director was quoted: "The thing I wanted to avoid when I took the job…was that it would turn out to be transitional. As it turns out, that's exactly what happened." Tiknis told Turegano that he had not been told by the people who interviewed him in

Buffalo of the actual, poor contributed income situation. "I fixed the marketing parts, filled the hall, stimulated the SummerPops, hired a better staff, and basically that killed me. Contributed revenues did not come in as expected. I was led to believe it was not as serious as it turned out to be. The board didn't do its part to address the contributed-revenue situation…"

Finger-pointing was endemic. Kessler, in his interview with me, took considerable umbrage at Tiknis's comments about the board. Kessler described the board as hard-working, heavy contributors. Again, he repeated his opinion that the contributed income was not the problem that the earned income was. Tiknis's accusation, however, that he did not know the seriousness of the financial situation when he took the San Diego job appears totally unrealistic. There was probably not a symphony executive in this country who was not aware of the years-long problems of this city's orchestra. Insofar as the figures were concerned regarding earned vs. contributed income, these were always readily available in the books of the orchestra. If any snake oil salesman from San Diego was trying to slip one over on Tiknis in order to get him to come here, it surely would have been expected that he would have been smart enough to check the orchestra's books for the past number of years before accepting a job here.

If Preston Turegano could write a history of the symphony's contributed income in his May 16, 1995, *Union-Tribune* article, the dreadful figures would certainly have been available for Tiknis to find before he accepted the job. The 1980s, of course, were critical years for both contributed and earned funds, but a clean slate was obtained in 1990 when four banks and two wealthy patrons forgave the symphony's debts to them to the tune of $4 million, and an additional gift of $2.5 million from Helen Copley brought Symphony Hall out of hock. Turegano wrote, "During the last two years of former executive director Wes Brustad's six-year tenure, the symphony's contributed income dropped from $3.4 million in 1991 to $2.9 million in 1992. Most of the decline was in membership contributions and government support. During the 1992-93 season, Tiknis was the executive director for the last two months of the fiscal year. Contributions rose to $3.7 million that season, but only because the symphony prematurely applied about $300,000 remaining in a $1 million incremental gift made a few years earlier by a symphony patron…For the 1993-94 season, which has yet to be audited, contributed income again dropped, to $3.4 million…Despite the improved attendance picture, symphony expenses continued to outdistance revenues…" And although the subscription ticket holders increased considerably, the over-all improved attendance figures were obtained in part by the use of discounted tickets, with occasional overt papering of the house. The enormous million dollar-plus deficit had never been reduced from the end of 1991-92. The figures are all simple enough. It takes no accountant to realize the desperate straits the symphony had been in when Tiknis took over, and the even more desperate straits it developed by the time he left.

Valerie Scher wrote about him in her own May 16, 1995, *Union-Tribune* column. She noted that, like his two predecessors, he was hailed as a savior, "...as if the expertise of one person could rectify decades of faulty financial thinking. Also like his predecessors, Tiknis is departing under a cloud of concern...particularly dark because he has left the orchestra in worse financial shape than when he encountered it...He is undoubtedly a complex and controversial figure. While in power, he could be persuasive yet prickly, passionately articulate but often unyielding — a controlling personality energized by almost manic determination..." He was a remarkable salesman who was energetically able to carry the board and the staff along with him. He provided excitement, and his marketing abilities drew crowds. But the crowds did not create enough revenue. Nor could they provide the other funds so sorely needed — the millions required from corporate, governmental and individual donors. Did Tiknis forget that American symphony orchestras simply can not be self-supporting? I certainly doubt that. Rather, he seemed to be carried away by the force of his own ideas about bringing the public into the house.

In the July, 1995, *San Diego Magazine*, David Gregson quoted Talmi's tribute to Tiknis. "When I first arrived in town, I was told, 'Forget about it! There is no audience for classical music in San Diego during the summer!' But when Michael Tiknis took the helm, I found a man in love with classical music and willing to take the risk. Well, the first try, we had full houses, and not only did we not lose our shirts, we made good money...So I wanted to go further with a Beethoven cycle for the first time. Tiknis was the one brave enough to say we will venture it..." Gregson continued, "In light of the current crisis, these comments are tinged with irony. Tiknis resigned in May...Now we're all crossing our fingers...Lovers of the symphony may pray that the Tiknis legacy of bravery flourishes, and that this valuable local institution of ours continues its superlative work under Maestro Talmi's artistic guidance."

Bravery may or may not have been the appropriate attribute, and the "good money" was, in actuality, not good enough. Others may have, and still do consider Tiknis's actions and decisions as reckless instead of brave. But, somehow, the music continued and the public came. In mid-July, the "Great Performers Series," planned by Tiknis and Talmi, opened as planned with Emanuel Ax starting to play the cycle of Beethoven piano concertos under Talmi's baton in San Diego and in Escondido. The musicians, however, received only part of their pay for their work done after July 1. Tom Morgan, the Association president, said that about half of the required $260,000 payroll was available for the July 15 payday. The SummerPops series had also started. Their first star soloist,

Doc Severinsen, was not paid completely nor was Emanuel Ax, and then Jaime Laredo, the second soloist of the "Great Performers Series" was also left high and dry. The balance of the July 15 salaries were finally paid about a week late, and the August 1 shortfall was not as great.

Worse luck, the summer nights were unusually cold at Embarcadero Marina Park South, and attendance at the 1995 SummerPops, with the exception of the performance of the touring Boston "Pops" Orchestra, was disappointing. The mid-August appearance of Kathleen Battle, herself fighting a plummeting career due to marked, highly publicized personality dysfunctions, created considerable resentment among those who came out to hear her — and among the orchestra under Yoav Talmi who was actually making his SummerPops debut. It was the summer's highest-priced ticket. Battle was, at best, distant and uncaring about the appearance, and immediately drove away after her last programmed number. No encore deterred her from racing to the waiting limousine. Later, Talmi confided that she did not show up on time for rehearsal, so that was quite limited, and her attitude did not make the attempts any easier. His comments confirmed the gossip I had heard from several orchestra members.

In mid-August, the city helped out by approving a lump-sum payment to the Association of the remaining revenue from the hotel-motel room tax that it had been scheduled to receive during the 1995-96 fiscal year. The city paid more than $218,000 to the orchestra, allowing the latest payroll to be met. But later in the month, more bad news afflicted the symphony when it was reported that, not just the one already known, but a total of three former symphony employees were suing Michael Tiknis. The allegations were that his verbal and sexual harassment forced two of them to quit, and that he fired the third without cause. That kind of publicity, of course, provided no help for the symphony's desperate fund-raising efforts. Later in the fall, Tiknis left San Diego to assume a job as a developer of an outdoor amphitheatre near New York City. Characteristically, he described it to Preston Turegano for the latter's September 25, 1995, *Union-Tribune* column, as the "...future Tanglewood of New York." He stayed there for a while, then managed the Honolulu Symphony for several years before winding up managing a mid-level orchestra in Michigan.

The summer concerts went on, regardless, but only under marked duress. In mid-August, the chairman of the Symphony's fund-raising campaign, "Symphony 2000," resigned. He had also been chairman of the San Diego Host Committee for the 1996 Republican National Convention, and he resigned from that, too. He and his family, with little notice, simply picked up and left for the east coast where he was to resume his work in finance and investments. The community was shocked, and contributions, of course, slowed. Natalie Cole nearly cancelled until a certified check was presented to her manager immediately before her scheduled performance. And Yoav Talmi entered the show-saving scene when he convinced Misha Dichter to accept partial payment to be followed by payment of the balance. The musicians in the orchestra took home only half of their expected September 1 pay.

The next payroll was simply postponed. Tom Morgan, the Symphony's president, said that he hoped that the musicians could be paid by the following week, but he was not at all sure. Hopes were high, though, because the summer finale with John Denver was attracting large audiences. But right after the final concerts, the general manager, Craig Hajduk, resigned. He had been trying to serve in Tiknis's place. Later that month, the musicians, themselves, offered to help with a plan of their own. They proposed that they be paid as per their three-year contract demands, but that a significant portion of the payroll be set aside in savings by the Association. Then, at the end of three years, if the symphony had succesfully operated without missing a payroll, that sum would be handed to the association as a gift, to be incorporated into the endowment. Preston Turegano reported in the September 30, 1995, *Union-Tribune*, that the symphony's board approved the musicians' plan and adopted it.

The 1995-96 season opened as scheduled, but a *Union-Tribune* editorial on the morning of the first concert, October 6, 1995, warned that dangerous times lay ahead for the city, and for the community if the orchestra vanishes. "Declining cities like Buffalo and Oakland have lost their orchestras in recent years because of inadequate community support. But we must never let that happen to San Diego." The editorial quoted Yoav Talmi: "It has become apparent to me that unless we do something urgent, the symphony will fall within a period of two or three weeks..." Elsie Weston assumed the symphony presidency, and predicted that at least a million dollars would be forthcoming from unnamed prominent local philanthropists, and the rest of the needed $2 million from the public. The philanthropists who came through early were Qualcomm, Inc., Ellen Revelle Eckis and John Moores. Their total was $700,000, and others contributed in somewhat smaller amounts. Warren Kessler's opinion is that Elsie Weston deserved a medal instead of the brickbats she received from a number of sources. She took over at a terrible time, he said, and worked harder than anyone thought possible to keep the symphony going. "She made such an incredible commitment to try to save the symphony..."

The audience favorite, *Carmina Burana*, opened the season, and Valerie Scher wrote in the October 9, 1995, *Union-Tribune*: "As music director Yoav Talmi conducted Cowell's 'Hymn for Strings,' Beethoven's Choral Fantasy, and Orff's 'Carmina Burana,' the first of this week's three concerts confirmed what a splendid musical organization this is...Talmi expertly synchronized 'Carmina Burana's' massive musical forces..." In a different vein, columnists in the media, such as financial expert Don Bauder, and Professor Wayne Cornelius blasted both management and the symphony board for over-estimating potential income and not planning realistically. Almost as if to answer these criticisms, the beleaguered Elsie Weston announced to the press that the next soloist, Yitzhak Perlman, had been paid. The musicians, however, donated their services for that special, expensively ticketed benefit, "President's Night" with Perlman. There was also an auction as well as the music, and a few thousand more dollars were raised. By a few days later, it was announced that just over half of the two million dollar goal was raised. But Elsie Weston was quoted by Preston Turegano in the October 19, 1995, *Union-Tribune*, that, "We need a major response from the corporate community." She noted that the public contributions were, "...not going to cut it."

The significant cuts being made by the Association were becoming more apparent to the audiences. For example, the program booklets were no longer being produced. Instead, beginning with the October 20 concert, conducted by Pinchas Zukerman, who also soloed on the violin, stapled pages of photocopies of computer-printed information were distributed. The audiences began to dwindle so that, at times, the hall was only half-full. Poor Yoav Talmi was becoming more depressed by the day about the financial mess, and then he took another uppercut with the assassination of his country's prime minister, Yitzhak Rabin, whom he knew. Moreover, Talmi's college-age daughter had been in a potentially dangerous position in the midst of the peace rally crowd in the Tel Aviv square when that happened. But Talmi proceeded with his work, and the orchestra followed him into its fourth Naxos recording in its Berlioz series. The concert reviewed by Valerie Scher in the November 20, 1995, *Union-Tribune* was a rehearsal for the recording. The performance of the *Symphonie Fantastique* was highly praised — and eventually it made a superb recording that, for one or another reasons, was not released by Naxos for several years.

Meanwhile, the board was debating policy, and some members were beginning to consider the possibility of bankruptcy. They failed to adopt a budget for 1995-96. The revenues for the fiscal year were projected at $6.5 million and the expenses as $9.5 million. An executive director was still being sought, and even Wes Brustad was briefly considered for the post. He had left his job in Oregon and had returned to San Diego where he was teaching at El Cajon's Christian Heritage College. However, it was rumored that at least six board members threatened to resign if he were hired as interim executive director.

Downsizing was a term being bandied about within the board and in the media reports of the rumors spreading throughout the town. Welton Jones, in his November 21, 1995, *Union-Tribune* column, blasted the entire concept pithily. "All too soon, a 'downsized' orchestra will become an orchestra not worth bothering over…" He concluded on another tack. "And, finally, it's time for our elected leaders to get busy. If Mayor Golding and the City Council can find a way to rebuild the library, then the symphony should represent a manageable problem. Hard work and passion from everybody. When we discard all the stuff that hasn't worked, those are the only answers left." Jones continued his tirade against downsizing over the next several weeks. In the December 12, 1995, *Union-Tribune*, he wrote, "Please, no more talk of downsizing the San Diego Symphony. Kill it or keep it but quit kidding around. There are no such things as downsized symphony orchestras, partial virgins or near-fatal deaths…"

A budget was finally developed for 1995-96, but it represented a severely cut estimate, based upon cutting the orchestra itself from eighty-one to seventy-five players, cutting the basic salaries from $835 weekly to $790, and cutting the work year from thirty-six to twenty-seven weeks — all despite the contract signed and sealed the year or so before. Talmi's response was, "If such a process meant the firing of musicians from the orchestra, I will not be a part of it. I will oppose it as strongly as I can…" Talmi was paid only through November, and he voluntarily requested a pay cut, in accordance with the new budget, despite his prior contract.

Valerie Scher noted a decrease in the orchestra's response to Talmi's conducting when she reviewed the November 24 concert. It was felt that this represented a collective depression on the parts of the musicians rather than any feeling about the conductor. The next concert was to be conducted by Vladimir Feltsmann, the famed pianist who had made a sensational hit with the orchestra during the summer "Great Performers" series a couple of seasons before. But his appearance was cancelled. Elsie Weston said, "We are in no financial position to afford him, and maybe some other future artists…" Jung-Ho Pak led the concert, and Scher's review in the December 11, 1995, *Union-Tribune,* was far from charitable. "Pak — an extremely promising young maestro — guided the orchestra…But he doesn't use a baton when he conducts, and his rather convoluted gestures appeared to prompt synchronization problems…There was the sense that Pak was so involved with interpretive details that he didn't sufficiently emphasize balance and clarity, melodic tension and rhythmic momentum…"

More staff layoffs followed in the symphony office, and by the time of Preston Turegano's year-end review of the arts in San Diego, in the December 25, 1995, *Union -Tribune,* he was able to write, "You would have to be as deaf as Beethoven not to have heard that the area's top arts story during 1995 was an old one — the San Diego Symphony's dire financial straits…" He noted that, despite Welton Jones' and other pleas against it, the orchestra was reduced in size to seventy-five players from its earlier eighty-one. In her own year-end column on that same date, Valerie Scher commented, "Through it all, the orchestra persevered, displaying admirable professionalism in everything from Beethoven to Tchaikovsky, from Orff's mighty *Carmina Burana* to downsized versions of Handels "Messiah."

The first article about musicians leaving for elsewhere came just a couple of days later, when it was reported that Arlen Fast, long-time symphony bassoonist, was leaving for the New York Philharmonic, and that the principal bassoonist, Dennis Michel, was leaving in the spring for a year-long Fulbright Fellowship in Vienna. Valerie Scher wondered if Yoav Talmi would leave, too. On December 31, 1995, she wrote, "The 52 year-old Israeli maestro — whose contract expires in September, 1997 — has demonstrated unusual resolve during difficult times. He has helped with fund-raising and morale boosting while providing strong musical leadership under stressful circumstances. But the board's decision to chop the annual budget...involves major cuts in the orchestra's size and season..." Talmi's "unusual resolve" was tested greatly by Mayor Susan Golding, in whose anterooms he had waited for three consecutive days to speak with her. He never got into her office. She never granted him an interview. He had hoped that she would do something — anything — to stave off what he saw coming.

The role of the Mayor was a strange one. It gave rise to many theories, rumors and even some substantiated notions. The most prominent of these was that she was in favor of the orchestra's collapse because she needed to demonstrate to the Republican Party that she was strongly anti-union. Letting the orchestra vanish would be a devastating blow to the union. Susan Golding had long harbored fantasies of climbing up the political ladder. She wanted to become either senator or governor, and believed that the 1996 Republican National Convention in San Diego would provide a springboard for those ideas. "Busting" the Musicians' Union, it was reported, would possibly newly endear her to the conservative wing of the party and provide an impetus for her ambitions. Her cold-blooded attitude toward the Symphony and its public did her no good, however. The rest of the mistakes she made while in office doomed any and all of her hopes for political advancement.

The first concert of the new year had been scheduled and was played — but with a reduced program. The reduction was in the size of the orchestra required and in the music to be played. Instead of Stravinsky's pageant-like, "Song of the Nightingale," Faure's Suite from "Pelleas and Melisande" was offered. As David Gregson wrote in the January, 1996, *San Diego Magazine*, "With his organization on the brink of financial disaster, the San Diego Symphony's superlative music director, Yoav Talmi, recently found himself wrestling with some real-life demons... Talmi tells me of his heartbreaking plans to downsize the classics themselves in order to save around $50,000. Music readers may not realize it, but some music costs more to perform — sometimes lots more." Talmi told Gregson that he would also have to forego the First Symphony by John Corigliano, as well as the longed-for Mahler Ninth Symphony, "…for me, the center of the entire season, musically…"Talmi explained that there was no money to rent the extensive Stravinsky score and parts. Jeffrey Kahane's appearance as piano soloist was also cancelled due to lack of funds to pay him, so instead of the Ravel Piano Concerto the orchestra was to play Debussy's "Petite Suite."

Finally, the January 10 issues of the *Union-Tribune* were headlined, "The Saddest Day." The decision made the previous day by the board was that the symphony would close its doors over the weekend and file for bankruptcy the next week. Elsie Weston, the president, noted that the Association had only $22,000 on hand and faced debts of more than $3 million. The Association called for a Chapter 7 bankruptcy, which really represented a total liquidation of the Association as well as the orchestra — and the loss of all of the assets, including the hall, business equipment, the music library, and the instruments. The uproar in the media was remarkable, with negative comments about the decision from nearly everyone. Editorials decried the situation. Letters to the editors abounded. Interviews with everybody involved were printed. But there was no financial savior this time. The board met with the mayor in a day-long session. The option of filing a Chapter 7 bankruptcy was discussed, as well as a possible proposal to keep the orchestra in business, at least temporarily.

The orchestra tuned up and Talmi rehearsed them for its last concerts. However, according to the January 13, 1996, *Union-Tribune*, "As scores of concertgoers watched in disbelief, deputy county marshals armed with a court order raided the Copley Symphony Hall box office, collecting money for a florist who hasn't been paid more than $3,000 by the organization. The raid occured at 7 p.m., one hour before the orchestra's first of two final concerts…"Nonetheless, the review of the concert was superlative-rich. Valerie Scher's January 14, 1996, *Union-Tribune* headline was, "Brahms, Mozart Come Alive as Orchestra Dies." She wrote, "During the Brahms, it seemed as if the ghosts of Arturo Toscanini and Wilhelm Furtwaengler were perched on Talmi's shoulders, inspiring one of the most splendid performances this critic has heard in nearly 12 years of reviewing this orchestra…"Talmi and the orchestra gave an encore, Bach's Air from his Third Suite, described as, "…handsomely shaped and thoughtfully paced, it was an elegiac ending made all the more poignant by the realization that these were probably the last notes this symphony would ever perform…"The house was packed. Funerals always attract people. Ordinary subscription concerts had failed to do so.

Talmi left soon after that concert because he had previously-contracted dates to guest conduct in Pittsburgh and in Europe. The proposed guest conductors who would have been on his San Diego podium during his scheduled absence had been notified not to come. The mayor became defensive in the press, taking exception to the criticism heaped upon her by many that the city had not helped the symphony in the same manner in which it helped the Chargers football team. The date for the filing of a Chapter 7 bankruptcy was put off for a time. The reason given was that there was a possible group of potential donors. Meanwhile, the City Council and *Union-Tribune* editorials urged that the board consider Chapter 11 reorganization instead of liquidation. Welton Jones, on January 23, 1996, commented in his *Union-Tribune* column, "This certainly doesn't feel like a city resigned to a bankrupt symphony orchestra. Popular reaction against the threatened hara-kiri by the...board is swelling daily...A majority of City Council members has called for reorganization rather than unconditional surrender. A grass roots support group called Voice of the Symphony Audience (VOSA) is scrambling for momentum. Radio talk shows bubble with input; people talk on street corners. Even newspaper reporters are receiving letters, telephone calls and faxes..."

Seemingly, everyone had his own plans to revive the Symphony, often starting with the resignation of the board and the founding of a new organization to take their place. Even Isaac Stern got into the act, when he was interviewed before his recital in Escondido, although he proposed no specifics. Welton Jones, on January 30, 1996, proposed the Nederlander Organization, a theater management firm that sponsors touring shows, as a possible group to mobilize a new symphony orchestra in San Diego. Meanwhile, Elsie Weston announced in early February, 1996, that Sol Price and Irwin Jacobs, two very distinguished long- (and large-) giving San Diego philanthropists, might be willing to donate what she described as, "...an undisclosed amount of funds that will enable the San Diego Symphony Orchestra to avoid bankruptcy and to resume concerts." The plan called for the Association to raise $20 million over five years as an endowment. The fund would be in a separate foundation and would be controlled and invested by a separate board, independent of the symphony board. The plan also required that the symphony board spend the rest of February and March raising $3 million in additional funds to finance the balance of the winter season and make some payments to creditors.

The plan was titled, "A Commitment to Financial Integrity." It recommended suspending the contract with the musicians and placing them on a fee per service basis. Elsie Weston clarified that concept, saying that it really meant a reduction of the minimum scale received by the musicians from that point until the end of the winter season, late in May, 1996. Welton Jones decried the plan as, "...another quick-fix band-aid," in the February 11, 1996, *Union-Tribune*. Talks with the musicians proceeded, but at what Elsie Weston called a, "snail's pace." Nonetheless, the talks and the plan had succeeded in at least postponing the planned bankruptcy. Meanwhile, Irwin Jacobs donated some money to hire a consultant, Tom Bacchetti, who had been executive director of the Atlanta Symphony Orchestra, as negotiations continued. A tentative accord was reached with the musicians late in February, and finally approved officially. The players agreed to a lump sum payment of $1,550 each instead of the thousands they would have received if they had performed the five weeks of concerts originally scheduled since mid-January. The Price and Jacobs money had allowed the doors to open in Copley Symphony Hall.

The orchestra would return to the concert stage at Copley Symphony Hall on March 15, under Talmi's baton, but the renowned soloists that had originally been announced at season's beginning would not appear. When Talmi returned to San Diego from conducting in Europe, he was interviewed and noted, "I've lost quite a few section leaders, at least temporarily. It's a big loss. We need to produce the same quality that the audience is expecting from us even though we don't have the same players…" Concertmaster Igor Gruppman had left to work with the London Symphony Orchestra on a tour of Spain, and eventually with it, as well as with the Royal Philharmonic Orchestra, on tours to the USA. He eventually joined the Royal *Concertgebouw* Orchestra of Amsterdam as one of its four concertmasters, and then became principal concertrmaster of the Rotterdam Philharmonic Orchestra. Nick Grant, the assistant concertmaster, went to Los Angeles to do studio work. Principal violist Karen Dirks joined the Chicago Symphony's viola section. Valerie Scher quoted Talmi in the March 12, 1996, *Union-Tribune*: "These are not normal circumstances, but we will try to do our very best…"

They did their best, playing excerpts from Smetana's "The Bartered Bride," and the Rachmaninoff Second Symphony. First hornist John Lorge played the Mozart Second Horn Concerto. Standing ovations greeted the orchestra, conductor and soloist. Valerie Scher quoted the conductor in her March 19, *Union-Tribune* column as saying, "I am almost afraid to be happy. So much has been accomplished in recent weeks, but we still don't know what will happen to the orchestra…" Scher contnued, "Talmi — whose contract expires in September, 1997 — remains devoted to the ensemble he has headed since 1989. Even though it means being a musician, mediator, psychologist and collective conscience rolled into one…" She also quoted Elsie Weston's comments about Talmi. "I can't speak highly enough of him. Yoav desperately wants to save the symphony. When he's in town, his whole being is devoted to the orchestra." And, as Scher quoted the musicians, "He's a father figure to the orchestra. The best thing about Talmi is his sincerity. Deep in his heart, he's trying to do the best he can for the music and for the orchestra…"

The new first cellist, Brinton Smith, was the soloist in the March 22, 1996, concert. It was his twenty-seventh birthday. There were too few celebrants in the half-filled hall. A week later, Preston Turegano reported that the symphony would not make its payroll that week, only two weeks following resumption of its operations after a nine-week shutdown. The next symphony performance was to be a film showing of Chaplin's "City Lights," with the orchestra accompanying. But the producer backed out because the Association still owed him $9,500 for films he produced for them last year. The payroll date of April 15 also passed without payment to the musicians. Welton Jones wrote, characteristically colorfully and provocatively, in the April 16, 1996, *Union-Tribune*: "In the game of strip poker being played by the San Diego Symphony musicians and board of directors, the climax has arrived. The hands are being laid down and, sometime this week, either the musicians get paid or the board members stand as naked as they would have in bankruptcy. Under terms of the February agreement, all salaries due as of the regular payroll date yesterday plus the $1,500 lump sum owed each of the contracted 79 musicians for concerts missed earlier this year...would be paid in full or....Or the musicians would gain possession of the music library, the stands, the chairs and the instruments belonging to the symphony. Yesterday afternoon, no checks appeared...So, in effect, everybody is waiting..."

The payroll was made the next day for the symphony staff but not for the musicians. Nonetheless, they continued playing, in a scheduled subscription concert conducted by Murry Sidlin. Meanwhile, after a guest conducting appearance in Salt Lake City, the board there was considering offering the post of music director of the Utah Symphony to San Diego's nearly out-of-work conductor. That orchestra also had a big deficit, and they had cut their season's budget by $800,000. However, they also had an endowment of $12.6 million. Talmi's concert, reviewed by Jeff Manookian in the April 14 *Salt Lake Tribune*, was strongly praised: "This level of music-making rarely has graced Salt Lake City's Abravanel Hall."

On May 7, 1996, the musicians finally refused to rehearse and said that they would not play in the next scheduled concerts unless overdue back wages were paid them. Talmi had been at home in Israel, but some symphony officials had called him and advised him to return immediately because of the chance of a positive resolution of the crisis. When he came, he was quoted by Preston Turegano in the May 8, 1996: *Union-Tribune*: "I understand the musicians' decision. You cannot pay your mortgage or buy groceries just on the inspiration of beautiful Schubert and Mozart. I have to respect what they decided. I wish, though, that we could end the season. There are only two more concerts to give..." They were not given. The Association cancelled them, and scheduled a meeting for the following week to discuss Chapter 11 reorganization. Some contributions came in and allowed the musicians to be paid about a third of two weeks' salary. It was not enough. On May 16, 1996, the *Union-Tribune* reported

Talmi's interview with Preston Turegano. "I really don't know if I'm returning to San Diego. If things do not improve, I must make myself available for orchestras that are interested in my services. I am terribly disappointed and frustrated. I was hoping to conclude this season, and to leave an impact on the public that this was not an organization they could abandon…Instead, the very long *diminuendo* of this season has finally ended with the softest *pianissimo*…"

The city decided to withhold the annual payment to the symphony of the hotel-motel room tax revenue. On May 29, 1996, the symphony board decided to liquidate via a Chapter 7 bankruptcy petition, reaffirming its original, January decision. This called for a federal bankruptcy referee to organize whatever assets remain with the symphony, including Copley Symphony Hall, and sell them in order to pay creditors to whom the organization owes over $4.5 million. Elsie Weston said that Irwin Jacobs and Sol Price had been unable to persuade other wealthy individuals to donate toward the proposed endowment fund and to provide some operating funds for the orchestra. The bankruptcy papers were filed on May 31, 1996.

Tom Bacchetti had returned to Atlanta after the conclusion of his three-month contract here as a consultant. Preston Turegano called him in Atlanta, reporting on that interview in the June 2, 1996, *Union-Tribune*. Bacchetti said, "The San Diego Symphony has been so preoccupied with managing its operations on a day-to-day basis, and chasing cash flow, that the kind of market research I'm accustomed to has never been done there. No demographic profile has ever been done." Regarding the resignation of Michael Tiknis and the lack of anyone to fill his job, Bacchetti said, "Having someone with professional orchestra management experience in there might have made a difference…but that's entirely speculation on my part. Still, I can't help but think about it…"

Valerie Scher's June 10, 1996, *Union-Tribune* column featured an interview with Yoav Talmi. "Every minute of every day I feel sad about the San Diego Symphony. I am sad for the musicians who have been deserted. Sad for the community which lost a great ensemble that brought immense joy to many people. And I am sad for myself. I have lost an orchestra that I dearly loved and to which I was dedicated for almost seven years…" The article pointed out that not all of the symphony's musicians were as loyal to Talmi as he had been to them. The previous month, a tin can labeled, "Send Yoav to Utah," appeared in the musicians' lounge at Copley Symphony Hall. It generated four dollars in donations in a single day.

Talmi commented on that by saying, "It's not worth discussing. A few of the musicians needed an outlet for their anger and I was a convenient choice. I do not judge people on their agony and their anger…" On the other hand, Scher reported that Talmi was "…unabashedly upset at the civic leaders and potential donors who, in his words, 'Turned their backs on the orchestra,' and chose not to save it. In contrast, he commended the earnest efforts of Elsie Weston, Irwin Jacobs, Sol Price and Ellen Revelle Eckis. As he told me much later, most of his anger was directed toward the mayor, whose help might have been invaluable. But it was never offered, and the orchestra fell, in part, as a result of her own failed political ambitions.

Regarding his relations with the musicians, in late 2003 Talmi pointed out to me, "I can proudly say that I never fired a San Diego Symphony musician. In 90 percent of the cases, it wasn't necessary. I found a fantastic team of wind players, and I appointed Sheryl [Renk] after the former first clarinetist left. I knew he was going to leave soon so I had no reason to be too anxious. Karen Dirks moved to the first viola chair from assistant concertmaster. I hired a new principal cello, who couldn't teach or lead the section. Then Brinton Smith came for two years until the orchestra began to collapse. Igor [Gruppman] was in *tutti* until Fabio Mecchetti decided to make him concertmaster. I took the very disciplined material I had inherited from Atherton, and started to work on finesse and subtlety, and more expression. I worked to try to bring all the sections to the same good level. It became a more sensitive orchestra. I got everybody to play at a level of engagement that they never had before..." Warren Kessler agreed. "Talmi really brought the orchestra along...He was really great for them at that stage..."

Talmi did not go to Utah. Instead, he embarked on a series of guest conducting engagements that, after a time, led to his accepting two simultaneous music directorships, in Hamburg, Germany, and in Quebec City. Germany was not unfamiliar to him. He had served as principal guest conductor of the great Munich Philharmonic Orchestra under the legendary Sergiu Celibidache many years before. Quebec was the home of the oldest established symphony orchestra in Canada, and Talmi took to that job with great pleasure and enthusiasm. He continues to thrive there, after gradually reducing his time in Hamburg, where he is now conductor laureate. Talmi compares the Quebec Symphony to the San Diego Symphony favorably in terms of their great attitude and eagerness to do well.

I was able to attend the centenary concert of the Quebec orchestra (they gave the Mahler Second Symphony on November 6, 2002), and it was apparent that he is truly idolized there by the musicians and by the public, significantly including the provincial government. In these days of financial crises severely affecting Canadian as well as American orchestras, the Quebec Symphony appears to be on solid financial round due to the support they receive from the government of the province. Also, the audiences there are large and enthusiastic. Talmi celebrated the hundredth anniversary of the orchestra not only with that centenary concert but also by touring with the orchestra across Canada. The reviews everywhere were fine. The orchestra is recording for a Canadian firm, and also presents broadcast concerts.

This does not mean that Yoav Talmi has forgotten about San Diego. He has many friends here and misses the orchestra. Certainly, it also does not mean that San Diego has forgotten about him. Through the entire history of the orchestra, he is the only ex-music director to have been invited back as a guest conductor following the appointment of a successor. During the 2003-04 season, he returned to conduct the Bruckner Fourth Symphony, a performance that Otto Feld, the long-time symphony violinist, called the best performance the San Diego Symphony ever gave. "They played better then than they had ever played as far as I can remember." In November, 2006, he will reappear here as a welcome guest.

Talmi has no wish to return here as music director. "That time is over," he told me, "and I am truly very happy in Quebec. But I would love it if they made me a permanent or principal guest conductor, or conductor laureate, so that I could give a concert or two here every year or so…" Many San Diegans who know and appreciate the rarified standard of music-making that characterized most of Talmi's performances here would also love it.

CHAPTER XV

Crucifixion and the Agonizing Resurrection

"It's dead," he said.

"It" was the San Diego Symphony. "He" was Richard Kipperman, quoted by Preston Turegano in the June 11, 1996, *Union-Tribune*. Kipperman had been appointed as the U. S. Bankruptcy trustee overseeing the Chapter 7 liquidation of the San Diego Symphony Orchestra. According to Turegano, Kipperman saw himself as a mortician. "The only thing that can change the symphony's situation is if it goes to court and files a motion to dismiss on the grounds that it has the funds to immediately pay off all its creditors. I don't think that's going to happen..." When the Association filed for bankruptcy on May 31, 1996, it reported assets of $6.4 million, including Copley Symphony Hall, and liabilities of $5.2 million. It was estimated that there were more than a thousand creditors, including individuals, employees and businesses.

Real estate agents had already contacted Kipperman about the hall, and he also had an inquiry regarding the music library, valued at over $90,000. It was to be determined if the hall could be sold, and also if the musicians could seize the music library, music stands and instruments. All of those, other than the hall, had been listed as security in the March 28, 1996, agreement that allowed the musicians to take the items if they had not been paid back wages by May 31, 1996. There had been no payment. The labor contract with the musicians would also need to be negated.

Meetings galore were held by the musicians, by various independent groups determined to protest the death of the symphony, and by VOSA, the "Voice of the Symphony." VOSA had been organized by a group of concerned music-loving citizens the prior year when the crisis had reached proportions serious enough to mean the likelihood of the death of the symphony. Musicians gave impromptu concerts in small groups all over downtown, and on at least one occasion a large group of VOSA members formed themselves into a kazoo band and played part of Tchaikovsky's 1812 Overture in front of Copley Symphony Hall. During the Republican National Convention, the musicians demonstrated at the Community Concourse, joined by Yoav Talmi, who, at the time, was in town trying unsuccessfully to sell or rent his Hillcrest condominium. Talmi also appeared at a benefit recital that raised $11,000 for the musicians.

Everybody was upset, everybody wanted the orchestra to continue. No one, however, seemed to have either the wherewithal or the creative capacity to turn the situation around.

The possible loss of the music library was the most serious and acute possibility. Nancy Fisch, the orchestra's long time librarian, estimated that replacement costs for the lost library would top $150,000. Costs would mount even more when scores were needed that were no longer in the public domain, and would have to be rented. The city refused to consider buying either the library or the hall. "We own one too many theatres already," according to the city manager, "And none of them makes any money for us..." On June 23, Preston Turegano reported in the *Union-Tribune* that none of the previous large donors to the symphony were interested in either of those assets. Turegano interviewed Bill Silva, the Pops promoter, as well as Ellen Revelle Eckis, Sol Price and Irwin Jacobs. None expressed any interest. Jacobs said that neither he nor his wife were interested in supporting a new entity or orchestra.

On June 27, 1996, the city council voted to earmark $500,000 from future hotel-motel room taxes (TOT funds) for an endowment fund if a new symphony orchestra is created to replace the defunct San Diego symphony. The council emphasized that the funds were to be earmarked, not allocated. The amount was greater than the mayor's plan to set aside only $200,000. Ben Haddad, Mayor Golding's Chief of Staff, was said to be working to bring together an interested and active group to work on the symphony situation, but no names were mentioned in the media.

Some of the musicians obtained part-time employment in a freelance orchestra organized by Silva to accompany the popular artists he was presenting during the summer here, and in Phoenix and San Bernardino. Murry Sidlin would not be at its helm. He was as out of work in San Diego as Yoav Talmi, although Sidlin remained as resident conductor of the Portland Symphony Orchestra for several more years, and as the director of conducting studies at the Aspen Festival. Jung-Ho Pak had obtained an appointment as associate conductor of the Spokane Symphony Orchestra, and continued as director of the Disney Youth Symphony.

In July, 1996, the musicians initiated a movement to replace Kipperman as trustee. They hired their own attorney, who announced that the musicians had requested to nominate their own Chapter 7 trustee, and that this was allowed under the federal bankruptcy code. The musicians and their union were critical of Kipperman because he had not contacted any of the musicians but, rather, communicated mainly with the board and management.

At the end of August, a hearing was held during which Kipperman filed a number of objections to the musicians' claims. The referee then determined that he could not rule on whether the musicians' claims were validly in dispute. The legal hassles continued at a snail's pace. Meanwhile the mayor and Ben Haddad were said to be forming a task force of about twenty-five people, described in the October 8 *Union-Tribune* by Valerie Scher as "...a broad mix of prominent business and cultural leaders who will examine what kind of orchestra San Diego can sustain..." That announcement fell on the anniversary of the opening of the last season provided by the orchestra, a year before.

Three days later, the bankruptcy judge ruled that the musicians could not replace Kipperman. The musicians appealed but, despite the appeal, Kipperman was proceeding with attempts to sell the Association's assets. The Athenaeum, in La Jolla, bid $30,000 for the music library, and competitive bids would be open until November 12. After a brief hearing, the sale to the Athenaeum was postponed to December 19. The Athenaeum planned to keep the library in trust until a new orchestra would be formed.

On December 15, 1996, the *Union-Tribune's* annual year-end article on the state of the arts, by Preston Turegano, detailed the creeping aspects of the bankruptcy. Turegano wrote, "Starting anything at all here seems just wishful thinking. When the San Diego Symphony filed for bankruptcy, Mayor Susan Golding vowed to do all she could to see that a new orchestra was formed. She persuaded the city council to set aside $500,000 in future TOT revenues for a new orchestra's endowment..." Actually, the mayor had suggested $200,000, but the city council over-ruled her and earmarked $500,000. Turegano continued, "...It appears to many observers that Golding has dropped the ball in forming a task force that would look at ways a new ensemble might be formed. In June, she said she would form the panel, but by November only three individuals had agreed to serve... Golding became preoccupied with the Republican National Convention in August (held in San Diego), and campaign endorsements for the November election. Now she is exploring the possibility of running for the U. S. Senate in 1998. In her state of the city address December 4, Golding spoke at length about education reform and jobs but said nothing about a symphony orchestra or her task force. Today, Golding's aides pass the buck to each other, with none able to say anything definitive about the task force..."

Five days later, a bombshell exploded when local businessman Larry Robinson offered to take the Association out of bankruptcy by contributing $2 million. That would pay off some of the orchestra's creditors and eliminate the need to sell the assets. Robinson and his wife, Ewa, were prominent socially in San Diego, and had been generous supporters of a number of local arts institutions as well as Scripps Memorial Hospital. Robinson had owned, sold and developed land in many areas of the country, most often in Colorado. "Soft-spoken, genteel, self-effacing and very successful at making money," is the way Larry Robinson was described in a profile by Preston Turegano in the January 26, 1997, *Union-Tribune*. Turegano quoted Robinson, very surprised at all the commotion he had stirred, as asking, "Does it matter who I am? Do you somehow have to be anointed by some process to do good works? Why can't anonymous types do the same thing?" Robinson had always requested that his name not be listed among donors in the program books of the organizations to which he gave money. His prior largest gift had been to UCSD when he donated $2 million to finance the four-building Graduate School of International Relations and Pacific Studies on the Muir College Campus.

Robinson's offer delayed the sale of the music library to the Athenaeum. His proposal would pay taxes owed on the hall, a second trust deed held on the hall, liens held against the hall, and the administrative bankruptcy costs. The remainder of the $2 million would pay other creditors. However, there was no mention of anything for the musicians as far as back pay was concerned, or possible forgiveness of other Copley Symphony Hall debt. Furthermore, much would depend upon large additional donations from others in order to fund a season of indeterminate length that would possibly commence in the summer. Robinson's proposal, however, depended upon a possible conversion of the bankruptcy from a Chapter 7 liquidation to a Chapter 11 reorganization, as requested by the musicians — and, it seemed, by a great many outside interested parties as well.

A January 27, 1997, date for the consideration of the conversion was set by the referee. The musicians, with Ted Graham as their attorney, filed court documents about the change. These stated, in part, that the reorganized Symphony would be run by a reconstituted board and a professional manager, and that the hall would be leased to Robinson through January 31, 2000, in exchange for his $2 million and an agreement for the orchestra to be able to use the hall for a certain portion of the year. Robinson would also be granted an option to buy the hall for an additional $225,000 if paid prior to January 31, 2000, and that, if purchased, Robinson would donate the hall back to the symphony on or before January 1, 2015, if the symphony would continue to be operating at that time. Crucial to the proposal would be an agreement by the Bank of America not to demand payment on the $2.1 million note it held on the hall. That bank represented the consortium of banks that forgave the mortgage debt on the hall in 1990 — provided that the symphony did not sell the hall before December 31, 1999.

Other portions of the court statement filed by Graham and agreed to by the referee caused the cancellation of the proposed sale of the music library because that would hinder the proposed reorganization. Kipperman, the bankruptcy trustee, revealed that four other bids had been made for the music library at prices above that offered by the Athenaeum. However, on January 27, 1997, eight months after the symphony board filed its bankruptcy petition, Chief Bankruptcy Judge Louise Adler approved the conversion of the symphony's Chapter 7 liquidation to a Chapter 11 reorganization. That step saved all the assets and, most dramatically, prevented the immediate loss of the invaluable music library. She appointed Thomas Lennon as the court's officer to oversee the reorganization.

In his Sunday, February 2, 1997, *Union-Tribune* column, Welton Jones created a list of heroes in the battle over saving the symphony. Larry Robinson and the musicians themselves (as well as their counsel) headed the list, along with Bankruptcy Chief Judge Adler. On the other hand, Jones noted, "…Leadership was not provided by Mayor Golding, who ignored the crisis for months while muttering about a 'task force' she might get around to appointing. Apparently, such a group was formed as 1996 drew to a close, and even met once amid the secrecy that suddenly seems to mark much of what happens in the mayor's office…"

After all the sense of relief and the huzzahs, however, not much seemed to be happening. Preston Turegano reported in the March 17, 1997, *Union-Tribune*, that, "…the reorganization of the San Diego Symphony is off-tempo…" No new executive director had been hired, no new board had been identified, and a business plan had not been formulated. Ted Graham, the musicians' attorney, responded, saying that he remained encouraged by the reorganization, and that he was holding meetings every week with various elements of the community. But in April, a Citizens' Symphony Committee announced its formation, stating its independence from the mayor, and its intention to sponsor summer pops performances as a means of jump-starting the symphony. That committee at least presented a program. That made it different from the many individuals and groups that had developed their own, often widely disparate plans for reconstituting the orchestra. Most of those foundered on the shoals of impracticality.

Later in April, it was determined that a task force organized by the mayor had actually been meeting, sometimes with and sometimes without her. Ted Graham noted that he had been talking with some of the people on that committee. "They identified themselves," he said, "As the 'old mayor's task force.' I was told that the task force no longer existed…" The secrecy decried by many was necessary, it was explained, because none of the members wanted to be lobbied by any of the disparate groups that had their own plans for the symphony. Members named included Fred Baranowski, vice-president of the Bank of America in San Diego; Sandra Pay, Chairperson of the city's Commission on

Arts and Culture; attorneys Victor Vilaplana and Pat Shea; Pete Savage, a businessman; and Joe Charest, a public relations representative for the Gable Group. Ian Campbell and Tom Hall, of the San Diego Opera and Globe Theatre, respectively, had dropped out due to conflicts over the possible financial planning.

The identification of the task force was accompanied by a document signed by the mayor, entitled, "Principles for a New Orchestra." In the April 22, 1997, Union-Tribune, Welton Jones reported on that document. He commented that it, "…rightly notes some obvious realities — there is no 'quick fix,' the music has to start again as soon as possible, the former symphony board should not be part of a new organization — but there are other phrases that raise more questions than answers." Jones commented further on the phrase, "Leave behind the baggage of the past," saying that it ignores some bankruptcy realities. Also, the Principles' declaration that a multi-million fund-raising goal is not realistic "…hints at a lack of financial perception, and 'a new orchestra committee would be elected by a new orchestra' displays a shocking lack of tact in dealing with a very bruised labor union. If this committee thinks it can produce a credible symphony orchestra without the full cooperation of the American Federation of Musicians, then it is hopelessly naïve…"

Negotiations soon broke down about a possible summer season. The Committee had planned to present three concerts in the Convention Center over the summer, paid for on a per-performance basis, without a union contract. The orchestra had agreed to everything in the negotiations except for the status of three musicians, concertmaster Igor Gruppman, librarian Nancy Fisch and personnel manager Jim Hoffman. The Citizens' Committee wanted them replaced. Meanwhile, new names were released of Committee members. The additions were Berit Durler of UCSD Extension; Bill Geppert of Cox Communications; cultural activists Esther Burnham and Judith Harris; Ellen Foster of Sanyo North America; and Ted Roth of Alliance Pharmaceuticals. The name of a consultant to the Committee was also released, Tom Gerdom, formerly with the St. Paul Chamber Orchestra. Finally, as Baranowski revealed, Jung-Ho Pak was being considered as the new music director of the revitalized orchestra. Pak, himself, stated, "I can't talk about that because the situation is very political, but I feel very hopeful and eager."

Early in May, 1997, the mayor finally spoke. Referring to a breakdown in negotiations, she said, "They (the Committee) told me that they were unable to reach any kind of agreement (with the musicians). I am very discouraged…" Further, she commented, "I think we should stop giving hope until we know that there is a way to get there. I don't think we can as long as we are in Chapter 11." No plan had emerged that was acceptable to both the Committee and the musicians. The musicians' attorney, Ted Graham, fired back at the mayor, pointing out that the Chapter 11 reorganization plan saved the symphony's assets, "And it offers the great potential for the Robinson gift to kick-start the symphony." The mayor's attitude appeared to validate those who had originally accused her of wanting to "break" the orchestra and the union by liquidating the ensemble, regardless of the tremendous losses represented by the hall, the instruments and the library.

Welton Jones entered that particular fray in the May 6, 1997, *Union-Tribune*, beginning with, "Finally, the 800-pound gorilla has been heard from…" Jones noted that the mayor had been convinced by her advisors, including bankruptcy attorney Pat Shea, that the Chapter 7 plan was by far the best route. She had been dismayed, he reported, when the orchestra musicians successfully won over the Chief Bankruptcy Judge who converted the plan to a Chapter 11 reorganization. "It worries me," Jones wrote, "That the mayor seems to be waiting for what she calls 'the musicians' plan' to fail so that she can restart her Chapter 7 scenario. Exposing the orchestra assets to public bidding just doesn't make any sense when there's an alternative as viable as Chapter 11. If the problem is old labor contracts, then a combination of the Robinson settlement plan and the local musicians' historic flexibility — they've never finished a union contract without giving back something — should solve that…"

The glacial pace of possible resolution continued. On June 22, 1997, Preston Turegano reported in the *Union-Tribune* that, "The bureaucratic rituals and legal maneuvering that defined the Chapter 7 proceedings only gave way to Sisyphean Chapter 11 reorganization meetings, negotiations and discussions. Tom Gerdom, the consultant (paid for by the San Diego Foundation) developed a plan to establish a new non-profit entity, the "San Diego Music Society," that would hire musicians "with a positive attitude and under a flexible contract" to present summer concerts in the summer of 1997, as well as a winter season, all under the batonless hands of Jung-Ho Pak. Although at least a million dollars would be needed to fund the summer season, only John Moores, the owner of the San Diego Padres, had come forth with any money. He pledged $100,000. But the dispute over the three musicians referred to above, as well as some other reservations held by the musicians, prevented the plan from coming to fruition.

Even I got into the press during the long, dreary days of trying to figure out what was happening, and how things were being done. The situation was increasingly complex and un-understandable due to the over-all secrecy, as well as to all the varied approaches continually being touted by others aside from the mayor's so-called Citizens' Committee. I had organized a small group consisting of Philip Klauber and Dallas Clark, who, with me, had been officers of the symphony board during the 1960s. I had specifically asked them to join with me because of their positions in civic circles. Each had, in former years, been a "Mr. San

Diego," and their names and reputations were widely known and respected. Also included were Jules Pincus, a respected local businessman, and Charles Cheney, a representative of VOSA. Our goal was to try to get the various groups to work together in an attempt to develop a coherent plan that all could eventually agree on, instead of competing with each other.

Preston Turegano quoted me in his June 22, 1997, *Union-Tribune* article: "Our group is not VOSA. We are simply monitoring the reorganization process. We are not expecting to be a new board for the symphony. We just want to see that the preliminary reorganization stuff is done correctly. We all believe that the symphony ought to be an organization that provides total community service, and in order to do that there can't be anything hidden under any rock." But things continued to be hidden. Turegano reported in that article that the mayor's position on the symphony was unchanged. She continued to favor the Chapter 7 liquidation that an attorney had told her would be the best fate for the orchestra. That appeared to contradict the position of her appointed Citizens' Committee that was to negotiate with the musicians who had succeeded in avoiding the destructive Chapter 7. Suspicion levels were high all around.

Of course, negotiations cannot generally be carried out in the open due to the likelihood of sides being taken and disruptions occurring that would only serve to widen the gap between the parties. But that general rule was being compounded by the gross mistrust between the musicians and the so-called Citizens' Committee formed by a mayor who appeared to want the orchestra and its union to sink under a Chapter 7 liquidation. Further, competitive ideas rising within a number of the disparate groups promoting their own plans for re-establishing an orchestra only muddied the waters. Had there, for example, been actual leadership from the mayor's office, had she worked to establish a committee that would have offered to hold open meetings or at least meet with interested parties in town, a totally different fabric of feeling would have been created about re-establishing the symphony. All sides would have been heard from, and the disparate and often mutually contradictory ideas about how to re-start the orchestra would have been resolved or otherwise dealt with. Most important, the aura of suspicion that clouded everything that was purported to be happening within or from the Citizens' Committee would have disappeared, and everyone would have been working together toward a common goal via a common road.

Characteristically, our group was turned away by the Citizens' Committee at the entrance to what had been billed as an open meeting. It was not made open to us, however, and we had little choice but to give up the good fight and continue monitoring from a distance. We never did get to talk with the Citizens' Symphony Committee or with any of its members, although we had some good communication and understanding with other pro-symphony groups, including the musicians and their attorney.

The lack of trust among the many sides was remarkable, and it became obvious that egos were becoming increasingly paramount over the hoped-for eventual result. VOSA, on the other hand, remained active and provided protests, newspaper stories and innumerable ideas about how to start the orchestra and how the orchestra should function in the community. Insofar as any meaningful response to all of that by the supposed powers-that-be, by and large they talked to walls, although Ted Graham always provided a ready ear and encouragement..

Hope, however, reared its by then-weakened head again later in July when the city manager, Jack McGrory, became associated with the negotiations in a manner that was not quite clear at first. He had scheduled his official resignation as city manager for fall, after which he was to start working for Sol Price. Price, of course, had been a staunch symphony supporter. It appeared as if the impetus for McGrory's participation came from the mayor, who commented, "A lot of the trouble has been labor-related, and Jack has a very extensive background in labor negotiations." Again, the Golding obsession with labor troubles rather than fund-raising or earned income troubles further intensified the impression that she was out to "break the union" as a ploy toward obtaining higher political office as an avowed conservative. Negotiations are hard enough when they center around a single agenda, but the mayor had her own.

On August 11, it was announced that a meeting with forty musicians and the representatives of the mayor's office "established working conditions for when the orchestra apparently resumes concerts this fall." The quotation is from Preston Turegano's article in the August 12, 1997, *Union-Tribune*, which provided some details. A two-year season was called for, with a seventy-eight-member orchestra. A new board would be comprised of individuals selected from throughout the community, and "...all parties agree to live within a predetermined budget, to do what is best for the overall San Diego community, and to participate in several musical educational programs..." The minimum pay for the musicians would be $20,000 for the first season and $25,000 for the second. It was assumed that Jung-Ho Pak would be appointed music director by the reconstituted board, and would have "final authority" on any new musicians. The mayor was quoted: "We felt it was prudent to announce this first baby step. This is a very financially conservative agreement, one that I think any donor would be comfortable with. There's a lot left to be done..."

A week later, in his *Union-Tribune* column, Welton Jones was markedly critical. "The struggling remnants of the San Diego Symphony sank further last week into the bog of politics...After months of empty promises, Mayor Susan Golding summoned the press to City Hall...Music-loving hearts quickened everywhere, because it had long been obvious that no orchestra revival is possible until the mayor decided to lead, follow or stand aside..." Jones decried the facts that there were no scheduled concerts, no conductor, no manager, no board, no bankruptcy agreement, no full-time wages, no money and no plan — "...just an exhausted surrender by less than half of the former musicians, who didn't even bother to take a vote." The result formulated by Jones was that "...the union musicians who once made up the San Diego Symphony have agreed to return to the status of part-time players in a community orchestra..."

The next week, though, there was management, paid for by the city. Thomas Gerdom had become the official managerial consultant, and had been given a nine-week contract for $30,000. Rumors began about a likely season opening early in October, but that came and went without anything — including without Gerdom, who had gone back to Ohio. When telephoned by Welton Jones, Gerdom responded that he was, "...waiting for some calls." Meanwhile, as Preston Turegano reported in the October 21, 1997, *Union-Tribune*, Larry Robinson remained waiting in the wings, a suitor without takers. His $2 million that had been offered was still available. It was being held in a certificate of deposit at Grossmont Bank. Meanwhile, talk had begun about the Convention Center taking over Copley Symphony Hall and operating it as a performance and meeting facility. How that would work when (and if) the symphony needed dates would have to be worked out.

Unfortunately, also meanwhile, the ongoing expenses of unused Copley Symphony hall had caused Thomas Lennon, the bankruptcy trustee for the symphony, to begin tapping the endowment money held in trust for the symphony at the San Diego Foundation. Lennon, like the musicians, had been unpaid during the extended stalemate, but he, like they, continued to try to make an orchestral future. As Lennon said in the Turegano article, "The symphony has languished in Chapter 11 for 10 months now. The only accommodation has been the musicians' readiness to perform at substantially lower pay. It's time for the other parties to make their contributions. We need a corpus of people and corporations willing to step forward and make contributions."

Finally, according to Welton Jones' November 20, 1997, *Union-Tribune* article, "After months of rumors, secrecy and missed deadlines, a citizens' committee stepped forward yesterday to take responsibility for the San Diego Symphony. Sandra Pay, until recently the chairman of the San Diego Commission on the Arts and Culture, and Ted Roth, vice-president of Alliance Pharmaceuticals, will serve as co-chairmen of the interim board of directors...It will take over from the old board which placed the orchestra in bankruptcy 16 months ago." Jung-Ho Pak would become artistic director and conductor, and Tom Gerdom would serve as interim executive director. "So far, in addition to Pay and Roth, the new board includes Bill Geppert of Cox Cable; banker Fred Baranowski; Berit Durler, operations director for UCSD Extension; Phil Blair of Manpower; Keith Johnson of the Fieldstone Corporation; and Elizabeth Oliver." The first concerts would be given in March, 1998, followed by a summer season — and funds would need to be raised in order to cover a planned budget of $7 million.

Then, on December 11, 1997, all ten of the new board members resigned because the old board refused to do so! The old board had met for only the fourth time since the decision to file for Chapter 7 sixteen months before. They then decided to wait for a court-ordered reorganization plan — and to remain on the reconstituted board that, they said, could have room enough to include them. Of course, they had not been asked to continue to serve by anyone on the newly named board. According to the sentiment felt throughout town, too, the rest of the community would not have them, either — but they refused to resign and simply turn over their function to the new board. To paraphrase Tonio, in his final lines of the opera, *I Pagliacci*, "*La Commedia e non finita.*"

Meanwhile, a gift was given as a Christmas token for the still out of work musicians. An un-named foundation, operated through the San Diego Foundation, gave a thousand dollars to each of the musicians. In the midst of the roller coaster running seemingly out of control all around them, it was a welcome Christmas present to all of them.

The new year started without any apparent progress in the board stalemate. On January 4, 1998, Valerie Scher wrote in her *Union-Tribune* column that it was likely that Jung-Ho Pak would become the orchestra's next musical director, "…if — still a sizeable 'if' — the San Diego Symphony resumes playing in a few months…" She offered a few comments about him. "Since joining the San Diego Symphony staff in 1994, Pak has demonstrated intelligence, insight and artistry in leading an array of orchestra concerts…He likes conducting without a baton, something that distinguishes him from most other conductors. The question is whether, baton or not, his talent and good intentions are enough to lure patrons back to symphony concerts. And to keep them coming back."

Finally, in the January 13, *Union-Tribune*, Welton Jones was able to report, "The old San Diego Symphony board is gone at last, but the new one isn't quite ready to take over. Eighteen months after the last concert, the bankruptcy referee remains in charge, the musicians still aren't working, the donors are silent and there's far more talk than action…" The old board finally submitted letters of resignation to the trustee, with the exception of retired Judge Alfred Lord, a holdover requested by the new board. The new board met after that and listened to Jung-Ho Pak's hopes for the orchestra, but made no specific moves toward reorganization. The trustee commented, "If the lawyers can get together, I can go into semi-retirement. If nobody steps forward, it may be time for me and the musicians and one or two other arts groups in town to take over..."

Three and a half months later, Welton Jones reported in the April 28, 1998 *Union-Tribune*, "After two years of dark, silent bankruptcy, the San Diego Symphony is preparing to make music again. A citizens' group has assembled more than $2.5 million in donations and pledges...The first concert is projected for July 24, possibly on Navy Pier...'We've never been closer,' said Sandra Pay, former chairwoman of the city's Commission for Arts and Culture." Jones reported that a drive for a $3 million start-up fund had been mounted, and when that sum would be raised the group plans to become the new San Diego Symphony Board of Directors — but not until then. Larry Robinson, San Diego Padres owner John Moores, and Joan and Irwin Jacobs pledged a combined total of $2 million. Tom Gerdom came back to town to work on a new operations plan, having resigned as executive director of the Ohio Chamber Orchestra. His fee, as well as the expensive maintenance of Copley Symphony hall, was being paid by income from an endowment managed by the San Diego Foundation. Sandra Pay said that all funds raised would be routed through the San Diego Foundation. The reorganization plan was expected to be presented to the bankruptcy court in mid-June. At April's end, even the mayor provided a cautious note of grudging encouragement. "For the first time, I feel confident enough to support releasing some of the city funds set aside for a new symphony — when we get court approval for the reorganization."

The reorganization plan was prepared and mailed to the creditors, who needed to vote to accept or reject it. Larry Robinson's original offer of $2 million for a seventeen-year lease on Copley Symphony Hall was a basic premise of the plan. He would allow the orchestra full use of the facility. Also, he would retain an option to buy the hall for $100,000 during the course of the lease, and then would have to donate it back to the orchestra by 2015. It was hoped that the $2 million would satisfy all debts not waived or invalidated by the court. Each of the seventy-nine orchestra members would be paid a minimum of $25,000 annually over the next three seasons. Although Jung-Ho Pak would be the major conductor and artistic director, a nationwide search would be made for a new music director, and a new executive director as well.

The June 16, 1998, *Union-Tribune* reported, "The San Diego Symphony is out of court and back in business. Yesterday," according to the Welton Jones article, "Two years and 15 days after the orchestra was shoved into bankruptcy, Chief Bankruptcy Judge Louise Adler officially accepted the Symphony Association's reorganization plan, overruling last minute claims on Copley Symphony Hall by the owners of the surrounding Symphony Towers." The summer series of pops concerts at Navy Pier were to begin, and the regular fall season would begin in October, with eight sets of classical concerts as well as special events.

Judge Adler complimented the trustees and the attorneys, as well as, "... the musicians and trade creditors who have given up a lot to achieve this resolution...The ballots had an interesting flavor. Even though they will be getting only a small return, many creditors emphasized that they are happy to see symphonic music back..." The June 17 *Union-Tribune* editorial began, "They're back at last!"

The announcement of the programs for the summer series was made by Jung-Ho Pak, as well as by Tom Gerdom and board members. Pak was beginning to demonstrate his crowd-pleasing capacities, including a remarkably articulate manner combined with a near-constant smile. The SummerPops series would consist of 18 performances of 8 programs, beginning with "Truly Tchaikovsky" and ending in mid-September with "Fiesta Mariachi." On July 7, 1998, Welton Jones reported in the *Union-Tribune* that over $110,000 in ticket sales were made before the Independence Day weekend, "...and that's 10 percent of the potential million dollar gross for the 18 concerts..."

With all the possible hoopla readily available, the symphony did, indeed, open its summer series at its new summer venue, Navy Pier. Valerie Scher reviewed the proceedings in the July 27, 1998, *Union-Tribune*, saying, "Small wonder that champagne corks supplied festive competition to the opening night's percussion effects. Long-starved for pops fare, patrons in then near-capacity audience happily toasted the orchestra..." She noted the absence of many of the former principals, and realized that it would have been unrealistic to expect the orchestra to play as it had in the past. "But the symphony still played well...in everything from selections from The Nutcracker to the Violin Concerto...to the 1812 Overture, complete with cannons" and the Navy Band. "Conductor Pak provided genial introductions to the music without turning the concert into Music Appreciation 101..." In the finale, "Cymbals crashed, chimes clanged, strings and winds surged. And four, 105 mm. Howitzers manned by Camp Pendleton Marines fired blanks through the climactic moments, causing smoke to waft through the seating area. It's too early to tell whether the San Diego Symphony has won the war for long-term stability. But Friday's concert was an important victory."

The religious among us would point out, nodding with justification, "There is life after death."

CHAPTER XVI

Survival and Salvation

Much to the amazement — as well as to the gratification — of most San Diegans, the newly-breathed life of the reconstituted San Diego Symphony Orchestra continued. It was not an easy task for anyone — musicians, conductor or audience, but it worked. As Welton Jones wrote in the August 2, 1998, *Union-Tribune*, "Even with the miserable parking situation, the long intermission lines for too few portable toilets, and the occasional putt-putting of passing power boats, the return concert was a triumph, an evening of delights made emotional by the central reality: the Symphony was back."

By the end of the summer season, Valerie Scher was able to summarize it on a very positive note. In the September 13, 1998, *Union-Tribune*, she wrote that, "As a conductor, alternating with guest maestros, Pak displayed earnest-ness, intelligence and a welcome sense of humor, though he sometimes came close to sounding like an eager-to-please new faculty member on campus. It's the music, not the mini-lectures, that lure pops audiences. The musical perfor-mances revealed a gifted orchestra that was still finding itself, still recovering from its most devastating crisis in its 88-year history. There was spirit, if not always cohesiveness; ability, if not always interpretive refinement…" At the end, she wrote, "In the meantime, here's wishing for a slew of successful innovations when the symphony launches its Copley Symphony Hall season next month. As the SummerPops demonstrated, good ideas and never-say-die determination do make a difference."

Scher contributed a very lengthy and warm profile of the Symphony's young conductor in the October 4, 1998, *Union-Tribune*, on the Sunday prior to the opening of the indoor subscription season. Newly married and expect-ing their first child, the Paks were in the process of moving to their new home in Point Loma. In the article, Sandra Pay, chairman of the Association's board, noted that there had never been any question that Pak would succeed Yoav Talmi if the orchestra revived. "We never mounted a search for a new conductor. I thought that if we could keep him here there would be some continuity, and his enthusiasm is what we need to get this orchestra back on its feet and moving into the next century…" Pak's background was spelled out in some detail in the article. His parents had emigrated from Korea about three years before Jung-Ho was born in Burlingame, California. There is one older sister. The father had formerly served as a translator for the Korean Army. In America, he worked his way through pharmacy school by moving boxes at a canned food factory. He did become a pharmacist but then decided he wanted to go further. Dental school beckoned, and he went into practice when Jung-Ho was in fifth grade. The father did not approve of his son's wish to become a musician, and his mother was said to have been horrified. However, they eventually saw that there was genuine talent there. Finally, when he became a professor at the University of California, Berkeley, the parents were mollified.

As always, Scher commented on Pak's not using a baton. She quoted his reason. "I don't use one because I see it as a symbol of authority, of control. I want to make music with people, not at them..." Apparently, this worked for him. The musicians quoted by Scher felt very positively about him. His contract for the forthcoming season had not been finalized. He received $20,000 for organizing and conducting the summer season.

Following a rapid, herculean cleaning and refurbishing job, Copley Symphony Hall welcomed the audience for the opening concerts of the 1998-99 season on October 9, 1998. Three days later, in the *Union-Tribune,* Valerie Scher's review stated that the orchestra played with, "...a resonant conviction that earned cheers and standing ovations from a near-capacity audience. [The] season opener was a triumphant homecoming..." Appropriately, the concert opened with a piece by one of the orchestra's musicians, John Lorge, principal horn, who would contribute a number of his remarkably orchestrated pieces to be played by the symphony over the years. Lorge's "Jubilations," was well-received. Scher wrote that the Tchaikovsky Fifth Symphony was played exceptionally well by the orchestra. "There was sentiment but not sentimentality, fire that lit up the score without scorching the nuances. Call it a controlled burn..."

Pak followed the opening concerts with the first of his new series, called the "Light Bulb Series," planned as reworked lecture-demonstration-multimedia programs. Pak hoped to capture a new audience. But the advance sales for the concerts that were to be presented in El Cajon were pitifully small, so those were cancelled. Only three more would be given downtown. The regular series at Copley Symphony Hall was continuing to draw reasonable audience numbers, at least over the first several programs. The November 6 concert featured soloists from the orchestra in Moncayo's *Sinfonietta* as well as in Haydn's *Sinfonia Concertante.* Scher concluded her November 9, *Union-Tribune* review: "Watching Pak's progress is another reason for concertgoers to attend the symphony, as opposed to staying home with their CDs. We're watching the maturing of a maestro, and the symphony is sure to be better because of it." More praise was forthcoming from Scher for Jung-Ho Pak in her January 3, 1999, *Union-Tribune* article reviewing the year. "1998 was undoubtedly the biggest year of Pak's career. He confidently took leadership of the San Diego Symphony, his first professional symphony orchestra, and became top maestro of the newly solvent ensemble..."

Catherine Comet was the first of the season's guest conductors. She conducted an all-French program, with Awadagin Pratt as piano soloist. He played Saint-Saens virtuosically. Musically, the performances seemed to be getting increasingly solid, although other, non-musical situations continued to cast shadows. On February 2, 1999, Welton Jones reported in the *Union-Tribune* that the orchestra is making less than projected for the initial post-bankruptcy season, but that it is also spending less than anticipated. "At present, there's a net loss of $130,200 but, as the spring proceeds and more donated income clicks in, the prospects are still for a season-ending $113,600 in the black." Cash flow was not mentioned in the article. Two weeks later, Jones reported that, "...Gerdom says things are going pretty well. The last 'Light Bulb' concert earned about $6,000 more than expected...And the December 31st progress report showed the orchestra $259,566 in the black, which is not quite as good as projected...but still...in...the...black..."

Stanislaw Skrowacevski was the season's second guest conductor, and he made such a great impression on both orchestra and audience that Jonathan Saville wrote a glowing review in the March 11, 1999, *San Diego Reader,* which had not been demonstrating as much interest in reviewing the orchestra as it had in the past. Saville contrasted Skrowacevski's Beethoven's Fifth Symphony with the recent performance of the same piece in town by Salonen and the Los Angeles Philharmonic. Salonen lost badly in the comparison. Valerie Scher, too, was enthusiastic. In the March 1, 1999, *Union-Tribune*, she wrote, "This was Beethoven that bristled and roared, brooded and triumphed...In the process, Skrowacevski demonstrated that he is, in the best sense, a maestro of the old school, whose meticulous approach recalls that of the...late George Szell..."

In retrospect, the impression is gained that this concert may have provided the impetus for many to look just a bit more critically at Jung-Ho Pak. As a conductor who was definitely learning on the job, and as a personality, Pak was doing just fine. But the Skrowacevski concert may have demonstrated to the waiting audience that there was more to music-making than was being heard gratefully by ears that had not heard any for too long. Scher's review of the next Pak-led concert, in the March 29, 1999, *Union-Tribune*, demonstrated more reserve than praise. Pak conducted the Mahler Fourth Symphony. "...Pak's conducting revealed good ideas and admirable impulses, especially when encouraging emotional warmth to infuse the playing. At age 37, Pak is still fairly young for a conductor, and his interpretations will doubtless grow. No one expects him to be as explosive as the young Leonard Bernstein, or as excitingly authoritative as Sir Georg Solti was in his prime. That's not his style. But Pak should resist the tendency to slow down during expressive passages, as in the dark and dance-like second movement and the exquisite variations in the third movement, which could be as soft as a caress. His tempos sometimes dragged, sacrificing tautness for the sake of tenderness. With experience, he may learn to maintain both…"

Jung Ho Pak. *Photo courtesy San Diego Symphony.*

The final program of the season was reviewed in the May 22, 1999, *Union-Tribune* by Valerie Scher. Pak was criticized for his reading of the suite from Stravinsky's, "The Firebird.""…It may not have been the most magical, or the most colorfully opulent. Pak's tempos were sometimes a bit slow; his phrasing, a mite bland…"

I recall being impressed on most occasions by Pak's persistence in maintaining a very tight ensemble, although many of his interpretations seemed to sacrifice nuance, reflection and emotionality for that tight ensemble. As for the Mahler described above by Valerie Scher, Pak's was, of course, a young man's Mahler, not the seasoned, wiser, reflective Mahler taught us by such as Bruno Walter. Interviews with some of the orchestra musicians around that time were indicative of their own agreement with that opinion. A bit of dissatisfaction was beginning to be aired when, before, there was nothing but happiness that we did, indeed, have an orchestra again.

Moreover, it was reassuring to know that the orchestra was a reasonably good, if undersized one. Certainly, the loss of some of the principals was especially damaging. Nick Grant, back from the studios, worked valiantly as the acting concertmaster, but no one really expected him to serve as a realistic replacement for Igor Gruppman. The string section was small, often presenting only twenty or twenty-two violins *in toto*. The rest of the strings were proportionate in number and also without their former principals, but the winds were fully staffed. However, their former star principals were also gone. Nonetheless, the substitutes (or in the case of the clarinets, Cheryl Renk, the only remaining woodwind star) did quite well and the orchestra's playing was generally fine. Intonation was usually on the button. When Janos Starker, the eminent cellist, was soloist with the orchestra in April, he remarked, "The San Diego Symphony sounds pretty damn good for a resurrected dead body!"

Optimism rode high when the summer season was announced, to be held as it had been the prior year, at Navy Pier. There was to be a ten-weekend series, with twenty-two performances. The series was sponsored by Qualcomm and the Port of San Diego. And soon after the announcement was made of the summer season, it was revealed that Jung-Ho Pak had been selected as principal conductor of the New Haven, Connecticut, Symphony Orchestra. His guest conducting engagement there was reported as so impressive that the orchestra's search committee stopped looking and offered him the job. Pak would remain as San Diego's artistic director but he would leave his positions at USC and the San Francisco Conservatory. In contrast, he would retain his position as director of the Disney Young Musicians Symphony Orchestra, a post providing him with great publicity and annual TV appearances watched by large viewing audiences. Moreover, the City's Commission on Arts and Culture awarded $300,000 to the San Diego Symphony from the proceeds of the Transient Occupancy Tax.

The finances of the orchestra were reported on by Welton Jones on May 30, 1999, in the Union-Tribune. The projections were that the end of the fiscal year, on June 30, would show income of over $7.5 million, and expenditures of over $6.9 million. The regular concert series was fairly well attended, but the silent films, the "Light Bulb" programs and the rush-hour concerts were disappointing draws. The 1999-2000 budget would again be about $6.9 million, but there would be no more special, start-up funds available. The annual fund drive goal was to be raised to $2.25 million, and afterwards, for each year, the goal would be $2.5 million. Optimism was expressed about the big donors coming back next year. Sandra Pay, symphony board chair, said, "I wish we had 25 Jung-Hos. He's a terrific fund-raiser and he's out there in the community..." Season ticket sales for the summer series were already ahead of the prior year's total.

The 1999-2000 series was announced. There would be ten pairs of programs, with three repeated on Sunday afternoons in Escondido. Jeffrey Kahane, Leonid Grin, Gerard Schwartz and Enrique Diemecke would guest conduct. Jung-Ho Pak would close the season with the Beethoven Ninth Symphony. "Light Bulb" and rush hour series were also announced. As Jung-Ho Pak said during the press conference announcing the season, "Everything bigger — and better!"

Valerie Scher reviewed the summer series in a September 6, 1999, Union-

Tribune article. The weather did not cooperate well, and much of the season was cold, breezy and overcast. Nonetheless, it was a financial success. Although Scher criticized Pak's major cutting of the 1812 Overture at the end of the last concert, she also wrote, "…The symphony relies on Pak's leadership. As the Pops' host, he became increasingly relaxed and genial. As its resident conductor, he became ever more confident…"

At the beginning of the summer season, Tom Gerdom left, and, after a time, Richard Ledford assumed the position of part-time administrative consultant to the orchestra. It was assumed that he would stay on the job for no more than six or seven months, until a definite replacement for Gerdom would be found. In the meantime, season ticket sales were up by nearly a third more than the prior season, despite the lack of a full-time marketing director. Ledford was quoted, "We have a pledge to live within our income. It may not be pretty but we're doing it." In a profile written for the October 3, 1999, *Union-Tribune*, Valerie Scher quoted percussionist Jim Plank as saying, "I've never seen a more reasonable and committed group of people than the ones who are running the orchestra now. They're in touch with the real world…"

The season opened with another John Lorge piece, "Homage," dedicated to the people who helped the orchestra survive through their financial gifts. Garrick Ohlsson played Chopin, and the major orchestral work was the Brahms Fourth Symphony. Only 1,400 attended — a bad omen, especially for an opening night program. The new series, "Intimate Encounters," featuring works for small orchestra and soloists, only attracted about 500 listeners to Copley Symphony Hall. Apparently, the encouraging figures about the season ticket sales were not reflected in the attendance.

Attendance continued to be a nagging problem, although the figures for the Connoisseur Series sometimes picked up a bit as the season progressed. The search for a new executive director continued, and Richard Ledford was staying on in his interim position longer than he or anyone anticipated. He was attempting to prepare for negotiations with the orchestra over their new contract, due over the summer. On January 8, 2000, Welton Jones reported in the *Union-Tribune* that Ledford said that the consultant hired for the executive director search, Richard Cisek, had five good candidates. It was also announced that Joan and Dr. Irwin Jacobs would guarantee the new executive director's salary, estimated to be in the $100,000-$150,000 range, for three years.

On January 29, 2000, Jones reported that the symphony had increased its direct-mail fund raising fivefold over the prior year, and appears to be on track to fulfill its goal for the season. The Jacobses, characteristically working hard for the orchestra, had created a challenge grant to match the first $200,000 raised during the campaign just finished, which brought in $528,000. Last year, it was said, that the appeal had raised $94,000. The board had contributed its expected $100,000 right away, according to Ledford, "And now they're out hustling other returning donors..."

Jung-Ho Pak continued leading most of the Connoisseur Series concerts. In her February 7, 2000, *Union-Tribune* review of the prior weekend's all-Russian program, Valerie Scher especially noted the contributions of a number of the ensemble's principals. She also wrote that, "...throughout the evening, Pak conducted with reliable élan, attentive to both interpretive details as well as the overall design." Elmar Oliveira was the violin soloist in the Glazounov Concerto. Scher reported that only 1,300 attended on Friday night.

The big news came when the symphony hired its new executive director, Douglas Gerhart, described by Welton Jones in his March 27 *Union-Tribune* article as, "...a 41 year-old ex-trumpet player who already has steered orchestras in Alabama and Tulsa out of bankruptcy." Gerhart was quoted: "I love turnarounds and start-ups. If you want the status quo, don't call me." He was coming to San Diego after a three-year stint in Birmingham, Alabama. The orchestra there had been revived after declaring bankruptcy, and Gerhart increased their budget by forty-four percent, to $4.6 million. Before that, he had revived the Tulsa Philharmonic after a year-long bankruptcy interval.

Gerhart's musical background was impressive. He graduated from the august Peabody Institute in Baltimore, and earned a master's degree in trumpet performance at the Eastman School in Rochester, New York. He decided to shift his career to management and administrative responsibilities while playing first trumpet in Sioux City, Iowa, where he also taught at Morningside College and served as personnel manager for the orchestra. He became a management fellow with the American Symphony Orchestra League, and in 1990 he became the executive director of the Louisiana Symphony Orchestra in Baton Rouge, where he stayed for five years before going to Tulsa. The San Diego Symphony is the largest orchestra, member-wise and budget-wise, with which he ever worked. Gerhart's wife was a band director in Iowa when they met. They have a seventeen-year-old son, a percussionist, and two younger daughters.

Valerie Scher produced a lengthy profile of the new man in the May 14, 2000, *Union-Tribune*. She noted that he and Jung-Ho Pak are enthusiastic about working with each other. Gerhart referred to the conductor as, "...incredibly energetic, visionary and very bright. One always hopes to work with an artistic director who understands the financial implications, and Jung-Ho certainly does." And, according to the artistic director, he and Gerhart, "...will make a very good team. He's a musician who happens to enjoy numbers. And we're both looking for a friend, not just a working partner. I'd like to be yin to his yang..."

In the same issue, but in a different article, Scher noted the continued improvement of the San Diego Symphony over the season just ending. "Under the intelligent and accessible leadership of Jung-Ho Pak, the orchestra has made strides toward becoming the outstanding regional orchestra it was before the financial collapse of 1996-98, which prompted the departure of a handful of key players. Pak and the orchestra are an increasingly confident team…This season, Pak's conducting has become more focused as he refines his baton-less technique with a large orchestra. The symphony, meanwhile, has become increasingly expressive, whether in delicate textures or sonorous outpourings…"

The season ended with a performance of the Beethoven Ninth Symphony. The May 8, 2000, review in the *Union-Tribune* by Valerie Scher opined that "The music-making reflected scholarship and spirited involvement, emphasizing the brisk tempos included in the new Barenreiter Edition. Pak conducted with such energy that, at times, he practically hopped on the podium…"That performance and that review make a remarkable contrast to the early 1960s performance under Earl Bernard Murray in the orchestra's much more juvenile days. At that time Alan Kriegsman, the reviewer, quoted in an earlier chapter here, wrote mainly about his gratitude that the massive work had been done at all, regardless of the orchestra's obvious inability to cope genuinely successfully with it.

Much to Richard Ledford's relief, Gerhart's first major task in San Diego was to address the new orchestra contract, due on July 1. The contract negotiations ended successfully with a good compromise. A new, one-year contract was approved, allowing a three percent raise to the musicians, and also buying time for the thirteen musicians (more than Scher's "handful") who had returned their contracts but had not rejoined the ensemble full time since the financial crisis. They would have another year to determine what they wanted to do, although it frankly was not expected that those who had joined rich, well-established orchestras in Chicago, Los Angeles, Pittsburgh and elsewhere would be coming back. Gerhart's first task was handled with aplomb, and the future looked good.

The summer season began on the weekend preceding the July Fourth holiday. Valerie Scher reported that the Friday and Saturday night concerts were both sold out at the 2,700 seat Navy Pier venue. In her July 3, 2000, review, Scher commented about the improved appearance of Navy Pier, with white picket fences, as well as better buffet dinner service. More improvement was noted in the orchestra's financial situation as well. On August 4, 2000, Welton Jones reported in the *Union-Tribune* that the last fiscal year had ended with a surplus of more than $200,000. The current summer season's attendance had been disappointing at times, according to Gerhart's comments in the article, but it nonetheless had earned ninety percent of its anticipated ticket sales, and it was still only half-way through the series. Gerhart announced an increase in the

Summer Pops at the Embarcadero. *Photo courtesy San Diego Symphony.*

symphony's budget for 2000-2001 to $7.1 million.

In his article, Jones commented about the symphony's lack of a significant endowment fund that would help it in its need to earn more needed funding from donors. Jones pointed out that the average American orchestra with a good endowment earns 12.7 percent of its annual income from endowment interest. Gerhart pointed out that long-range planning depended upon the establishment of a real endowment. He established a new, unique, "Partner with a Player" sponsor program, in which certain level donors to the general fund partner with individual musicians. They do not pay the musicians' salaries, but they may develop close relationships with the musicians they select, and thereby get to know and understand more about the mechanisms of a working orchestra. That program, albeit very creative, could not compare with what an endowment could do. "My concern," Gerhart stated, "is can we fund a comparable salary when we're paying $30,000 for a player who would get $120,000 in Minnesota?"

Four days earlier, the *Union-Tribune* published a pretty powerful editorial, praising the symphony's new, solid financial footing and also praising its new leadership. The editorial warned, however, that the budget remains a terribly lean one, and that the symphony continues to live hand-to-mouth. "The reality is that, over the long term, the symphony will remain in a precarious financial situation until it establishes a healthy endowment to undergird its operating budget and ease its reliance on repeated cash infusions from a handful of generous patrons...This is the ideal moment for the symphony to initiate an endowment drive..."

The music continued. A special concert was held in Copley Symphony Hall, filled for the occasion at the end of August by fans of Garrison Keillor, who appeared with the orchestra. The 2000-2001 season was announced. Ten subscription series programs would be given, all at Copley Symphony Hall. Pak would conduct only half of them, having asked for some respite due to the demands of his bicoastal commuting, as well as those of his now 18 month-old daughter. The guest conductors scheduled included Max Bragado-Garman, Leslie Dunner, Nicholas McGegan, Yoav Talmi (in his first return to the orchestra he had headed before the crash), and Maximiliano Valdes. There would be no Escondido performances on Sunday afternoons, nor would there be the silent movies series. The rush hour concerts, geared to the downtown professional and business people, were also cancelled. By the time of the opening concerts in October, the season subscription sales had reached $670,000 of the $750,000 goal. The WinterPops series had been budgeted for $25,000 in ticket sales, but before the first of that series the advance was already nearly $69,000. The emphasis was on earning instead of expenditure. The new, "Partner with a Player" campaign had raised $304,000 by the time of the opening concert; the goal was set at $1.2 million.

The reviews of the Connoisseur Series were continually good but the audiences remained too small. Too many empty seats were too apparent to the audience and to the orchestra. An exception to the usual good reviews was the one in the October 23, 2000, *Union-Tribune*, when Valerie Scher wrote about "rough passages" in the concert guest conducted by Max Bragado-Dorman, of the Louisville Orchestra. Billed as a concert of Spanish music, it held scores by only two Spanish composers, and used Spanish-themed pieces by Rimsky-Korsakoff and Lalo for the rest. Interviews with the musicians indicated that they were not generally positively impressed. A generally loud, blockbuster type of program was conducted by Pak over the December 1, 2000, weekend. Generally well-played, it featured music by Khatchaturian (music from "Spartacus" and the Piano Concerto, with Dickran Atamian as soloist), as well as Respighi's "Pines of Rome," with effective, augmented brass in the side balcony and Hollace Jones pumping the electric organ on stage. The old pipe organ's console needed extensive repairs (or replacement), but the Symphony Association was not yet in any shape to consider the large expense of refurbishing that instrument. Instead, the console was lifted to a perch backstage and stored there. As of this writing, it is still there, although talk is beginning about possibly doing something about it.

A number of audience comments about these two programs indicated the impression that, to them, they represented cheap, "dumbing-down" programs, geared to pleasing the lowest denominator of attendees. On the other hand, they did not attract more than the usual, relatively small crowds of little more than 1,500 per night. The musicians, likewise, were not enthused about the music. In contrast, the program of the previous season in which Pak conducted the Mahler Sixth Symphony was praised enthusiastically by Valerie Scher in her year-end review of the concert season, published in the December 24, 2000, *Union-Tribune*

The new year brought some guest conductors who generally received better reviews than the first one of the season the previous autumn. Nicholas McGegan, the genial, well-recorded and very busy specialist in early, baroque and classical period music, came to the San Diego podium in mid January and led a characteristic McGegan program of Rameau, Handel, Bach and Haydn. The smallish orchestra responded well to his bouncy, always spirited conducting, and so did Valerie Scher in her January 15, 2002, *Union-Tribune* review.

Pak came back to lead several more concerts, and then Yoav Talmi returned to his former orchestra early in March. His program was enormously well-received by orchestra and audience, and also by Douglas Gerhart, who commented to me after the concert that the orchestra was playing in a different league that night. Scher described it as a "watershed" event. Although the playing was not quite up to the remarkable standards Talmi had instilled until five years before in San Diego, the then-current orchestra, with its roster of substitutes and missing principals from that earlier era, did very well. The second half, featuring the Brahms First Symphony, led to an ovation.

Although his announcement must have been planned for a while, it seems somewhat ironic that, immediately following the Talmi performances, Jung-Ho Pak stated his intention to leave the San Diego orchestra after his last concert of the 2001-2002 season. The temptation is strong to assume that the young artistic director may have become aware that he could not bring the orchestra to the level reached by Talmi — but the real truth is that Pak did not hear that concert. He was in Connecticut, rehearsing his east coast ensemble for its next concert. In a telephone interview with Valerie Scher, reported in the March 6, 2001, *Union-Tribune*, Pak was quoted: "The international world is calling. It's not feasible to continue in San Diego at the level I want. Why not leave on top?" Scher asked Pak if the fact that he had never been given the title of music director had anything to do with his decision. He had always been artistic director through his three generally successful seasons as the orchestra's head. Interestingly and somewhat provocatively, he responded, "That's not the bulk of it..."

Ben Clay, the president of the Symphony board, praised the young maestro, pointing out that he led the orchestra with, "...a modern vision that has spoken to the arts community and the community at large." There is no question about the truth of that statement. Pak was the man to have at the time he was here, and the orchestra and the city was lucky to have him here then. Not only did he save the show, he reached out to the community as no conductor had ever done before. Although his music (practically always well-performed, especially with tight ensemble playing) often led to some grumbling about a lack of warmth, reflection or relaxation, there was never a complaint about the person whose broad, incredibly welcoming smile lit up the hall — and lit up whatever space he was occupying. As a number of the musicians said to me, "In twenty years, he'll really be a fine conductor!" Some of the other musicians disagreed strongly.

A few days later, Scher wrote, "Pak did much to restore artistic stability and credibility to the orchestra that nearly perished in a financial crisis. Eager to succeed in his first major post leading a professional symphony orchestra, he saw not the limitations but the possibilities. Though not as accomplished as such predecessors as Yoav Talmi or David Atherton, Pak displayed his batonless style to fine effect in music spanning connoisseur concerts and Pops programming. And Pak...excelled in people skills, becoming an uncommonly accessible maestro who delighted in hosting and conducting his pet innovation, the Light Bulb series..."

At the end of March, 2001, the next season was announced. Pak was to lead six of the ten programs in the subscription series, leading off with a special concert on September 9, featuring Yo-Yo Ma soloing in the Dvorak cello concerto. James dePreist, Jo Ann Falletta, Angel Romero and Julian Wachner were listed as guest conductors, and, of course, rumors started spreading immediately that they, as well as countless other *maestri*, were candidates for the post of San Diego's music directorship. Many of the rumors were far-fetched but the media picked them up and, for that matter, added fuel to that fire by making suggestions in the press. Valerie Scher quoted Douglas Gerhart in the April 17, 2001, *Union-Tribune:* " It's safe to say that the next musical director will be someone who has already been a musical director. We're leaning toward someone with an emerging career, not a youngster. In the last four days, I've had calls from all over the world, from agents and from conductors themselves. We already have a list of thirty names. It changes every meeting. Of course, identifying the names is the easy part..."

The music went on. Maximiliano Valdes guest conducted late in April, and Cynthia Phelps, formerly principal viola in San Diego (now principal viola for the New York Philharmonic) made what Valerie Scher called a welcome return, playing the Bartok concerto. Scher did not care for Valdes' podium style, describing it as "stiff and stuffy" in her April 30, 2001, *Union-Tribune* review, although she acknowledged that his results were, "largely satisfying." The dean of San Diego composers, David Ward-Steinman, whose music had in the more distant past been heard with more frequency in his home town, was finally featured again in Pak's finale for the season on May 25, 2001. His "Millennium Dances" were praised and welcomed warmly by the audience. Pak received a standing ovation at the end of the concert. As expected, the newspapers were filled with letters to the editor saying that he should be retained. But Pak insisted that he was going, and the Symphony Association kept its search committee busy, again headed by the indefatigable Dr. Warren Kessler.

The summer season began late in June, mainly featuring popular stars. James Darren received an especially good review from Valerie Scher in the July 9, 2001, *Union-Tribune*. The Navy Pier venue was pretty well filled for most of these concerts. A very insightful and somewhat provocative review of another concert was made by James Varga, the popular music critic of the *Union-Tribune* in the July 27, 2001, issue. The famous rock group, Yes, were the featured attraction — with the orchestra. Varga questioned, "Can a symphony orchestra and a well-amplified rock band co-exist on the same stage, performing the same material? Can the orchestra make an impact if it must struggle to be heard above the rock band?" Varga continued, "The answers were simultaneously encouraging and troubling, sometimes for the same reasons." The biggest reason was the inability of the orchestra to reach sonic parity with the heavily electronically amplified band. Larry Groupe, the arranger for Yes, had made several "charts" for the band and the orchestra, and these were deemed successful, but the vast bulk of the music might as well not have been played by the orchestra when the band was on stage. The lesson was that better arrangements were needed whenever a rock group appeared with any orchestra, as well as better sound engineers.

Regardless of the lack of those better arrangements, the rock groups continued to appear every summer, the orchestra continued to make some usually indecipherable noise behind them, and the audiences continued to eat it up. According to the Varga article, the attendance at the first Yes concert for that weekend was 4,800, in a venue seating 2,800! The money was good, but no one was continuing to pretend that the orchestra was training future listeners to serious music. The money was good in other areas as well. The fiscal year that ended on June 30 revealed that the symphony had earned a surplus of $200,000. The summer season surpassed its ticket goal by $180,000, racking up a record $1.3 million in revenue, obviously boosted by the disparate rock group/orchestra programs disparaged by George Varga and many others.

The new season began in early October, with an advance subscription sale of about $900,000. That welcome news, however, was clouded just a bit by Gerhart's comments to the press, indicating that there was still a great deal of work to be done because there was no safety net of an endowment. The orchestra itself was staffed in great part by substitute musicians hired on an annual (or, sometimes, even shorter) basis, due to the relative lack of formerly contracted players who had left. In the 2001-2002 season, these substitutes included an acting principal oboe from Honolulu and an acting principal bassoon from Los Angeles. Many of the substitute string players had been recruited from the available pool of University of Southern California veterans who had played under Pak in the fine music school's fine orchestra. The size of the string section, however, remained small, with about the same number of violins (twenty-two for most concerts) as before.

On the day before the opening of the season, the good news was announced that a new contract had been signed with the musicians' union that allowed for an increase in basic salaries and an increase in the length of the contracted seasons. The contract was for a five-year span, and was written to be retroactive to the prior July 1, replacing the temporary one-year contract that had gone into effect on that date. Everybody was happy about this, and both symphony spokespersons and union executives praised the pact. The contracted season would expand to forty-one weeks from the present twenty-six, and the base salaries would increase to $45,750 from the present $25,920. A bonus for the musicians would be a four-week paid vacation by the end of the 2005-2006 season, when the contract ends. Educational concerts would also be increased. The dozen or so formerly contracted members who had left for other posts were given two years from the date of the signing of the new contract to let the local orchestra know if they will be returning. It was not expected that many would return because they had found work at established, relatively crisis-free orchestras, but the agreement held that they had the right of return.

The feeling of optimism engendered not only by the new contract but also by the underlying sense of developing, increased financial security that led to that new contract permeated the atmosphere of the opening concerts. Just as it had when the orchestra returned to work in 1998 after the bankruptcy, John Lorge's "Jubilations" opened these concerts as well, giving a bright tone to the evening. It provided an antidote to the sense of dread that was part of the country's collective emotion following the September 11 terrorist disaster. Leila Josefowicz played the Tchaikovsky Violin Concerto, and Pak led the Tchaikovsky Fourth Symphony to considerable acclaim.

James DePreist, the first scheduled guest conductor, led the next set of programs, and he created considerable excitement with his reading of the Mahler First Symphony. Christof Perick came for the next set of concerts, and his conducting also won praise. Were these people candidates? DePreist was retiring as music director of the Oregon Symphony, and Perick had just begun his tenure in Charlotte, North Carolina. In her November 5, 2002, Union-Tribune review, Valerie Scher wrote about her satisfaction in hearing "...wonderful music so well-performed...The orchestra...was admirably responsive, both in broad strokes and interpretive details. All of which suggests that, if Perick isn't already a candidate for music director, he should be..."The year ended with a good performance of Handel's "Messiah."This was under the direction of Julian Wachner, a young, early-music specialist from Boston and Montreal. He was not considered a candidate, but Valerie Scher wrote in her December 17, 2002, Union-Tribune review that "...he deserves to conduct more choral concerts here."

The new year began with some very stimulating and provocative news. Two special concerts had been arranged for two seemingly special conductors who were felt to be prime candidates for the musical directorship. These special, conductor debut single concerts were to be given in January, first under the direction of Peter Oundjian and the second under the baton of David Robertson. Oundjian was a string quartet violinist who chose a conducting career and became director of the Caramoor Festival in upstate New York. Robinson, a native Californian, had been busy with a successful European career. Music director of the French *Orchestre National de Lyon*, Robinson, like Oundjian, had begun a busy round of American guest conducting appearances. The quickly-arranged appearances by these two apparently strong candidates created enormous interest. They certainly demonstrated the strong direction and purpose of the conductor selection committee.

Big news, indeed. But who would expect the real big news that exploded in the *Union-Tribune* only two days after the announcement of these concerts. That news became the likely most significant announcement about the San Diego Symphony Orchestra in its history, galvanizing not only the local community but the entire musical world.

CHAPTER XVII

The Jacobs Gift: The Key to a Future

As expected, the new year began with an aura of excitement about the newly-energized conductor search. Valerie Scher's January 7, 2002, *Union-Tribune* report was headlined, "Opening Movement: concert series tryouts will launch symphony's search for a new conductor." She began by opining, "If the San Diego Symphony had a list of new year's resolutions, finding a new music director should be at the top. Nothing is more important than hiring a successor to conductor Jung-Ho Pak, who will leave in May. And nothing else will have as profound an impact as a new conductor, affecting everything from the orchestra's repertoire and reputation to ticket sales and donations.

"The selection process will get underway in earnest this week with the opening of the two-part series, 'Conductor Debuts!' at Copley Symphony Hall, when Canadian-born Peter Oundjian — who's artistic director of New York's Caramoor Festival — leads the orchestra Thursday. Then, on January 18, Santa Monica native David Robertson, who's music director of France's *Orchestre National de Lyon*, will conduct the local symphony... Officially, the concerts are not being called auditions. Yet, insiders say that Oundjian and Robertson are two of the ten or so conductor candidates who will try out this season and next..."

Who knew? Of course, at that time the need for a conductor was rightfully believed to be the primary need of the San Diego Symphony, and the search for the right man or woman was paramount in most interested peoples' minds. It was only two days later, however, that the orchestra's even more impor-

The Jacobs at the ceremony for the bestowing of their gift, January 14, 2002. *UT Photo.*

tant primary need was fulfilled by a coup that left the entire orchestra world gasping — and the non-orchestral portions of the arts world in general. Valerie Scher had something even more important to write about in the January 9, 2002, *Union-Tribune*. The front-page banner headline on that day was, "Multimillion Dollar Gift to Boost Orchestra: once bankrupt San Diego Symphony to receive unprecedented donation."

Scher wrote, "The once-bankrupt San Diego Symphony is on the brink of a multi-million dollar gift from longtime supporters Joan and Irwin Jacobs that is expected to be the largest individual donation ever given to a U. S. symphony orchestra. The money — thought by some in San Diego's arts community to be as much as $100 million — eventually could place the orchestra's endowment near the top of U. S. orchestras and bring unprecedented stability..."

" 'It's a major gift — no denying it," San Diego Symphony president and CEO Douglas Gerhart said yesterday. It will propel us forward in a dramatic way.' Irwin Jacobs, the co-founder, CEO and chairman of the board of Qualcomm, was in Beijing yesterday for the launch of a wireless network based on Qualcomm technology. He declined to comment on the gift, but said, 'We love music!' "

"Although the San Diego Symphony sought to embargo the information until the official announcement planned for Monday, it is the *Union-Tribune's* policy to decide when or how to report the news..."

Scher waxed enthusiastic about Gerhart. "No administrator has been as successful in correcting the problem...[i. e., the lack of a significant endowment]...as Gerhart, 43, who has served in the orchestra's top job since May, 2000. He previously had voiced his concern about the insufficient endowment, calling it 'a missing safety net'..."

The now topped, previously biggest news, the conductor search, merited a paragraph at the end of the story, almost parenthetically. "The orchestra is seeking a new conductor who is almost sure to receive more than Jung-Ho Pak's $150,000 salary. Canadian-born Peter Oundjian will have an unofficial tryout tomorrow at Copley Symphony Hall..."

Upstaged as he was by the latest news of the anticipated multi-million dollar gift, Peter Oundjian led the orchestra in a lengthy but generally well-performed program of chestnuts. The program included the Vaughan Williams *Fantasia on a Theme of Thomas Tallis*, the Rachmaninoff Second Piano Concerto (with Adam Neiman as soloist) and the Beethoven *Eroica* Symphony. The hall was packed, but everybody was really waiting for the official news about the Jacobs gift. How much was it — truly? Never mind the rumors and the obvious leaks. How was it to be given? In any event, Oundjian, a very genial man and obviously a very fine musician, pleased the audience, orchestra and critics despite the lack of any pronounced dramatic bent that might have enlivened or darkened the mighty

Beethoven symphony. Perhaps he was already aware that he was a prime candidate to become the music director of his own, home town orchestra in Toronto. A year after his initial appearance here, I saw him conduct the Toronto Symphony just two weeks before the announcement was made of his hiring there, and at that time he appeared to be in much firmer dynamic and emotional control as a conductor. After several successful seasons as music director in Toronto, he returned to San Diego in 2004 as a welcome and esteemed guest conductor.

The January 15, 2002, issue of the *Union-Tribune* finally told it all. Valerie Scher wrote,

> "It's official! The San Diego Symphony has a $100 million endowment pledge, thanks to Qualcomm billionaire Irwin Jacobs and his wife, Joan. As if that's not enough, the couple disclosed yesterday in a ceremony at downtown's Copley Symphony Hall that they will be kicking in an extra $20 million over the next 10 years toward the orchestra's operating expenses...The gathering in the hall amounted to a lavish outpouring of gratitude to the couple who have secured financial stability for the once-bankrupt San Diego Symphony. The Jacobses' donation is the largest single contribution ever made to a U. S. orchestra. And beyond speeches, musical performances, champagne, *hors d'oeuvres* and standing ovations was the realization that the ninety-two-year-old institution is the envy of arts organizations across the nation...
>
> " 'Today is the greatest day in our history,' symphony president and CEO Douglas Gerhart said during the official presentation before an invited audience of 1,600 invited guests...
>
> 'Today, we celebrate a great new beginning. And it was Gerhart...who Jacobs said, 'Stayed after us,' with the idea that it was important that the symphony have a substantial endowment...Under the provisions of the Jacobs endowment contribution, an initial $50 million will be donated at $5 million per year over the next ten years. Another $50 million will come in the form of a bequest. The extra $20 million will tide the organization over, via grants of $2 million per year for 10 years, until substantial interest starts being generated by the massive endowment..."

It was, indeed, a lovely and very heartfelt presentation. If anything, Scher's description of "…a lavish outpouring of gratitude…" was an understatement. Sarah Tuck, acting principal flute, spoke movingly on behalf of the orchestra, saying that this was a dream come true. Matt Garbutt had quickly rehearsed the orchestra in the Dvorak "New World" Symphony, and they played their hearts out for him and for us. The Jacobses, with their four married sons and their spouses, were on stage and all received tumultuous applause.

Irwin Jacobs spoke simply and modestly, but in his talk he was careful to outline the way the endowment was to be handled. It was, he said, to be administered by, "…a separate foundation, perhaps administered by one or two of the existing non-profit foundations in the city…I believe that the board of the symphony should have some input into what was happening, but I think that a separate board will have its own fiscal responsibility to maintain and to grow the endowment…" It was very obvious that Jacobs was not ignoring history here. He knew only too well that a prior symphony board had lost the endowment that had been seeded many years ago by a Ford Foundation grant. Jacobs also noted that he knew improvements were needed in parts of the hall, and that they were going to be made over the next few seasons. He also spoke of the necessity to increase the orchestra's outreach and educational programs. Joan Jacobs also spoke, seconding all of her husband's remarks, and adding her own hope that the orchestra would eventually be able to tour and to become as famous and as respected in wider circles as it should be. As Irwin Jacobs had said to Valerie Scher via long-distance telephone from Beijing the previous week, "We love music!"

In their characteristically gracious way, the Jacobses were kind enough to receive me in their lovely, contemporary La Jolla home so that I might interview them for this history project. I saw them there in April, 2004. We spoke for several hours, and afterwards Dr. Jacobs demonstrated his joy in the new music room added only recently to the house. A Steinway concert grand had been installed there and had been played by a number of visiting artists. As befits not only a serious music loving family but also a man with a doctorate in electrical engineering, there was also an almost unbelievable audio-visual system. Dr. Jacobs told me that he and his wife really do listen to it during their leisure times at home that have unfortunately become scarcer due to their travel demands.

Irwin Jacobs grew up in New Bedford, Massachusetts, in a family that was not especially musical or even particularly music loving. Although he says that he was never serious about it, he took lessons for a time on the clarinet and saxophone. In fact, he related, he had never heard or seen a live performance by a symphony orchestra until he and his then-new wife, Joan, attended a concert at Boston's Symphony Hall during his graduate school days at MIT. "We were on a tight budget in Boston…" They both enjoyed that first concert and they went again whenever they could. They also tried to attend as often as possible the summer series of the Boston Symphony Orchestra at Tanglewood, "…but we didn't get really involved with music other than record collecting. I started that as an undergraduate…" Greater involvement began only after the Jacobses moved to San Diego in 1966, when he was hired as a faculty member at UCSD. Eventually, after settling down here, he became involved with the La Jolla Chamber Orchestra, organized by Peter Eros in the early 1970s, and staffed mainly by San Diego Symphony musicians. "I always enjoyed being with the musicians and talking with them."

As he related, "Over time, I just got increasingly involved." Jean Rice, at the time the development director of the San Diego Symphony, convinced him to join the symphony board. By then, he had left the university and had helped organize the Link-a-Bit Corporation, in which he held a high executive position, and which was the progenitor of Qualcomm. "The company was small then, so I was pretty heavily involved with it. I was always directed toward situations that I thought could grow, like the company and possibly like the symphony. The '70s were the times of the first high-giving boards…" He was involved in the planning to purchase the Fox Theatre. He left the symphony board a little later, though, prior to the Atherton financial/labor crisis. "I was off the board when Yoav [Talmi] came, but I became close to Yoav…"

He shook his head sadly as he described himself watching from the side-lines the disastrous (his term) situation centering around Michael Tiknis. He lent money to the symphony in order that they might have a summer season, and he was repaid. Dr. Jacobs went on to describe Elsie Weston, then Symphony president, as "heroic" during the difficult days that followed. He and Sol Price teamed up to help but they both became discouraged when they saw that the attendance at the concerts simply continued to fall off. "So we both decided to make no further contributions, and the bankruptcy followed." Dr. Jacobs told me that he never thought that he would be giving any more money to the symphony that never seemed to attract enough listeners or any genuine community appreciation, mainly due, he believed, to its remarkable negative history. He said that he certainly never wanted to be the only principal donor. "But then Larry Robinson came out of the blue and made his offer, and that restimulated our interest. We weren't going to be alone!"

"I felt strongly about supporting the orchestra," he said, "because they are a large organization, employing a lot of people in the community — people who really live and work here." Dr. Jacobs contrasted that with several other southern California orchestras whose musicians are not residents of the city for whom those orchestras may be named and in which they play. Instead, for the most part, those musicians commute from Los Angeles, where they make most of their money doing studio work. He also commented more about the educational function of the orchestra, which he considers extremely important. He is quite sensitive to the lack of arts education in the public schools of today.

Dr. Jacobs and I spoke about the previous gifts he and his wife had given to the orchestra. "The shell was very successful," he noted, and laughed when I pointed out that I had been so impressed by it that I donated the podium to match it as the best I could do under the circumstances. He laughed harder when I told him that I had warned Yoav Talmi to wipe his feet before stepping onto the then-white carpet-covered stand. It has since been recovered in red. He spoke about the reports out of Carnegie Hall when it was being redone. He paid particular attention to the problems there based upon the concrete stage floor. That led to his recognition that Copley Symphony Hall needed a wood floor so that the sound of the orchestra would resonate better. That was installed last year, and the orchestra indeed sounds better, and also looks better, especially now that new risers were also added to the stage setting.

At this point, Mrs. Jacobs joined us and entered the conversation. She pointed out her own feelings about the "front of the house," indicating that this was her primary interest as differentiated from her husband's major concerns about the stage and the acoustics. In no way, however, does she abdicate her role as a critical listener to what goes on inside the hall. But, as she said, "A dilapidated looking facility simply isn't valued, and it won't attract people." She told me that she had brought her own interior designer to Copley Symphony Hall to provide suggestions regarding upgrading the appearance of the nearly three-quarter century old former movie palace.

With the interior designer's aid, Mrs. Jacobs has overseen the installation of new mirrors in the lobbies. In the hall itself, she ordered new, subtle lighting to illuminate the large oil paintings on the sides of the main floor beneath the balcony. She and her husband have also seen to the installation of a new elevator off the main lobby to allow stress free access to the balcony for audience members who enter through the main B Street entrance to the hall.

The Jacobses also underwrote the renovation of the symphony staff offices on the Seventh Street side of Copley Symphony Hall. It was expected that the staff would have its enlarged and better laid out facility before the beginning of the 2004-05 season, and they did. Mrs. Jacobs commented that the symphony needed a larger staff in order to, among other things, take better care of the donors and make them feel more appreciated. "A successful organization needs a large staff," she said. Then she added that they ought to be well-housed and have good feelings about where they work, and about the organization for which they work. Mrs. Jacobs also pointed out the need for railings along the stepped aisles of the balcony and said that she would get to that soon. She did. Further, "I want to establish a flower fund." She envisions fresh flowers in the lobbies as well as possibly lining the lip of the stage as had been done in some seasons past. "I'm not a clubwoman," she told me, "although I'm a member of a number of philanthropically-oriented organizations. I'm an instigator and an innovator."

Mrs. Jacobs was born and reared in Manhattan, in an arts-conscious family. Perhaps surprisingly, however, music was not the family's primary artistic consideration. The Boston Symphony Orchestra concert spoken of above by Dr. Jacobs was also Mrs. Jacobs's first live orchestra experience — and, like her husband, she got the bug right away. As a child, she was taken regularly to the theatre for Saturday matinees, and also to the city's great museums before lunch and curtain times. The theatre was her major artistic love when she was growing up. The couple has expressed that philanthropically by their generous gifts to local organizations such as the Olde Globe, and especially to the La Jolla Playhouse. Joan and Irwin Jacobs met as undergraduates at Cornell University. As she told me in that 2002 interview, in September, 2004, they will celebrate their fiftieth wedding anniversary. There is no question; they are quite a team!

We spoke at some length about the endowment gift itself. The couple had always been disturbed about the orchestra's hand-to-mouth existence. They talked about it a lot at home, they said. They were very much aware that considerably increased financial support was necessary for the orchestra to obtain the necessary services of a necessarily good conductor. They also were very aware that a long-term, mutually beneficial contract with the musicians was mandatory. The couple had been impressed by Doug Gerhart's work as CEO of the orchestra, at least insofar as his financial acumen was concerned. They were, however, also aware that he had some difficulties in the interpersonal area, especially with some of the musicians and with some of the staff. But they were positively impressed by his ideas and his achievements, such as establishing the new contract with the musicians. Also, as Dr. Jacobs told me, "Doug developed the idea of the opera hiring the symphony, subcontracting the orchestra to the opera."

It was Gerhart, they said, who brought the couple into the actual giving area that led to the endowment, although they had both been thinking about "something like that" for a long time and, of course, had given the orchestra numerous major gifts before. Once, however, they found "...evidence of increasing stability in place," then the concept of the endowment was crystallized, "sitting around our dining room table." As Dr. Jacobs said, "Joan decided on the figure. I had suggested $50 million. Joan said that we should do a hundred. She always likes round figures..." In discussing the gift, the Jacobses each recognized the need for ongoing funds for the orchestra as well as the need for the endowment, so they jointly formulated the plan of the annual $2 million grants.

I asked the Jacobses quite frankly about the San Diego Opera, headed by Ian Campbell. I did this because Campbell (who has always been my good friend) has been exceedingly successful as the local opera impresario. Much of that success was due to his aggressive courting of many of the city's wealthiest citizens to become significant opera donors, and to continue to support it for many years. Quite bluntly, I wondered about the Jacobses not having directed their principal giving there instead of to the symphony. In fact, as they pointed out, the Jacobses had indeed donated a great deal of money to the opera over the years — and to many other arts and educational institutions, as well as to the Jewish Community Center and many other community service institutions. The San Diego Symphony is not their only philanthropic target but, fortunately for the orchestra, it seems to have become their favorite. As Dr. Jacobs put it, "They were the ones who needed it the most, and besides, they picked up the ball and ran with it…"

The Jacobs gift changed everything, especially the morale of the orchestra, the staff and the audience. As interesting as the conductor search had been before, the community really perked up its collective ear to hear the next contestant, David Robertson. With the Jacobs gift, the orchestra had become a winner, and San Diegans love winners. The interest level in the orchestra and its search for a new conductor became heightened throughout the entire community. Valerie Scher's review of Robertson's concert in the January 21, 2002, *Union-Tribune* was rather puzzling to many who had been in the audience, as well as to many members of the orchestra who, in agreement with the audience, felt that this young conductor was nothing short of sensational. Robertson had been making the guest conductor rounds of American orchestras and, for a time, had been considered as a possible successor to Loren Maazel at the New York Philharmonic. They decided not to hire him for that post, however, but to allow the increasingly aging and not too popular Maazel to continue.

Robertson's program consisted of the brief Charles Ives piece, "The Unanswered Question"; the Copland Clarinet Concerto, featuring the orchestra's superb principal clarinetist, Sheryl Renk; and the Berlioz *Symphonie Fantastique*. Scher wrote, "What's unclear is whether conservative concert-goers — who consider Ives a stretch — would be happy with Robertson's programming. And whether Robertson could be persuaded to help a once-bankrupt orchestra to gain new prominence. Though he's not the kind of thrilling conductor who makes the heart race, Robertson was wonderfully assured on the podium. His combination of skill and insight prompted many fine efforts from the orchestra…"

In marked contrast to Scher's observations, many of the attendees and musicians did, indeed, feel their hearts racing because Robertson's concert was one of the most exciting — and excitingly played — performances heard in recent years at Copley Symphony Hall. Scher referred to the conductor's "exceptional attributes" and commented that, "Robertson and the orchestra deserved the standing ovation that they received…"That standing ovation, in fact, was one of the longest and most enthusiastic heard in the hall by this long-time attendee, and the number of the conductor's curtain calls far exceeded the usual.

Perhaps one problem bothering Scher was Robertson's penchant for addressing the audience about the music, as he did at Copley Symphony Hall and in Chicago's Orchestra Hall where, gratefully, I also heard him a year later. He also did it when conducting the New York Philharmonic at Lincoln Center, as reported by the reviewer in *The New Yorker*, who described Robinson as, "…a conductor who cultivates bright colors and driving rhythms." In any event, Robinson is quite articulate and, fortunately, a native English speaker with a good speaking voice. He does not repeat anything already in the program notes but, instead, says interesting and sometimes provocative things about the music from a conductor's point of departure. At the end, after quieting the standing ovation, he called out to the audience, "Don't you think this orchestra really deserves a hundred million dollars?"The answer was another enormous ovation, in which the conductor joined.

It turned out to be a great night at the symphony but, be that as it may, Robinson turned out not to be a candidate after all. He was frankly interested in a more prestigious post, preferably in the east or Midwest where he could have easier access to his beloved other position in France, which he did not want to give up. Eventually, he was chosen by the St. Louis Symphony.

More candidates were to follow in San Diego, though, and most of them were genuine candidates. As Valerie Scher noted in her February 4, 2002, *Union-Tribune* article, Jung-Ho Pak continued to be a non-candidate, despite the number of symphony listeners and petitioners who wanted him to continue on the San Diego podium. Scher wrote, "A lame duck conductor who was never awarded the customary title of music director, Pak did not speak or conduct at last month's ceremony saluting the Jacobses' largesse and the founding of the orchestra's New World Endowment Campaign. This new world will do without him and any dreams he might have for the symphony's artistic future…According to board president Dokmo, the symphony gave Pak the option of throwing his hat into the ring and becoming one of the candidates…'It was his own choice and he chose not to,' Dokmo says. 'He said he did not want to do that.'

Scher continued, "Who first suggested that Pak should leave? Was it Pak or the symphony? When asked, Pak hunkers down into a self-protective shell. 'It's a little bit like trying to figure out which came first, the chicken or the egg,' he responds. 'I can't say anything productive toward that.'"

Despite the obvious cloud hanging over his withdrawal, Pak had no reason to leave without his head hanging high, and he had no need to "hunker down." He did well by and for the orchestra, and for the community. He saved the show as the right man in the right place at the right time, and he continues his career unblemished in New Haven, Connecticut. More recently, he also obtained another position that almost exactly and ideally matches his greatest strengths and enthusiasms as an educator to young people. He has become the director of orchestral training at the famed Interlochen Summer Music Camp in Michigan. His stature as a conductor and educator will continue growing, and it would be no surprise at all to see him guest conduct in San Diego, perhaps in the Light Bulb Series that was closest to his heart.

In the midst of all this mainly positive excitement, subsequent to Ling's appointment, Douglas Gerhart suddenly left the San Diego Symphony. Rumors began floating that he had been offered the position of executive director of the Pittsburgh Symphony Orchestra, and he openly acknowledged his interest in the job. He said that he was leaving the job in San Diego because he did not want to hurt the administration of the orchestra by being a lame duck executive whose mind may be in two places at once. There were also some stories about difficulties in his marriage, and a possible separation, but he did not discuss these. In the end, Pittsburgh did not hire him. Another, new search committee was formed to find a replacement for Gerhart.

A fairly lengthy search resulted in the hiring of Edward B. ("Ward") Gill from Minneapolis, where he was serving as the deputy executive director of the famed Minnesota Orchestra. No one could argue with that pedigree. Genial and quite personable, he is much more of a people person than Doug Gerhart was. He is liked by the staff and by the musicians, with whom he has developed good relationships. On the other hand, he maintains a strict and healthy respect for the continuing cash flow problems that affect all arts organizations. New staff members have also been added in the development, marketing and public relations areas, and all are very pleased to have moved back to their newly renovated offices at Copley Symphony Hall.

The parade of guest conductor/candidates continued. The roster included Eduardo Diazmunoz, from Tijuana and Mexico City; Miguel Harth-Bedoya, associate conductor of the Los Angeles Philharmonic; Andrey Boreyko, from the Winnipeg, Canada, Symphony; Giancarlo Guerrero, from Eugene, Oregon; Daniel Hege, music director of the Syracuse Symphony; and Mathias Bamert, associate guest conductor of the London Philharmonic Orchestra. In brief, none of these seemed to capture the imagination of most of the audience or most of the musicians as had, for example, David Robertson, although each had their own champions. One other, Jahja Ling, had conducted before in San Diego. He had, in fact, been an alternate selection to Yoav Talmi in the late 1980s.

Ling had been resident conductor in Cleveland for eighteen years, until 2002, and music director of the Blossom Music Festival outside of that city, featuring the great Cleveland Orchestra. Ling had also developed another talent as producer of the longstanding series of radio concerts given by that so-called "Cadillac of orchestras." Before his appointment in Cleveland, Ling had served as associate conductor of the San Francisco Symphony Orchestra. In more recent years, he also served as the very successful music director of the Florida Philharmonic Orchestra in the Tampa Bay area for fourteen years. He had been a frequent guest conductor with most of the major American orchestras as well as in Europe, and he also served as music director of the orchestra in Taiwan.

At his 2002-03 appearance as a guest conductor/candidate in San Diego, Ling led the orchestra in a fine performance of the Mahler Fifth Symphony, which caused many in the audience to be reminded of the exceptional quality of the orchestra under Talmi and Atherton. The orchestra was also impressed, and it appeared that the choice was pretty much unanimous for him to assume the position of conductor designate for the 2003-04 season, and to become music director beginning in 2004-05.

Jahja Ling was born in Jakarta, Indonesia, to Chinese parents who encouraged his early musical gifts. He began to study the piano when he was four years old and, at age seventeen, he won the Jakarta Piano Competition. A year later, he was awarded a Rockefeller grant that allowed him to train further at Julliard, in New York City. He studied piano there with Beveridge Webster and Mieceslaw Munz. He also began to study conducting there with John Nelson. Julliard granted him a master's degree, after which he studied conducting further at Yale, under Otto Werner-Mueller. He received a doctorate in musical arts there in 1985. Five years before, however, he had been accepted as a Leonard Bernstein Conducting Fellow at Tanglewood, and two years later Bernstein selected him as a Conducting Fellow at the Los Angeles Philharmonic Institute. Bernstein had become one of his most influential mentors.

In 1988, Ling received the Seaver/NEA Conductor's Award, a career development grant given to American conductors who had demonstrated exceptional promise. Ling continued his piano career as well, and won a bronze medal at the 1977 Artur Rubenstein International Piano Master Competition in Tel Aviv. In 1987, three years after assuming the post of resident conductor in Cleveland, he made his piano debut with that orchestra. He has appeared as piano soloist with a number of other orchestras as well as a guest conductor.

Ling jumped into the fray as soon as the announcement was made of his selection as San Diego's music director designate. He began planning auditions for new and replacement musicians for an orchestra that he insisted would be larger and fuller, as well as better. Prior to the beginning of his inaugural season as music director, he started to build and rebuild. He also continued and maintained the constructive attitude that he had also successfully injected into the eagerly waiting public. That attitude is one that says that this orchestra has the capacity to become great — and that he will see to the job. The entire city awaited his tenure as music director, holding high hopes for him and for his ability to live up to the revitalized faith established in the community by the Jacobs gift. The future was seen as Ling's to formulate and ours to appreciate.

EPILOGUE

Ring-a-Ding-Ding: DazzLING, TingLING
Jahja Ling

San Diego Symphony

He definitely began to formulate, and the audience began to appreciate, often rather wildly. The public relations push began far more aggressively and imaginatively than ever before in the Symphony's history. The billboards went up all around town, and the banners began to fly along the main streets of the center city. The pun on the new conductor's name, exemplified in this chapter's title, proved the heart of the campaign, with huge pictures of the maestro in action, and with those puns emblazoned at the top of the signs. The neo-gerundic endings accented the name by capitalizing it. Imagination sometimes went over the top a bit, as, for example, in the legend, "Pure AdrenaLING" that headlined the cover of the season's first program booklet. But they were catchy.

Jahja Ling proved to be an engaging, sometimes quite funny, talkative subject for interviews. He was seen on local TV and was heard on talk shows. Also, he had conducted the orchestra in the last of its 2003-04 Masterworks Series concerts. The second half of the program was devoted to what turned out to be a sensational performance of the Tchaikovsky Fifth Symphony. Many attributed at least part of the sensation to the fact that Ling was conducting a full string section, featuring thirty violins, twelve violas and the same number of celli, as well as eight basses. That rich a string choir had not been seen on the San Diego Symphony stage since the mid-1980s! The sections had been augmented by using substitute musicians who had been filling in at times over the previous several seasons. The woodwind and brass sections were full, and the totality and quality of the sound that emerged from the stage were overwhelmingly satisfying.

Ling had let it be known far and wide that he would not accept the reduced orchestra that had been playing at Copley Symphony Hall in the past. But it was not only the fact that more musicians were playing that made the performance memorable. The very sensitive reading of the score as well as the remarkable control Ling demonstrated over the very responsive orchestra were the major factors. The large, gratefully demonstrative audience eagerly awaited the beginning of Ling's own first season. Some of them had heard the maestro's short speech in the Revelle Room following that last 2003-04 concert. He broke them up, saying, "Wait, you ain't heard nothing yet!" And in what was to become true to form for Ling, they hadn't.

In his welcoming article in the program booklet for the first 2004-05 concert, executive director Ward Gill announced, "The orchestra of the 21st century opens its 2004-05 season with a whole new look. Our long-awaited new music director…will be taking over the helm of an orchestra ready for greatness. Jeff Thayer, our new concertmaster, adds to this excitement, as we continue the process of filling over 20 positions, including eight principal chairs…" The orchestra committees worked hard auditioning hundreds of players eager to fill vacancies, and Jahja Ling spent many hours with them. The large orchestra that greeted the new season continued to feature a number of longstanding substitutes, especially in the strings, but also showcased some new members who had been selected by audition. Jeff Thayer, formerly the associate concertmaster of the Atlanta Symphony, had been one of a surprisingly large number of candidates for the concertmaster's chair. Later in the 2004-05 season, the Jacobs family, thankfully continuing as the orchestra's major benefactor, purchased the "Sir Bagshawe" Stradivarius violin and lent it to Thayer to use in his position. It (and Thayer) sounded just fine in the Mozart Fourth Violin Concerto in early March, 2005.

New first chair musicians also filled the posts of principal viola (Che-Yen-Chen), principal cello (Daniel Lee, who, unfortunately, was recruited soon after for higher pay elsewhere), principal bass (Jeremy Kurtz), principal flute (Demarre McGill) and principal percussion (Cynthia Yeh). Frank Rosenwein and Valentin Marchev became the official principals of their respective oboe and bassoon sections, which they had formerly headed as acting principals. Rosenwein's San Diego career was, however, cut short after just a couple of seasons. He was selected to replace the great John Mack, the long-time, famous oboe soloist for the Cleveland Orchestra. The caliber of musicians being hired by the San Diego Symphony can be measured by the quality of the orchestras who raided our personnel. Danny Lee had left to assume the first chair position in the St. Louis Symphony's cello section. Jeannette Bittar assumed the position of acting principal oboe. All of these had won their posts by audition. Sheryl Renk returned to lead the clarinets following her maternity leave.

The prior season's last concert had featured a performance by Horacio Gutierrez of the Chopin First Piano Concerto. Emanuel Ax was the soloist in the 2004-05 opener, playing the same composer's Second Piano Concerto beautifully, but the *piece de resistance* followed the intermission when Ling led a performance of the Mahler First Symphony. A justifiable ovation followed. The audience responses and the *Union-Tribune* reviews continued to be positive, and the season progressed accordingly.

There were high points at every concert, and enthusiasm continued to run high. This was marked not only by the applause for the concerts but also by the colder statistics that measure success. By February, 2005, only two-thirds of the way through the 2004-05 season, the total attendance at the Masterworks Series concerts to that time had exceeded that of the entire prior season, and so did the proceeds. Subscriptions were up. Management was happy. The audience was happy. The musicians were happy. As Otto Feld told me — and it must be recalled that he is one of the more experienced and perhaps most cynical members of the orchestra, "He's wonderful! I just hope we can keep him…"

One further happifying event was a management coup — not the result of Jahja Ling's exertions, although he was as happy about it as anyone else. This was the long-awaited (and even longer-negotiated) contract with the San Diego Opera. The Opera had hired its own orchestra for its performances, although the bulk of the personnel were San Diego Symphony players. However, the Symphony's principals were not always the Opera orchestra's principals, and other such actual and potential difficulties abounded under that system. The San Diego Opera season had been set up for a number of years to last over a five-month long period, from January through May. Their schedule of performances made for considerable difficulty in Symphony scheduling during that time. But the new contract was finally agreed upon by both parties by the opening performance of the January, 2005 initial opera performance, to the delight of all concerned, including most of the orchestra.

Basically, the new agreement stated that the San Diego Opera would hire the San Diego Symphony Orchestra — or, at least as many as would be needed in the pit per opera performance. The new system allows for more performances and obviously far more continuity in orchestral performances. It also provides far more financial stability for many of the musicians.

Perhaps the highest point of all the fine performances in Ling's first season was the performance of the Bruckner Seventh Symphony, played on the same program that featured Jeff Thayer's Mozart, noted earlier. David Gregson, the long-time music critic for a number of San Diego publications, felt that the performance of the Bruckner represented the finest playing that he had ever heard from the stage of Symphony Hall. Jahja Ling had programmed the work as a labor of love, and the audience responded with great affection, although the work was, indeed, a very long sit. Even earlier in the season, Ling and the orchestra especially gleamed in their performances of Debussy's *La Mer*, the Mendelssohn "Scottish" Symphony, Richard Strauss's *Don Juan*, and Bartok's Suite from *The Miraculous Mandarin*.

Jahjah Ling also fulfilled his pledge to honor his commitment to contemporary music, sometimes to the grudging admiration of some of his listeners. He introduced the San Diego audiences to new works by John Corigliano, Marc-Andre Dalbavie and Inouk Demers, as well as providing a contemporary favorite, Peter Maxwell Davies' *An Orkney Wedding, With Sunrise.* The requisite kilted piper paraded down the main floor aisles tootling away to the great amusement and satisfaction of all concerned. Guest conductors during Ling's initial season as music director included Michael Stern, soon to become the music director of the Kansas City Symphony, and Otto Werner-Mueller, a distinguished teacher of conducting at Juilliard, Yale and Curtis. He had been one of our own music director's principal teachers.

Critically speaking, the orchestra even made it into the supposed "big time." Mark Swed, music critic for the *Los Angeles Times,* reviewed the orchestra's late February concert featuring the Ives Second Symphony and the Copland *El Salon Mexico.* The *Times* had not reviewed any performances by the orchestra since the early 1990s, when its former music critic, Pulitzer Prize-winner Martin Bernheimer, provided very enthusiastic reviews of several concerts he had heard under Yoav Talmi, whom he described as "brilliant."

Swed's article, in the February 28, 2005 issue of the *Times,* noted that, "The San Diego Symphony, broke, shut down in 1996. Two years later it was back with a flashy young conductor, Jung-Ho Pak, and trying every condescending trick under the ever-present San Diego sun to raise its profile. It was hard to take it seriously.

"Three years ago, it became impossible not to take it seriously when a tele-communications executive gave the orchestra $100 million, with another $20 million promised over the next 10 years. San Diego went conductor shopping and hired Jahja Ling, an Indonesian best known as the music director of the Cleveland Orchestra's summer music series, the Blossom Festival. This is his first season in San Diego, and his program Saturday was ambitious and all over the map.

"Copley Symphony Hall, the renovated, amusingly neo-Gothic 1929 Fox Theatre now embedded in a drab office tower, was so packed Saturday that one had to fight one's way through the intermission crush for a hit of Starbuck's choc-olate. The audience was surely unlike any other symphony crowd — socialites in mink coats, teens on dates dressed for clubbing, surfers in Hawaiian shirts, aca-demics in tweeds….After intermission, Ling turned to Ives' Second Symphony. He gave it a sincere, careful reading, and the orchestra played it strongly. That was all it took. The Copley has an agreeable acoustic [...*note: this from a writer who constantly praises the acoustics of the new Disney Hall in Los Angeles to the skies...*], and Ives' craziness (a little toned down here, but only a little) created an irresist-ible exuberance. Copland's 'El Salon Mexico' was an unnecessary finale and a too obvious gesture to the nearby border. Still, it did raise the temperature yet another degree…"

This was not a "damned with faint praise" review, despite some of the relatively patronizing aspects. The orchestra is far better than anyone had a right to expect after the past several years, and is now playing at the level of the finest regional orchestras in the country, or maybe even better. The audiences, including the characteristically broad spectrum of attendees noted by Swed, have continued to be enthusiastic. Moreover, they continued to come, not only for the remainder of the initial Ling season but the following one as well, when the management planned a more extensive season of fourteen Masterworks sets. As Ward Gill commented to me then, "This will be a real test, and I think we can do it."

They did do it. The performances were received enthusiastically by a gradually growing audience throughout the season. Guest conductors during the 2005-06 season included Gerard Schwartz, who had not conducted here for several years, as well as James Paul, William Eddins and Stefan Sanderling. Schwartz led a remarkably intense performance of the Shostakovich Eleventh Symphony. Among the many highlights led by Ling during the 2005-06 season was a reverent reading of Mendelssohn's oratorio, *Elijah*. Following a pre-intermission, hyper-virtuosic performance by both soloist Yefim Bronfman and the orchestra of the Rachmaninoff Third Piano Concerto, Ling closed the season with a raise-the-roof reading of the Tchaikovsky Fourth Symphony. The rousing cheers from

Jahja Ling in Copley Symphony Hall. *Photo courtesy Marc Tule.*

the audience assisted greatly in the roof raising.

Management has reached out more than ever to audiences. Not only the free samples of Starbuck's chocolate drink noted in the *Los Angeles Times* article provided impetus for increased attendance. For example, although pre-concert talks had been given for a number of previous seasons, they have become increasingly popular and appreciated. Eric Bromberger and especially Nuvi Mehta have provided entertaining information to increasingly large numbers of attendees who would come early to hear them. The program booklets began to contain more information for the readers, including a column of material about program building gleaned from interviews with the conductors, *Why This Program? Why These Pieces?* By and large, the audience has been increasingly drawn into the concerts instead of simply remaining as passive listeners. The wide range of people described in the Swed *Los Angeles Times* article are the broad spectrum the orchestra wants to draw in more and more. Its future depends upon that.

Further attempts to attract younger, perhaps more-with-it, audiences were described by the Association's marketing director, Greg Parry. "Since I began my tenure here," he related, "We have very much made the internet a central part of our marketing, and we are always striving to be at least aware of the latest technologies. Currently, for example, we have the largest e-mail list of any arts organization in the city, and this summer we are selling over 20 percent of our tickets on-line. The actual percentage is much higher if you look at just single ticket sales, because we don't as yet sell subscriptions or renewals on-line. We have begun pod-casting as well to promote our concerts, and have a variety of multimedia features on our busy web-site, including audio and video, as well as the new, 'view from your intended seat' feature for on-line ticket purchasers. We have also been experimenting with the 'bill my cell' feature, where patrons can purchase tickets using their cell phones. This is still quite experimental in this country, but it is the wave of the future."

For a number of years, the American Symphony Orchestra League has been addressing the problems of attracting younger audience members, and also advising orchestras about trying to use the internet. It can be seen that considerable energy has been applied in both of these directions, and it is likely that the San Diego Symphony is somewhere near the vanguard among American orchestras in working with 21st century technology. How better to combat the age-old stereotype of the stodgy, stuffed shirt symphony orchestras?

In late July, 2006, Ward Gill sat down with me and discussed a number of changes, some that have already occurred and others that are planned, but all of which are intended to boost the image, attendance and artistic aspirations of the orchestra. Swed's *Los Angeles Times* column accented the number of younger people attending the concerts. Because they represent the audience the orchestra needs to attract the most, the "Thursday Nite Lite" series had been an experiment that needed to catch on. That informal hour of good music, well performed, especially attracting younger downtown workers and dwellers, with cocktails and *hors d'oeuvres*, grew slowly. The final performance in the 2005-06 season drew 1,300 attendees, and the series will definitely continue. Ward Gill enthused, "Everybody had a great time!" Also, Marvin Hamlisch has been contracted as the director of the winter "pops" programs. Seven programs are projected for the 2006-07 season, and, according to Gill, due to Hamlisch's star quality, the expected earnings for that series should be more than a half-million dollars. Further, it is expected that more winter "pops" programs will be added season after season.

During 2005-06, according to Ward Gill, the symphony reached 28,000 children via the Symphony Hall Young Peoples' Concerts, as well as via outreach programs in which musicians went to the elementary schools to perform and teach the students about their instruments and the music they play. "We want to reach 50,000 kids this coming year, and we're working with Dr. Carl Cohn (the San Diego Unified School District Superintendent and, not so incidentally, new Symphony board member) to try getting there. Every fourth grade student in the District will get to Symphony Hall at least once. The Parker Foundation has been helpful with a grant for that"

The Jacobs Masterworks Series has been expanded to thirty-nine concerts over the past season (2005-06), from its original thirty performances. Ticket sales were up by twelve percent in 2005-06, and it is expected that subscriptions will grow further, as well as individual ticket sales. Ward Gill took great pride in talking about the increased level of performance quality demonstrated by the orchestra under Jahja Ling's guidance, and believes that this will be recognized by more and more listeners. Section principals are outstanding. New for the coming 2006-07 season are Toby Oft, as first trombone (from the Buffalo Philharmonic), and Karen Basrak as first chair cellist (from the Houston Symphony), both former principals in their previous orchestras. Demarre McGill is returning as first flute, after a season on leave as principal with the Pittsburgh Symphony. New string players in the stands are also to be seen and heard. The contracted personnel list remains at seventy-nine, but for the Masterworks Series the strings are generally augmented by a dozen or more players, with proportionate gains in the winds, as needed. The orchestra's list of substitute or extra players represent a group of excellent, well-routined musicians. As Ward Gill noted, "Last year, we lost nobody! I really like the new stability of the orchestra. The artistic quality is really solid!"

The Association's new Finance Director is Seth Goldman, CPA. He related the very pleasant news that the orchestra has been in the black since the

1998-99 season. There are no significant liabilities or deficits being carried over. For the last three years, he told me, the annual budgets have been in the range of twelve to fourteen million dollars. "We expect that it will be a little higher for the 2006-07 season." In the 2003-04 season, the Symphony earned $4,230,000 from ticket sales, and that figure reached $5,675,000 during 2004-05. During the 2005-06 season, a total of more than 95,000 people attended the San Diego Symphony winter season concerts. The summer season, having been moved back to its best location, Embarcadero Park South, drew over 61,000 fans in 2005, and reports indicate that even more will attend during 2006. When all the figures come in and are carefully checked, it is expected that the 2005-06 earned income will exceed $6,000,000.

Such opportunities as celebrating the 75th birthday of the hall during the 2004-05 season also provided some special excitement, as have the newly-instituted tours of Symphony Hall. Although most of the tour attendees are at least occasional concert goers, their enthusiasm for the tours has often caused them to "spread the word" among their friends, and new listeners began to attend.

All of this ought to work, based upon the renewed, constantly increasing excellence of the orchestra and the continuing excitement generated by its music director. During the 2006-07 season, Yoav Talmi will return for his third guest appearance after having been music director in the 1990s. David Atherton will also return to this podium. He has not conducted the orchestra since the mid-1980s, when he was music director. It is strongly anticipated that all the guests will be delighted with what they find here. Jahja Ling will make his first appearance here as a pianist during the season, with his wife, Jessie Chang. They will play the Mozart Double Concerto, with Ling's former conducting Professor, Otto-Werner Mueller, leading the orchestra. The 2006-07 season will provide a remarkable series of programs. Maestro Ling will open the initial concert with William Schuman's American Festival Overture, and close the final concert with the Beethoven Fifth. In between, a broad spectrum of music is scheduled to be presented. Contemporary works range from a favorite, Bernstein's *Chichester Psalms*, to novelties by Messaien and Bright Sheng. A new double bass concerto by John Harbison will be premiered here by our first chair player, Jeremy Kurtz. Tried and true audience favorites include the Franck D-Minor Symphony, under Yoav Talmi, and, under Ling, *Scheherazade*, the Tchaikovsky "Pathétique" Symphony, Mendelssohn's music for "A Midsummer Night's Dream," and, as a spectacular showpiece with great music, the huge Berlioz Requiem.

Moreover, the orchestra itself is happier, due to the hard work by both management and the orchestra committee in reaching a mutually agreeable, negotiated settlement regarding the forthcoming salary contract. The fact that it was reached before the start of the new season is somewhat exceptional among

American symphony orchestras. They often have had to begin their seasons in the midst of sullen dissatisfactions regarding contracts — if they would begin at all. The San Diego contract was adopted with time to spare, but it must be recognized that, characteristically, the task of reaching mutuality was a long and hard one for both sides. The negotiations began in March, 2006. New wages and work rules were adopted near the end of June, 2006, for seasons running through 2010-11.

According to the press release written by Stephen Kougias, the Symphony's public relations director, "The new, five-year agreement covers the 79 full-time musicians of the San Diego Symphony for 41 weeks for the first three years, and 42 weeks annually for the fourth and fifth years. Minimum salary increases for each of the five years include six percent for the first year and four percent for each of the four remaining years of the contract. The minimum salary in year five will be $57,776, including an electronic media guarantee. The current minimum salary is $45,750."

All systems appear to be more "go" than ever for the San Diego Symphony Orchestra. Ward Gill's comments about increased stability are genuinely heartening. But perhaps *The Los Angeles Times'* Swed should continue to be quoted here. "The San Diego Symphony is ready, under Ling, to go places. I hope it throws fiscal caution to the wind and spends its millions on hiring the best players and splurging on rehearsal time..." Those particular last words need a bit of comment, however. The best available players have already been selected to fill the principals' chairs, and more are constantly being selected to fill the other vacancies in the orchestra as well. They will eventually eliminate the need for the continued, routine use of substitutes when new contracts open the door to more than seventy-nine full-time players. And as for "throwing fiscal caution to the wind," the millions that Swed and almost everyone else seem to talk about are really not the orchestra's to spend now, other than any interest gained from the annual Jacobs installments.

The large, $100 million pledge is simply not spendable. There was no sudden gift of $100 million dollars in cash. It is to be given at $5 million annually, for ten years, to a permanent endowment fund, with the $50 million balance to be given to the same fund as a bequest by the Jacobses. It is restricted to an endowment that, it is hoped, will *eventually* generate enough interest income to allow the ongoing expenditures of the orchestra to be greatly augmented.

The continued growth as well as the basic existence of the San Diego Symphony depends upon continued good attendance at its performances, as well as by the continued generosity of donors whose contributions either eliminate deficits or pare them down to manageable levels. Hopes remain high that all of this will happen — and, realistically, there seems to be no reason why there should not be optimism here.

But to continue Swed's remarks, and to allow him, finally, the last word: "Let its good works then attract more money and keep bringing in its delightfully eager and oddly mixed crowd."

Viva that odd mixture!

Viva Ling!

It IS all spine-tingLING!

Jahja Ling *Photo courtesy Marc Tule.*

APPENDIX

MUSICIANS
Season 2006-2007

VIOLIN
Jeff Thayer, Concertmaster
Nick Grant, Principal Associate
  Concertmaster
Jisun Yang, Associate Principal I
Alexander Palamidis, Principal II
Jeff Zehngut, Associate
  Principal II
Randall Brinton
Yumi Cho
Hernan Constantino
Alicia Engley (L)
Lynn Feld
Otto Feld
Patricia Francis
Kathryn Hatmaker
Angela Homnick
Hyun Ok Kang
Tricia Lee (S)
Laurence Leeland
Martha Nilsen
Igor Pandurski
Susan Robboy
Shigeko Sasaki
Edmund Stein
John Stubbs
Pei-chun Tsai
Jing Yan
Joan Zelickman

VIOLA
Che-Yen Chen, Principal
Nancy Lochner, Associate
  Principal
Rebekah Campbell
Chi-yuan Chen
Wanda Law
Qing Liang
Thomas Morgan
Yoko Okayasu
Dorothy Zeavin
Gareth Zehngut

CELLO
Margo Drakos, Acting Principal
Yao Zhao, Associate Principal
Marcia Bookstein
Glen Campbell

Michael Deatherage
Karla Holland-Moritz
Richard Levine
Ronald Robboy
Mary Oda Szanto

BASS
Jeremy Kurtz, Principal
Susan Wulff, Associate Principal
Greg Berton
Travis Gore
Margaret Johnston +
Sam Hager
Allan Rickmeier
Michael Wais

FLUTE
Demarre McGill, Principal
Sarah Tuck
Elizabeth Ashmead

PICCOLO
Elizabeth Ashmead

OBOE
Dwight Parry, Principal
Betsy Spear
Sidney Green

ENGLISH HORN
Sidney Green

CLARINET
Sheryl Renk, Principal
Theresa Tunnicliff
Frank Renk

BASS CLARINET
Frank Renk

BASSOON
Valentin Martchev, Principal
Ryan Simmons
Leyla Zamora

CONTRA BASSOON
Leyla Zamora

HORN
John Lorge, Principal
Keith Popejoy, Assistant
  Principal/Utility
Warren Gref

Tricia Skye
Douglas Hall

TRUMPET
Calvin C. Price, Principal
John McFerran Wilds
Mark Bedell

TROMBONE
Toby Oft, Principal
George Johnston
Richard Gordon +
Michael Fellinger

BASS TROMBONE
Michael Fellinger

TUBA
Matthew Garbutt, Principal

HARP
Elena Mashkovtseva, Acting
  Principal

TIMPANI
Tatsuo Sasaki, Principal

PERCUSSION
Cynthia Yeh, Principal
James Plank

PIANO/CELESTE/ORGAN
Mary Barranger

PERSONNEL MANAGER
Douglas Hall

PRINCIPAL LIBRARIAN
Nancy Fisch

ASSISTANT LIBRARIAN
Kimberly Miller

PIANO TECHNICIAN
Earl Kallberg

(L) On Leave
(S) Full Year Substitute Musician
+ Staff Opera Musician

All musicians are members of
the American Federation of
Musicians Local 325

BOARD OF DIRECTORS
Season 2006-2007 and Past

SAN DIEGO SYMPHONY BOARD OF DIRECTORS

Mitchell R. Woodbury, Chairman
Steven R. Penhall, Chair Elect
Paul Chacon, Vice Chair
Theresa J. Drew, Vice Chair / Treasurer
Dennis V. Arriola, Secretary
Claude Benchimol, Ph.D.
Joye Blount
James Lewis Bowers, Ph.D.
Tanya M. Brandes
Julia Brown
Carol Cebron
Ben G. Clay
Carl A. Cohn, Ph. D.
Theodore J. Cranston, Esq.
Robert Crouch
Harold B. Dokmo Jr.
Ephraim Feig, Ph.D.
Lew Haskell
Paul Hering
Barbara M. Katz
Takashi Kiyoizumi, M.D.
Anil Kripalani
Evelyn Olson Lamden
Elizabeth Hamman Oliver
Nathaniel L. Oubré
Peter Platt
Shearn Platt
Edward H. Richard
Craig A. Schloss, Esq.
Charles Simpson
Donald M. Slate
David R. Snyder, Esq.
E.M. Strauss
Carol Stensrud
Debra A. Thomas
Hubert Wolff
Stephen T. Worland, Ph. D.
Kenneth Y. Yun, Ph. D.
John Zygowicz

HONORARY DIRECTORS

Warren O. Kessler, MD
Anne Ratner
Ellen Revelle
Herbert Solomon

SAN DIEGO SYMPHONY ADVISORY BOARD

Peter Platt, co-Chair
John R. Queen, co-Chair
Robert Caplan
Charles H. Cheyney
William S. Cooper
Dr. Peter Czipott
James R. Dawe, Esq.
Diane Eggleston
Daniel J. Epstein
Martin Fenton
John V. Forrest
Mary Lou Fox
Martha A. Gafford
Audrey Geisel
John M. Gilchrist
Michael S. Grossman
Ronald H. Kendrick
James Lauth
Richard C. Levi
Sandra Levinson
Alfred Lord
Richard Mau
Judith A. Moore
Veryl J. Mortenson
Larry Papay
John A. Porter
Kathleen H. Porter
Cathy Rempel
A. J. Schaps
William A. Tribolet

SAN DIEGO SYMPHONY FOUNDATION BOARD OF DIRECTORS

Joan K. Jacobs, Chairman
Robert Caplan, Esq., Vice Chairman
Warren O. Kessler, MD, Secretary
Marjory Kaplan, Treasurer
Murray Galinson
Edward B. Gill
Robert A. Kelly
Mitchell R. Woodbury

PAST BOARD PRESIDENTS

1927	Ed H. Clay
1928-29	Willett S. Dorland
1930-33	Mouney C. Pfefferkorn
1934-37	Mrs. Marshall O. Terry
1938-39	Mrs. William H. Porterfield
1940-42	Donald B. Smith
1952-53	Donald A. Stewart
1953-56	Mrs. Fred G. Goss
1956-58	Admiral Wilder D. Baker
1959-60	Dr. G. Burch Mehlin
1960-61	Fielder K. Lutes
1961-63	J. Dallas Clark
1963-64	Oliver B. James Jr.
1964-66	Philip M. Klauber
1966-68	Michael Ibs Gonzalez
1968-69	Arthur S. Johnson
1969-70	Rober J. Sullivan
1970-71	Simon Reznikoff
1971-74	L. Thomas Halverstadt
1974-76	William N. Jenkins
1976-78	Laurie H. Waddy
1978-80	Paul L. Stevens
1980-82	David E. Porter
1982-84	Louis F. Cumming
1984-86	M.B. Det Merryman
1986-88	Herbert J. Solomon
1988-89	Elsie V. Weston
1989-93	Warren O. Kessler, MD
1993-94	David Dorne, Esq.
1994-95	Thomas Morgan
1995-96	Elsie V. Weston
1998-00	Sandra Pay
2000-01	Ben G. Clay
2001-03	Harold B. Dokmo, Jr.
2003-04	John R. Queen
2004-05	Craig A. Schloss, Esq.

ADMINISTRATION

EXECUTIVE OFFICE
Edward B. Gill, Executive
Director
LeAnna Zevely, Office Manager
Laurie Gallagher, Receptionist

ARTISTIC/ORCHESTRA OPERATIONS
Robert Wilkins, Chief
Operating Officer
Shelly Stannard Fuerte, Director
of Artistic Planning
Jennifer Ringle, Production
Manager
Tamara Broitman, Stage
Manager
Magdalena O'Neill, Artistic
Coordinator
Douglas Hall, Orchestra
Personnel Manager
Nancy Fisch, Principal Librarian
Kimberly Miller, Library
Assistant
Kayrl Garbutt, Library Assistant

CONCERT PRODUCTION
Tom Resenbeck, Carpenter/
Steward
Donnie Clifton, Electrician
Mark Wildman, Property
Manager
Michael Winston, Soundman
David Leyton, Sound Engineer
Walker Vision Interarts, Live
Video Production
Sound System provided by
Power Plus Sound and
Lighting
George Kutchins, House
Manager
Shaun Davis, Assistant House
Manager

House Staff: Marian Fowler,
Billy C. Gomez, Sue Gomez,
Mary Hodge, Sharon Karniss,
Jackie Stetter
The stage crew employed by
the San Diego Symphony are
members of the International
Alliance of Theatrical Stage
Employees (IATSE),
Local 122, AFL-CIO.

DEVELOPMENT
Christine Deardorff, Director of
Annual Fund
Megan Pogue, Director of
Corporate Development
Chaz Dykes, Associate Manager
of Individual Giving
Joani Nelson, Special Events
Coordinator
Michelle Wohlers, Development
Office Manager
Art Fuerte, Development
Assistant
Libby McClendon,
Development Assistant
Barbara Broderick, Consultant

EDUCATION
James Miles, Manager of
Education & Outreach
Programs
Donna Bullock, Volunteer

FACILITIES
Dennis Legg, Director of
Facility Operations
Virginia Tunnell, Facilities
Operations Assistant
Facilities Assistants: Pete Perez,
Robert Saucedo, Scott
Garbutt, Patrick Paul,
John Yancy

FINANCE
Seth Goldman, Director of
Finance
Mariellen Oliver, Assistant
Controller/Human Resources
Manager
Garrett Shields, MIS Manager
Tim White, Network
Administrator

MARKETING
Greg Parry, Director of
Marketing
Stephen Kougias, Public
Relations Manager
J.D. Smith, Manager of Single
Ticket Sales and Outreach
Jeffrey Young, Subscriptions
Coordinator

DIRECT SALES
Gerry Gagliardi, Direct Sales
Manager
Direct Sales Representatives:
Marc Beccia, Sandra Hawkins,
Yolanda Moore, Patrick
Murphy, Vaughn Rainwater,
Esther Sundel

TICKET OFFICE
Lisa Baker, Ticket Services
Manager
Octavia Person, Assistant Ticket
Services Manager
Ticket Office Representatives:
Pablo Amador, Sharon Chen,
April Cross, Saloun
Echeverria, Cheri LaZarus,
Kymberlee Pappas.